Roy D'Andrade has written a lucid historical account of the growth and development of the field of cognitive anthropology. The origins of cognitive anthropology can be traced back to the late 1950s when anthropology was grappling with the problem of understanding native systems of categorization. This book starts with an evaluation of these formative years, portraying the way in which research evolved across more than thirty years to the present. It traces the way in which the early notions about semantics and taxonomies evolved into more sophisticated theories about prototypes, schemas, and connectionist networks, seen as the cognitive mechanisms underlying the organization of folk models and reasoning in ordinary life. This is followed by a review of the most recent research on the social distribution of cultural knowledge and the relation of cultural models to emotion, motivation, and action. The final section summarizes the general theoretical perspective of cognitive anthropology, which treats culture as particulate, socially distributed, variably internalized and embodied in physical structures – a view which opposes structuralist, interpretive, and post-modern conceptions of culture.

The development of cognitive anthropology

The development of cognitive anthropology

ROY D'ANDRADE

University of California

PUBLISHED BY THE PRESS SYNDICATE OF THE UNIVERSITY OF CAMBRIDGE
The Pitt Building, Trumpington Street, Cambridge, United Kingdom

CAMBRIDGE UNIVERSITY PRESS
The Edinburgh Building, Cambridge CB2 2RU, UK http://www.cup.cam.ac.uk
40 West 20th Street, New York, NY 10011–4211, USA http://www.cup.org
10 Stamford Road, Oakleigh, Melbourne 3166, Australia
Ruiz de Alarcón 13, 28014 Madrid, Spain

First published 1995
Reprinted 1995, 1996, 1997, 2000

Printed in the United Kingdom at the University Press, Cambridge

A catalogue record for this book is available from the British Library

Library of Congress Cataloguing in Publication data
D'Andrade, Roy G.
The development of cognitive anthropology / Roy D'Andrade
p. cm.
Includes bibliographical references.
ISBN 0 521 45370 4.–ISBN 0 521 45976 1 (pbk.)
1. Ethnopsychology. 2. Cognitive and culture. I. Title.
GN502.D36 1995
155.8–dc20 94–4749 CIP

ISBN 0 521 45370 4 hardback
ISBN 0 521 45976 1 paperback

SE

Contents

Figures

Tables

Preface

I wrote this book with two major goals in mind. At present, there is no single book to which outsiders can go to find out about cognitive anthropology. Work in cognitive anthropology has been published in articles spread across a range of journals and edited collections. One goal, then, is to bring some thirty years of work together in one place.

The second reason, related to the first, is that many social and cognitive scientists do not know about recent work in cognitive anthropology. The common view of the field was set in place by work done in the 1960s on kin terms and plant taxonomies. Research during the 1980s and 1990s on cultural models, reasoning, consensus, emotion, memory, motivation, and distributed cognition is less well known. While I have not been able to do a complete review, this book is intended to provide reasonable coverage of current research and thinking.

This book is not a standard textbook; it is too particular in its perspective and involved with current controversy. Nor is it a history of the sort historians of science write, since I have been more concerned with the presentation of ideas than with the intricacies of chronology and first authorship. However, it does try to show how the field of cognitive anthropology developed over time. I wrote it to tell what I believe is an interesting story about a fascinating problem.

What is the problem? The problem is the nature of human culture. One can conceive of a society's culture, in Ward Goodenough's famous phrase, as "whatever it is one has to know or believe in order to operate in a manner acceptable to its members." Certainly humans do learn an enormous amount of cultural knowledge. The problem comes when one tries to understand what that knowledge *is*. Is it lists of propositions? Organized structures of contrasting attributes? A storehouse of images? A collection of taxonomies? A set of computer-like programs? Is it totally language based, or does it include images and physical skills?

Along with these questions about the character of cultural knowledge comes a related set of questions about how other mental processes might effect how that knowledge is organized and used, such as the limitations of short-term memory or degree to which knowledge is necessarily involved with emotion and motivation. In turn, these questions lead to other questions about how what is learned affects other mental processes, such as long-term memory and reasoning. And underlying all of this is the crucial issue: how can one formulate these questions so that they can be investigated?

The field of cognitive anthropology has "grown up" with the other cognitive sciences. There has been a constant exchange of ideas across fields, although the practitioners in each discipline are often unaware of the parallel development of the fields or believe that these parallel developments are due to borrowing from their own field. In my experience, I have found that a good idea appears almost everywhere at once across the cognitive sciences, although how seriously and effectively a particular idea is pursued may differ greatly by field.

Overall, the agenda of cognitive anthropology has held to the idea that the study of cognition should be more than a series of propositions which are based solely on laboratory experiments. There is nothing wrong with a laboratory; a great many questions can only be answered through experimentation. However, a general goal of anthropology is to understand the natural world of human life, as it is found. What the anthropologist needs is a theory which will help in understanding how ordinary people normally organize and use knowledge.

Along with the idea that cognitive anthropology should try to understand the way knowledge is used in ordinary life, there is also the notion that cognitive anthropology should study the way in which knowledge is conventionalized into *culture*. Human knowledge is much too precious a thing to be carelessly discarded each generation with the hope that it will be rediscovered in the next. Human knowledge is carefully preserved and passed from one generation to another. Most of what any human ever thinks has been thought before, and most of what any human ever thinks has been learned from other humans. Or, to put it another way, most of what anyone knows is *cultural* knowledge. Cognitive anthropology investigates cultural knowledge, knowledge which is embedded in words, in stories, and artifacts, and which is learned from and shared with other humans.

The number of anthropologists who have been involved in creating the field of cognitive anthropology has not been large. At various times the number of anthropologists and linguists involved in cognitive research may have reached two hundred or so. About a hundred and fifty anthropologists and linguists are cited in the following chapters, along with about a hundred psychologists. Most of the work has been carried out by a shifting core which has never been larger than about thirty persons. Within this group there has been a remarkable spirit of collaboration and good will; the personal attacks and exaggerated claims to precedence and prominence typical of much writing in the social sciences have been notably absent from the cognitive anthropology literature.

This book is dedicated to those who set the agenda of cognitive anthropology: Floyd Lounsbury, Ward Goodenough, Anthony Wallace, Harold Conklin, and A. Kimball Romney. And to the fine folks who helped with this manuscript, many thanks.

1 Background

Cognitive anthropology is the study of the relation between human society and human thought. The cognitive anthropologist studies how people in social groups conceive of and think about the objects and events which make up their world – including everything from physical objects like wild plants to abstract events like social justice. Such a project is closely linked to psychology because the study of how particular social groups categorize and reason inevitably leads to questions about the basic nature of such cognitive processes.

Early history

The story of cognitive anthropology begins in the late 1950s. To make comprehensible what was happening at this time requires understanding certain aspects of the history of anthropology. Anthropology started as a professional field of study in the late nineteenth century. The original charter of anthropology was to fill in a missing piece of human history – or, more accurately, human "prehistory," the period of time before written history and the rise of the classic civilizations. Part of the motivation for this agenda was western society's discovery of the native peoples of the Americas, the Pacific, and the far Orient. European savants speculated with great interest and imagination about where these people might have come from and what their history might have been. Obtaining facts to resolve these questions rapidly grew into a recognized field of scholarly endeavor in the late nineteenth century.

This "prehistoric" agenda of anthropology had three different methods of investigation. One involved the direct investigation of the past through exploration of the physical remains. This became the field of *archaeology*, which started with the professionalization of the techniques that had been developed by gentlemen scholars interested in ancient Greek, Roman, and Egyptian antiquities. Methods of careful excavation were developed to work out from the stratigraphy of materials buried in the earth the chronology of early peoples. Interest spread from the study of the chronology of early Middle Eastern and European civilizations to the prehistory of North and South

American Indians, and eventually to the general study of the prehistory of humanity.

By the 1950s an enormous amount had been learned about human prehistory. A detailed chronology had been worked out beginning with the evolution of early hominids several million years ago. This chronology includes the development of hunting and gathering technologies in the paleolithic, the shift to food cultivation in the neolithic 8,000 to 10,000 years ago, and the rise of the six great independent centers of civilization over the past 5,000 years in Egypt, Mesopotamia, the Indus, the Yangtze, Mesoamerica, and the Peruvian coast.

A second method of investigation developed at the end of the nineteenth century was called *ethnography* – the observational study of the ways of life of primitive peoples. By obtaining and comparing objective accounts of the social and cultural institutions of primitive people around the world, it was thought that the historical connections and course of evolutionary development could be worked out, complementing the results obtained by the archaeologists. According to Radcliffe-Brown in 1909: "A meeting of teachers from Oxford, Cambridge and London was held to discuss the terminology of our subject. We agreed to use 'ethnography' as the term for descriptive accounts of non-literate peoples. *The hypothetical reconstruction of 'history' of such peoples was accepted as the task of ethnography and prehistoric archaeology*" (italics added).[1]

Early ethnographers were interested in the way in which particular cultural traits diffused from one society to another, and the way in which simple societies could be grouped on the basis of overall similarity into geographic clusters of societies, called *culture areas.* They were strongly divided on whether or not societies *evolved* in a series of stages from simple hunting people to complex urban civilization or were simply involved in non-evolutionary, non-directional, multiple process of *change* – an argument that is still not entirely resolved.

The third method was the investigation of human physical types. Unfortunately, this work became contaminated with the racist ideas common in western societies in the nineteenth century. However, the basic project was reasonable. This project was to collect data on physical similarities and differences between human groups so that patterns of migration and historical relations between groups could be determined, and special environmental adaptations discovered. With modern techniques of direct genetic comparison there is some hope that this agenda can now be undertaken without falling into racist typologizing.

Thus anthropology began with three fields – ethnography, archaeology, and what is now called "biological anthropology." These three fields are still found

[1] Quoted in Kuper (1983:2). Radcliffe-Brown's statement goes on to contrast "ethnology" with "social anthropology" which was defined as the *comparative* study of the institutions of primitive societies.

in most modern departments of anthropology. It is interesting that while the general project of working out the history of early civilizations and primitive peoples has long since retreated to a minor place in both the fields of ethnography and biological anthropology, the coalition of the three fields remains fixed in the institutional framework of university and college departments.

The field of linguistics has also played a part in the general development of anthropology. From the very first it was recognized that similarities and differences in languages gave crucial information about historical relationships. Since languages change slowly, historical relationships and connections between very different societies can sometimes be discovered by linguistic comparison. While there was still controversy about the grouping of some of the major stocks, by the fifties most of the languages of the world had been classified and described in some detail (Ruhlen 1987).

Another tie between anthropology and linguistics is based on the practicalities of learning unwritten languages. To carry out ethnographic research it is a great help to know the language of the people being studied. And to transcribe and learn to speak unwritten languages, one needs to know how to transcribe exotic sounds and to know how to analyze rules of word formation and syntax. Thus linguistics became part of the field training curriculum of many departments of anthropology. Although today most universities have separate departments of linguistics, linguists are often still found in a variety of departments from anthropology to Slavic literature and cognitive science.

It might seem from the description given above that anthropology is primarily a kind of historical study. Certainly part of it – *archaeology* – is, and certainly all the fields of anthropology have contributed to our general understanding of what has taken place in human prehistory. Ethnography, however, drastically changed its goals. This change in goals is an example of an interesting phenomenon in anthropology and the social sciences which I call *agenda hopping*. Agenda hopping is different from a *paradigm shift*, a process made famous by Thomas Kuhn in his book *The Structure of Scientific Revolutions*.

According to Kuhn, at any particular time a science will have a number of examples of what is excellent science – "examples which include law, theory, application, and instrumentation together – [which] provide models from which spring particular coherent traditions of scientific research" (1970:10). Working within an established scientific paradigm is called *normal science* and involves a kind of puzzle solving activity in which the major problem is to fit new pieces of information into an already known pattern. However, there comes a time at which more and more pieces of information are found which do not fit into the pattern. Anomalies accumulate. At some point maverick scientists break out of the old paradigm and try to develop a new conceptual framework which can account for these anomalies. Such times are periods of intense controversy. Reinterpretation of the old facts into the framework of the new paradigm is often a matter of intense debate. The shift from the Newtonian mechanics to quantum mechanics is an often cited example of such a paradigm shift.

Agenda hopping is quite a different process. What happens in agenda hopping is that a given agenda of research reaches a point at which nothing new or exciting is emerging from the work of even the best practitioners. It is not that the old agenda is completed, or that too many anomalies have accumulated to proceed with equanimity. Rather, what has happened is that as more and more has been learned the practitioners have come to understand that the phenomena being investigated are quite complex. Greater and greater effort is required to produce anything new, and whatever is found seems to be of less and less interest. When this happens, a number of practitioners may defect to another agenda – a new direction of work in which there is some hope of finding something really interesting. Note that in agenda hopping there is no reinterpretation of the old findings into a new framework as there is in a paradigm shift. Rather, there is simple abandonment of the old venture in favor of a new set of problems.

Although the old agenda may still be a reasonable endeavor (except for its dullness and difficulty), the defectors to the new agenda will usually attack the old agenda with great vehemence. They may say the old agenda simply cannot be done (since they could not do much with it), and therefore is unscientific or irrelevant, or that it is just too incomplete (since it does not cover the phenomena they are now interested in), or more simply and brutally that it is "old-fashioned" and "out-of-date." These attacks on old agendas are unfortunate, since they often denigrate a record of considerable accomplishment.

Agenda hopping often begins quite early in the history of a field. By the time of World War I a number of ethnographers had already begun to abandon the historical agenda for the study of simple societies. Adam Kuper describes the situation as follows:

> But if one were to characterize the mood of British anthropology in the first decades of this century one would have to stress the over-riding concern with the accumulation of data. The ultimate goal might still be the reconstruction of culture history, or evolutionist generalizations, but these interests were overlaid by a strong resurgence of British empiricism. There was a feeling that the facts which were increasingly becoming available made *facile evolutionist and diffusionist schemes look rather silly.* (Italics added) (1983:5)

These are the perceptions of scientists about to abandon an old agenda for a new one. The old agenda had become entangled in problems as data was collected. Rather than modifying the evolutionist and evolutions schemes so that they would *not* look "silly," the decision was to move on to a new agenda in the name of empiricism. Bronislaw Malinowski, the great ethnographer of the Trobriand Islands, developed a series of intricate arguments for why historical study was irrelevant to the study of primitive societies.[2] Radcliffe-Brown, who had done pioneering ethnographic work among the Andaman Islanders and Australian aborigines in the first decade of the twentieth century, also made his contempt for "conjectural history" quite clear. Although Franz Boas, who had founded the first department of anthropology in the United States at Columbia University and trained the first elite cadre of professional anthropologists in America, remained affiliated with the old historical agenda of anthropology, by the 1930s most American ethnographers were primarily engaged in the new agenda.

It should be stressed that there is nothing wrong with agenda hopping: indeed it is a good thing if the new agenda has scientific potential. And the new agenda of the early twentieth-century ethnographers proved to have real potential. This new agenda was focused on *the detailed examination of how the institutions of society are integrated together to make society function.* According to the new agenda, the institutions of a society are not just a jumble of traits, but rather a set of *learned and prescribed activities which are coordinated with one another to bring about a satisfactory way of life and maintain social order.*

While they wrote about their data using the general term "society," these anthropologists were in fact exclusively interested in the functioning of simple, kinship-based, non-literate societies – an inheritance from the previous "pre-historical" agenda. To carry out such a detailed examination required extensive field work, with the ethnographer spending months and sometimes years living intimately with the people being studied, observing and participating in the ordinary routines of life. A special aspect of this kind of field work is that the anthropologist *learns* a significant part of the culture – an anthropologist knows he or she understands a kinship system, for example, when he or she can classify kin and anticipate what kin will do the same way a native of the culture can.

The result of field work was expected to be one or more lengthy monographs – *ethnographies* – which would describe in a series of chapters the technology and techniques of providing for material needs, the composition of the village or local group, the composition and roles of the family and extended kinship grouping, the organization of politics and leadership, as well as the nature of magic, religion, witchcraft, and other native systems of belief. For cultural and social anthropology, ethnography – published in books, monographs, and articles – is the basic data of the discipline.

This agenda remained in force as the dominant project in social and cultural anthropology until the 1950s. Central work on this agenda was done by British social anthropologists who completed a series of outstanding ethnographies which became the exemplars for the entire field. Australian aborigines, African pastoral and horticultural groups, Pacific Islanders, Burmese tribal peoples, all

[2] See Ernest Gellner's delightful paper "Zeno of Cracow *or* Revolution at Nemi *or* the Polish revenge: A Drama in Three Acts" (1987).

were described in meticulous detail and presented in a way that made the organization of these societies vividly apparent. In the thirties there was a shift from a "functional" to a more "structural" approach, that is, from an emphasis on how institutional activities related to individual and social needs to an emphasis on how such institutions were organized into an encompassing structure through the kinship system and political activity. Overall, however, there was considerable continuity from the functional to the structural periods; both emphasized the detailed description of institutional forms of activity which made society possible. An excellent account of the development of this new agenda, which had become a full-fledged scientific paradigm by the late 1930s, can be found in Adam Kuper's *Anthropology and Anthropologists: The Modern British School.*

For those who have never read an ethnography, the account given above gives little sense of the real accomplishment of this work. Today, the standard ethnographies written for undergraduate classes follow almost exactly the course laid out by these pioneers (for example, Napoleon Chagnon's *Yanomamö* or Richard Lee's *Dobe!Kung*). Good ethnography has the ability to immerse one in a strange and different world, which, while exotic, nevertheless is comprehensible.

While the central core of the classic ethnographic paradigm was developed by British social anthropologists, the Americans constructed a number of variations around this core. The Americans did not abandon the historical agenda as completely as the British. One American school, lead by Leslie White and Elmer Service, emphasized the process of social evolution. The social evolutionists argued that human societies have evolved from band-based hunting and gathering societies to simple tribal forms of organization, and then to more and more powerful chiefdoms, and eventually to the development of the state. The "motor" for evolutionary advancement to more complex forms of organization has been generally thought to be technology and economy, especially the technical means by which energy is captured and put to human use. This school is still flourishing, and its practitioners have made common cause with archaeologists to build a sound "non-conjectural" prehistory of human societies.[3]

Another American variant within the ethnographic agenda was the *culture and personality* school. The distinctive characteristic of this school was an emphasis on the way in which socialization practices shape the personality of the members of a society, making them more likely as adults to behave in certain distinctive ways and more likely to adopt certain cultural institutions. The culture and personality school was split into two camps. One camp, lead by Ruth Benedict and Margaret Mead, emphasized the way in which each society is marked by a particular *ethos* – a common emotional and characterological way of responding to the world which could be seen throughout the

[3] See Johnson and Earle 1987.

range of cultural activities performed by members of a society.[4] According to Benedict and Mead culture and personality are basically the same thing; culture can be seen as group personality "writ large."[5] The members of this camp, most of whom were students of Boas, used as evidence detailed ethnographic materials to show that a particular culture is infused with a particular emotional ethos.

The other camp, initiated by Abraham Kardiner, a psychoanalyst, and Ralph Linton, an anthropologist, took as their task working out the ways in which particular child rearing practices give rise to particular personality problems which are then expressed in specific cultural activities and beliefs.[6] This group relied more on the analysis of comparative and cross-cultural data and has been more specific about the psychological mechanisms by which socialization practices are linked to cultural activities and beliefs than the Mead and Benedict camp. John and Beatrice Whiting's *Children of Six Cultures* is a good exemplar of this field. A good historical review of the entire culture and personality field can be found in Phillip Bock's *Continuities in Psychological Anthropology.*

While each of these schools had a different explanations of how social life was organized, these were differences *within* a general paradigm. Overall, the task was agreed upon – *to find out how institutionalized systems of action are organized.* The means to carry out the task was also agreed upon – intensive ethnographic research. While Malinowski held that much of the organization was based on the satisfaction of human needs, and Radcliffe-Brown held that much of the organization was based on the requirements of the functioning of society, and Mead and Kardiner held that much of the organization was based on personality as formed by early experience, and White and Service held that much of the organization was formed by the means and modes of production, these differences were primarily matters of emphasis.

Each of these schools agreed on the centrality of kinship and face-to-face relationships in understanding "primitive" society. Even more basically, they agreed – without needing to say it – that *the basic unit for scientific analysis consisted of learned and prescribed systems of action*, variously called "customs," or "traits," or "institutions." By the 40s George Murdock and his collaborators had developed an *Outline of Cultural Materials* containing a listing of over 500 categories of institutions classified under eighty-eight general headings like "agriculture," "family," "religious practices," etc.

By the early 1950s, this kind of ethnography had become "normal science." A good social or cultural anthropology graduate student could be expected to return from a year's field work with a solid description of the institutions which comprised the technology, economy, kinship, politics, religion, and magical practices of the people studied, and could be expected to put these facts together

[4] See Benedict 1934 and Mead 1950.

[5] See LeVine 1973 for a devastating methodological critique of this assumption.

[6] Kardiner and Linton 1949.

into an argument about how these facts were organized by functional or structural or economic or personality factors. From 1920 to 1950 excellent ethnographies were written on a large number of societies spanning the entire world. Murdock's *Social Structure*, a cross-cultural study published in 1949, lists 250 societies on which information was complete enough to determine the major social institutions. By 1957 Murdock's "World Ethnographic Sample" included 564 societies, and probably included less than a quarter of the societies on which a reasonable amount of ethnographic material had been published.[7]

Success, however, has its cost. As more and more ethnographies appeared, the value of each new one decreased. As more and more facts became known, the idea that any one school would be able demonstrate that its central concept was truly *the* primary organizing factor became more and more unlikely. It was not that the questions were settled and nothing new remained to be discovered. It was just that adding anything really *new* had become increasing difficult. The time for agenda hopping had again arrived.

A new agenda in anthropology and the great paradigm shift

As the agenda for the study of the organization of social institutions was reaching a point of exhaustion, a genuine scientific revolution was taking place in psychology and related fields. By the 1920s *behaviorism* had replaced "introspectionism" as the dominant paradigm in psychology. The basic assumption of the behaviorist paradigm was that psychology should be the study of the *observable*. One can observe the responses and the stimuli which impinge on an animal; therefore the task of psychology is to work out how *stimuli* are lawfully related to *responses*. "S–R" or "stimulus–response" theory retained its hegemony for more than thirty years. A basic principle of the behaviorists was that no theoretical construct about what goes on "inside the mind" should be introduced into psychological theory unless it could be *tightly* connected to measurable external events. Thus behaviorists could talk about "drive" as a state of the "organism" because it could be measured directly from external events – typically the number of hours of deprivation (of food, water, exercise, etc.) the animal had experienced. Similarly, one could talk about the "reinforcing" or rewarding properties of certain stimuli because reinforcement simply referred to the fact that an animal was more likely to perform a response if it was immediately followed by the presentation of a certain class of stimuli. A pellet of food, presented to a rat after pressing a lever, when the rat had not eaten in twenty-four hours, was a reinforcement because the rat was now more likely to press the lever than it had been before the pellet was presented.

7 Today it would probably be possible to give an account of the major economic, social, political, and cultural institutions of over 2,000 societies based on professional ethnographic descriptions. *The Encyclopedia of World Cultures*, edited by David Levinson, for example, presents summaries of the cultural institutions of more than 1,500 societies.

While all the behaviorists agreed on the necessity for this kind of tight connection between observables and theoretical terms, there was a split between the purists, such as B. F. Skinner, the eminent psychologist at Harvard, and those willing to use "hypothetical constructs" such as Clark Hull, the eminent psychologist at Yale. According to Skinner, even constructs like "drive" were unnecessary; all that one should talk about was number of hours of deprivation. Nothing was gained, according to Skinner, by postulating states of the organism one could not *observe* directly. Those with less pure inclinations, however, maintained that the use of *hypothetical constructs*, such as "drive," "habit," "frustration," "anxiety," "expectancy," etc., properly tied tightly to observable events, allowed the development of a more powerful theory.

Although behaviorism had begun as a healthy corrective for the subjectivism of the introspectionist schools of psychology, by the fifties a large number of anomalies had made the tight constraints of the behaviorists seem like an intellectual prison. Tolman, an experimental psychologist at Berkeley, had performed careful experiments with rats that demonstrated beyond any reasonable degree of doubt that even as simple a creature as the common rat had in its mind a complex *map* of its environment which it could use to make decisions, and that this map could not be reduced to some complex of S–R connections. Jean Piaget, in Switzerland, had been doing interesting work on the intellectual development of young children, showing that as children develop they construct more and more complex models of the world around them. Jerome Bruner, a cognitive psychologist at Harvard, had shown how college students use a variety of strategies in concept attainment tasks.[8] None of these findings could be easily assimilated to the behaviorist paradigm.

In 1957, when I went to graduate school, the arguments on both sides of the behaviorist dispute were well known. The counter argument of the behaviorists to the growing list of anomalous findings was that while it was true that there were lots of things one could not account for with the behaviorist paradigm *at this point*, nevertheless the thing a good scientist should do is stick with what can be *really* understood, and gradually work one's way to the more complex phenomena. Various findings might seem anomalous now, but would most probably prove to be nothing more than some special combination of simple S–R processes *when the truth was known*.

Despite such arguments, the behaviorist paradigm collapsed quickly. In my view, a major factor in the rapidity of the death of the behaviorist paradigm was the influence of the modern digital computer. In the late 1950s computers were becoming a major part of the university scene. With the development of higher level programing languages it became possible to write computer programs ranging from simple statistical analyses to programs capable of playing checkers and chess. These game playing programs had memory, could plan ahead,

[8] See Bruner, Goodnow, and Austin 1956.

and could even be constructed to make good guesses about what would happen in situations too complex to calculate exact answers.

Since computers gave a mechanical example of how a mind *could* work, they began to serve as a model for how the human mind *did* work. By 1958 Newell, Shaw, and Simon had extended what had been learned about solving problems with computers to human problem solving.[9] George Miller, one of the pioneer psychologists in the cognitive revolution, said in an interview about this period of time:

> My thinking was influenced by computers perhaps earlier than most people's. Even while I felt that I should be behavioristic, I was willing to play around with other ideas. The generation before me felt that *you couldn't use a term without having a physical instantiation of it.* And on that criterion, *we now have physical instantiation, by means of computers, of fabulous things!* Things that they had never dreamed of. So, just accepting that as your license to talk . . . you could talk about memory, syntactic rules, plans, schemata, and the like. We didn't believe that computers were giant brains, but *we could see the similarities.* (Italics added) (Baars 1986:205)

The cognitive revolution was not limited to psychology. Prior to 1956 most theory in linguistics was also behavioristic in approach. The ideal was one in which the linguist transcribed into a phonetic alphabet the speech of a competent speaker of some language, and once transcribed, analyzed these written symbols in a relatively mechanical, algorithmic way, with minimal reference to meanings, to discover the various levels of structure of the language. Little or nothing was assumed about the mind, or about anything psychological. Noam Chomsky's *Syntactic Structures*, published in 1957, changed all this. This book had an enormous impact on both the field of linguistics and the field of psychology. What Chomsky was able to demonstrate was that *one could not learn a language like English by just learning what words can follow other words.* As George Miller put it in a personal interview:

> As I thought about Chomsky's arguments, it occurred to me that if you try to learn English using purely statistical approximations to English – by learning transitional probabilities between words – then when you look at the size of the set of sentences 20 words long, it turns out that you have to learn an astronomical number of connections in order to generate just exactly the set of English sentences and no others. I think it works out that the average number of possible transitions following any word in a sentence is on the order of 10 – that is, at any point in a sentence there is an average of about 10 words that can follow that word. So, in sentences about 20 words long – which is not very long, that's about the average length of sentences in the *Reader's Digest* – that would lead to 10 to the 20th power number of sentences. And there are less than 10 to the 10th seconds in a century.
>
> So if you imagine that you have been learning one transitional probability per second since your were born, you would not have had enough time to learn more than a tiny fraction of all the sentences you can in fact produce and understand. (Baars 1986:208)

[9] See Newell, Shaw, and Simon 1958.

In summary, *to be able to speak a language a speaker must learn a grammar – a relatively small set of rules that will generate all and only those sentences which are grammatical in that language.* This grammar is a mental object. In *Syntactic Structures* Chomsky presented a rigorous formal proof that such a grammar could not be described or accounted for in stimulus–response terms.

The paradigm shift from behaviorism to cognition has been widely commented on and written about. Howard Gardner's *The Minds New Science* is an accessible and wide-ranging account of the development of the cognitive sciences, covering cognitive developments in psychology, artificial intelligence, linguistics, anthropology, and neuroscience. Bernard Baars' *The Cognitive Revolution in Psychology* gives a good description of the behaviorist paradigm and includes a series of interviews with major figures in psychology in both camps. If there is any controversy about the cognitive revolution, it is not about whether such a shift occurred, or who was involved, or what the change in the general conceptual framework consisted of, *but whether or not to call what happened a true paradigm shift.*

The issue here, of course, is how the word "paradigm" is to be defined. According to Kuhn, one does not have real paradigms in the social sciences because the examples, research strategies, instruments, etc., which provide the models from which a tradition springs are not *completely and firmly shared* – as they are in the physical and natural sciences. Speaking of "pre-paradigmatic" science, Kuhn says:

> fundamental disagreements characterized, for example, the study of motion before Aristotle and of statics before Archimedes, the study of heat before Black, of chemistry before Boyle and Boerhaave, and of historical geology before Hutton. In parts of biology – the study of heredity, for example – the first universally received paradigms are still more recent: *and it remains an open question what parts of social science have yet acquired such paradigms at all.* History suggests that the road to *a firm research consensus* is extraordinarily arduous. (Italics added) (1970:15)

So, from the Kuhnian viewpoint, what I have been calling "paradigms" in the history of anthropology and psychology should really be called something else – perhaps "pre-paradigmatic traditions" or "quasi-paradigms." However, what we find in psychology or anthropology also consists of "accepted examples of scientific practice" which "provide models from which spring particular coherent traditions of scientific research." What is different about them is that *the paradigms in the social sciences are less widely accepted than the paradigms in the physical and natural sciences.* This is easy to understand – the physical and natural science paradigms are *better* than the paradigms in psychology and anthropology. That is, the paradigms in physics, chemistry, and biology fit a broader range of facts, are more precisely stated, and give more effective predictions than the paradigms in the social sciences and psychology. The high degree of sharing and firmness of commitment of the physical scientists to their conceptual schemes, exemplars, research strategies, etc., is not due to anything special about the intrinsic character of their conceptual schemes, exemplars, and research strategies as such, but to their superiority in explaining the world. In my view it would be a mistake to make a *high degree of sharing* the criterion by which one decides what is or is not a paradigm. It is like refusing to call someone a "runner" unless they win a race.[10] But in any case, whatever we call it, the revolution occurred.

The cognitive revolution was more indirect in its effect on anthropology than in its effect on psychology and linguistics. Anthropology had been less behavioristic in its orientation than psychology and linguistics, and so the revolutionaries had less to change. However, anthropology had arrived at a point where the dominant agenda was reaching exhaustion. In fact, by the time the cognitive revolution hit psychology, anthropology had already begun to move towards more ideational, mental, and cognitive concerns – the study of ideas, beliefs, values, and cosmologies. In 1955, J. Beattie, a respected British social anthropologist, wrote a paper titled "Contemporary Trends in British Social Anthropology." In this paper he says:

> Evans-Pritchard suggests that *the full understanding of human societies requires that they be studied as moral or symbolic systems*, not simply as "natural" systems . . . This general broadening of theoretical approach . . . has led to a marked advance in the study of beliefs and ideas . . . Recent studies, therefore, have undertaken the study of *systems of ideas and beliefs* not exclusively from the functional point of view, but also *as systems in their own right*. (Italics added) (1955:12)

The shift from the study of institutional behavior – "natural systems" – to the ethnographic study of "idea systems" or "symbolic systems" appears to have been a very general trend. George Mandler has suggested that a major cause of this shift was the tremendous expansion of the importance of communication and information technology throughout industrial societies by mid-century.[11] The dependence of society on the growth, organization, and retrieval of information was becoming clearly apparent in the development of telephone, radio, television, phonograph, and film industries. The computer was not the cause of the cognitive revolution in psychology, but rather the new piece of technology that symbolized in physical form the power of information manipulation.

This trend in the social sciences towards the study of idea systems occurred in Britain, France, and the United States, although each country had its own particular direction. In the United States Clyde Kluckhohn had moved from the functionalist perspective found in his 1949 classic work on *Navaho Witchcraft*

[10] In the second edition of *The Structure of Scientific Revolutions*, Kuhn explicitly recognizes this distinction between "cognitive content" as paradigm versus the "consensus of the scientific community" as paradigm, a distinction he admits is conflated in the first edition, but which he does not completely renounce in the second edition. See pp.174-190.

[11] Personal communication.

to the study of Navaho concepts and values. One of his first publications in this area was an attempt to lay out the basic philosophic ideas of the Navahos. Below is Kluckhohn's summarization of the Navaho concept of the universe:

1. The universe is orderly: all events are caused and interrelated.
   a. Knowledge is power.
   b. The quest is for harmony.
   c. Harmony can be restored by orderly procedures.
   d. One price of disorder, in human terms, is illness.
2. The universe tends to be personalized.
3. The universe is full of dangers.
4. Evil and good are complementary, and both are ever present.
5. Morality is conceived in traditionalistic and situational terms rather than in terms of abstract absolutes.
6. Human relations are premised upon familistic individualism. (1949b)

Despite Kluckhohn's great knowledge of Navaho culture, these results are not impressive. The propositions are too abstract, too general, almost disembodied. Many tribal groups could be described in these terms. It is unclear to what degree the selection of these particular propositions depended on Kluckhohn's special interests. Kluckhohn's pioneering attempt to state Navaho philosophic assumptions did not appear to be the best way to get at cultural "idea systems'.

Shifting from very general "conceptions of the universe" Kluckhohn turned to the study of *values*. He defined "values" as "conceptions of the desirable" – that is, a special class of socially shared *ideas* about what is "good". In the early fifties he organized a project in the American Southwest in which the cultural values of five different societies – Zuni, Navaho, Morman, Texan, and Spanish American – were to be analyzed and related to ethnographic descriptions of social, economic, and religious institutions in each of these societies. This work aroused considerable interest in anthropology and the social sciences in general.[12] However, the results were generally agreed to be disappointing.[13] The major problem seems to have involved the *identification* of values. If a universal classification system was used, like Florence Kluckhohn's universal framework for the analysis of values, specific cultural values were left undescribed and unanalyzed.[14] But no procedures had been developed to determine specific cultural values. By the late fifties Clyde Kluckhohn had lost interest in the study of values and shifted his interest to new work in communication and linguistic anthropology.

There were other examples of this new tendency to change the "ethnographic object" – that which is to be described – in the direction of idea systems. Meyer Fortes, an outstanding British social anthropologist, wrote a monograph titled

[12] For a summary of this work see Vogt and Albert 1966.
[13] A good review of Clyde Kluckhohn's work on values is Edmunson 1973.
[14] See Kluckhohn and Strodtbeck 1961.

Oedipus and Job in West African Religion, which was first published in 1959. It gave an outline of religious concepts which define the relationship of the individual to Tallensi society in great ethnographic detail. Robin Horton, in an introductory essay to a second publication of *Oedipus and Job*, argues that Fortes was attempting to look at a religious system as a kind of folk "social psychology" in which supernatural forces can be understood as internalized psychological forces.

Another more controversial example is Edward Banfield's *The Moral Basis of a Backward Society*, published in 1958. Banfield gives a brief ethnographic description of Montegrano, a small and then desperately poor town in the province of Potenza in southern Italy. As a political scientist, Banfield begins by pointing to the lack of any effective local political organization in Montegrano along with the lack of any sense of shared community for which people are willing to make some sacrifice. His book is an attempt to answer the question "what accounts for the political incapacity of the village?" The answer Banfield found was that the usual explanations of poverty, a history of oppression, and class antagonisms were insufficient – that basically the resources for political action were present, but stopped by a *value system* of "amoral familism." The idea that it was a set of ideas, rather than structural or material conditions, that prevented social progress was intensely debated. Roy Miller, who did a study of "amoral familism" in a village near Montegrano, cites an "almost acrimonious exchange" between Banfield and Robert Redfield, an eminent American anthropology, during a seminar at the University of Chicago (1974). Given Redfield's legendary good humor and kindliness, the thesis that a bad life might be due to bad values must have provoked Redfield greatly.

Perhaps the most challenging new agenda in anthropology in the late fifties was an amalgam of ethnoscience with linguistic anthropology. Ethnoscience had long been a minor sub-field of ethnography concerned with the study of what native peoples knew about biology, zoology, astronomy, and related topics. This interest had always been a part of Boazian ethnography, which had from its inception been concerned with the rich variety of cultural knowledge to be found in any society. In the Yale department of anthropology, influenced by George Murdock, a strong program in ethnography had developed. The anthropologists trained at Yale had been concerned to raise the standards of ethnography to the kind of precision that linguists were able to obtain in their descriptions of native languages. In this endeavor they were supported and inspired by Floyd Lounsbury, an anthropological linguist at Yale who had worked with American Indian languages and was specially interested in kinship systems.

Lounsbury and Ward Goodenough published a pair of papers in 1956 on the semantic analysis of kinship terms. Lounsbury analyzed an American Indian kin term system, Pawnee, which had a complex kind of generational skewing (to be described later), while Goodenough analyzed a kin term system from

Truk in the Pacific which had a similar kind of skewing. These two papers had a great impact on the field.

To understand why these papers by Lounsbury and Goodenough had the effect they had, and understand how these papers came to form the basis of the early theories of cognitive anthropology, we must leave our historical overflight and enter into the more detailed world of ethnographic description.

2 Towards an analysis of meaning

It is one thing to be interested in the ethnographic study of idea systems. It is another thing to be able to carry out this type of investigation successfully, as Kluckhohn's work with Navaho philosophy indicated. The basic problem revolves around the issue of *identification*; that is, *the development of a method by which an ethnographer can reliably identify cultural ideas, beliefs, or values.* At first the issue did not seem particularly problematic. It seemed one could simply interview the people one was studying, and from these interviews determine the native systems of ideas.

Indeed, there had been a number of studies in anthropology which used this approach. Malinowski had interviewed the Trobrianders about their beliefs about magic and religion and Evans-Pritchard had interviewed the Azande about their beliefs about witchcraft, to cite two well-known examples. Such interviewing was sufficient to investigate the specific ideas surrounding a specific set of institutions. However, ordinary interviewing did not get at deeper, more general understandings which were not related to any particular set of cultural practices.

Further, there was a general intuition that cultural systems of ideas consisted of more than just *lists* of statements. The intuition was that there was something *organized and systematic* about culturally shared ideas, that they had some kind of *structure* or form. Note the continual use of the terms "system" and "systematic" in the quote from Beattie in the previous chapter. But what form did these systems have? Conceptual clarification of these questions had to be forthcoming before real ethnographic research could be carried out.

One of the early formulations concerning the nature of cultural idea systems was presented in a paper by Anthony Wallace on "Revitalization Movements" (1956). Wallace defined a revitalization movement as a "deliberate, organized, conscious effort by members of a society to construct a more satisfying culture." Such attempts at drastic and rapid change are typically found in nativistic, revivalist, and messianic movements in which a society, stressed by rapid social change, attempts radically to restructure its institutions to bring about a new, more effective way of life.

According to Wallace, revitalization movements are brought about by a charismatic leader who has a vision which serves as a guide to a new way of life. This vision constitutes a restructuring first of the prophet's and eventually a whole segment of the society's *mazeway.* A mazeway, as defined by Wallace, is "a mental image of the society and its culture." It includes "perceptions of both the maze of physical objects of the environment (internal and external, human and non-human) and also of the ways in which this maze can be manipulated by the self and others in order to minimize stress."

The concept of a "mazeway" – *a mental image* of the objects in a person's world and how they can be manipulated – proved useful in describing the kind of change brought about by visionaries such as Handsome Lake, the Seneca prophet who established a new religion and way of life among nineteenth-century reservation Iroquois. However, while useful as a formulation broader in scope than traditional terms like "religion" and "magic," the "mazeway" concept still left unspecified the problem of how to identify the elements of the "mental image" and how to determine how these elements are organized.

Structure

The reason that the kinship terminology papers by Lounsbury and Goodenough had such a large impact was that they presented a rigorous method for identifying "idea units" and analyzing the organization or structure of these units. While developed specifically for the analysis of kinship terms, it appeared that the general principles involved in identification and analysis could be extended to other domains. It was this body of methods and goals which was to become the agenda of cognitive anthropology.

The basic ideas used by Lounsbury and Goodenough were not novel. In fact, the development of these ideas goes back at least to the 1920s in linguistics. At the First International Congress of Slavic Philologists, the Prague Linguistic Circle, including such figures as Roman Jakobson and N. Trubetzkoy, presented a *Thèse* which introduced the concept of "structure" as a key theoretical term. Influenced by linguists such as Ferdinand de Saussure and Baudouin de Courtenay, the Prague Circle went against the standard philological agenda of historical study and the construction of etymologies for particular words. The new agenda was to study language as a *system* of communication. The major question was to work out how the parts of a language fit together – how they make up a structure. A central idea was that the units of the structure could be identified only *in terms of their relationships with other units*. In making up the structure, the parts define each other, and in defining each other, the parts make a structure.

Jakobson and other linguists of the Prague School were able to apply the general concept of structure to various aspects of the study of language with notable success. Their exemplary work was in the area of phonology – the analysis of the sounds of a language. One basic idea that had been assimilated into

American linguistics through Jakobson and Halle's influential *Fundamentals of Language* was the notion of *distinctive features*. Briefly, rather than treating the "chunks of sound" (the sort of thing we recognize with letters of the alphabet) as the ultimate units, the distinctive feature approach decomposed each sound chunk into "features" which distinguish it from other such sound chunks.

Take, for example, the spoken word "pat." The sound represented by the "p" contrasts with the sound of "b" in "bat." The difference between the sounds is that the "p" sound is *unvoiced* – that is, the vocal chords do not vibrate when pronouncing "p," unlike the "b" sound in which the vocal chords do vibrate. The sound represented by "p" also contrasts with the sound of the "t" in "tat." Here the distinction between "p" and "t" is that for "p" the passage of air is first cut by closing the lips, then releasing the pressure, while for "t" the passage is first cut off by blocking the air with the tongue against the *alveolar* area immediately behind the teeth. Thus "p" is characterized by the articulatory feature of being a *bilabial stop*, while "t" is an *alveolar stop*.

Not all of the features of a particular sound in a particular word are necessarily distinctive. Some features may be *conditioned* by the surrounding environment of the word, and may not signal a true difference. For example, when pronouncing the word "pat," English speakers produce a small puff of air which can be felt by holding one's hand in front of one's mouth. This puff of air is called *aspiration*. However, when we pronounce the word "spat" we do not produce this puff of air. Yet in both cases we hear the same "p" phoneme because "aspiration" is non-distinctive in English (although aspiration is a distinctive feature in many languages).

There are other kinds of differences in pronunciation which are also non-distinctive – we may say "pat the cat gently" to a child, pronouncing the "p" with much less force than "push off!" to someone who is annoying us. Such stylistic and emphasis related features do not signal a difference in word meaning, and so are also non-distinctive.

What we hear, then, when we hear a word, is not exactly what is actually pronounced. What we hear are the distinctive features bound into bundles which form perceptual units called "phonemes." The phonemic analysis of a language uncovers the phonemes by determining the distinctive features of the language – that is, the structure of the distinctions which make up these units.

By the 1950s phonemic analysis had become a well-known exemplary model for the analysis of cultural materials. A programatic extension of this idea had been proposed by Kenneth Pike (1967), who argued that these same concepts and methods could be used in the analysis of other kinds of cultural materials, such as games or folktales. The important idea was that one could find structure *in* cultural materials by discovering distinctive contrasts between different aspects of these materials. Pike called such analyses *emic* analyses, based on the "-emic" suffix of the word "phonemic." To carry out an *emic* analysis one began with a set of categories brought in by the scientific observer and then tried to find out which of those categories really made a difference with respect to the way the natives understood and responded to things. The categories the scientific observer brought to the material prior to the *emic* analysis were called *etic* categories (after the term "phonetics', which is the study of the actual speech sounds produced in speaking a language).[1]

The importance of the idea of structure in the 1920s and 1930s was apparently quite general, and included mathematics as well as the physical, natural, and social sciences. Perhaps the importance of the concept of structure was due to the great power of such physical science achievements as the periodic table of elements and the analysis of the structure of atomic and sub-atomic elements. Certainly in the study of social institutions, the term "structure" was of central importance to social anthropologists. The term was used by social anthropologists in a variety of senses, ranging from "structure" as the organization of the actual activities of real people to "structure" as the abstract and never fully realized model that lay behind the actual activities of real people. The definition of "structure" was intensely contested, but its importance remained unquestioned.

The particular idea of structure promulgated by the Prague Circle had a major influence on many anthropologists. For example, the model of phonemic analysis greatly influenced Claude Levi-Strauss, a French anthropologist, who met Jakobson in New York during the years of World War II. Levi-Strauss developed a method he termed "structural analysis" which he applied with imagination to kinship systems and to a variety of other materials such as myths and folktales. Clifford Geertz, David Schneider, and Victor Turner, in their different ways, developed similar agendas, called *symbolic anthropology* or *interpretative anthropology*, for the analysis of cultural symbols. Some discussion and critique of these alternative agendas will be presented in later chapters.

The feature analysis of kin terms

Among simple, non-literate societies, kinship constitutes the major social institution. That is, the roles that make up the social organization of the society are primarily kinship roles: in such societies most of one's positions are assigned on the basis of kinship and most of what one will be expected to do will be based on the kinship positions one is assigned. One of the things that ethnographers discovered early on was that the kinship systems in these societies were different than the kinship system of modern western society.

1 There has been a good deal of dispute about just what the terms "etic" and "emic" mean. According to Marvin Harris (1968), "emic" analyses are criteria and explanations given by informants, while "etic" analyses are criteria and explanations used by the scientific observer. This is not what Pike meant by the terms at all. For example, if one asked a typical American informant what the vowels of English are, one would not get anything close to a real phon*emic* analysis, but rather a rough approximation to English orthography. Harris' confusion on this matter seems to be motivated by his irritation with the philosophic idealism implicit in much of the research on the structure of idea systems.

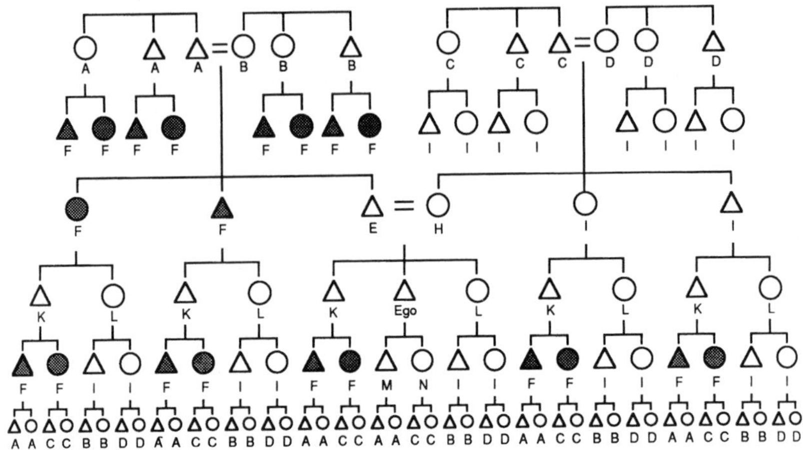

Key for Chiricahua kin terms

A cìnálé	E cìtàà	F cìdèèdèè’	K cìkìs
B cìt’cìné	H cìmáá’	I cì¥ó¥é	L cílà’
C cìtsóyé	M cì¥è’		
D cìtcó	N cìyát’cé’		

“c” is pronounced like the “sh” in “shell”
` represents a low tone
´ represents a high tone
¥ is a voiced velar fricative

Figure 2.1 Chiricahua kinship terms

Along with a different organization of kinship roles, these societies typically had systems of kinship terminology which were also different from those of western societies. With no outstanding exceptions, ethnographers were able to find “marriage” and “parent/child” relationships in every society. In every society these two basic genealogical relationships were organized into complex categories, such as *uncle* or *sister-in-law* in English. However, the complex kin categories of non-western societies frequently did not correspond to anything like the organization of kin terms in English, French, or German.

Consider the genealogical chart (Figure 2.1) for Chiricahua kin terms, taken from Bellah (1952:71). This chart is a standard format for presenting the organization of kin terms. The triangles stand for males, the circles for females. At the center of the chart is a person, called “ego,” who is center of the entire network of relationships. Each of the females (circles) and males (triangles) are connected by a pathway of lines to ego. Vertical lines stand for parent/child relationships, horizontal lines stand for sibling relationships. The equal sign stands for a marriage relationship.

While the chart presents a diagram of ego's genealogical relationships to a variety of types of kin, it is an idealized diagram – a real person might have three sisters, no brothers, six father's brothers, etc. However, on the chart ego has exactly one brother, one sister, one father's brother, etc. The chart has been idealized so each *kind* of relationship is represented by a pathway to a single triangle or circle.

Under each circle or triangle is a letter. This letter stands for the actual *term* used by the Chiricahua for that kin type. For example, ego's father's brother is labeled with term F, *cìdèèdèè'*. Ego's father's sister is also labeled with term F, *cìdèèdèè'*. All the kin types labeled with term F have been filled in with cross-hatching to make visually apparent the wide variety of kin types to which this term applies.

It would be hard to find a translation term for the Chiricahua term *cìdèèdèè'*. Our term "uncle" would not be right, since the Chiricahua term includes such kin types as father's sister (whom we call "aunt,") brother's son (whom we call "nephew"), and brother's daughter (whom we call "niece"). Also mother's brother (whom we also call "uncle") is labeled with term I *ci¥ó¥é* by the Chiricahua, not *cìdèèdèè'*.

The chart presented here is for a male ego. The terms are almost the same for a female ego with two exceptions. First, the K and L terms are reversed for a female ego – a woman refers to her brother and male cousins by term L and her sister and female cousins by term K. Second, a woman's son's child would be referred to by term B and a woman's daughter's child by term D, rather than A and C as they are for a male ego.

It should be mentioned that the terms presented in the chart above are *terms of reference*, not *terms of address*. That is, the terms on the chart are roughly what an informant would answer if one asked "What is Jose Yaze, your mother's brother, to you?" The question can be put in a number of ways, but the idea is to get the name of the relationship. This term may differ considerably from the way the informant will "address" Jose Yaze when they meet – the informant may address him by his first name, "Jose", or perhaps by some special term of affection, or perhaps by the same term that the informant would use to "refer" to Jose Yaze when speaking of him to another person. Generally, anthropologists emphasize the analysis of terms of reference more than terms of address, which tend to be highly variable and often affected by situational factors.

The problem that Lounsbury and Goodenough solved was how to analyze the organization or structure of a kin term system. This method was called *componential analysis*, although the term *feature analysis* is more common at present. The procedures presented here are basically an adaptation of Lounsbury and Goodenough's methods developed by A. K. Romney.[2] These procedures consist of an explicit step-by-step process to carry out a componential analysis of kin

2 See Romney and D'Andrade 1964.

terms. The first step in the analysis is to see what is common about each term. For example, let us begin with term F. There are twenty different kin types on the chart above which all are labelled by term F. What do they have in common?

To illustrate diagrammatically what the different kin types labelled F have in common, let us begin with a simple reduction of two kin types in a single more encompassing expression. As described above, it makes no difference whether *ego* is *male* or *female* with respect to term F. For example, a *male ego* calls his *father's brother* by term F, and so does a *female* ego. Since the sex of ego does not matter, the two expressions can be combined into a single form using *a square to stand for a person who can be either a male or a female* (see Figure 2.2). Continuing the analysis, both ego's father's brother and ego's father's sister are referred to by term F. In Figure 2.3 below the two kin types are presented and then combined into a single form again using the square to stand for a person who can be a male or a female.

What has happened in Figures 2.2 and 2.3 is that the sex markers indicated by the triangle and the circle have been replaced by squares because it does not matter with regard to term F whether ego is *male* or *female* and it does not matter whether one is referring to one's father's *brother* or father's *sister.* The sex difference at these points in the expression makes no difference. Romney calls this the *rule of minimum difference*. This is the first rule one applies in finding out what kin types have in common.

Two other kin types referred to by term F are brother's son and brother's daughter. Again it does not matter whether ego is male or female – both a man and a woman call their brother's son and their brother's daughter by term F. Figure 2.4 below illustrates these relations and combines them into a single form on a repeated application of the rule of minimum difference.

Looking at Figures 2.3 and 2.4, we can see that both summary forms can be combined into a single form, since the second form is simply the *reciprocal* of the first form. Or to put it in another way, if person *X* calls person *Y* by term F, then person *Y* calls person *X* by term F. In English, only the term "cousin" is completely reciprocal – if someone calls you "cousin," you call them "cousin." For Chiricahua the use of reciprocal terms is much more common than in English. This next step of combining kin types is presented in Figure 2.5.

Romney calls this the *rule of reciprocals* – where two expressions labelled by the same term differ only in being reciprocals of one another, they can be combined into a single expression.

There are still a number of kin types labelled F that are not included in our current summary expression. All of ego's father's parent's sibling's children are also labelled F. (Here I have already applied the minimum difference rule – the complete list of kin types would include ego's father's mother's sister's son, ego's father's mother's sister's daughter, ego's father's mother's brother's son, ego's father's mother's brother's daughter, etc.)

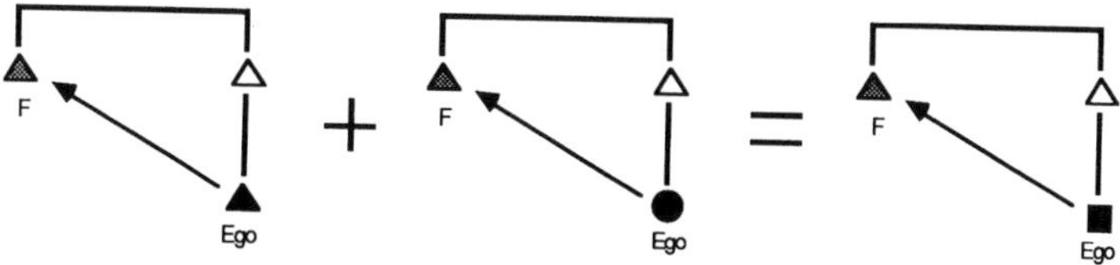

Figure 2.2 Sex of ego reduction of term F kin types

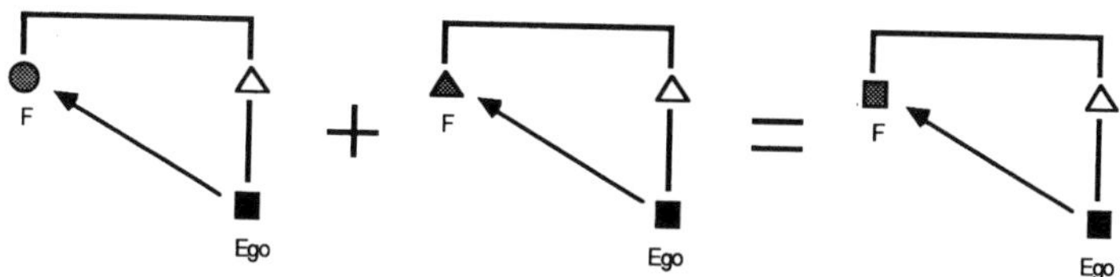

Figure 2.3 Sex of alter reduction of term F kin types

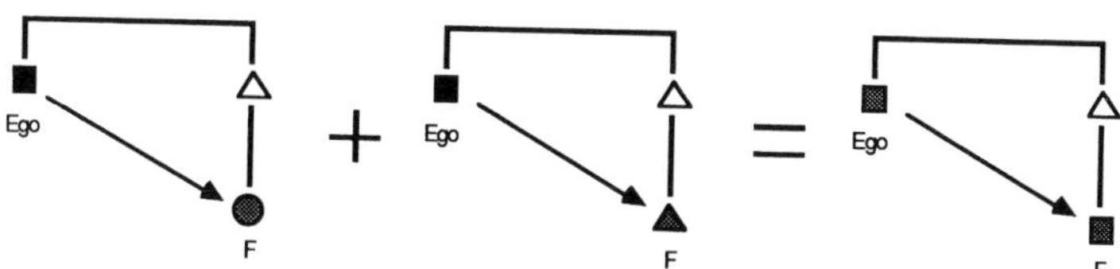

Figure 2.4 Further sex of alter reduction of term F kin types

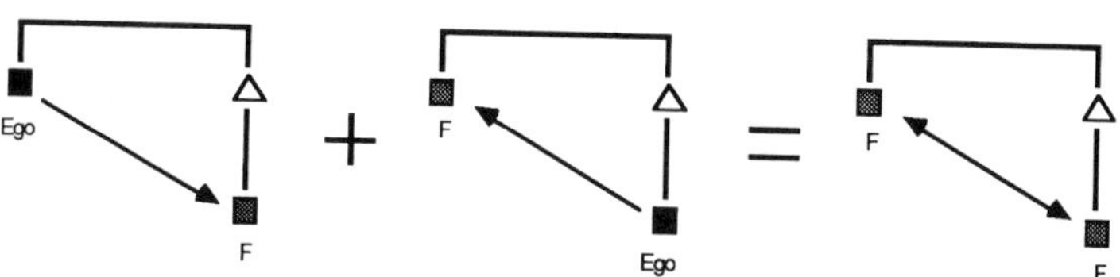

Figure 2.5 Reciprocal reduction of term F kin types

Another set of kin types labelled F that are not included in our summary expression are all of ego's male cousin's children. (Here again the rule of minimum difference has been applied to summarize the full set of kin types which would include ego's father's brother's son's son, ego's father's brother's son's daughter, ego's mother's brother's son's son, etc.) If we diagram these two sets of terms, it can be seen that they are, in fact, simple reciprocals of each other, and can be combined into a single expression by the reciprocal rule (see Figure 2.6).

We have now collapsed the different kin types labelled F into only two expressions. The two expressions, presented in Figure 2.7, differ only in the

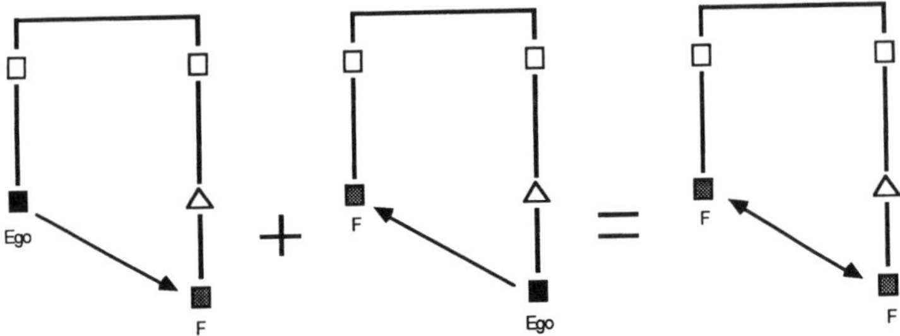

Figure 2.6 Further reciprocal reduction of term F kin types

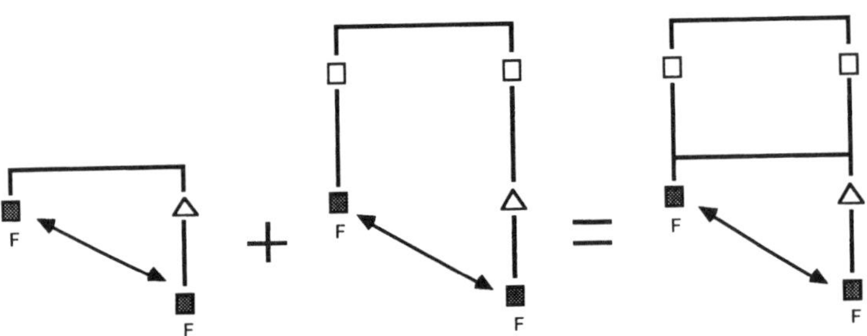

Figure 2.7 Sequence difference reduction of term F kin types

presence of additional genealogical links in one expression that are not present in the other expression. These two can be combined because of the fact that they are labelled by the same term, indicating that these additional genealogical links are a difference that makes no difference. Romney calls this kind of reduction the *rule of sequence difference*. The summary expression shows *two* paths by which persons labelling each other with term F may be related; in the ascending direction one path goes from ego's father to his sibling, in the ascending direction the other path goes from ego's father to his parent and then to his parent's sibling and finally to ego's father's parent's sibling's child.

The final summary expression can be read – the following kin call each other by term F: *ego's father's sibling or cousin and the reciprocal of that relationship*. In examining the summary expression we see that the crucial thing is that the relationship go through a *male* link between generations. In a more technical fashion we might define term F as *a consanguineal relative of my parent's generation who is on my father's side of the family*, or, for the reciprocal descending relationship, *a consanguineal relative who is the child of a man of my generation*.

At this point the reader may have begun to experience a kind of vertigo which overtakes people who are not used to thinking about exotic kinship relationships. It is really not that the material is complicated. It is mostly quite simple

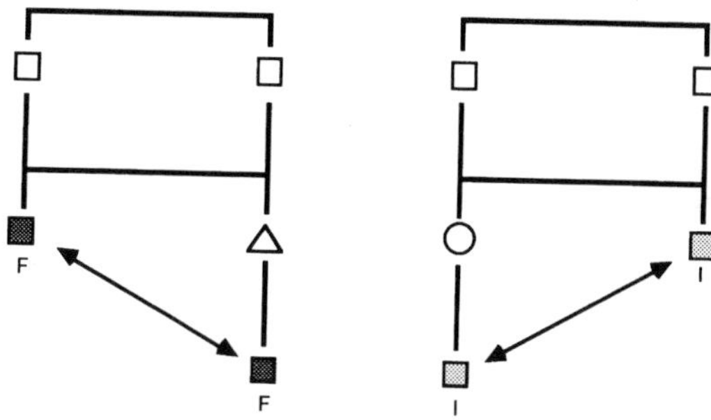

Figure 2.8 Reduced expressions for Chiricahua terms F and I

– when one thinks in other categories. Our own English groupings of kin – the "aunts and uncles," the "cousins," the "grandparents," our "parents," our "siblings" – seem easy and obvious to us. The way the Chiricahua divide the world seems more complex and confusing. However, the principles in both cases are equally simple.

We have seen how a term can be reduced to a single expression (or diagram) which collapses the distinctions which do not make a difference and retains the distinctions which do make a difference. Using the same strategy of combining forms, term I can also be reduced to a single expression or diagram. The reduced expressions for term F and term I are presented together in Figure 2.8. Comparing terms F and I it can clearly be seen that the terms are identical in all respects except that term F is distinguished by relations through a *male* while term I is distinguished by relations through a *female*. Both terms include only *consanguineal relatives* (not linked through any relatives by marriage), both terms involve kin who are separated by exactly *one generation*, both terms are *self-reciprocal* (if you call someone F they call you F, if you call someone I they call you I), and both terms involve *collaterals* (that is, relatives like English "aunts" or "nieces" who are related to one through a *sibling link*).

The point of doing the reductions so that each term is represented by a single diagram is to allow a direct comparison between terms. In looking at the full kin term chart for Chiricahua the differences between term F and term I are not obvious in the way they are in Figure 2.7.[3]

[3] The diagrammatic scheme used here is not the only way in which kin types can be represented. Romney developed a notational system using "m" for male, "f" for female, "a" for a person of either sex, "=" for marriage, "+" for a child to parent link, "–" for a parent to child link, and "o" for a sibling link. Such a system is much easier to write than the diagrams presented above. Despite its ease of use, Romney's notation system did not become standard for the field, perhaps because the letters conflicted with the standard notational system (e.g. the standard notation for ego's mother's brother's daughter's husband is "MBDH" or sometimes "MoBrDaHu", while in Romney's notation it is "a + f o m – f = m"). With Romney's notation symbols can be rewritten and manipulated in an algebraic manner, making a kin term feature analysis much less complex and laborious.

What the analysis of the two Chiricahua terms does is to give us a simple model of how an analysis of meaning can be done. Note that the list of the different kin types was *not* considered to be the meaning of the term. Recall that the kin types are all the particular relationships labelled by a term – kin types for term F, for example, are ego's father's brother, ego's father's sister, ego's mother's sister's son's son, etc. Using the language of Charles Morris, the kin types are the *denotata* of the term – the things to which the term "refers." What we have done is to analyze the list of kin types for a particular term and try to find out what the referents all have in common that contrasts with the kin types of other terms. We will call these properties by which one term contrasts with another *distinctive features*.

The distinctive feature that distinguishes between term F and term I is the kind of link between kin on one generation and kin on the generation above. This is quite different than English kin terms for "uncle" and "aunt" where the sex of the linking relative does not matter – only the sex of the person being classified. A standard format to show the feature composition of term F and I would be:

F = consanguineal	1 generation from ego	collateral male link
I = consanguineal	1 generation from ego	collateral female link

Besides terms F and I, the other generation one terms are just as they are for the English terms *father*, *mother*, *son*, and *daughter*. Given the simplicity of these terms, reduction by various rules to a single expression is not necessary. The feature composition of these terms is:

E = consanguineal	1 generation from ego	direct	ascending	male
H = consanguineal	1 generation from ego	direct	ascending	female
M = consanguineal	1 generation from ego	direct	descending	male
N = consanguineal	1 generation from ego	direct	descending	female

The feature *direct* contrasts with the feature *collateral*. Direct relatives are those that are linked to ego through parent/child links only, no sibling links being present. For these four terms the female vs. male link distinction is not relevant.

Unlike the English system, the Chiricahua system does not distinguish between siblings and cousins. Brothers, sisters, and cousins are all called by the same terms. The distinction of sex is also made quite differently among the Chiricahua. There are two terms, K and L. Term K refers to those siblings and cousins who are of the *same sex* as ego, while term L refers to those cousins and siblings who are of the *opposite sex* from ego. The feature composition of these terms is:

K = consanguineal	same generation as ego	same sex as ego
L = consanguineal	same generation as ego	opposite sex from ego

The final set of terms, A, B, C, and D are grandparent/grandchild terms. There are four of these terms in Chiricahua. They are like the F and I terms in that in all cases the terms are self-reciprocal – if you call someone by term A, that person calls you by term A. Thus the distinction we make between ascending generation terms (*grandmother*, *grandfather*) and descending generation terms (*granddaughter*, *grandson*) is not made for these Chiricahua terms. Nor does the sex of the relative make a difference – each of the four terms refers to both males and females.

The important feature which distinguishes these four terms is, like terms F and I, whether the link to ego is *through* males or females. However, for these terms the *mother's side* vs. *father's side* distinction is *iterated*, so that term A, for example, is a relative two generations away from ego connected to ego through *two male links*. Thus term A applies to relatives linked to ego through *ego's father's father* going up the generational chain, or to relatives linked to ego through a male of ego's generation followed immediately by another male in the next generation. What is also different about these four terms compared to the F and I terms is that the *collateral* vs. *direct* feature does not apply – it does not matter whether A is ego's father's father (a direct relative) or ego's father's father's sibling (a collateral relative). The feature composition of these terms is:

A = consanguineal	2 generations from ego	male–male link
B = consanguineal	2 generations from ego	male–female link
C = consanguineal	2 generations from ego	female–male link
D = consanguineal	2 generations from ego	female–female link

Given that such an analysis does tell us about the meaning of Chiricahua terms, of what general use is it? One answer concerns the understanding of Chiricahua society. The Chiricahua ranged across southern New Mexico, Texas, and northern Mexico. With the acquisition of the horse, most Apachean groups, of which the Chiricahua were one, turned to raiding. The raiding complex put the Apachean peoples in conflict first with the Mexican government and then with American settlers and the US Army. In the period from 1861 to 1886 the Chiricahua were reduced from more than 1,000 to 400 people. After Geronimo's capture, and the removal of the tribe to Florida, there was an eventual resettlement of the Chiricahua to the Mescalero reservation in New Mexico.

Among the Chiricahua, the most important functional social unit was the *local group*. Each local group had a war leader, and the most important war leader functioned as the leader of a larger collection of local groups called a "band," which intermittently acted as a unified group in warfare. Each local group had a geographical base in a fairly impregnable mountain area. The local group served as the main economic unit for raiding and multifamily activities. Within the local group, the matrilocal extended family, composed of a number of nuclear families related through marriage, formed the main domestic unit. The matrilocal extended family was typically composed of a woman and her husband, one or more of her daughters and their husbands, along with their children. The matrilocal extended family was the primary economic unit, organizing hunting and gathering on a daily basis. Food was prepared in the mother-in-law's dwelling and distributed from there to other family members. Each nuclear family had its own dwelling.[4]

This brief description makes some sense of the distinction between terms F and I, and between the grandparent terms A, B, C, and D. Apparently the Chiricahua saw the world outside parents and children as divided into two halves – the relatives through one's father in contrast to relatives through one's mother. This contrast corresponds roughly to the way the kinship world was divided because of the matrilocal extended family. This distinction is further elaborated with respect to the grandparents, partitioning the world of relatives into father's father's side, father's mother's side, mother's father's side, and mother's mother's side, reinforcing the basic *side* distinction even further. However, this distinction was not made with respect to the same generation terms of *same* vs. *opposite sex* sibling or cousin – it is often the case in kinship systems around the world that same generation terms do not make as many distinctions as the parental generation terms.

This use of componential or feature analysis of kin terms is intended to give a sense of the mental world – the "real" categories – by which a culture made sense of its family and kin organization. Where kinship is the major social institution in a society, such an accomplishment has great ethnographic utility. Scheffler's work on Australian kinship terminologies, for example, uses a variety of this kind of semantic analysis to deal with a whole series of complex issues still surrounding Australian aboriginal kinship and social organization.[5] For those interested in pursuing further the semantic analysis of non-western kin term systems, Harold Scheffler and Floyd Lounsbury's book *A Study in Structural Semantics* is an excellent source.

A feature analysis of English kin terms

A kin term analysis is perhaps less centrally informative about American culture than about Australian aboriginal culture, since kinship is just one of many social institutions in our society. However, it is easier to present a feature analysis of English kin terms than Australian or Chiricahua kin terms because we, as English speakers, have already learned the distinctive features of this system. It would be possible to proceed in the same way we did with Chiricahua terms F and I, first reducing all the kin types to single expressions,

4 See Bellah 1952 and Opler 1937 for descriptions of Chiricahua society and culture.
5 Scheffler 1978.

		direct		collateral	
		male	female	male	female
G2	+	grandfather	grandmother		
	-	grandson	granddaughter		
G1	+	father	mother	uncle	aunt
	-	son	daughter	nephew	niece
G0		brother	sister	cousin	

Figure 2.9 Feature analysis of English kin terms

then discovering the characteristics which distinguish each of the expressions. Such an exercise is carried out in Romney and D'Andrade's (1964) paper "Cognitive Aspects of English Kin Terms." However, such reductions are not necessary for a non-technical presentation of English kin terms. A feature analysis, using a box diagram representation of English consanguineal kin terms is presented in Figure 2.9.

The *male* vs. *female* contrast is present in all terms except *cousin.* All terms are specific with respect to generation, although *cousin* in its extended sense can refer to higher or lower generation relatives.

The feature of *generation* refers to the absolute number of parent/child links between ego and the relative. Thus both an *uncle* and a *nephew* are in generation 1 because there is an absolute difference of one parent/child link between them. The difference between an *uncle* and a *nephew* is that the first is in an *ascending* generation, while the second is in a *descending* generation.

The contrast between *direct* vs. *collateral* relatives involves the distinction that collateral relatives are linked to ego through an *ascending sibling link,* while direct relatives are not linked to ego through an ascending sibling link. By this definition, ego's own siblings are not collaterals, while cousins are. One's *great-aunts* and *great-uncles* (the *brothers* and *sisters* of one's *grandparents*) would, of course, be collaterals, since they are linked to one through an ascending sibling link.

Not all analysts of English kin terms agree with the analysis presented here. The reasons for preferring this analysis will be presented later in a discussion concerning the psychological reality of feature analyses.

There is another point to be made concerning the usefulness of componential or semantic feature analysis. The analysis of kin terms served as an exemplary model of how to investigate cultural systems of meaning. The feature analysis of kin terms served as a central part of a particular paradigm which attempted to achieve precision and naturalness. In such an analysis the native categories are derived from an emic analysis of the way the natives discriminate things in their world rather than by imposing categories from the outside.

Thus one can trace a direct path from the call for structural analyses by Saussure, through the feature analyses of phonemes by the Prague School, to the semantic feature analyses of kinship terminologies. This is a line of research which served at the time as an example of the very best work done in the field. Those who rejected this kind of analysis of kin terms generally did so *not* because they had a better method for the analysis of these terms, but because they rejected either part of the agenda (that the road to understanding native systems of thought lay primarily in the analysis of native systems of terminology rather than the analysis of ritual or social action), or rejected the entire agenda (native systems of thought are not of interest because that is not the way to understand society and culture).

It is difficult to explain the beauty which a semantic analysis of kinship terms held for some anthropologists in 1960. In the present intellectual milieu, this type of analysis seems specialized, arcane, and formalistic. In 1960, the effect was quite different. Then such an analysis was experienced as a nearly magical process of discovery in which elegant simple patterns emerged from an initial jumble of kin terms and kin types. The patterns came out of the data, and, once seen, were unforgettable. In present day anthropology the field is less interested in discovery procedures and formalization. What was once generally considered exemplary work is now a matter of interest to only a very small number of kinship specialist.

3 The classic feature model

The particular kind of structure found for kinship terms is termed a *paradigm* – a different sense of the term than the "paradigms" of Kuhn's scientific revolutions. *In a complete paradigm all possible combinations of features actually occur.* An example of an almost complete paradigm in English is composed by the terms *man*, *woman*, *boy*, *girl*, and *baby*. The features here are *male* vs. *female* and *adult* vs. *immature* vs. *newborn*. A box diagram of this paradigm is presented below in Figure 3.1.

A similar paradigm for the domain of horses is presented in Figure 3.2. In both cases the paradigm is not fully complete because the term for a newborn – *foal* or *baby* – leaves sex unspecified, and for horses there are no terms for neutered females or neutered immature or newborn horses (perhaps because such types would be a rare occurrence).

	male	female
adult	man	woman
immature	boy	girl
newborn	baby	

Figure 3.1 Paradigmatic structure of English terms for *humans*

	male	female	neuter
adult	stallion	mare	gelding
immature	colt	filly	
newborn	foal		

Figure 3.2 Paradigmatic structure for English terms for *horses*

	subject	object	adjective	possessive
1st person singular	I	me	my	mine
plural	we	us	our	ours
2nd person singular	you	you	your	yours
plural	you	you	your	yours
3rd person singular male	he	him	his	his
female	she	her	her	hers
plural	they	them	their	theirs

Figure 3.3 Paradigmatic structure for English pronouns

	subject	object	adjective	possessive
2nd person singular	thou	thee	thy	thine
plural	ye	you	your	yours

Figure 3.4 Paradigmatic structure for second person pronouns used in King James Bible

The pronouns in current English constitute another well-known paradigm (see Figure 3.3). This paradigm is incomplete in that the distinction of gender is not made for 1st or 2nd person, or for 3rd person plural. Although the 2nd person has the same external form for singular and plural, the plural forms of *you* and the singular forms of *you* are actually different terms – context usually makes clear which sense is intended. In the King James version of the Bible – c. 1610 – the plural and singular 2nd person forms of the terms were clearly differentiated, as shown in Figure 3.4.

An interestingly different pronoun system is found in Hanunóo, a Philippine language. Harold Conklin (1969), who did the analysis of this system, found a complete paradigm constructed from three binary dimensions: *inclusion* vs. *exclusion of the speaker*, *inclusion* vs. *exclusion of the hearer*, and *minimal* vs. *non-minimal membership*. Conklin notes that the pronoun systems in Tagalog, Ilocano, Maranao, and some other Philippine

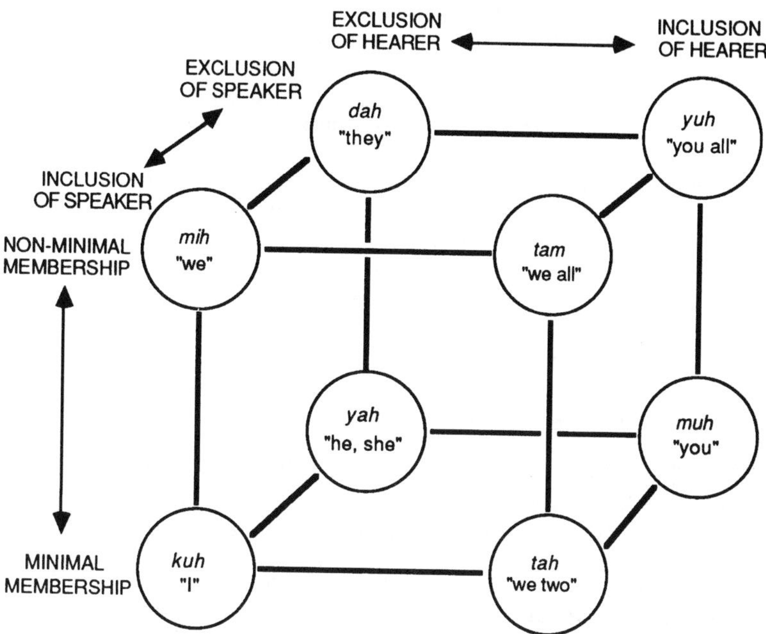

Figure 3.5 Paradigmatic structure of a Hanuóo pronominal set (adapted from Conklin 1969)

languages have a similar structure. The structure of this system is presented in diagrammatic form in Figure 3.5. It has a symmetric beauty that English lacks.

Complete paradigms turned out to be relatively rare in natural languages: typically only a few domains in each language display this type of structure. A possible reason that complete – or even partially complete – paradigms are so rare is that the world does not usually present us with sets of objects which display *all* possible combinations of features. The most extensive paradigms are usually found in domains that involve relationships, such as kin terms and pronouns, probably because of the greater combinatorial possibilities created by relationships. And, in many cases, even where distinctions could easily be made (we could have separate terms for baby boys and baby girls), people are not always motivated to make them.

Feature analysis, however, is not limited to analyses of paradigms. Feature analysis can be carried out on any set of contrasting terms. As Frake put it:

> In a few fields, notably in kinship studies, anthropologists have already successfully pushed an interest in terminological systems beyond a matching of translation labels . . . The recognition that the denotative range of kinship categories must be determined empirically in each case, that the categories form a system, and that the semantic

contrasts underlying the system are amenable to formal analysis, has imparted to kinship studies a methodological rigor and theoretical productivity rare among ethnographic endeavors. Yet all peoples are vitally concerned with kinds of phenomena other than genealogical relations; consequently *there is no reason why the study of a people's concepts of these other phenomena should not offer a theoretical interest comparable to that of kinship studies.*

The analysis of a culture's terminological system will not, of course, exhaustively reveal the cognitive world of its members, but it will certainly tap a central portion of it. Culturally significant cognitive features must be communicable between persons in one of the standard symbolic systems of the cultures. A major share of these features will undoubtedly be codable in a society's most flexible and productive communication device, its language . . . *To the extent that cognitive coding tends to be linguistic and tends to be efficient, the study of the referential use of standard, readily elicitable linguistic responses – or terms – should provide a fruitful beginning point for mapping a cognitive system.* (Italics added) (Frake 1962)

A theoretical vocabulary developed rapidly in the late 50s and early 60s for this "study of the referential use of standard, readily elicitable linguistic responses." The basic terms of this vocabulary are presented below.

A *lexeme* is a lexical unit which has a meaning which cannot be derived from the meaning of its sub-units. For example, a *white house* (a house which is white) is a complex term consisting of two distinct lexemes, while the *White House* (the residence of the president) is a complex term which comprises a single lexeme.

A *domain* is an area of conceptualization like space, color, the human body, kinship, pronouns, etc. Not all domains in a language are labeled with a single lexeme. Typically a domain is differentiated by more specific *lexemes*.

A class of objects – things in the world – referred to by a linguistic term may be called a *segregate*, or *denotata,* or if the things are biological, *taxa* (singular *taxon*). *Taxa* may correspond to groupings at the species, genera, families, or phyla level.

The objects in a segregate will usually share a number of *attributes* – properties they hold in common. A *semantic feature* of a term corresponds to a *criterial attribute* of the objects in a segregate, that is, to an attribute which distinguishes the objects in this segregate from objects in other segregates.

A *dimension* consists of a set of contrasting features. For example, the dimension of *sex* consists of the contrasting features *male* vs. *female,* and the dimension of *relative age* consists of the contrasting features *elder* vs. *younger.*

A series of terminologically contrasting segregates form a *contrast set.* Charles Frake (1962) uses the example of someone ordering food at an American lunch counter where the most inclusive segregate would be the

<table>
<tr><td colspan="5">something to eat</td></tr>
<tr><td colspan="2">sandwich</td><td colspan="2">pie</td><td>ice-cream bar</td></tr>
<tr><td>hamburger</td><td>ham sandwich</td><td>apple pie</td><td>cherry pie</td><td>Eskimo pie</td></tr>
</table>

Figure 3.6 Taxonomy for *something to eat* (adapted from Frake 1962)

class of available foods. One contrast set would include the segregates referred to by terms like *sandwich*, *hamburger*, and *apple pie*. Frake makes the point that a "rainbow" – while distinct from any of the other segregates – does not form a part of this contrast set because it does not function as an uncontrived alternative to any of the other items.

A *taxonomic* relation occurs when one segregate or taxon *includes* other segregates or taxa; for example the segregate referred to by the term *pie* includes the contrast sets *apple pie* and *cherry pie*.

Frake presents the small taxonomy of lunch counter foods (Figure 3.6). Whether a set of terms forms a paradigm or a taxonomy depends on the way in which the distinctive features are structured. Thus, given the terms L1, L2, . . . Ln, and the contrasting features a1, a2, b1, b2, . . . z1, z2, if a set of features is structured:

L1 = a1 b1
L2 = a1 b2
L2 = a2 b1
L2 = a2 b2

the terms will form a paradigm because all possible combinations of the "a" and "b" features occur. For example:

uncle	=	ascending generation	male
aunt	=	ascending generation	female
nephew	=	descending generation	male
niece	=	descending generation	female

which can be represented as in the box diagram for English kin terms in the preceding chapter. However, if the features are structured:

L1	=	a1	—
L2	=	a1	b1
L3	=	a1	b2

where "—" stands for the absence of any feature specification, the result will be that L1 is taxonomically related to L2 and L3. For example:

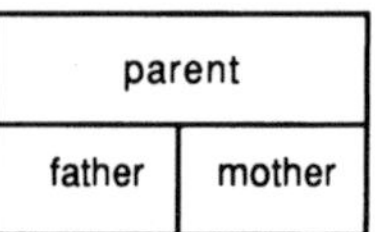

Figure 3.7 Taxonomy for *parent*

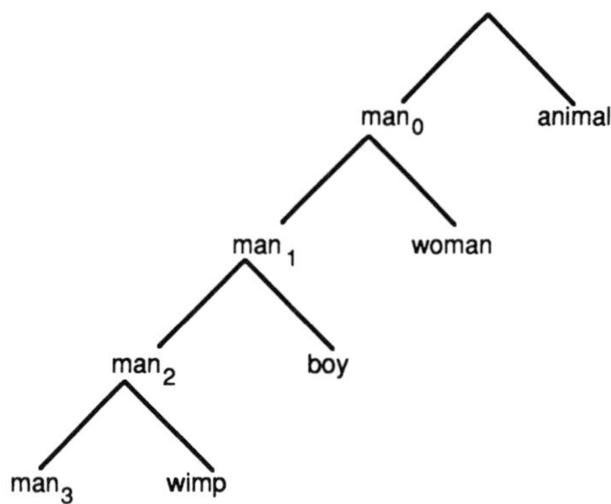

Figure 3.8 Taxonomic representation of polysemous sense of *man*

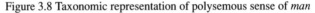

parent	=	consanguineal ascending	direct —
father	=	consanguineal ascending	direct male
mother	=	consanguineal ascending	direct female

The term *parent* is unspecified for gender. Except for the gender features *male* vs. *female* the terms *father* and *mother* have exactly the same features as the term *parent*. A standard box diagram for this small taxonomy is shown in Figure 3.7.

The point here is that *the way in which a set of terms is organized is derived from the way the features of these terms are structured relative to each other.* A complete paradigm, or incomplete paradigm, a taxonomy, or a mixture of a taxonomy and a paradigm can all be created by simple patterns of distinctive features.

Polysemy

A notable fact about most natural language terms is that they are *polysemous* – that is, most terms have more than one sense. A classic example is the term *man*. The term *man* has a number of related meanings which can be represented in a simple taxonomic hierarchy (see Figure 3.8). With respect to the feature structure of these senses of man, we find the following:

man_0	=	human			
man_1	=	human	male		
man_2	=	human	male	adult	
man_3	=	human	male	adult	courageous

In linguistics, when there are a pair of terms like *man* and *woman*, and one of the pair (*man*) has a more general sense that includes both members of the pair, this term is called the *unmarked* term. The term which does not include both (*woman*) is called the *marked* term. This type of situation is very common in all languages, and occurs not only in lexical items as illustrated above, but also in phonology and grammar (Greenberg 1966). In the case of *man* each of the senses (*man_1*, *man_2*, and *man_3*) is unmarked with respect to its oppositional senses (*woman*, *boy*, and *wimp*) because in each case there is a more general sense of *man* which includes both of the more specific senses. Note that the marked term *woman* is also morphologically *marked* by the addition of *wo-* to *man*. Similarly, *fe-male* and *author-ess* are also morphologically marked. However, *boy* and *wimp* are not morphologically marked, but are *semantically* marked). Thus, sometimes, but not always, the semantically marked term also has a special morphological marker.

This phenomena of marking is very general. It occurs at the phonological and grammatical levels of language as well as the lexicon, and is found in all languages. As Joseph Greenberg says:

> The pervasive nature in human thinking of this tendency to take one of the members of an oppositional category as unmarked so it represents either the entire category or *par excellence* the opposite member to the marked category can be shown to operate even within the austere confines of mathematical and logical symbolism. Thus negative is always taken as the marked member of the positive–negative opposition; –5 is always negative, but 5 by itself is either the absolute value of 5, that is 5 abstracted from its sign value, or +5 as the opposite of the marked negative category. So, in logic *p* was used ambiguously either as the proposition *p* abstracted from its truth value as either true or false or, on the other hand, for the assertion of the truth of *p*. Note that logicians use the term "truth value", involving the unmarked member, not "falsity value" to express the over-all category which has truth and falsity as members so that, as usual the unmarked member stands for the whole category in the position of neutralization. (1966:25-26)

A common kind of marking occurs with pairs of contrasting adjectives such as *good–bad*, *many–few*, *long–short*, *wide–narrow*, *deep–shallow*. In each of these pairs the first term is the unmarked case. It is the first term which is unmarked because it is the first term which refers to the entire dimension. We ask "how good is the wine?" if we do not know whether wine is either good or bad, thus using the term *good* to refer to the entire dimension. We only ask "how bad is the wine" if we already know it is bad, and we want to know *how* bad.

It is generally the case that the unmarked term occurs with higher frequency than the marked term. Table 3.1, taken from Greenberg (1966), gives the Lorge magazine count for the frequency of these adjective pairs in English. There are

Table 3.1. *Lorge magazine count*

Term	Frequency	Term	Frequency
Good	5,122	*Bad*	1,001
Many	3,874	*Few*	2,730
Long	5,362	*Short*	887
Wide	593	*Narrow*	391
Deep	881	*Shallow*	104

a number of possible explanations for the fact that the unmarked term usually occurs more frequently than the marked term. One explanation is that because the unmarked member is typically of greater interest to people, it is both referred to more frequently and perceived as more appropriate to serve as the more general term. Another explanation is that it is cognitively more efficient to make the high frequency term the unmarked term, since if one of the pair of terms is to be used as the upper level term the more frequent term will come to mind more easily. A third explanation is that since the unmarked term has at least two senses it therefore has more chance to be mentioned than the marked term. Probably all these factors have varying degrees of influence on the frequencies depending on the particular set of terms.

Conjunctivity (or non-disjunctiveness)

In all of the examples used so far, it has been assumed that the features which define a term are conjunctively related; that is, they *jointly* define the term and so are connected together by the logical relationship *and*. For example, an *uncle* is a collateral *and* a relative one generation above ego *and* a male. Such a term is conjunctively defined. However, one can define a class of kin types quite differently – one could define some relative (say a "blove") as someone who is *either* a female relative *or* a younger generation relative. When a term is defined as *either* X *or* Y, it is said to have a *disjunctive* definition. Such terms are relatively rare. It could be said that polysemy is a kind of disjunctiveness, and polysemy is quite common. For example, the term *man* could be said to refer to *either* a human, *or* a human male, *or* a human adult male, *or* a courageous human adult male. The standard analysis is to say that these are different but related *senses* of the term *man*, rather than one sense which is defined by a disjunctive set of features.)

A good example of an English word which has a particular sense requiring a disjunctive definition is the term *strike* in baseball. A strike can be:

(a) *either* a "swing" at the ball by the batter which did not hit the ball,
(b) *or* a ball thrown over the plate between the knees and the shoulders and called a "strike" by the umpire,

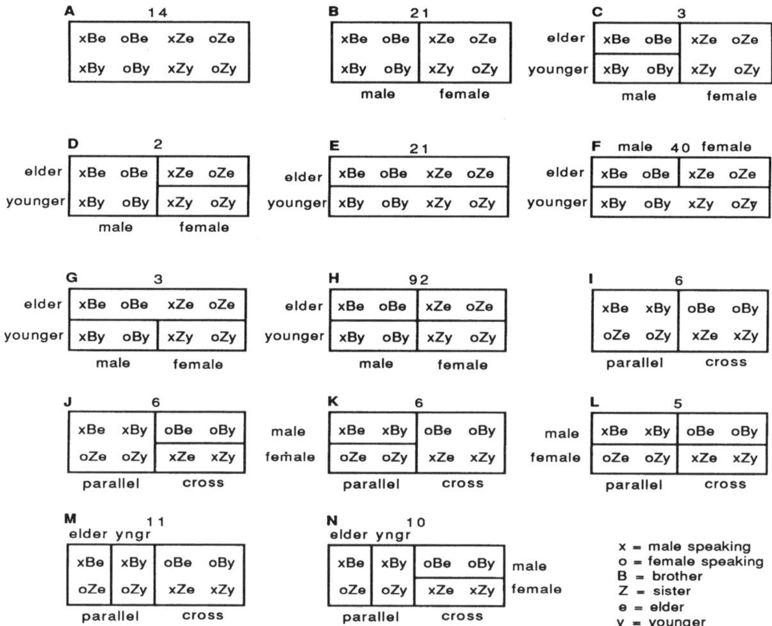

Figure 3.9 Types and frequencies of sibling terminology

(c) *or* a ball hit "foul" and not caught (unless the batter already has two strikes, in which case the uncaught "foul" does not count as a strike).

Note that such definitions are hard to learn – there are Americans who occasionally watch baseball who have not fully learned what a strike is. Disjunctiveness is thought to be rare because it is much more difficult to learn disjunctive classes than conjunctive classes (Bruner, Goodnow, and Austin 1956). Furthermore, in this particular case, the various classes of events that are all called *strikes* are not totally unrelated. The prototypic *strike* is a swing and miss – the batter should have hit the ball into the field but did not. The *called strike* and the *foul ball strike* are also instances in which the batter should have hit the ball into the field but did not. Thus the different classes of events called a *strike* are related to each other; they are all examples of failures of the batter. Thus we can say the connection between the different senses of *strike* are *motivated*, meaning they have reason to be grouped together. George Lakoff, in his book *Women, Fire, and Dangerous Things,* gives numerous examples of categories like *strike* which have core classes and motivated extensions.

This does not mean that purely disjunctive categories never occur. In a cross-cultural study of sibling terms Sara Nerlove and A. K. Romney (1967) found that the overwhelming majority of terms were conjunctively defined, but there were a small number of disjunctive cases. Figure 3.9 presents a summary of the

Nerlove and Romney data. Each of the boxes from A to N presents a type of sibling terminology. The number at the top of the box gives the frequency with which this particular kind of sibling terminology occurs in a world-wide sample of 245 societies. These are all the types which occur more than once out of the 4,140 logically possible types of sibling terminologies which can be created from eight kin types[1], not counting four societies which had disjunctive systems – about 1.6% of total, and one society (Pawnee) which had a unique system.[2]

In each box are the eight kin types that can be constructed by distinguishing sex of relative, sex of speaker, and relative age. For example, the expression "xBe" stands for a *male ego's elder brother*, while the expression "oZy" stands for a *female ego's younger sister.* (The symbol Z rather than S is used for "sister" because in single letter kin term notation S usually stands for "son.") Fourteen societies in Figure 3.9 have type A sibling terminology – a simple system in which no distinctions are made, and there is just one term – "sibling." Type B, found in twenty-one societies, divides the eight kin types into two terms, one consisting of *male* siblings, the other consisting of *female* siblings. English is an example of this kind of system. Type C is like type A except that it has three terms; elder brother is distinguished from younger brother, but there is just one term for sister. The most common kind of sibling term system is type H, occurring in ninety-two societies, in which there are four sibling terms, one for older brother, one for younger brother, one for elder sister, and one for younger sister.

Types G through L have a basic distinction which is not found in English, but which we encountered in Chiricahua. All of these types make the *cross-sex* vs. *parallel-sex* distinction, in which a sibling of the same sex as ego is distinguished from a sibling of the opposite sex as ego. Type G presents the simplest version of this kind of system with just two terms, one for *cross*, the other for *parallel* siblings. The other five types add other features to the *cross/parallel* partition, resulting in systems with more than two terms. Type L, for example, which occurs in ten societies, has three terms, one for elder parallel sibling, one for younger parallel sibling, and one for any cross-sex sibling.

Figure 3.10 presents the Hopi sibling terminology system (Eggan 1950). This is a disjunctive system – one of the four in the Nerlove and Romney sample. It has four terms. Three of the terms can be conjunctively defined; the

1 4,140 is a surprisingly large figure for the number of kinship terminologies which can be created from just eight kin types. Combinatorial problems of this sort often produce unexpectedly large numbers of possibilities. The mathematics is presented in detail in Nerlove and Romney 1967.

2 Types F, H, M, and N include twenty-one societies which also made tertiary distinctions in sibling terms (a "tertiary" distinction subdivides a secondary distinction of two kin types into single kin types). These tertiary distinctions do not create disjunctive terms, and so do not contravene the conclusions based on the simplified types.

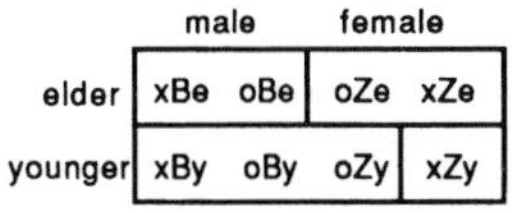

	male		female	
elder	xBe	oBe	oZe	xZe
younger	xBy	oBy	oZy	xZy

Figure 3.10 Hopi sibling terminology

first as *elder brother*, the second as *elder sister.* The third term is used only by a *male ego* for a *younger sister.* The fourth term, however, consists of either a *male ego* referring to a *younger brother* or a *female ego* referring to a *younger sibling*. There is no simple conjunctive definition for this term. In summary, for a Hopi male the sibling system looks like type F, with primary distinctions of both relative age and sex of relative, while for a Hopi female the system looks like type E, where relative age is a primary distinction and sex of relative is only a secondary distinction subdividing the elder side.

The cross-cultural sibling data[3] indicates that there is an extremely powerful tendency for humans to define terms conjunctively rather than disjunctively.[4] However, it should be pointed out that the sibling data used here examines only *one sense* of these sibling terms – the *genealogical* sense. Just as English has a number of senses for the terms *brother* and *sister* (a *sister* can also be a woman in a religious order, or two objects which have some kind of common historical origin, such as *sister languages*, etc.) so we can expect that in most if not all of the 245 societies in the sample there were a variety of other senses for their sibling terms. What the sibling data actually shows is that there is a powerful tendency to define each *particular sense* of a term conjunctively. Paradoxically, it is probably because of the powerful tendency to expect things to be susceptible to conjunctive definition that we abstract out the different senses of a term – otherwise we would simply define every so called "polysemous" term with a long disjunctive definition rather than presenting different conjunctive definitions for each sense.

So far this chapter has presented a brief outline of part of what is called *ethnographic semantics.* A fuller presentation of work in ethnographic semantics can be found in Stephen Tyler's *Cognitive Anthropology* and in Oswald Werner's *Systematic Fieldwork.* The point of the materials presented in this chapter has been to show that the feature model, first successfully applied to

3 There is a controversy about the status of the term "data." Some people say that "data" is a plural noun (with "datum" as the singular). However, to be a plural it must be a count noun – only count nouns have plural forms. Count nouns are things one counts: "one house, two houses, a thousand houses." Yet no one says "two data" or "a thousand data." Why not? Because "data" is almost always used as a mass noun, like "sand" or "water," not a count noun, and mass nouns are treated as singular.

4 Nerlove and Romney's sibling data has been analyzed further by David B. Kronenfeld (1974). See also Epling, Kirk, and Boyd (1973) for an analysis of the historical relations between sibling terminologies among twenty-three Polynesian societies using Nerlove and Romney's classification methods.

Table 3.2. *Kinship terms in six cultures*

Society	Number of terms	$\log_2$ of N in terms	Society size	Technological level
Kariera (Australia)	23	4.52	Hundreds	Foraging
Comanche (US)	37	5.21	Hundreds	Foraging
Lapps (European Arctic)	49	5.61	Hundreds	Nomadic herding
Truk (Micronesia)	14	3.82	Thousands	Horticulture and fishing
Japan	39	5.29	Millions	Modern industrial
United States	37	5.21	Millions	Modern industrial

kin terms by Lounsbury and Goodenough, was quickly generalized to the study of the entire lexicon with the explicit agenda of providing, as Frake (1962:87) puts it, "a fruitful beginning point for mapping a cognitive system." Rather than move further into the details of ethnographic semantics, the rest of this chapter will attempt to show some of the ways the feature model was found to be related to other cognitive processes, such as memory, analogizing, and making similarity judgments.

Short-term memory

One interesting connection between the feature model and the limitations of humans as information processors was made by Anthony Wallace (1964). Wallace's starting point was the observation that *although the social and technological complexity of societies vary hugely, the size of the system of terms for kin does not* (see Table 3.2).

In order to transform the number of terms of a system into a number which has the capacity to measure information complexity, Wallace computed $\log_2$ of 1/L, where L equals the number of terms in a system. This figure gives the number of binary choices necessary to produce a terminological system of size L. From this table Wallace concluded:

> Two facts are apparent, even when this small group of terminologies is considered: first, there is no *necessary* relation between complexity of the kin terminology system and the size and technological level of the society; and second, *each of the systems can be accommodated by a taxonomic space requiring only six binary dimensions or less.* (Italics added) (1964)

With six binary dimensions it is possible to create a maximum of sixty-four categories, but not more. Wallace goes on to discuss the size of other *taxonomic spaces*, or *institutionalized systems of discrimination* – what is called here a "contrast set." He points out that the number of segmental phonemes reported for natural languages ranges between thirteen to forty-five. The number of grammatically significant forms of the English verb is less than sixty-one; there are fifty-two playing cards in a standard deck of cards, sixty-four squares on a chess board, twelve combinations in a pair of dice, less than sixty-four basic number terms in English, fewer than sixty-four military ranks, fewer than sixty-four kinds of players on various sport teams, etc.

Considering why there should be such a strong limitation on "institutionalized systems of discrimination," Wallace points out that since such limitations are found in a variety of domains and across a wide range of kinds of societies, it is reasonable to assume the limitation is of a psychobiological nature. Wallace notes that his results correspond closely to Miller's, although he had not read Miller's famous 1956 paper "The Magical Number Seven, Plus or Minus Two: Some Limits on our Capacity for Processing Information" until a reviewer pointed it out to him. This correspondence is especially impressive given the very different kinds of data and method involved.

Miller's 1956 paper is a case of Kuhn's point that certain pieces of research become prototypical examples in the formation of a new paradigm. This paper, which shows with the most carefully collected experimental data that the number of simultaneous discriminations that individuals can make falls off rapidly at about seven bits of information, became a central facet of the new cognitive models of the mind. Uniting work in communication theory and basic psychophysical measurement, it gave evidence of inbuilt constraints and structure in cognitive processing. It showed the direction in which a new theory of the mind might be constructed.

The strong limitations on the number of discriminations that humans can make simultaneously also limits the number of levels of folk taxonomies. After careful review, Berlin, Breedlove, and Raven (1973) concluded that folk taxonomies, unlike scientific biological taxonomies, rarely exceed five levels, although sometimes there are a few items at a sixth level. The reason for this comes directly from the structure of features in a taxonomy. As illustrated above, each lower level of a taxonomy adds a *new* feature dimension to the preceding level. If there were more than six levels, there would have to be more than six features present in the lowest level term.

It is important to note that this limitation in information processing – usually called the 2^7 rule after Miller (rather than 2^6 after Wallace) applies only when a person must make a number of simultaneous discriminations. Simultaneous discriminations divide the world into some number of things which one is holding in mind at the same time. This type of memory is called *short-term memory* or *working memory* by psychologists.[5] While there are a number of unresolved complexities about this type of memory, it is clear that it contrasts sharply with *long-term memory.* Humans have huge long-term memories,

[5] *Short-term memory* is the older term. Currently most psychologists use the term *working memory* to refer to a system of limited temporary storage and information manipulation. Working memory is thought to be divided into three subsystems: a phonological loop which stores and rehearses speech sounds, a visuospatial sketch pad which stores and manipulates visual images, and a central executive which controls attention. See Baddelely 1990.

remembering many hundreds of thousands of things. However, these items cannot all be brought to mind at the same time, but rather *serially* – one remembers first one thing, then another.

In a sense, this limitation makes an odd creature out of the human. With a capacity to remember many hundreds of thousands of things, every item that gets placed in memory must first be discriminated and placed in short-term memory which can only contain six or seven discriminations. This creates a tight bottleneck in the flow of information from the world to long-term memory. It limits the complexity of our terminological systems, our phonology, our artifacts and instruments, our art – all of culture.

Chunking

Given this tight bottleneck, human culture would not be possible were it not for the process of chunking. This process, described in Miller's 1956 paper, is the means by which we are able to circumvent the limitations of short-term memory. Basically, in chunking humans group a number of things together into one thing. A common example is the chunking of digits. Given a random set of digits it is hard to hold a very large number in mind long enough to be able to repeat them. However, if the digits can be grouped together into a small number of units, there are fewer things to remember. For example, if presented the digits

69325754

most people will have a hard time recalling all eight numbers. But given the digits

19891990

most people will have an easy time recalling the digits. This is because most people hear only two numbers in this sequence – *1989* and *1990*. So instead of having eight distinct things to remember, one has only two easy things to remember, and remembering these two things generates the eight digits.

The power of the process of chunking is even more apparent with letters than numbers. For example, compare the difficulty of remembering

lsnsyaia

with the ease of remembering

analysis

The letters are the same, but the organization of the letters corresponds in the second case to a well-practiced chunk. With letters and phonemes the chunking not only extends to syllables and words, but to whole phrases and even sentences.

This kind of chunking also occurs with the respect to semantic features. Consider terms like *buy* and *sell*. *Buying* involves a complex set of discriminations: (1) one person is the *buyer*; (2) another the *seller*; (3) there must be some object to be *purchased*; (4) the *ownership* of the object changes from the *seller* to the *buyer* (5) in exchange for *money* (6) whose *ownership* changes from *buyer* to *seller*. Charles Fillmore (1977) has called this the basic "commercial event" scene.

Note that in the analysis given above six major discriminations need to be made. Six discriminations is within the capacity of short-term memory. However, each of these discriminations is itself quite complex. For example, what is involved in making the discrimination that something is *owned* by someone? *Ownership* involves discriminations about the kinds of *rights* that someone has over something; typically these include the *right* to *use*, *give*, or *exchange* the object whenever one wishes. And to have a *right* means roughly that there is a *social agreement* that one can take some actions with regard to some class of objects without *interference* from others. So in the discrimination of *ownership* there is the chunking of a number of other discriminations contained in the notion of *rights*. As a result of chunking the discrimination of *ownership* becomes a single feature of the term *buy* despite its complexity.

Without this kind of chunking we humans would be extremely limited in what we could discriminate and hence remember. We might have some number of very simple discriminations which we could make and use as features of terms, but the building of level upon level of complexity, so typical of human culture and human language, would not be possible. Simple discriminations, like *who* is in physical *possession* of *what* might be made, but more complex discriminations involving things like "rights" would be improbable without chunking, and even more complex discriminations built out of exchanges of kinds of rights over kinds of things (like *buy*, *loan*, *mortgage*) would simply be impossible. Even more complex discriminations built out of certain kinds of *failures* for certain kinds of commercial exchanges to occur (like *steal*, *default*, and *defraud*) would be wildly impossible. In general, for successive levels of chunking to occur there must be symbols of some type to hold the meaning of chunked information in a single unit. Thus there is a tight relation between the limitations of the human as an information processing system and the structure of language and human culture. *Complex human culture would be impossible if there were no linguistic symbols to help as chunking devices in making complex discriminations.*

Analogy

Another process which has a direct relation to semantic features is the process of *analogizing*. Standard analogies are of the form: *water* is to *wine* as *bread* is to *cake*. In this analogy *water* and *wine* are both "things to drink", but *wine* is the more "expensive" and "celebratory" drink. The same pattern of features are found for the terms *bread* and *cake.* Both are "things to eat," but *cake* is the more "expensive" and "celebratory" food.

It is common to give analogies as problems. For example: *father* is to *son* as *aunt* is to *whom*? We can represent this problem in feature form as follows:

father	:	*son*	::	*aunt*	:	(*niece*)
direct	=>	direct		collateral	=>	(collateral)
G1	=>	G1		G1	=>	(G1)
+	=>	–		+	=>	(–)
male	=>	male		female	=>	(female)

The rule used to produce the parenthesized features is simply to repeat the *relationships* that occur with respect to the first pair of terms: if a feature stays the same for the first pair of terms then the corresponding feature should also stay the same for the last pair of terms. But if a feature changes, the same change should occur in corresponding features for the second pair of terms. Thus both *father* and *son* are *direct* relatives, so no change should be made for the corresponding feature of *collaterallity* with respect to the second pair of terms. With respect to the *ascending* (+) vs. *descending* (–) features, however, *father* is *ascending* while *son* is *descending*, so since *aunt* is *ascending* the missing term should be *descending.*

Once the missing features have been filled in by this simple pattern matching process, the term that corresponds to these features is selected. In English, a *collateral, one generation from ego, descending, female* is a *niece.*

This kind of simple pattern matching of features is not the only way of computing an answer to analogy problems. For instance, consider the following analogy problem: *grandfather* is to *father* as *uncle* is to *whom*? The feature pattern matching procedure yields the following results:

grandfather	:	*father*	::	*uncle*	:	(*brother*)
direct	=>	direct		collateral	=>	(direct)
G2	=>	G1		G1	=>	(G0)
+	=>	+		+	=>	(+)
male	=>	male		male	=>	(male)

The relative who is a *direct, zero (or same) generation, ascending male* is an *older brother.* Since English does not have a distinct term for one's older brother (although many languages do) the best answer is simply *brother.* However, approximately 50% of a class of undergraduate university students give a different answer to this problem. They say that the answer is *cousin.* When asked why they gave this answer, they said that just as a *father* is the child of a *grandfather,* a *cousin* is the child of an *uncle.* These respondents are doing a different kind of computation to get from term to term in the analogy. Instead of doing a *same/different* pattern matching with features, they compute a *relative product* relation between terms. The relative product in this case is computed with the relation *parent of/child of*. Other common relative product relations found for kin terms are A is the *spouse of* B and A is the *sibling* of B.

In some cases, both methods will give the same answer. For example: *father* is to *mother* as *uncle* is to *whom*? Both feature matching and relative product computation yield the same answer – *aunt*. Using relative products, we can see that just as a *mother* is the *spouse of* a *father* so an *aunt* is the *spouse of* an *uncle*. The pattern matching of features is:

father	:	*mother*	::	*uncle*	:	(*aunt*)
direct	=>	direct		collateral	=>	(collateral)
G1	=>	G1		G1	=>	(G1)
+	=>	+		+	=>	(+)
male	=>	female		male	=>	(female)

Finally, consider the following problem: *father* is to *mother* as *brother* is to *whom*? Here the relative product result would be *sister-in-law* because just as *mother* is the spouse of a *father*, so *sister-in-law* is the spouse of a *brother.* However, given this question, the great majority of respondents give the pattern matching answer; *sister.* Perhaps so few people use the relative products transformation in this example because it moves outside the domain of *consanguineal* kin to *affinal kin*, and this is felt to violate some domain boundary condition.

We have examined here just one aspect of the process of analogizing. A considerable amount of research has been done in cognitive psychology on the way people create and learn analogies. Real world analogies may be much more complex in form than indicated by the simple *A is to B as C is to D* format. An often cited real world example is the analogy created by Rutherford between the solar system and the hydrogen atom. In such an analogy there is a set of objects (the sun, the planets) and relations among the objects (the planets circle the sun, the sun is more massive than the planets, the sun attracts the planets, etc.). The relations found among the objects in the solar system are then mapped on to the objects of the atom – the nucleus is matched to the sun, the electrons to the planets, with the expectation that, as in the solar system, the electrons circle the nucleus, the nucleus is more massive than the electrons, the nucleus attracts the electrons, etc. As in kin term examples presented above, what remains constant is that the relations between *A*, *B*, *C* . . . in the original domain should be the same as the relations between *D*, *E*, *F* . . . in the target domain.

This kind of *structure-mapping* theory of analogy has been worked out in detail by Dedre Genter (1983, 1989), who has found that a major problem that people have in learning or making analogies is overcoming the surface differences in the attributes that characterize the objects in the two domains so that the underlying similarity of relations can be perceived. The difficulty in creating or understanding a good analogy is in finding the same structure of relations between *apparently* very different kinds of objects. To do so, people must distinguish between *attributes* of objects, which are simple one place predicates (x is red, x is a male, x is hot), and *relations*, which are two or more place predicates (x is greater than y, x is the opposite of y, x is identical to y, x is between y and z). Analogies ignore differences in attributes and point out similarity in relations.

Similarity judgments

The feature composition of terms can also be used to predict similarity judgments. To see how this works, let us consider a simple type of similarity task called the "triads test." In the triads test the respondent is presented with three objects and asked to select the object which is *most different*. For example, a respondent might be given the following three kin terms:

father uncle son

and asked to select the term which is most different in meaning. To do this the respondent must compare the three terms with respect to their features. For *father*, *uncle*, and *son* the semantic features are:

father	consanguineal	male	G1	+	collateral
uncle	consanguineal	male	G1	+	collateral
son	consanguineal	male	G1	–	direct

Note that *uncle* and *son* are different from each other with respect to *two* sets of features – *direct/collateral* and *ascending/descending* – while the other two pairs of terms (*father/son, father/uncle*) differ on only one feature. On the basis of this pattern of features, the respondent might reasonably choose either *uncle* or *son* as the most different, but never *father*. This is because if the respondent chose *father* it would leave *uncle* and *son* as the most similar pair of terms despite the fact that they have the *greatest* feature difference.[6]

In some cases the choice of the "most different term" is quite obvious. Given the triad:

mother daughter nephew

nephew is clearly the "most different." This can easily be seen by comparing the features of these terms:

mother	consanguineal	female	G1	+	direct
daughter	consanguineal	female	G1	–	direct
nephew	consanguineal	male	G1	–	collateral

[6] A detailed psychological model concerning the relations of similarity judgments to features has been presented by Tversky (1977).

Table 3.3. *All possible triads for the set* father, mother, son, daughter

1.	Father	(0)*	Mother	(4)	Son	(6)
2.	Father	(3)	Mother	(0)	Daughter	(7)
3.	Father	(5)	Son	(0)	Daughter	(5)
4.	Mother	(3)	Mother	(7)	Daughter	(0)

*Figures in parentheses indicate the number of times a term was selected as most different in meaning from the other two terms by ten respondents.

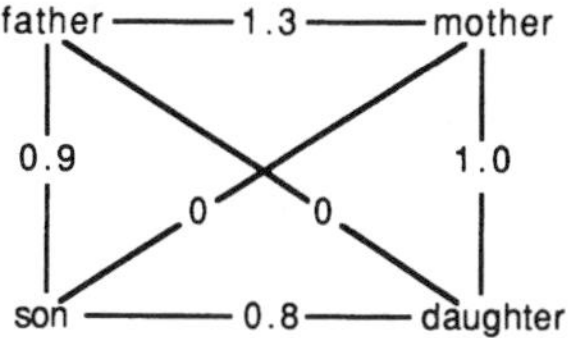

Figure 3.11 Pairings of selected kin terms.
Frequencies represent mean number of times terms were classed together

Nephew differs from *mother* on three features and from *daughter* by two features, while *mother* and *daughter* differ on only one feature.

The same technique can be used for more than three terms, simply by presenting all possible triads of these terms. For example, given the four terms *father*, *mother*, *son*, and *daughter*, four possible triads can be constructed. A sample of ten high school students was given a test in which these four possible triads were presented in random order and the students were asked to pick out the term which is most different imeaning in each triad. The results are presented in Table 3.3.

To construct a graphic representation of these results, we can compute the mean number of times each pair of kin terms are grouped together by summing the number of times each pair of terms is *not* selected as the most different term and dividing by the number of respondents. Thus in the table *father* and *mother* are classed together six times in the first triad and seven times in the second triad for a total of thirteen pairings, or a mean of 1.3 pairings. Figure 3.11 presents the data for mean pairing for all four terms. These results conform well to what we would expect on the basis of feature similarity. Note that no respondent paired the two terms that differed on *both* of the relevant features.

So far we have used the features of terms to predict similarity judgments. It is also possible to make the prediction in the other direction. That is, from similarity judgments it is possible to infer something about which terms share the most features. This means that *similarity judgments can be used to test hypotheses about the feature arrangements of a set of terms*. Most importantly, where there are different ways of analyzing a set of terms, similarity judgments can be used to decide which analysis corresponds best to the way individuals

<table>
<tr><th></th><th colspan="2">lineal</th><th colspan="2">co-lineal</th><th>ablineal</th></tr>
<tr><th></th><th>male</th><th>female</th><th>male</th><th>female</th><th></th></tr>
<tr><td>G+2</td><td>grandfather</td><td>grandmother</td><td rowspan="2">uncle</td><td rowspan="2">aunt</td><td rowspan="5">cousin</td></tr>
<tr><td>G+1</td><td>father</td><td>mother</td></tr>
<tr><td>G0</td><td colspan="2">[ego]</td><td>brother</td><td>sister</td></tr>
<tr><td>G-1</td><td>son</td><td>daughter</td><td rowspan="2">nephew</td><td rowspan="2">niece</td></tr>
<tr><td>G-2</td><td>grandson</td><td>granddaughter</td></tr>
</table>

Figure 3.12 Wallace and Atkins (1960) feature analysis of English kin terms

actually discriminate among terms. For example, several different analyses of English kin terms have been presented in the literature. The model we have been using, developed by A. K. Romney, presented at the end of Chapter 2, is just one of these alternatives. An earlier analysis presented by Wallace and Atkins (1960) had the form shown in Figure 3.12.

There are several major differences between the Wallace and Atkins analysis and the Romney analysis of English kin terms. Generation is treated in the Wallace and Atkins model as a *signed* distance up or down from ego, rather than as two features, one consisting of *absolute distance from ego*, the other consisting the *ascending/descending* dimension. The Wallace and Atkins analysis also has a three feature *lineal* vs. *co-lineal* vs. *ablineal* dimension in contrast to the two valued *direct/collateral* dimension used in our analysis in Chapter 2. Third, the terms *uncle*, *aunt*, *nephew*, and *niece* in Wallace and Atkins refer to both first and second generation kin types (i.e., not only is a parent's brother an *uncle*, but a grandparent's brother is also an *uncle*), and the term *cousin* is given as referring to any generation.[7]

It is important to understand that both the Romney analysis and the Atkins and Wallace analysis are equally effective at assigning the right *terms* to the relevant *kin types*. Both analyses work as models which individuals *could* use to refer appropriately to their kin. The question is, which model *do* Americans use? How do Americans conceive of kin – with three values of collaterallity, or two? With signed generation differences, or absolute generation differences? Which categories do Americans really use?

[7] For most English speakers these are *extended* uses of the basic meaning of the terms *uncle*, *aunt*, and *cousin*. Discussion of the distinction between basic and extended terms is presented in Chapter 5.

The issue of which analysis corresponds best to the way the natives actually categorize things is called the issue of *psychological reality.* As Wallace and Atkins state:

The psychological reality of a individual is the world as he perceives and knows it, in his own terms; it is his world of meanings. A "psychologically real" description of a culture thus is a description which approximately reproduces in an observer the world of meanings of the native users of that culture. (1960:75)

Wallace and Atkins discuss a number of problems involved in trying to determine the psychological reality. They conclude:

A problem for research, then, must be to develop techniques for stating and identifying those definitions which are most proximate to *psychological reality.* This is a formidable task. The formal methods of componential analysis, even with refinement and extension of their logico-semantic assumptions, will not yield discriminations between psychologically real and non-psychologically . . . real meanings . . . Ethnographers like Goodenough and Lounsbury obtain clues to psychological reality from observations on the cultural milieu of the terminology such as residence and marriage rules or historical changes. But the only way of achieving definitive knowledge of psychological reality will be to study the semantics of individuals both before and after a formal, abstract, cultural-semantic analysis of the terms has been performed. Simple demands for verbal definition, the use of Rivers' genealogical method, and analysis of the system of kinship behaviors may not be sufficient here: *additional procedures, by individual representative informants, of matching and sorting, answering hypothetical questions, and description of relationships in order to reveal methods of reckoning will all be required.* (Italics added) (1960:78)

In order to determine whether Romney's model or Wallace and Atkins' model corresponded most closely to the psychological reality of standard American-English speakers, a triads test was administered to 150 public high school students for the male kin terms by Romney and D'Andrade (1964). This test consisted of presenting in random order all the triads of the seven basic male kin terms (*father*, *son*, *brother*, *grandfather*, *grandson*, *uncle*, *nephew*) plus *cousin*. It would have been more comprehensive to use both male and female kin terms. However, a major drawback to the triads methods is that the number of triads increases drastically with the number of items. There are 56 possible triads for 8 kin terms, but 455 possible triads for 15 kin terms.[8]

After checking the questionaire forms for incomplete responses, failure to understand the instructions, etc., 116 forms were accepted for analysis. The results are given in Table 3.4 for mean number of times each pair of terms was classed together across all triads. Mean responses have a possible range from 0.0 to 6.0. The table has a skewed distribution of scores, with nine scores with frequencies above 2.0 and nineteen scores with frequencies below 2.0.

[8] The formula to compute the number of possible triads which can be constructed from n objects is n * (n-1) * (n-2) / 6.

Table 3.4. *Mean number of times each pair of kin terms was classed together*

Grandfather	Father	Brother	Son	Grandson	Uncle	Cousin	Nephew
Grandfather	*3.9*	1.0	1.4	*4.3*	1.5	0.6	0.9
Father		*2.4*	*3.9*	1.6	2.0	0.6	0.6
Brother			*3.8*	1.6	1.6	1.7	1.5
Son				*3.1*	0.6	1.4	1.2
Grandson					0.7	1.1	1.7
Uncle						*3.5*	*3.7*
Cousin							*4.2*

(n = 116) Scores over 2.0 appear in italic.

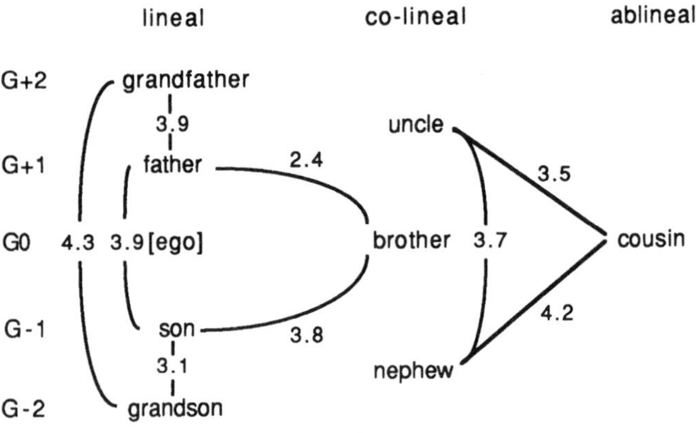

Figure 3.13 Diagrammatic representation of Wallace and Atkins (1960) feature analysis of English male kin terms
Connecting lines indicate terms paired together with high frequency. Numbers present mean frequency of pairings

Which model does this data support? It is hard to see the answer just from viewing a table of numbers. To make the results more apparent the two models have been put into diagrammatic form and the nine most highly similar pairs of terms plotted onto the diagram. Figure 3.13 gives the results for the Wallace and Atkins model. If the model had a good fit to the data, all the highly similar pairs would be adjacent to each other.

It is apparent that the Wallace and Atkins model does not fit the data very well. *Grandfather* and *grandson* are judged to be highly similar but are at opposite ends of the Wallace and Atkins dimension of generation. *Father* and *son* are both strongly paired with *brother,* although according to the Wallace and Atkins analysis a *brother* is different from *father* and *son* in being a collateral and a different generation. Similarly, *uncle*, *nephew*, and *cousin* show the same pattern of discrepancy.

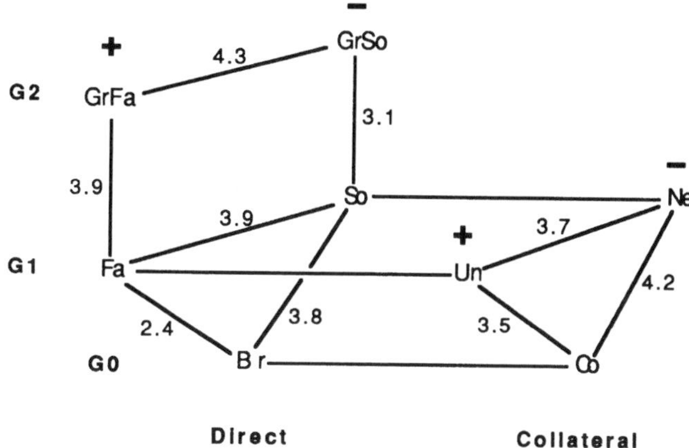

Figure 3.14 Diagrammatic representation of Romney feature analysis of English male kin terms
Connecting lines indicate terms paired together with high frequency. Numbers present mean frequency of pairings

Figure 3.14 presents the results for the Romney model. The diagram has been rearranged from the diagram in Chapter 2 into a three dimensional format to make it possible to visualize the orthogonal relation of the three dimensions of generation, collaterallity, and the *ascending/descending* dimension.
The data fits the Romney model very neatly. All of the high frequency pairings connect immediately adjacent terms.

From these results we can conclude that for Americans (or at least our sample of high school students) the basic male English kin terms are distinguished as in the Romney model by a dimension of absolute generation, an *ascending/descending* dimension, and a *direct/collateral* dimension. The evidence is counter to the Wallace and Atkins model which defines these dimensions differently.

A later study by Michael Burton and Sara Nerlove (1976) included both male and female terms in a balanced incomplete triad block design, in which a subset of all possible triads is selected such that all pairs of terms occur the same number of times. Using all sixteen basic English kin terms, they found four distinct dimensions; one was clearly a *male* vs. *female* dimension, while the other three were the same as the Romney dimensions described above. Other similarity judgment studies of the eight male English kin terms have also found the same general pattern of results.[9] With the use of multidimensional scaling programs, such as non-metric scaling and correspondence analysis, a direct graphic representation of English kin terms can be constructed from similarity

[9] See Wexler and Romney 1972 and Nakao and Romney 1984.

judgments alone; an early example of such an analysis is presented in Romney and D'Andrade (1964).

Overall, these various analyses show that it is quite feasible to use similarity judgments to test hypotheses about the psychological reality of different models. This result counters the objection made by Robbins Burling (1964) that the psychological reality of a componential analysis cannot be determined because there are too many logical possibilities. In the case of English kin terms, there is little doubt that the Romney model gives a better account of the way people make similarity judgments than the alternative model. The results are quite clear-cut. However, more important than these particular results, the discussion in the journals and articles concerning the alternative analyses of English kin terms concretized the issue of psychological reality. *The issue really has to do with the standards by which ethnographic descriptions are to be judged.* By the time the English kin term controversy was finished, a consensus had been built in cognitive anthropology that the models of how natives categorize the world should do more than account for what things get which labels; they should also account for the discriminations that individuals use to give things labels. Or, to paraphrase Wallace and Atkins, the ethnographic problem is not just to describe behavior, but to discover the individual's "world of meanings."

The feature composition of evaluative judgments

So far we have seen that feature composition strongly affects judgments of similarity. To what extent might feature composition affect other kinds of judgments, such as evaluations or preferences?[10] The hypothesis that responses to an object, such as evaluations and preferences, are influenced by the features of the object is called the *feature decomposition hypothesis.*

Let us continue with English kin terms to illustrate this hypothesis. A sample of American respondents is presented with a randomized list of all possible pairs of English kin terms (*mother/father*, *grandfather/son*, *aunt/daughter*, etc.), and asked to circle for each pair the relative "you would expect to be the warmer, friendlier, and more trustworthy person." For every respondent each kin term can be placed on a scale of warmth/ friendliness/ trustworthiness (*solidarity*) by counting the number of times each term is chosen. For the whole sample we can then obtain a mean *solidarity* score for each of the fifteen basic kin terms.

To what extent will these *solidarity* scores show the effects of feature decomposition? The most informative way to present such data is in a diagram, rather than a table of numbers. In Figure 3.15 the mean scores for a sample of

[10] Strictly speaking, *features* should apply only to lexical items, while the objects that the lexemes refer to are said to have *attributes*, such that the features of a term correspond to the criterial attributes of a class or object. However, for the sake of simplicity, *features* will be used both with reference to terms and the classes or objects labeled by these terms.

		direct		collateral	
		male	female	male	female
G2	+	grandfather 5.6 (6.1)	grandmother 8.3 (8.1)		
	-	grandson 4.5 (4.1)	granddaughter 5.9 (6.1)		
G1	+	father 9.9 (10.1)	mother 12.7 (12.1)	uncle 3.6 (3.9)	aunt 6.3 (5.9)
	-	son 8.4 (8.1)	daughter 9.7 (10.1)	nephew 2.0 (1.9)	niece 3.6 (3.9)
G0		brother 9.5 (9.2)	sister 10.8 (10.1)	cousin 4.1 (4.0)	

Figure 3.15 Observed and predicted *solidarity* scores for English kin terms (n = 65)
Predicted scores in parentheses; *r* between observed and predicted scores =.92.

sixty-five college undergraduates are presented within a feature diagram. In parentheses and to the right of each of the observed *solidarity* scores are the *predicted solidarity* scores. These solidarity scores were derived by first determining a *solidarity weight* for each of the features. To calculate the weight for a particular feature, the mean for all scores on a particular feature was calculated. This mean was subtracted from the mean of the matching terms on the opposing dimensional feature and the difference divided by two. Once the feature weights were found, the predicted score for a particular kin term was computed by adding together all the feature weights for that term plus an estimated grand mean. The predicted score for *nephew*, for example, consists of the sum of the weight for *male* (–1.0), *descending* (–1.0), *generation 1* (+2.0), *collateral* (–3.1), plus the estimated grand mean (+5.0), yielding a predicted score of 1.9.

The fit between the predicted and the observed scores is fairly good. The Pearson *r* between the two sets of scores is .91. It is interesting that the discrepancies between the predicted and the observed scores are also nicely patterned. In every case the ascending female terms (*mother*, *aunt*, *grandmother*) and the descending male terms (*son*, *nephew*, *grandson*) have higher *solidarity* scores than predicted by the feature scores, and the ascending male (*father*, *uncle*, *grandfather*) and the descending female (*daughter*, *niece*, *granddaughter*) have lower solidarity scores than predicted by the feature scores. It would appear one can expect a little more solidarity from senior females and junior males than either sex or seniority alone would predict.

Since the solidarity ratings used in this analysis are *aggregated*, these results do not indicate whether or not the same pattern occurs on the individual level. To check on the way individuals perform, individual respondents were selected and for each individual feature weights were calculated and checked to see how well they fit the observed scores. The correlation remains impressive, although slightly lower (the mean of these *r*'s was .82). For all respondents the feature weight for *female* was higher than for *male*, *ascending* had a greater weight than *descending*, and *direct* had a greater weight than *collateral*. Absolute generation showed much more individual variation, especially between *first generation* and *second generation* weights.

What this good fit between predicted and observed scores shows is that *in some cases* the way people evaluate a set of items can be predicted from the separate features which distinguish these items. For basic English kin terms, it appears that – at least in some tasks – what people do is average across features: how warm, friendly, and trustworthy a class of kin is expected to be is approximately the average of the *solidarity* weights for the features of sex, collaterallity, generation, and direction. These results would not occur if the actual criteria on which respondents made their judgments were not the same as, or highly correlated with, the linguistic features of the terms.

Another application of the feature model to psychological processes concerns child language learning. If features are the psychological discriminations that people make in determining which things belong in which categories, then the child, in learning to talk, will have the task of learning these discriminations. Since the child learns some features before others, there should be evidence for feature learning in the order in which children learn vocabulary. Terms with complex features should be learned later than terms containing only a subset of these features. Dedre Genter, for example, found that children understand the terms *give* and *take* before they understand the terms *buy* and *sell* (1978). In a general review, Eve Clark (1973) has argued that features play a significant part in child language learning, although complicated by other processes.

Summary

This chapter has presented the classic feature model which was developed in the late fifties and early sixties in anthropology. Because of their paradigmatic structure, kin terms were the prototypic example for most of this early work on features. The paradigmatic structure of kin terms made identification of genealogical features relatively straightforward, allowing the production of simple and compelling findings. Once a good example had been found, ideas about how features might be related to other phenomena could be tested and refined. The demonstration that features determined the structural organization of terms into paradigmatic or taxonomic forms, the analysis of the feature organization involved in multiple senses of a term, the development of the concept of "marking," the identification of the strong tendency towards conjunctive composition of features, the discovery of the relation between the small size of short-term memory and the extreme limitation on the numbers of features defining a term, the analysis of the feature transformations involved in analogy and the relation between similarity judgments and feature overlap, all "fell out" of an expanding research agenda with considerable rapidity. Such periods are exciting for the people working within the agenda. Certainly I found it that way. There was a feeling that things were coming together and making sense.

4 Extension of the feature model

Firewood

Kin terms served as an exemplary domain for investigation of the way semantic features can be related to short-term memory, analogy, polysemy, similarity ratings, and other cognitive phenomena. Necessarily, these findings depend on being able to determine the features of the terms. The techniques described in the preceding chapters for determining the features of kin terms had a long history of development. Out of years of research on kin terms came the techniques developed by Lounsbury, Goodenough, Romney, Hammel, Atkins and others which gave a high degree of precision to the feature analysis of kin terms; although there might be disputes about certain complex configurations, in general a high degree of consensus was obtained in the analysis of kin term systems.

Kin terms, however, are only one small terminological domain in the lexicon of any language. What about all the other domains which did not have the paradigmatic character of kinship terminologies? *The question quickly arose as to whether the same kind of feature model could be applied to other domains of cultural meaning.* The feature model might be quite important theoretically, but if it could only be applied to kin terms it would be of very limited use. Most of these other domains, however, had no long history of semantic analysis. To get at the feature structure of these new domains new methods had to be developed.

One of the early anthropological studies to try explicitly to identify features outside of the domain of kin terms was carried out by Duane Metzger and Gerald Williams (1966). Working in Tzeltal, a Mayan language spoken in the highlands of Chiapas, Mexico, they attempted to analyze the salient features of *firewood*. Since there has been criticism of Metzger and Williams for concentrating on a domain which seems to have little political or social importance, it is worth noting that whatever firewood means to us, it is not a trivial topic for Tzeltal speaking horticulturalists. Much of the land has been stripped of timber, resulting in a daily arduous search for firewood. Knowledge of the kinds of timber which make good firewood is a necessary part of any adult Tzeltal speaker's stock of knowledge. To criticize Metzger and Williams for studying firewood rather than things which seem more relevant to us is itself a kind of ethnocentrism in which *our* concerns about their lives are given much greater weight than *their* concerns about their lives.

Since the techniques for the analysis of kin terms in which the kin types for each term are used to find contrasting features have no clear analog in studying how people categorize firewood, Metzger and Williams developed a new set of techniques to uncover features. What they did was to adapt a kind of structural approach to the analysis of linguistic forms which utilizes *frames* and *slots.* This approach had been part of what was then called *structural linguistics* developed by Bloomfield and Zelig Harris, although the root ideas go back at least to Saussure and the Prague school. Basically, the idea is that one can get at the meaning of items through the way items are distributed in different environments.[1] The environment, or frame, consists of a well-formed series of items – say a phrase like *"___ is a kind of fruit"* which consists of a syntactically well-formed series of words which make a true sentence when filled in by the right kinds of items. Thus "*A pear* is a kind of fruit" makes a true sentence, while "*A flowerpot* is a kind of fruit" makes a false sentence.

Although the idea of *frame* and *slot* were basic to Metzger and Williams' approach, they found that it was often possible to transform frames into questions. Thus the frame "___ is a kind of fruit" can be transformed into a direct query "What kinds of fruits are there?" and obtain the same kinds of responses. Metzger and Williams say:

> Of basic importance in the formulation of frames is the use of bilingual informants who assist us in formulating relevant questions in the native language, the central problem being one of finding out from informants what things there are to be asked about, what relevant things may be asked about them, and what are the significant answers to be anticipated. (1966:390)

In the firewood example, Metzger and Williams began with the question of whether or not there is a category similar to the English category of *firewood.* They found that there was such a category, which they established by the following series of queries:

Q: How are they named, the things of mother earth in all the world?
A: There are many kinds.

Q: What is the name of the first kind?
A: There are people.

Q: What is the name of the second kind?
A: There are animals.

1 The idea that meaning could be uncovered by analyzing word distribution was an ideological position in the late forties and early fifties. This position collapsed with the advent of Chomsky and the generative-transformational revolution.

Table 4.1. *Evaluation of firewood*

Good	Poor
Hard wood	Soft wood
Burns strongly	Burns quickly
Dries rapidly	dries slowly
Its fire is hot	Its fire is only a little hot

Q: What is the name of (another of) a third kind?
A: There are "trees-and-plants".

Q: What is the name of (another of) a fourth kind.
A: There are no more (of a fourth different kind). (1966:391[2])

The same queries can be used to find out the kinds of people in the world, or the kinds of animals, or the kinds of trees-and-plants. When asked to name the the kinds trees-and-plants, informants respond with the Tzeltal terms for trees, shrubs, grasses, and vines. When asked what are the name of the kinds of trees, informants give a long list of trees including oaks. Repeating the same process for just oaks, informants are able to produce a list of a number of specific kinds of oak.

This kind of repeated query technique makes a highly formalized way of eliciting a taxonomy. Of course, such a taxonomy could be elicited in a more informal manner, but a part of Metzger and Williams' goal was to develop a process which was *interpretation free* – what they got was what you saw.

Next Metzger and Williams developed queries which asked for the *uses* for the items they have elicited. With respect to trees some of the uses are as wood for houses, axe handles, benches, etc., and finally firewood. About firewood, Tzeltal speakers say that "it serves us (in that) we put it in the fire." Using this somewhat lengthy procedure, Metzger and Williams are able to show where the category of "firewood" fits into the total Tzeltal classification of things – "firewood" is the use of certain trees which along with "people" and "animals" constitute the major kinds of living things.

Having established firewood as a natural category among the Tzeltal, Metzger and Williams go on to use the same kind of frame/query approach to discover the salient features of firewood. Informants know in detail which kinds of trees make the best and worst kinds of firewood, and readily produce such lists if presented with the appropriate query. Next Metzger and Williams develop two queries to uncover the features that make for good or bad firewood, which are glossed "Why is ___ good (as firewood)" and "Why is ___ not good (as firewood)." Responses to these frames produce four major dimensions (see Table 4.1).

These qualities of hardness, burning quality, drying quality, and heat are the

[2] In the original article both Tzeltal phrases and their English glosses are given.

Table 4.2. *Consequences of burning certain varieties of wood*

Because they say that __		if we burn __ in the fire
	our own bones will be burned	
	our chickens will die	
	we will be seized by insanity	
	we will not have children	
	our children will get epilepsy	
	a snake will come to our house	

major properties used in the evaluation of "firewood." However, for a few special kinds of wood the reasons given for why the wood is not to be burnt are quite different (see Table 4.2):

It appears that the burning of firewood has more to it than the ordinary pragmatics of heat production. In their article Metzger and Williams go on to discuss how firewood is prepared, cut into different size lengths, how the lengths are measured (in axe handles), how firewood relates to kindling and to charcoal. For each of these points they discuss the formulation of appropriate queries and the kind of responses made by informants.

The firewood example presented here illustrates well the general query technique developed by Metzger and Williams. Using the same set of techniques, they worked out a precise ethnographic description of the role of the curer in Tenejapa (a Tzeltal speaking municipio) (1963b), and a detailed description of the wedding ritual used by Tenejapa Ladinos (1963a). M. Black and Metzger presented a programmatic study of law, using as informants a second year Stanford law school student and a number of Tzeltal speaking Tenejapans (1965). Black also produced a detailed Ojibwa taxonomy of "living things" (1987).

The major impact of the work of Metzger, Williams, and Black in the mid-1960s was methodological – the basic thesis was that informant knowledge could be obtained in a reliable and replicable way, without imposing the ethnographer's conceptual framework on the elicitation procedure. Everything was put out in the open. The reader was confronted with the ethnographer's data. The attempt was to find out what the informant thinks in a highly *explicit* and *formalized* manner. In all of this, psychological considerations played a negligible part; the major goal was straightforward ethnographic description. Metzger and his associates were interested in cultural knowledge – something which they often found to be detailed, systematic, and sometimes surprisingly different than one might have expected from the perspective of American culture.

While the techniques of Metzger and his associates did not become a part of standard anthropological ethnographic technique, some of the general ideas about frames and queries were adopted by other anthropologists. For example, James Spradley's book *The Ethnographic Interview* uses the query approach to teach students how to do ethnographic research, as does Michael Agar's *The Professional Stranger.*

What did emerge most clearly from this work was the idea that in any culture there were certain appropriate questions which could be asked about a particular cultural category, and these question elicited kinds of *relationships* which informants understood to hold between cultural categories. For example, in the firewood paper, Metzger and Williams developed queries which asked about the "kind of" relationship, "use" relationships, and "evaluative attributes" of goodness and badness.

Semantic networks

One important effect of Metzger and Williams' work was to open up the general problem of understanding native thought from the analysis of simple features to an analysis of the relationships between categories. As Frake said in his paper "Notes on Queries in Ethnography":

> By presenting an inquiry (e.g. "What kind of tree is that?"), a native inquirer seeks to restrict the appropriate responses to a given set of responses (e.g., tree names), so that the selection of a particular response . . . conveys information significant to the inquirer. A description organized by linked queries and responses is simultaneously a program for finding out information, a program which can be replicated and tested by the reader of the description . . . Furthermore, the topic of a given query will be a response to some other query, making it possible to produce lists of utterances *interlinked* as topics and responses of specified queries. A pair of queries which interlink utterances as mutual topics and responses constitute the basic unit of these procedures, a unit we will call an *interlinkage*. (Italics in the original) (1964:134)

The ethnographic task that Frake uses to illustrate the way in which cultural knowledge can be modeled as an interlinked set of categories is the process of manufacturing *gasi*, a fermented drink used by the Eastern Subanun of the Philippines. In manufacturing *gasi* a starchy mash is reduced to sugar by certain fungi grown with yeast in cakes of rice flower. The fungi reduce the starch to sugars upon which the yeast can then act to bring about fermentation. Frake focuses his description of the yeast cakes and the selection of "spices" to add to the other yeast ingredients.

In trying to work out how the different items of "spices," "yeast," and "beer" (*gasi*) are interrelated, Frake found that he needed a series of linked queries. These queries were:

use: What is __ used for?
kind: What kind of __ is it?
what: What is __ (a kind of)?
ingredient: What is that ingredient of X?
part: What (separated) part of __ is it?
source: What does __ come from?

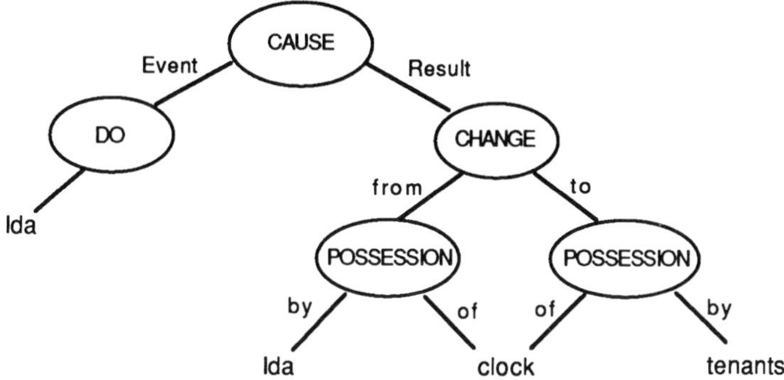

Figure 4.1 Example semantic network model (adapted from Genter 1978)

Frake points out that some of these queries are reciprocals of each other. Thus "yeast" is *used for* making "beer" and "beer" has an *ingredient* which is "yeast." Frake then uses these queries to analyze the relationship between the different items that go into making *gasi*. In carrying out this analysis, he found that some terms had a number of different senses, and that these different senses could be demonstrated by the kinds of relations each sense has to other items.

A similar semantic network model was developed in artificial intelligence by Ross Quillian, Allan Collins, and others in the late 1960s. In Quillian-like models, nodes of the network stood for objects, while lines stood for relationships of various kinds, especially subset/superset relations. This type of model was used in psychology primarily as a representation of the structure of long-term memory, and served as the postulated structure for a number of cognitive processing experiments (Collins and Quillian 1969). A modified version of this network model was developed by the LNR group at UCSD to represent complex word meanings (Peter Lindsay, Donald Norman, and David Rumelhart). Figure 4.1 presents a diagram of the feature structure of sentence "Ida gave her tenants a clock" using the LNR representational format (see Figure 4.1).

In anthropology, Oswald Werner extensively developed the use of semantic network models. In his book *Systematic Fieldwork*, written with G. Mark Schoepfle, the authors lay out a step by step method of doing ethnography using a small number of basic relationships as the building blocks for constructing networks. One of Werner's most extensive examples of a network analysis is *The Anatomical Atlas of the Navajo*, written in collaboration with K. Y. Begishe, M. A. Austin-Garrison, and J. Werner.

As a method, semantic network analysis has the capacity of creating an encyclopedia-like description of a culture. Basically, the networks consist of linked propositions. The problem with such networks is that everything is connected directly or indirectly to everything else, so there is no clear way of grasping what is important and what is peripheral. Instead of having a small number of features which reveal what is most salient to the native, one ends up with a great encyclopedia in which everything is as important as everything else. Of course, if you want to find out particular information about some cultural object, a good encyclopedia is the place to go.

Finding salient features through similarity judgments

In Chapter 3 the point was made that similarity judgments reflect the sharing of features. Terms which share many features will generally be judged to be more similar than terms which share few features. This "effect of shared features" was used in Chapter 3 to decide between alternative feature analyses of kin terms. It is also possible to use the "effect of shared features" on similarity judgments in cases in which no prior analysis has been made. To take a simple example, let us consider color terms. Without any prior analysis of the feature dimensions of color terms, it is possible to give a number of respondents a set of color terms and have them judge how similar every pair of terms is. Using the mean similarity judgment for each pair for the sample of respondents, it is then possible to analyze these scores to discover something about the structure of these terms.

One of the most widely used multidimensional statistical programs is KYST. The KYST program is the joint effort of a number of people, including Joseph Kruskal, Forrest Young, Roger Shepard, and Warren Torgerson.[3] What the KYST program does is to try to place objects in a spatial configuration in which the computer generated distances between objects corresponds as closely as possible to the original similarity scores between items. That is, objects which are similar to each other should be close together, while objects that are dissimilar should be far apart. For example, if one inputs the distances between various cities in the the United States to the KYST program and asks for a two dimensional output, the result will be a plot which looks just like the placement of cities on a map of the US. However, when the data is noisy, or when the similarities come from a cognitive structure which has many dimensions, the program will still produce, if asked, a two dimensional output, but the distances shown on the output will no longer correspond as closely to the similarity scores. The program gives a figure, called "stress," which indicates how closely the original input scores correspond to the output distances.

To return to the analysis of color terms: in a study by Samuel Fillenbaum and Amnon Rapoport (1971) in which twenty-six English speaking respondents ranked all possible pairs of fifteen color terms by degree of dissimilarity, the resulting output is presented in Figure 4.2. The stress for two dimensions was low; 0.085, which means the fit between the input scores and the output

[3] For a general introduction to multidimensional scaling, see Kruskal and Wish 1978.

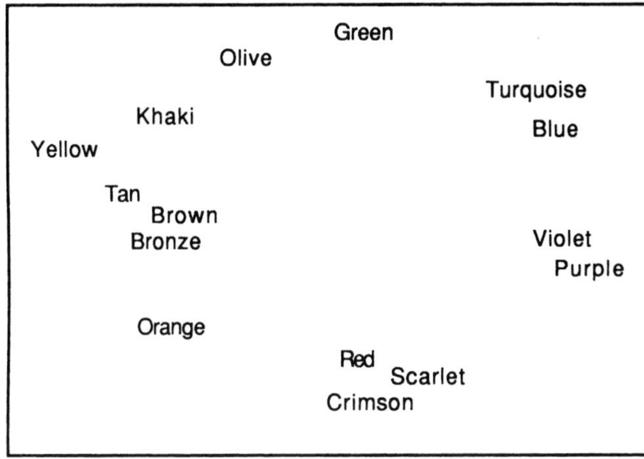

Figure 4.2 Two dimensional KYST representation of color terms (Adapted from Fillenbaum and Rapoport 1971)

distances is very good. This contrasts with what happens if the program tries to order the scores along a single dimension (instead of two dimensions); then the stress score rises to 0.339. The overall result corresponds closely to the normal image of the color wheel, with *red* and *green* on one axis and *blue* and *yellow* on the other axis.

In this color term example the *red/green* dimension and the *yellow/blue* dimension are not simple dichotomous values like *male/female* or *direct/collateral* in the analysis of kin terms. Instead, terms can have a graded position along a dimension. *Orange*, for example, is positioned towards the *red* end of the *red/green* dimension, but not as far out as *red* itself. *Orange* is also on the *yellow* side of the *yellow/blue* dimension, but again not as far out as *yellow* itself. One of the advantages of multidimensional scaling analyses is that they have the capacity of representing fine gradations along a continuum.

Given the ease and effectiveness of multidimensional scaling analysis, it is not surprising that this technique has been used frequently. Anthropologists, psychologists, and sociologists have all used multidimensional scaling of similarity ratings to try to discover the major dimensions underlying a variety of domains. Some of the domains which have been analyzed include American occupational terms (Burton 1972), American-English personality trait terms (Rosenberg and Sedlak 1972), nation states (Wish, Deutsch, and Biener 1972), American concepts of success and failure (Romney, Smith, Freeman, Kagan, and Klein 1979), Maasi personality terms (Kirk and Burton 1977), A'ara personality terms (White 1980), American interpersonal relationships (Wish 1976), interpersonal behavior traits (White 1980), fish shapes (Boster and Johnson 1989), and emotion terms (Russell, Lewicka, and Nilt 1989).

One can think of multidimensional scaling as a kind of sophisticated feature extractor. However, multidimensional scaling techniques generally do not get at the fine detail of minor feature differences. What these techniques usually do is to find a small number of the highly salient dimensions that apply to the majority of terms. The result is a smoothed out mapping of items in which general similarity relations are preserved but specific differences are lost. For example, in Figure 4.2, the color terms *bronze*, *tan*, and *brown* are all grouped together between *yellow* and *orange*. The differences between these three terms – the metallic sheen of *bronze* and the lighter shade of *tan* compared to *brown* – are lost in the two dimensional representation.

While at first the major use of multidimensional scaling was simply to explore the salient feature characteristics of different cultural domains, as the field became more sophisticated investigators began to use multidimensional scaling to test specific hypotheses. Kirk and Burton (1977), for example, were able to show that the salient features of role terms changed for Maasi males as they went through culturally marked life stages. Boster and Johnson (1989) were interested in comparing the knowledge of expert and novice fishermen about fish, and used multidimensional scaling to show these differences. Other studies, such as Russell, Lewicka, and Nilt (1989) and White (1980) were aimed at uncovering cross-cultural universals in the salient feature characteristics of emotion terms and interpersonal behavior traits.

Psychological reality again

It is interesting that some of the same questions that arose concerning feature analyses of kin terms arise again with respect to the results of multidimensional scaling. That is, given certain scaling results, did these results have any psychological validity or were they just some kind of computer output with no real psychological implications? Or, to put the question another way, what difference did it make that respondents rated some things as more similar than other things? After all, the multidimensional scaling results are just a summarization of a large number of similarity judgments, and cannot be expected to have any more psychological meaning than the original judgments.

Several kinds of experiments were undertaken to answer this question. Using a multidimensional scaling analysis of similarity ratings for common animals (*cat*, *dog*, *rabbit*, *monkey*, *lion*, *giraffe*, etc.) Rumelhart and Abrahamson (1973) developed a task using analogical reasoning to see if scaling results could predict respondent choices. The scaling results for common animals, carried out by Henley (1969), had an interpretable two dimensional solution. Figure 4.3 presents the two dimensional Henley analysis. The horizontal dimension is clearly *size*, with *elephant* on the far right and and the other animals in approximate order of size ending with *mouse* on the far left. The vertical dimension is *ferocity*, with *leopard*, *tiger*, *and lion* on the bottom of the diagram, and *cow* and *sheep* at the top of the diagram. For this test Rumelhart and Abrahamson first chose two animals, and then measured the direction and distance between these two animals. They then chose a third animal, and drew a line from the third animal in the same direction and distance as the line between the first two animals. Whatever animal came closest to the end of this line should be the best choice for an analogy. They gave respondents the following type of test:

CAT: LEOPARD :: MONKEY : ____
A. ANTELOPE
B. BEAVER
C. GORILLA
D. TIGER

Here the most appropriate answer is *GORILLA,* which is approximately the same distance and direction from *LEOPARD* as *MONKEY* is from *CAT.* The results of a series of such tasks supported Rumelhart and Abrahamson's hypothesis; a mean of 70% of the respondents gave the predicted animal as their first choice. It seems likely that respondents use the same kind of analogy searching procedure for this task described in Chapter 3. Given the A:B :: C: __ format, if the second (B) animal of the first pair is somewhat larger and somewhat more ferocious than the first (A), then select as an answer an animal which is equally larger and equally more ferocious than the first animal of the second pair (C).

Another simple test of the psychological validity of multidimensional scaling results for similarity judgments was developed by A. K. Romney (1989). The task consists of asking respondents to list all the common animals they can think of. There is a general finding in psychology that when respondents are asked to list items in free recall, the stronger the association between the items, the more likely they will be recalled together (Bousefield 1953). Using a statistic for the analysis of path lengths, it has been found that respondents are much more likely to list together animals that are close together in the scaling analysis. For example, a respondent might produce a list like *deer, sheep*, *cows*, *goats*, and *horses*, but would be very unlikely to produce a list like *gorilla*, *dog*, *camel*, *rat*, and *elephant*. This "clustering in recall" effect is quite robust and replicable (Romney 1989).

Another task to test the psychological implications of scaling of similarity judgments was developed by Nerlove and Romney (1976) using reaction time in a forced choice format. Respondents were shown a series of 70 slides with three animal terms in the following format:

HORSE

SHEEP ZEBRA

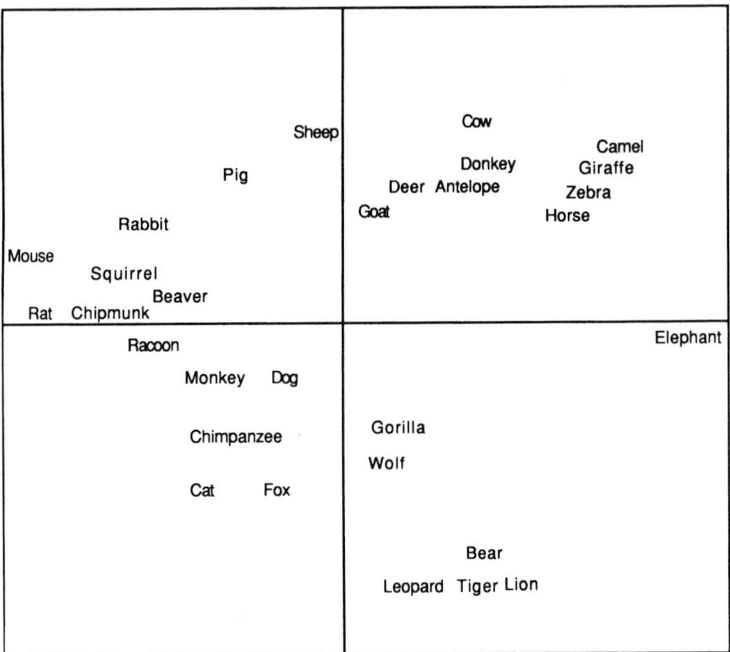

Figure 4.3 Two dimensional representation of judged similarity among common animals (adapted from Henley 1969)

The task for the respondent was to choose among the bottom two terms the term which is most like the top term. Respondents were told to make their choices as quickly as possible, and the response time it took the respondent to answer was recorded. In the example above *zebra* was chosen with a mean reaction time of 2.98 seconds. However, given the following triad

CAMEL

TIGER LION

the mean reaction time was much longer – 4.15 seconds. In their analysis of the data Nerlove and Romney found that two factors had a major effect on reaction time. First, respondents were quicker if the distance between the left and right comparison animals was large (e.g., the distance between *zebra* and *sheep* is much larger than the distance between *tiger* and *lion*). Second, respondents were quicker if there was a large difference between the distance of the top animal to one of the comparison animals versus the distance to the other comparison animal (e.g., *horse* is much closer to *zebra* than to *sheep*, but *tiger* and *lion* are just about the same distance from *camel*). Similar results for the domains of birds and fruits have been obtained by Hutchinson and Lockhead (1977).

In summary, multidimensional scaling of similarity ratings has certain advantages over traditional semantic feature analysis. Traditional semantic feature analysis works best when a few features partition a relatively large number of terms, as in a complete paradigm. But most domains have much more loosely defined contrast sets than kin terms and pronouns. For example, there are a huge number of features, physical and behavioral, which differentiate a *camel* from a *tiger* or a *pig* from a *gorilla.* Similarity judgments present the respondent with the task of finding those features which are most general and most salient in structuring a domain, since the respondent has to consider the ways in which all the different pairs of items in a domain are alike as well as they ways they are different.

Thus scaling analyses of similarity judgments tend to result in the identification of a few salient features which structure an entire domain. However, there is also a drawback here. In some analyses, the feature dimensions are relatively obvious. In the Henley animal analysis, for example, the dimensions of *size* and *ferocity* account nicely for the placement of most of the animals. However, in many analyses it is not obvious which features account for the way in which items are placed in the space. There have been a number of arguments, for example, about the dimensions which structure the domain of personality trait terms. Various techniques, such as having ratings of potential dimensions made on all terms, then finding the vector which correlates most highly with the dimensional ratings, can be useful in helping to select feature dimensions.[4]

Another problem involved in scaling analyses of similarity judgments is the fact that the number of pairs of items increases geometrically with the number of items (for n items, there are n * (n-1) / 2 pairs of items). Thus 10 items generate only 45 pairs, while 50 items generate 1,225 pairs. If the task consists of judging on a similarity scale every pair of items, large domains require too many judgments to be practical. The triads test – the easiest similarity task to administer to non-literate respondents – is even more time consuming than using all possible pairs, since the number of triads increases with the number of items even more rapidly than the number of pairs (for n items, there are n * (n-1) * (n-2) / 6 triads). There are ways around this problem using incomplete balanced block designs,[5] but there is always a concomitant loss of information in using such designs, as well as the difficulty of finding the right design. Another technique is to use a *pile sort* method, in which a respondent is given a stack of cards with one of the items written on each card, and then asked to sort the items into piles on the basis of similarity. One measure of similarity derived from the pile sorting technique is simply to count the number of times respondents place pairs of items in the same pile; the more times any pair of

4 For an example of this technique, see Rosenberg and Sedlak 1972.

5 In an incomplete balanced block design only a special selection of pairs or triads are used. Combinations are selected so that all items occur the same number of times. See, for example, Burton and Nerlove 1976.

items is placed in the same pile, the more similar the two items. It has been found that obtaining reliable measures with the pile sorting technique requires a relatively large number of respondents; fifty respondents is usually a minimum. Respondents can do this task with as many as a hundred items, although pile sorting a hundred items is a daunting task. A number of techniques for collecting similarity judgments are described and illustrated in Susan Weller and A. K. Romney's book *Systematic Data Collection.*

Item by feature matrices

So far we have dealt exclusively with multidimensional analyses of *similarity* judgments. However, it is possible to use multidimensional scaling techniques to analyze other kinds of data. For example, consider beliefs about illness. A normal American knows a number of disease terms – *colds, mumps, cancer, ulcers*, etc. A normal American also knows a number of things about these diseases – that some *bring on fever*, that some *can be caught from other people*, etc. The things that Americans know about diseases can be called *disease features*. Given a list of commonly known disease terms and a list of commonly known disease features, respondents can be asked to judge which features go with which disease terms. The result is an *item by attribute matrix* in which both disease features and disease terms can be analyzed together.[6]

A study by D'Andrade, Quinn, Nerlove, and Romney (1972) used item by attribute matrices to attempt to investigate standard American and Ladino Mexican categorizations of disease. We turned to this type of analysis because attempts to construct standard taxonomies of disease terms resulted in shallow, non-exclusive structures (i.e., the same diseases were said to belong to more than one superordinate category), while attempts to carry out standard semantic feature analyses resulted in confused attempts on the part of our informants to use the technical language of medicine.

The first step of the study was to collect a suitable list of disease terms. Lists of common diseases were collected and then a small number of informants asked to judge which terms were most common and least ambiguous. Table 4.3 presents a list of the final selection of disease terms.

To collect lists of features relevant to disease states a series of statements made by informants about diseases were collected from informal ethnographic interviews about beliefs about illness. These statements were then transformed into belief-frames. For example, a common statement was "you can catch colds from other people." This was transformed into the belief-frame "you can catch ___ from other people."

6 Some of the earliest analyses of item by property matrices were carried out by Volney Stefflre in marketing studies; see for example, Stefflre 1972.

Table 4.3. *American disease terms*

1. Appendicitis	2. Bronchitis	3. Cancer
4. Chicken pox	5. Colds	6. Dental cavities
7. Epilepsy	8. Gonorrhea	9. Heart attack
10. Influenza	11. Laryngitis	12. Leukemia
13. Malaria	14. Measles	15. Mononucleosis
16. Mumps	17. Pneumonia	18. Poison ivy
19. Polio	20. Psychosis	21. Rheumatism
22. Smallpox	23. Strep throat	24. Stroke
25. Syphilis	26. Tonsilitis	27. Tuberculosis
28. Typhoid fever	29. Ulcers	30. Whooping cough

Table 4.4. *American disease belief-frames*

1. You can catch ___ from other people.
2. ___ is caused by germs.
3. Most people catch ___ in bad weather.
4. ___ comes from being emotionally upset.
5. ___ runs in the family.
6. When you are overtired, your resistance to ___ is lowered.
7. ___ can not be cured.
8. ___ has to run its course.
9. ___ should be treated by miracle drugs.
10. ___ gets better by itself.
11. ___ is serious.
12. ___ is a fatal disease.
13. You never really get over ___.
14. ___ is a crippling disease.
15. You can have ___ and not know it.
16. ___ spreads through your whole system.
17. ___ is contagious.
18. If a woman comes down with ___ during her pregnancy it harms her child.
19. Feeling generally run-down is a sign of ___.
20. ___ affects the heart.
21. Your skin breaks out with ___.
22. Runny nose is a sign of ___.
23. Sore throat comes with ___.
24. ___ brings on fever.
25. Once you've had ___ you can't get it again.
26. ___ is a children's disease.
27. Most people get ___ at some time or other.
28. Some people have a tendency to get ___.
29. It is safer to have ___ as a child and get it over with.
30. ___ is a sign of old age.

In both Mexico and the United States, the interviews with informants produced large numbers of sentences about diseases. Once a large corpus of belief-frames had been constructed, informants were asked to select the most basic, unambiguous, and general frames for describing diseases. Table 4.4 presents the final selection of American disease belief-frames.

The American sample consisted of ten monolingual English speaking Stanford undergraduates. In a pretest it was found that American informants preferred to answer on a scale rather than give simple "yes–no" answers. A five point scale was developed for the final test form and administered using the following format:

You can catch ___ from other people.					
	definitely	probably	possibly	probably not	definitely not
1. Appendicitis :	_______ :	_______ :	______ :	___________ :	__________ :
2. Bronchitis :	_______ :	_______ :	______ :	___________ :	__________ :
etc.					

The Mexican informants preferred a simpler scale, with responses restricted to "yes" (*si*), "at times" (*a veces si, a veces no*), or "no" (*no*) The Mexican disease terms were selected the same way the terms for the American sample were selected. However, for the disease frames a small number of the American frames were translated into Spanish to facilitate comparisons between the two systems despite the semantic awkwardness of some of the translations.

Each American informant was asked to fill in an answer for all 30 disease terms for all 30 belief-frames, making a total of 900 judgments. The scale responses were averaged across respondents, and the mean for each belief-frame across the 30 diseases calculated. To simplify the data the responses were dichotomized by using the mean score for each belief-frame as the basis for deciding whether a score was to be considered a *yes* or a *no*. The results for the American sample are presented in Table 4.5. Each column of the matrix gives the dichotomized "yes" (x) or "no" (a blank) responses for a particular belief-frame, and each row of the matrix gives the responses for a particular disease. The rows and columns have been grouped on the basis of separate cluster analyses of disease terms and belief-frames.[7]

A special method of multidimensional scaling was used to analyze these data. The scaling program used, MDSCAL, was an early version of KYST. Using a special "missing data" option, it was possible to put into the program simultaneously both the belief-frame by belief-frame Pearson correlation matrix and the disease term by disease term Pearson correlation matrix. The result produced a representation in which both the disease terms and the belief are mapped into the same metric space. A two dimensional representation was found to fit the original data reasonably well, and to have a clear interpretation. The MDSCAL plot for both disease terms and belief-frames is presented in Figure 4.4. The abbreviations for belief-frames are in capital letters while disease terms are in small letters. Interpretation of this figure is fairly straightforward. There is a clear *seriousness* dimension running from right to left, with the most serious diseases and relevant belief-frames on the right hand

[7] The cluster analyses used the "average linkage" method – see Aldenderfer and Blashfield 1984:40.

Table 4.5. *American sample, dichotomized data for disease terms and belief-frames*

		Weathr 3	Throat 23	Fever 24	Itself 10	Nose 22	Resist 6	Catch 1	Contag 17	Germs 2	Drugs 9	Once 25	Safech 29	Childr 26	Most 27	Spread 16	Rundow 19	Pregna 18	Course 8	Seriou 11	Fatal 12	Heart 20	Skin 21	Inheri 5	Never 13	Nocure 7	Crippl 14	Tenden 28	Oldage 30	Emotnl 4	Notkno 15
Tonsilitis	26	x	x	x			x			x		x	x	x	x																x
Appendicitis	1			x								x	x		x					x	x										x
Poison ivy	18				x			x	x						x				x				x					x			
Strep throat	23	x	x	x	x		x	x	x	x	x			x	x				x												
Laryngitis	11	x	x	x	x		x	x	x	x	x			x	x				x									x			
Whooping cough	30	x	x	x	x	x	x	x	x	x	x	x	x	x				x			x										
Influenza	10	x	x	x	x	x	x	x	x	x	x				x	x	x	x	x												
Pneumonia	17	x	x	x	x	x	x	x	x	x	x					x	x	x	x	x	x										
Mononucleosis	15	x		x	x	x	x	x	x	x	x					x	x	x	x			x									
Colds	5	x	x	x	x	x	x	x	x	x					x	x	x		x							x		x		x	
Bronchitis	2	x	x	x	x	x	x		x	x	x									x								x	x	x	
Chicken pox	4			x	x		x	x	x	x	x	x	x	x	x	x		x	x				x								
Measles	14			x	x	x	x	x	x	x		x	x	x	x	x		x	x				x								
Mumps	16		x	x	x		x	x	x	x		x	x	x	x	x	x	x	x												
Smallpox	22			x				x	x	x	x	x	x	x		x		x	x	x	x		x								
Typhoid fever	28	x		x			x	x	x	x	x	x	x	x		x		x	x	x	x										
Gonorrhea	8							x	x	x	x							x		x	x		x				x				x
Syphilis	25							x	x	x	x					x		x		x	x	x	x				x				x
Polio	19							x	x	x	x	x		x		x	x	x	x	x	x	x				x	x	x			
Leukemia	12										x	x		x		x	x	x	x	x	x	x		x	x	x	x				x
Tuberculosis	27						x	x	x	x	x	x				x	x	x	x	x	x				x	x					x
Malaria	13			x						x	x					x	x	x		x	x	x			x						

Table 4.5. *contd*

		Weathr 3	Throat 23	Fever 24	Itself 10	Nose 22	Resist 6	Catch 1	Contag 17	Germs 2	Drugs 9	Once 25	Safech 29	Childr 26	Most 27	Spread 16	Rundow 19	Pregna 18	Course 8	Seriou 11	Fatal 12	Heart 20	Skin 21	Inheri 5	Never 13	Nocure 7	Cripple 14	Tenden 28	Oldage 30	Emotnl 4	Notkno 15
Stroke	24						x									x		x	x	x	x	x		x	x	x	x	x	x	x	
Heart attack	9						x											x	x	x	x	x		x	x	x	x	x	x	x	x
Cancer	3															x	x	x		x	x	x	x	x	x	x	x	x	x		x
Psychosis	20						x													x				x	x	x	x	x	x	x	x
Ulcers	29																							x	x			x	x	x	x
Epilepsy	7													x						x				x	x	x	x			x	x
Dental cavities	6														x									x	x	x		x			x
Rheumatism	21	x									x					x	x		x					x	x	x	x	x	x		x

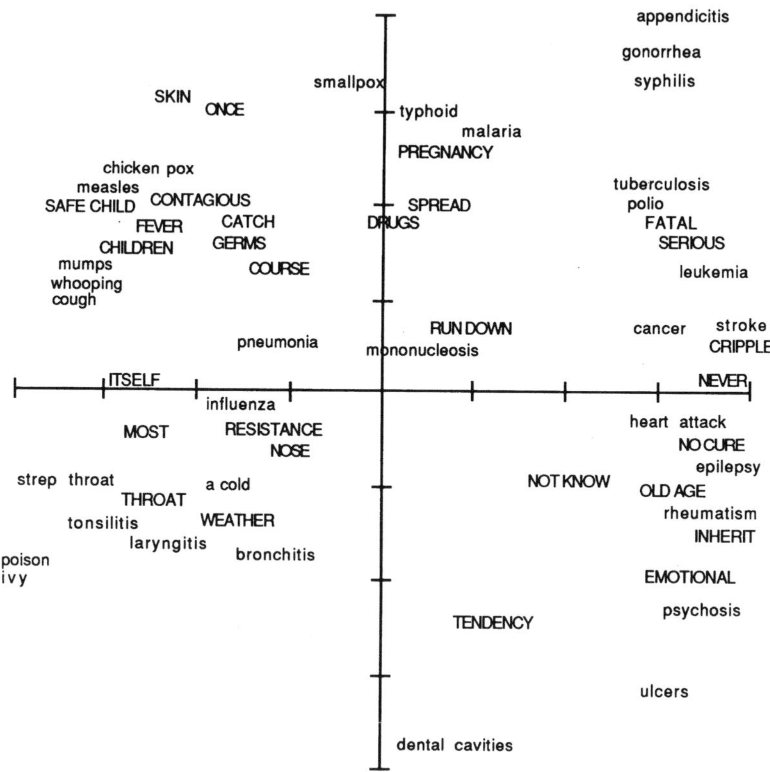

Figure 4.4 MDSCAL plot for American belief-frames and disease terms

side of the space and the minor and self-limiting illnesses and relevant belief-frames on the left.

The second dimension runs from the top left of the plot to the bottom right, and concerns *contagion*. At the bottom right are the old age, inherited, or emotion caused illness and belief-frames. The entire left side of the plot (with the exception of *poison ivy*) contains the simpler contagious diseases, such as *colds*, *influenza*, *chicken pox*, etc., along with belief-frames concerning the throat, resistance, germs, and diseases which are safer to have as a child and can only be gotten once. In the top right (with the exception of *appendicitis*) there are the serious systemic contagious diseases such as *syphilis*, *typhoid*, and *malaria*. At the far right are the crippling, non-contagious and often incurable diseases, such as *cancer*, *heart attack*, and *stroke*.

The Mexican data showed quite a different configuration than the American data. The MDSCAL results show a *hot–cold* dimension, marked most clearly by the kind of medicine one should take. For example, one should take a hot medicine when the disease involves getting wet, having a cold body or chills, and pains in the bones that go with illnesses which involve internal congestive, respiratory, and pulmonary complaints, as well as when there are problems with the milk of a nursing mother. The second dimension has the appearance of a *contagion* dimension with *measles*, *smallpox*, *colds*, and *whooping cough*, along with belief-frames concerning microbes, contagion, and children's diseases on one side of the dimension and illnesses which involve witchcraft, anger, stomach ache, diarrhea, and having fits on the other side of the space. It is interesting that the range of what is considered contagious appears in a different form in the Mexican data, with dysenteries and respiratory infections not near the "contagious" diseases and related belief-frames.

Another belief-frame by disease term matrix, using slightly different disease terms and belief-frames, was collected by James C. Young (1978) from a Spanish speaking Mexican-Tarascan town. Young used cluster analysis to determine both groupings of disease terms and groupings of belief-frames. To identify the most important belief-frames, Young developed a measure to determine which belief-frames best define particular disease clusters. The belief-frames which best define a particular disease cluster are those in which most of the illnesses in that cluster have that property, while most of the other illnesses in other clusters do not have that property. On the basis of the results of this measure, Young concluded that a major dimension for the Tarascans involved the distinction between *externally caused* illnesses, which result from contact with hazardous agents in the environment like weather, versus *internally caused* illnesses, which result from internally initiated imbalances, including *hot* versus *cold* diet imbalances.

As a general technique, the analysis of "item by feature" matrices appears to do a reasonably good job of identifying the salient features of a domain. However, for cognitive anthropology a distinct shift in the overall goals of analysis occurred as a result of using these kinds of data. In the feature or componential analysis of kin term paradigms, the overall goal was to identify the *criterial attributes* for each term – the *defining* features or properties of each term. In the multidimensional scaling analyses, whether MDSCAL or KYST or clustering, the goal was to find the most *general and salient features* which organize the field of items. However, the most general and salient features of a domain are not necessarily the criterial attributes of the objects in the domain. For example, the feature or property of being a *serious* illness is not a criterial attribute of any of the American diseases. *Cancer* is certainly considered a *serious* illness, but *seriousness* is not a criterial attribute of something being a "cancer." Nor does the fact that *colds* are *contagious* make something a "cold." Yet *contagion* and *seriousness* are two of the most salient features of illnesses for Americans.

The point is that a shift in the technique of analysis led to a shift in what was being looked for. *The shift from componential analyses of distinctive features to the analyses of belief-frame matrices resulted in a shift from trying to find features which could be used to define terms to trying to find features which people respond to most strongly.* Features which are not criterial but which are salient are often called *connotative* features (in contrast to *denotative* features, which consist of criterial attributes). What these new ways of collecting and analyzing data did was make apparent that sometimes connotative features of the items in a domain are of more interest to people than denotative or defining features. In some cases – as in disease terms – the denotative features or criterial attributes are not even known to most folk. It is the medical doctor who knows how to diagnose diseases, not the ordinary person. The categories of concern to most Americans with respect to illness are the conditions which bring about certain diseases and the conditions that these diseases produce.

Under certain conditions an attribute by item matrix data will produce results which correspond closely to direct similarity ratings. For example, in the case of the disease term and belief-frame data, a sample of fifteen American undergraduates were asked to make seven point similarity scale ratings between all pairs of the thirty disease terms listed above. These similarity scale ratings correlated highly (.87) with the number of belief-frame judgments shared by the pairs of disease terms. The reason that these similarity ratings are highly correlated with the degree to which two diseases share belief-frames seems to be because in both cases the same features are involved; that is, in making similarity ratings the rater makes judgments about the similarity of disease terms on the basis of the same features – *contagion*, *seriousness*, *fever*, etc. – that have been used to construct the belief-frames. Of course, if the belief-frames had been *irrelevant* to the features that Americans use to make similarity judgments about diseases, then the number of belief-frames shared by pairs of disease terms would not be correlated with the raters' similarity judgments for these pairs.

Rating correlations based on feature overlap

Ratings are a standard part of the technology of social science. They are used in public opinion attitude polls, in personality tests, and in a vast range of psychological experiments. An ordinary set of character trait rating scales is presented below:

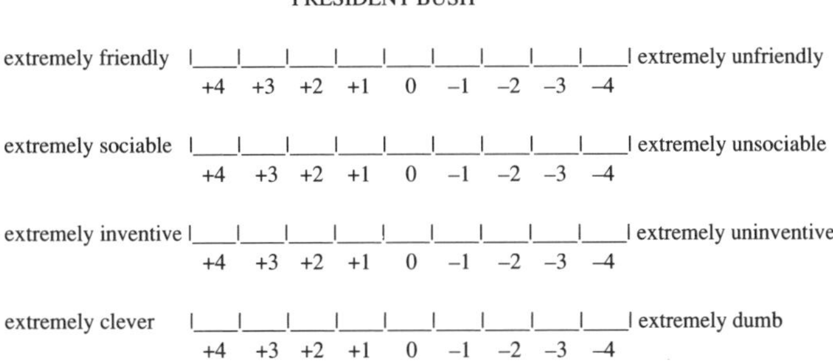

Table 4.6. *Character trait ratings of six notables*

	Bush	Einstein	Monroe	Starr	Nixon	Nancy Regan
Friendly/unfriendly	4	2	3	1	–3	–1
Sociable/unsociable	4	2	2	2	–1	2
Inventive/uninventive	–1	4	1	3	2	–2
Clever/dumb	2	4	–1	3	3	1

Table 4.7. *Pearson correlations for four character trait across six notables*

	Friendliness	Sociability	Inventiveness	Cleverness
Friendliness	1.00	.86	–.03	–.26
Sociability	.86	1.00	–.37	–.21
Inventiveness	–.03	–.37	1.00	.58
Cleverness	–.26	–.21	.58	1.00

The instructions would tell the respondent to place a check in the slot that corresponds best to their judgment of how "friendly" or "unfriendly" President Bush is. Typically ratings use adjectives (*friendly*, *unfriendly*) with adverbial modifiers (*extremely*) to indicate "strength" or "intensity" associated with some number scale. Below is a table of ratings from one informant for four scales (*friendliness*, *sociability*, *inventiveness*, and *cleverness*) for six well-known persons (George Bush, Albert Einstein, Marilyn Monroe, Ringo Starr, Richard Nixon, and Nancy Reagan). The result is a special form of *item by attribute* matrix, with persons as the objects and trait ratings as the attributes.

Early in the history of psychology such ratings were used in an attempt to measure individual differences in personality. A standard research technique is to find a social group in which all the members know each other relatively well, and then have every individual rate every other individual in the group on a series of adjective scales. The averaged ratings would then give a fairly good idea of the salient characteristics of each of the members of the group. A variant of this technique is to have a series of individuals rated by a small number of psychologists after an interview or after observing the person in the performance of some sort of task.

An issue that arose early in this kind of research involves the question of the degree to which. personality adjectives measure underlying dimensions of personality *or simply reflect the degree of feature overlap between terms*. Consider the four adjectives rating scales presented in Table 4.6. On the basis of feature overlap we would expect the *friendly–unfriendly* scale to correlate highly with the *sociable–unsociable* scale; that is, that someone who is given a high rating on *friendliness* will also be given a high score on *sociability*. We expect this because both scales are similar in *meaning* – that

Table 4.8. *Factor analysis of four character traits across six notables*

	Factor 1	Factor 2
Friendliness	**.97**	–.03
Sociability	**.94**	–.03
Inventiveness	–.08	**.90**
Cleverness	–.14	**.86**
Variance accounted for	46%	40%

is, the features used to identify someone as *friendly* are similar to the features that identify someone as *sociable*. Both involve features concerning interaction with people in which the interaction is characteristically emotionally pleasant, and the rated person characteristically shows an interest in and liking for other persons. The features of these two terms are not identical – somebody might involve themselves in a lot of social gatherings but not really act very warm to others, and so be rated as *very sociable*, but only *slightly friendly*. However, while we would not expect the correlation between *friendliness* and *sociability* to be perfect, we would expect on the basis of feature overlap that people who are high on one scale are also high on the other scale.

Similarly, we would expect the *cleverness* scale and the *inventiveness* scale to be positively correlated because of the feature overlap between these two scales; both traits involve being able to accomplish difficult intellectual tasks. However, in general we would not expect the *friendliness* scale to correlate with either the *inventiveness* or *cleverness* scale since *friendliness* has few if any features outside of general "goodness" which overlap with being *inventive* or being *clever*. We would also expect the same pattern with the *sociability* scale. Table 4.7 presents the correlations of the four scales across the six persons for the data in Table 4.8.

Of course, these correlation coefficients would change somewhat if a different set of persons were to be rated, or if the ratings were made by a different rater. For this sample we see that *friendliness* and *sociability* are highly correlated at +.86, and that *inventiveness* and *cleverness* are correlated +.58. This is generally what we would expect on the basis of feature overlap – *two traits that have overlapping features will be positively correlated because similar discriminations are used in making both ratings*. For this sample there are relatively small negative correlations between the "social" traits and the "intelligence" traits, which means that for this sample the persons who are *friendly* and *sociable* have a tendency *not* to be *inventive* and *clever*. One would expect that if ratings were made over a larger set of persons that these correlations would move closer to zero, since there is no apparent feature overlap –

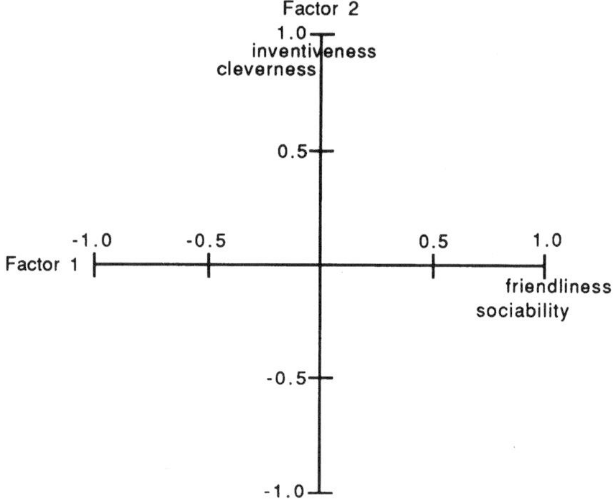

Figure 4.5 Factor plot for four character traits

positive or negative – between these "social traits" and these "intelligence" traits.

A factor analysis of these four traits yields two factors with eigenvalues greater than one.[8] The varimax rotated factor loadings are presented in Table 4.8. The factor loadings for the character traits show a clear pattern in which the social traits have high loadings on the first factor and the intelligence traits have high loadings on the second factor.

These results can be diagrammed in a two dimensional space, each dimension representing a factor. This diagram is presented in Figure 4.5.

The number of traits and ratings in the example above is too small to serve as a real test of our hypothesis. But if more extensive factor analyses of character trait ratings can be duplicated with just similarity judgments, this would indicate that such results are due primarily to feature overlap rather than to the co-variation of distinct attributes in the *external* world such as, for example, the correlation between the heights of fathers and sons.[9]

Over the past twenty years psychologists have developed a general consensus that there are five factors – called the "big five" – which account for most of the ratings using character traits (Digman 1990). Many kinds of raters have been used; teachers rating students, officer candidates rating each other, college

8 Factor analysis (in this case actually principal components analysis from SYSTAT) is a method of multivariate analysis in which the original matrix of correlations is resolved into a smaller number of orthogonal determinants. Like multidimensional scaling programs such as KYST, the resulting factor loadings can be given a spatial representation.

9 It is not being argued that *all* the correlations between ratings can be accounted for by feature overlap. Ideas about traits that go together, such as being "loud" and being "aggressive," can also be a source of correlational structure, whether or not these traits do, in fact, co-vary. For an exploration of this hypothesis with respect to personality traits, see Gara and Rosenberg 1981.

Table 4.9. *Factor loadings for twenty character scales*

Factor name and scale	Factor loadings				
	F1	F2	F3	F4	F5
1. Extroversion					
Talkative–silent	**90**	02	–02	04	00
Frank, open-secretive	**78**	–08	07	–03	07
Adventurous–cautious	**79**	15	–20	32	01
Sociable–reclusive	**86**	01	–18	–01	–02
2. Agreeableness					
Goodnatured–irritable	17	**80**	17	12	07
Not jealous–jealous	–10	**64**	20	49	07
Mild, gentle–headstrong	–20	**80**	27	19	10
Cooperative–negativistic	33	**74**	28	13	11
3. Conscientiousness					
Fussy, tidy–careless	–33	–08	**66**	–35	20
Responsible–undependable	–03	32	**86**	08	18
Scrupulous–unscrupulous	–30	–08	**66**	–35	20
Persevering–quitting, fickle	–05	28	**74**	12	27
4. Emotional stability					
Poised–nervous, tense	01	56	15	**61**	05
Calm–anxious	06	21	–10	**82**	–07
Composed–excitable	13	06	16	**71**	24
Not hypochondriacal–hypochondriacal	21	27	00	**65**	–09
5. Culture					
Artistically sensitive–insensitive	–04	08	39	–10	**75**
Intellectual–unreflective, narrow	–04	05	47	04	**74**
Polished, refined–crude, boorish	15	25	53	16	**46**
Imaginative–simple, direct	12	19	03	10	**68**

students rating each other, clinical staff rating trainees, etc. A variety of different trait adjectives have been used in a variety of rating formats. The results have been remarkably consistent, each study finding essentially the same five factors. Many psychologists consider these five factors to constitute the five major *dimensions* of human personality. Table 4.9 presents Warren Norman's 1963 factor analysis of these five dimensions which have served as a standard for other analyses.

In 1965 I attempted to test the hypothesis that these five factors were the result of feature overlap. I had a small sample of ten undergraduates rate the degree of similarity in meaning of all possible pairs of the negative poles (*silent, secretive, cautious,* etc.) for each of the Norman twenty bipolar scales.[10] The results produced five factors with almost exactly the same composition as the Norman analysis. A more elegant result was obtained by Milton Hakel (1974) who had a large number of respondents make co-occurrence judgments

[10] D'Andrade 1965. At the time multidimensional scaling programs were unavailable, so I treated the rows of the similarity matrix as subjects and the columns as variables to compute a correlation matrix which was then factor analyzed.

Table 4.10. *Multidimensional scaling of similarity ratings for Norman character traits*

	Factor loadings				
Factor name and scale	F1	F2	F3	F4	F5
1. Extroversion					
Talkative	**84**	–35	21	13	–15
Frank, open	**92**	11	–24	–06	–31
Adventurous	**60**	–51	48	–40	–38
Sociable	**80**	–59	20	–29	09
2. Agreeableness					
Goodnatured	–33	**92**	04	17	06
Not jealous	13	**84**	–01	40	08
Mild, gentle	09	**81**	43	13	15
Cooperative	–61	**65**	31	31	16
3. Conscientiousness					
Fussy, tidy	05	–63	**65**	–49	09
Responsible	–23	36	**84**	03	06
Scrupulous	–12	–26	**89**	–14	07
Persevering	–06	–09	**80**	38	19
4. Emotional stability					
Poised	–12	21	34	**82**	06
Calm	05	24	–08	**87**	–37
Composed	12	–45	42	**70**	–20
Not hypochondriacal	–33	08	–23	**85**	–06
5. Culture					
Artistically sensitive	–08	–46	30	–26	**80**
Intellectual	–48	10	47	26	**75**
Polished, refined	–53	**60**	54	–19	28
Imaginative	07	13	–11	–07	**103**

("Suppose a person is ____ – how likely is it that he is also ____?") on both sides of the twenty bipolar scales, resulting in a forty by forty matrix. A total of 480 respondents each judged 100 pairs of descriptors in a balanced block design in which no pair was repeated on the same questionnaire and each pair was represented thirty times across all questionnaires. The mean score for each cell was computed and the matrix analyzed with MDSCAL. Hakel's results for just the positive side of each scale are presented in Table 4.10. Out of the twenty positive trait terms, only one does not have its highest loadings on the factor predicted from the Norman analysis. The structural similarity of Hakel's and Norman's results is overwhelming.

The fact that the similarity ratings give the same dimensional results as a correlation matrix of traits does not mean that these dimensions or factors are worthless, or that the specific ratings are worthless. There is considerable evidence that personality trait ratings are both reasonably reliable and valid

[11] See Wiggins 1973 for a review of these issues.

descriptors of behavior.[11] For example, the fact that ratings about someone's "talkativeness," "frankness," "adventurousness," and "sociability" are likely to be positively correlated does not mean that these ratings are inaccurate, only that to some extent *they all measure the same thing*. The issue being contested here is that the correlations reveal something about *real dimensions of personality* rather than *a linguistic fact that these traits all overlap in meaning*.

Dean Peabody summarizes these studies as follows:

> Wiggins (1973) made a useful distinction between *external* structure (based on judgments about the traits of people) and *internal* structure (based on judgments about the relations between traits). The radical attack on personality, initiated by D'Andrade (1965) essentially claims that external structure is simply a projection of the internal structure of the judges. D'Andrade obtained judgments about internal structure (similarity of meaning) for Norman's 20 scales and claimed to find the same Big Five factors as in studies of external structure. Such a correspondence between external and internal structure is also widely accepted by defenders of personality, who argue that this correspondence does not preclude the validity of personality assessment. (1987:67)

How, then, do "defenders of personality" explain the high degree of correspondence between "external" ratings and "internal" judgments of similarity? Basically, they argue that the external structures exist – that is, that personality is really composed of these five major dimensions – and that people have observed and identified these dimensions and have over time encoded them as salient features of trait terms (Goldberg 1982). This could be true. Data from other cultures is needed to resolve the issue.

A number of other studies were carried out in which external ratings of various sorts were reproduced by similarity ratings. Richard Shweder showed that a factor analytic classification of interpersonal behavior, developed by F. Bales, could be replicated solely from similarity judgments (1972). Shweder also replicated with similarity judgments the Alpha factor of the Minnesota Multiphasic Personality Inventory (MMPI), a questionnaire used to diagnose forms of mental illness (1977). I replicated the Leary Grid organization of interpersonal behavior (1965), as well as the four dimensional structure of Overall's Brief Psychiatric Rating Scale (Shweder and D'Andrade 1980).

Memory based rating

All of the examples so far involve ratings in which raters judge on some kind of scale how strongly some target person displays some particular characteristic. A related type of data is often collected by psychologists and others interested in interpersonal behavior. In this kind of study the investigator begins with a classification of behavior acts. A group of people are observed and each time they perform one of these behavior acts, that act is counted. At the end of the observation period every member of the group can be characterized by a frequency count for how many times he or she performed each of the behavior acts in the classification system. Using the frequencies, the different behavior acts can then be correlated across persons and analyzed in various ways.

In a number of studies, not only were actual behaviors observed and counted, but *retrospective* data was also collected. The retrospective data consisted of the observer's *memory* of what happened. Typically the observers are asked to indicate on a scale running from *very frequently* to *not at all* how often each member of the observed group performed each of the behavior acts. These recalled frequencies can then be used to correlate the different kinds of behavior acts across persons in the same way the actual frequencies are used.

What is interesting is that typically the correlations for the immediately observed behaviors correspond only weakly to the correlations for the recalled behaviors (D'Andrade 1974). However, the correlations for the recalled behaviors correspond *strongly* to the judged ratings of the *similarity* of the different behavior acts. Across seven different tests of intermatrix correspondence taken from a variety of studies, Shweder (1982) found that similarity ratings and recalled behavior correlations show a mean *r* of +.75, while recalled behavior correlations and immediately observed behavior correlations show a mean *r* of only +.25 and immediately observed behavior correlations and recalled behavior correlations show a mean *r* of only +.26.

All this correlating of correlations gets somewhat confusing. Most simply, what this data shows is that, at least for the case of classifications of specific kinds of behavior (e.g. *informs*, *questions*, *explains*, *jokes*, etc.), people's memories do not reflect accurately what kinds of acts go together. What memory based ratings show is that what people remember as going together are the kinds of behavior they judge to be similar. Humans show a systematic distortion in their memories. They falsely recall "what goes with what" based on "what is like what." This effect has been demonstrated across a wide range of kinds of materials, not just behavior frequencies (for example, see Chapman 1967). Overall, these results throw doubt on a broad class of retrospectively based research data.[12]

While the seriousness of the problem of feature overlap and systematic memory distortion for personality assessment is still a controversial issue, the results reported above are much happier for the study of the organization of *cultural* features. That is, the evidence is that similarity judgments, item by property matrices, and external ratings all typically uncover cognitively shared salient features. Cognitively shared salient features are an interesting part of a society's culture. From an anthropological viewpoint, much of the research by psychologists on dimensions of personality traits and dimensions of interpersonal behavior can be seen as an investigation of western culture.

Consider, for example, the Norman "big five" dimensions of personality. If

[12] See Dawes and Pearson 1991 for an excellent review of the problems involved in retrospective questionnaire data.

we look at these dimensions as culturally meaningful ways of organizing our knowledge about people, we see that these dimensions presuppose a certain way of dividing up the individual's world. First, almost all trait terms are *evaluative* – either positively or negatively. This is a cultural system which is oriented towards evaluating how well people do certain things rather than just presenting neutral description. For example, the second dimension, called *Agreeableness*, consists almost entirely of traits which involve *interpersonal behavior*; they describe different ways of treating other people well or badly. The term "agreeableness" is simply one of the more general ways of describing a good way of getting along with others. A more accurate but less "personality" oriented way of describing this second dimension would be to call it the "evaluation of interpersonal behavior." Similarly, the third dimension, *Conscientiousness,* consists of evaluations of how well people do *work* – "responsibly," "with perseverance," "carelessly," etc. The fifth dimension, called *Culture* by Norman and *Intellect* by others, involves the evaluation of the person with respect to basic ideational systems of a society, such as knowledge and art. Only the first and the fourth factor are defined by qualities internal to the person. The fourth factor, *Emotional Stability*, focuses on the rich and varied emotional communication system carried by facial expression, tone of voice, and body language. It seems reasonable that evaluation of the quality of emotions a person communicates would be a salient feature of the individual in a world in which important social relationships, such as marriage and friendship, are based primarily on affective rewards. Finally, the first dimension, called *Surgency* or *Extroversion*, appears to be primarily a measure of *level* of social participation and expressiveness.[13]

Thus the "big five" dimensions of personality, viewed anthropologically, divide the world into *work*, *interpersonal relations*, *idea systems (knowledge and art)*, *emotions*, and *general activity.* Evaluation of people in terms of these domains makes sense in modern industrial societies. To date, the evidence, while somewhat sparse, indicates that these same dimensions are found in Germany, Japan, and Israel (Digman 1990). However, Geoffrey White, working in an A'ara speaking Solomon Island society, found what appears to be quite a different system of organization of personality traits (1978). These Solomon Islanders are primarily subsistence horticulturalists. Kinship and political leadership constitute the major institutional systems of their society. Working in the A'ara language, White collected thirty-seven common personality descriptors. Using a modified sorting method in which informants are asked for each term to choose the five other terms that are most like it in meaning, twenty-five male adults rated all terms. Using a median method,[14] White cluster analyzed the thirty-seven trait terms. The results are presented in

[13] This argument is made in more detail in D'Andrade 1985.
[14] Also sometimes called U-statistic clustering; see D'Andrade 1978.

Figure 4.6 using English glosses for the A'ara trait terms. The terms in italics have been added to emphasize what appear to be the most salient contrasts between the clusters. Basically, the A'ara system has two main dimensions; *good* vs. *bad* ways of behaving and *leader-like* vs. *follower-like* ways of behaving. This makes four clusters – *bad followers*, *bad leaders*, *good leaders*, and *good followers*.[15]

The overall argument here is that in a society with different social institutions, the *salient features* of personality trait terms are organized in a different way. White (1978) points out that the pattern found for the A'ara seems general for Melanesian societies in which leadership is highly valued, but where there are often also strong egalitarian values which conflict with domineering styles of leadership, leading to ambivalence about powerful leaders. A'ara personality terms certainly do *not* have an organization of terms like Norman's factors, throwing doubt on the cross-cultural universality of the "big five."

The material presented in this chapter has shown that similarity judgments, item by attribute matrices and external ratings all can be used to uncover general, salient cognitive features which people use in structuring a domain. This gives the cultural analyst a kit bag of techniques which can be used to investigate any particular topic. If there are not too many items, similarity judgments are a direct and simple way of finding out how the items are organized. To investigate simultaneously the organization of features and items, the analysis of an item by attribute matrix is preferable. If there is a large number of items and the domain is not one which has a clear item by attribute organization, external ratings are likely to be most effective method.[16]

The categorization of interpersonal relationships is a good example of a domain which is most appropriately investigated by means of external ratings. There are a great number of statements that people make about interpersonal relationships, making it difficult to use direct similarity judgments. Since these statements about interpersonal relationships are themselves attribute-like (e.g. *I feel at ease around* ___) it is possible to use external ratings of actual relationships to form a data matrix.

As part of a project to study the way Americans evaluate themselves and each other, I undertook an investigation in 1982 of the way in which Americans categorize relationships. The first step was to elicit statements which individuals normally use in describing their relationships. The statements were taken from a series of informal tape recorded interviews in which informants were queried about their family, friends, lovers, acquaintances, and enemies. From the transcripts a series of 300 statements were abstracted which had been used to characterize relationships. A small sample of informants were asked to

15 White (1978) carried out a KYST multidimensional scaling of these data which strongly supports this dimensional interpretation.

16 There are also a number ways of combining these three techniques; see Wish, Deutsch, and Biener 1972 for an example in which similarity ratings and external ratings are used together.

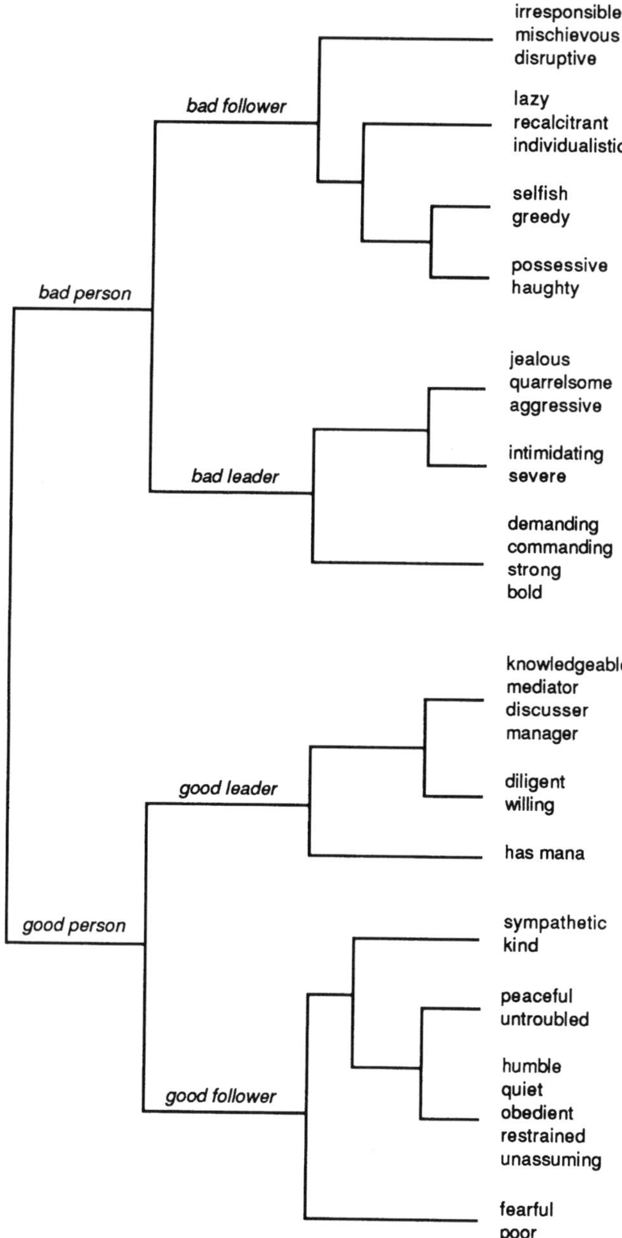

Figure 4.6 Hierarchical clustering of A'ara personality descriptors

choose "the most unambiguous statements which were also most diagnostic about the character of relationship being described." Fifty-eight statements were finally selected for analysis.

The second step was to have ratings made on these fifty-eight statements about specific relationships by a reasonably large sample of respondents. A total of fifty-two undergraduate respondents rated people they knew well. Each respondent was asked to select twenty persons with whom they had significant relationships, making sure that family/non-family, liked/not-liked, and male/female targets were included in the selection. For each person selected, the respondent was asked to rate on a seven-point scale how well each of the fifty-eight statements applied to their relationship with this person. All pairs of statements were then correlated with each other across relationships and respondents. The resulting correlation matrix was then cluster analyzed using the median method. The result is presented in Figure 4.7. The terms in capital letters have been added as interpretations of the clusters.

The clustering of propositions about interpersonal relationships divides neatly into three general groupings; *negative* relationships, *unbalanced* relationships in which the other person wants more from the rater than rater wishes to give, and *positive* relationships. The positive relationships have three distinct sub-clusters; one concerning relations of *mutual caring* and *closeness*, one involving the *dependability*, *support*, and *honesty* of the person being rated, and one concerning *romantic* relationships.

This clustering is notable for several reasons. First, the strong dislike of being controlled by others and being treated as an inferior person, often noted in studies of American national character,[17] comes through strongly. The opposite of this kind of domination is found in the sub-clusters of mutual caring and mutual sharing, in which an egalitarian relationship is maintained at the same time each person in the relationship both gives and receives material and emotional resources. The problem of inequality also arises in the clusters which involve one partner needing more than the other, making the relationship insecure. Overall, the strong anti-authoritarian and pro-egalitarian configuration of the clusters is impressive.

Applied research

The extended feature model has been used in applied research for both marketing and political polling. Volney Stefflre, for example, has developed a set of techniques by which predictions about preferences for different brands of commercial products can be made from the judged features of these brands (1972). The purpose of this research is not simply to predict product preference, but to help businesses develop new products which can compete successfully

[17] See, for example, Geoffrey Gorer's insightful study, *The American People*.

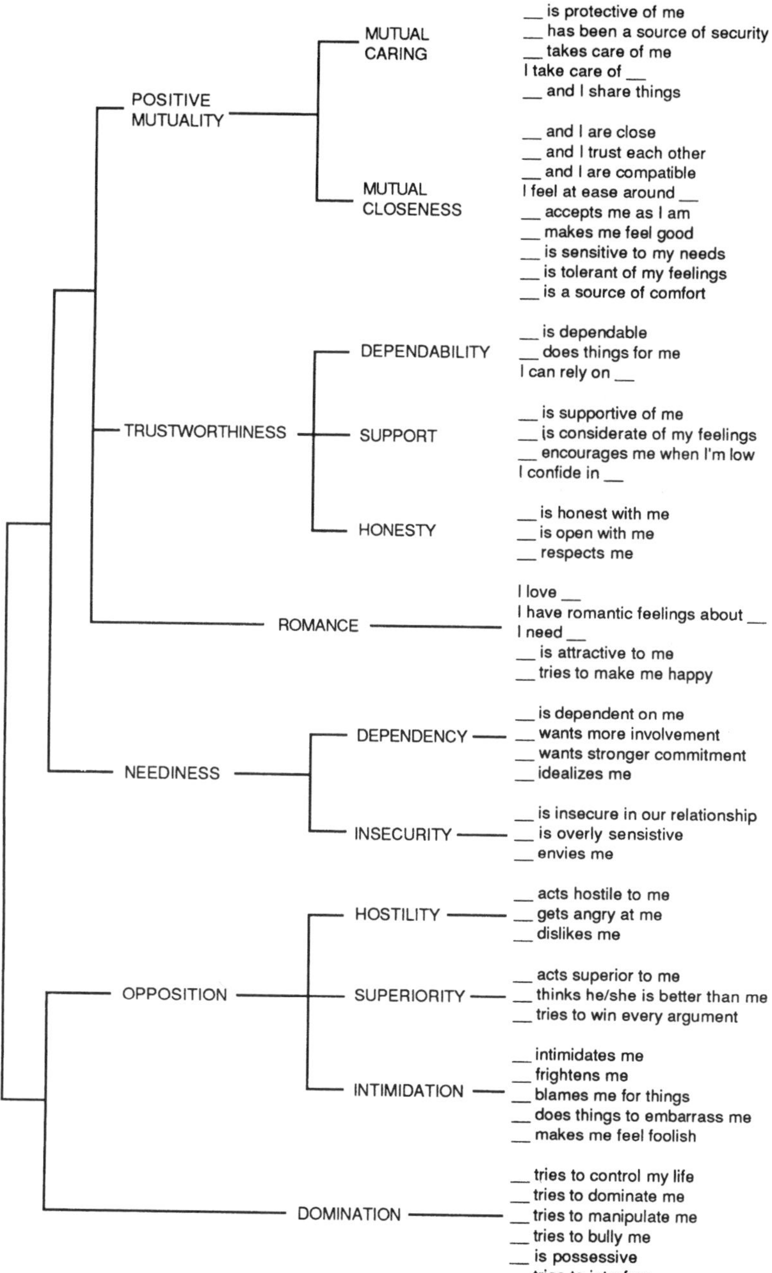

Figure 4.7 U-statistic hierarchical cluster analysis of ratings of propositions about interpersonal relationships

with their competitors' products but not their own. For example, Stefflre was employed by a coffee company to develop a feature profile for a new brand of coffee which would compete in the market with other competing companies' coffee brands. Based on various rating tasks, Stefflre developed a profile of a *light*, *clean*, *friendly*, and *mild* coffee. (One does not normally think of *friendly* as a coffee flavor, but apparently consumers use this term often in judging which coffees they like.) By varying bean selection and roasting processes, after a number of trials a new coffee was created which had these features of taste. This coffee did reasonably well in the market, taking away purchases from the seven brands with which it was expected to compete. The Pearson correlation between the predicted and obtained amounts which the new coffee drew from each of the other seven brands was .94 in a survey of performance in a national market.

Stefflre has pointed out that the relation between features and similarity judgments is not uniquely fixed; it depends on the context of judgment. With respect to *making* coffee, two instant coffee brands might be judged as quite similar to each other. However, with respect to *taste*, these same two coffees might be judged as quite different. The point is that features are judged with respect to the aims and goals of the individual, and as a result a small shift in aims and goals can make for large shifts in feature weights.

Stefflre has also pointed out that it is generally true that there is considerable agreement between individuals from the same culture in "what is like what," but considerable variability in "what is liked." Or, to put this another way, *preference judgments are more variable than similarity judgments.* Almost everybody will agree that chicken tastes more like turkey than steak, yet there is considerable variation with respect to judgments about which one tastes best. However, to predict preferences, one can expect that a person will like those things which are most similar to other things that person likes. A person who strongly prefers turkey to steak is likely to prefer chicken to hamburger.

In retrospect

During the middle and late sixties there was a large increase in techniques aimed at uncovering salient features. Many of these techniques were built on the number crunching power of the computer. Various multidimensional scaling programs made it possible to uncover the feature organization of a domain using new kinds of data, such as similarity judgments and external ratings. Psychologists were also interested in the feature model as a way of understanding the basic processes of categorization and added greatly to this new technology. However, in the development and application of these techniques of analysis, there was a shift in the model of feature analysis itself. Not only was there a shift away from the identification of defining or denotative features to the identification of whatever features were most salient to respondents, there was also a shift from the dichotomous features of most lexical analyses to a more continuous dimensional type of representation. Further, in the earlier work, much of the point of such analyses was an economical definition of the items in the domain. The goal of definition *per se* drops out of the later work, and the new emphasis is on finding which, out of the many features that potentially apply to a set of items, are the most salient and frequently used. The basic task was no longer to find out how particular terms are defined, but rather to discover the most general categories people use to understand their world.

5 Folk taxonomies

At the time the feature model of kinship was being developed, detailed field studies of folk biology were also being investigated by a number of anthropologists. One of the earliest systematic investigations of folk botanical knowledge – a field of study called "ethnobotany" – was carried out by Harold Conklin among the Hanunóo, a horticultural people of the Philippines (1954). He found Hanunóo ethnobotany to be an incredibly rich lexical domain, containing more than 1,800 specific plant terms. Conklin and later ethnobiologists focused much of their research effort on plant and animal terminological systems, and especially the taxonomic groupings of plants and animals.

There were good reasons for placing the primary emphasis on taxonomy rather than features in the study of folk knowledge of biology. The taxonomic relation, *x is a kind of y*, is one of the major ways in which people organize knowledge about plants and animals. It is not that features of plants and animals are irrelevant – Hanunóo or Tzeltal informants can talk at length about the features of particular specimens, and have rich vocabularies with which to do so. Rather, it is that when talking with informants about the differences between generic groupings of plants, such as the difference between oaks and orange trees, there are such a very large number of differences that, as Berlin, Breedlove, and Raven put it:

> verbal specification of distinctive features or characters is only in the roughest sense an adequate representation of what kinds of assessments our informants make in the actual identification of plant taxa . . . identification and placement of a particular specimen in some recognized class is often instantaneous and basically one of overall pattern (or undifferentiated Gestalt). (1974:154–155)

Eugene Hunn, who has worked on Tzeltal ethnozoology and Sahaptin ethnobotany, has been particularly interested in the hypothesis that the features of specific plants and animals tend to be perceived as a gestalt, or total configurational unity, rather than as a discrete list of properties. Using distinctions made by Bruner, Goodnow, and Austin in their classic work, *A Study of Thinking*, Hunn has considered the question of how, given the severe limitations of short-term memory, people categorize multiattribute objects (1976). According to Bruner, Goodnow, and Austin, there are two major techniques for reducing the load on short term memory. The first technique is *attribute reduction.* This consists of simply limiting the number of criterial attributes or features to a very small number – five or six – and ignoring the rest of the attributes. The second technique is *configurational recoding.* In configurational recoding, a number of features are "chunked" together to form a single attribute. As Bruner, Goodnow, and Austin say:

> Such reconstruction is possible because in fact the defining features of most objects and events are redundant with respect to each other. A bird has wings and bill and feathers and characteristic legs. But . . . if it has wings and feathers, the bill and legs are highly predictable. In coding or categorizing the environment, one builds up an expectancy of all these features being present together. It is this unitary conception that has the configurational or Gestalt property of "birdness" . . . When the conception is well enough established, it takes on the property of being able to serve as a discriminable and seemingly irreducible attribute of its own. (1956:47)

From this perspective, taxonomies use relations between *kinds of things* which have been recoded into "configurational attributes." A *collie* is a kind of *dog*, and "dogginess" is a configurational attribute – a configuration of large numbers of attributes "recoded" and "chunked" into a single gestalt of "dogginess." By virtue of being *a kind of* dog, collies "inherit" all the recoded attributes that make up the chunked quality of "dogginess" – nose, tail, yelp and all.

One of the major findings of ethnobiology, stated by Berlin, Breedlove and Raven (1973, 1974), is that folk taxonomies have a limited number of levels. Typically five levels can be distinguished in a folk taxonomy. This limitation, I argued in Chapter 3, is due more to the limitations of short-term memory than to the structure of plants. According to modern biology, there are at least twelve levels distinguishable in the plant domain. For example, a *dandelion* is classified as a member of the kingdom *plantae*, subkingdom *embryophyta*, phylum *tracheophyta*, subphylum *pteropsida*, class *angiospermae*, subclass *dicotyledoneae*, superorder *sympetalae*, order *campanulales*, family *compositae*, subfamily *liguliflorae*, genus *taraxacum*, and species *taraxacum officinale.*

Each level of a folk taxonomy forms a *rank,* or level of grouping. The very top of a taxonomy is rank zero. Rank zero consists of a single term which refers to everything included in the taxonomy, called the *unique beginner*, since by itself it "begins" the taxonomy. For example, in English the term *plant* can be used to refer to all kinds of trees, shrubs, vines, grasses, etc.[1] Similarly, the term *animal* when used to refer to the entire animal kingdom is a rank zero unique beginner term, although the term *creature* is perhaps truer to ordinary usage.

It is interesting that in a number of cultures there is no rank zero term for the plant domain. For example, there is no single term for "plant" in either Tzeltal or Aguaruna. This does not necessarily mean that there is no concept for "plant." The evidence that such a concept can exist without a term is quite strong for both the Tzeltal and Aguaruna. First, in the systems investigated to date which lack a zero level term, there are numerous terms for parts of plants and stages of plant growth which are applied *only* to plants. Second, as Berlin says of the Aguaruna, a Jivaroan speaking aboriginal people living in a Peruvian tropical rainforest:

> there is much informal evidence that the world of plants is recognized as a distinct domain . . . In collecting more than 20,000 specimens, informants, some of whom were monolingual, never selected organisms *other* than plants in actual field collecting situations; mushrooms and other fungi were not considered to fall within the domain. (1976:384)

Third, in pile sorting tasks, Berlin found that his Tzeltal informants always sorted plants and animals in different groups. Finally, as reported in Chapter 4, if asked most generally what kinds of things there are in the world, Metzger and Williams found that Tzeltal informants produced a classification system which partitioned the world of living things into "humans," "animals," and the polylexemic phrase "trees and plants."

Immediately below the unique beginner are the *life-form* groupings. The number of life-forms is quite small, and they always have a number of subordinate groupings below them. In English, *tree*, *bush*, *vine*, and *grass* are life-forms. In the plant domain life-forms are usually based on what Berlin calls "stem habit"; that is, the form of the trunk or stem of the plant. The Aguaruna, for example, have just four life-form terms:

numi "trees and shrubs exhibiting woody (non-pithy) stems with erect habit"
dáek "plants exhibiting twining stem habit, including woody liana and herbaceous vines"
dúpa "net-leaved plants and small shrubs exhibiting herbaceous or pithy stems"
sínki "palms, excluding the small reed-like and trunkless forms.

The life-form level tends to be based on major perceptual discontinuities – obvious differences between kinds of things like the difference between *birds* and *fishes* or *trees* and *vines*.

Below the life-form groupings at rank two are what Berlin refers to as *generics*. The generics are the basic core of the folk taxonomy. They constitute those groupings that share the most numerous characteristics of form and behavior. They are "natural kinds" of things; *dogs*, *mice*, *dandelions*, *oaks*, etc. It is

[1] The term *plant* is more commonly used to refer to a young tree, shrub, or herb that has just been planted or is ready to plant. The use of *plant* or *animal* to refer to an entire kingdom is a semi-technical use, as Anna Wierzbicka (1984) has pointed out.

knowledge about generics that makes up the greater part of folk knowledge about plants and animals.

The folk generics do not necessarily correspond exactly to the biologists' *genera* or to the biologists' *species*. It is difficult to match the folk taxonomy with the biologists' taxonomy to determine precisely how they correspond because the two different systems have different numbers of levels (Hunn 1975). However, most anthropologists who have done intensive ethnobiological research in ethnobiology have found a strong degree of congruence between folk generics and the classification system of scientific biology. Berlin found that of 471 Tzeltal plant generics, 61% corresponded to scientific species, while another 21% corresponded to two or more scientific species in the same genus (Berlin, Breedlove, and Raven 1974:102). Similarly, Hunn found 75% of Tzeltal animal generics corresponded to scientific species, and another 11% corresponded to two or more species in the same genus (1975). Boster, Berlin, and O'Neill (1986) found a tight correspondence between the scientific taxonomy of birds and the degree to which Jivaro informants were likely to use the same folk taxonomic terms to describe pairs of specimens. That is, birds which are close together in the scientific taxonomy are identified with overlapping lists of names, while birds that are distant from each other in the scientific taxonomy are identified with distinct lists of names.

Most folk generics belong to a particular life-form. A *lilac* is a *bush*, a *cricket* is an *insect*, and a *maple* is a *tree*. However, folk plant and animal taxonomies include generics which are either ambiguously classified in more than one life-form (for example, *willows* typically have a *tree* shape, but under some conditions have a *bush* shape), or are unaffiliated with any life-form term (for example, *mushrooms* are not included under any of the English plant life-forms, nor *octopus* under any of the English animal life-forms). Of Tzeltal plant generics, 4% were ambiguously affiliated, and 21% were unaffiliated.

There is some controversy about the reality of the generic level. Berlin argues that by taking linguistic, morphological, and psychological factors into account, a clear determination of level can almost always be made. Hunn (1976) has a slightly different perspective, arguing that it would be better to consider the entire field of terms as a "similarity space," rather like the spaces created by multidimensional scaling. In such a model, one could talk about the "spread" of a particular grouping as well as the "distance" between different groupings which are neither superordinate nor subordinate to each other in a way that cannot be represented in a pure taxonomy.

Below the generic level are the *specifics*. Most specifics occur in sets of two or three members. The differences between specifics in the same contrast set usually consist of a very small number of morphological features, such as color and size. Specifics are usually labelled by *secondary lexemes*. Secondary lexemes consist of binomial terms like *white oak* in which one part of the term consists of an immediately superordinate class (*oak*). For a term to be a true

Table 5.1. *Aguaruna plant generics by degree of cultural significance (adapted from Berlin 1976)*

	Cultivated	Protected	Significant	Unimportant	Total
Generic with no specifics	37 (61%)	31 (69%)	215 (80%)	177 (94%)	460
Generic with specifics	24 (39%)	14 (31%)	53 (20%)	12 (6%)	103
Total	61(100%)	45 (100%)	268 (100%)	189 (100%)	563

secondary lexeme it must occur in a contrast set in which other members are also labelled by secondary lexemes (*black oak*, *coast oak*, *cork oak*). Thus a form like *tulip tree* is a primary rather than secondary lexeme because it does not occur in such a contrast set – there are no *gladiola trees* or *marigold trees* contrasting with *tulip trees*. Instead, *tulip tree* contrasts with *oak*, *elm*, etc.

Most generics are *monotypic*; that is, they are not further divided into specifics. This is true for both folk and scientific taxonomies (Geoghegan 1976). Generics which are further divided into two or more specifics are called *polytypic*. The number of polytypic generics is between 10 and 20% in most folk botanical taxonomies (Berlin 1976). The likelihood that a folk generic will be further subdivided into specifics is strongly related to its *cultural significance*. Berlin has developed a four category scale of cultural significance to show this relationship. Most significant are the *cultivated forms*, followed by *protected plants* (not planted but not destroyed), *significant plants* (regarded as useful but not systematically protected), and *unimportant plants* (no known cultural utility). Table 5.1 presents the relevant data for Aguaruna plants.

From this table one can see that almost 40% of folk generics for Aguaruna cultivated plants are further subdivided into specifics, while only 6% of "unimportant" plant generics are subdivided. Comparable figures were found for Tzeltal plants (Berlin, Breedlove, and Raven 1976:389).

There are at least two possible explanations for this association. One is that there truly is more differentiation among the cultivated and protected plants, and that the scientific taxonomy for these plants would give the same results as the folk taxonomy. A second explanation is that people give more attention to plants which are important to them, and for this reason differentiate them more finely. The second explanation seems the most powerful. Berlin states:

> In fact, the actual numbers of biological species included in the generic taxa of little or no cultural importance is many times greater than those included in taxa of major cultural significance. Thus, unimportant generics exhibit more *potential* for further subdivisions than do culturally important forms. I would not discount . . . persuasive arguments that the objective genetic and morphological characters in cultivated plants caused by controlled breeding must also be considered an important factor in the recognition of subgeneric taxa. (1976:394)

At the most detailed level of folk taxonomy are the *varietals*. These are rare in any folk taxonomy. Varietals are always of strong cultural significance, and involve fine discriminations. For example, there are a number of varietals in English for highly specialized breeds of dogs, such a *toy poodle*, *border terrier*, *miniature collie*, etc. Relatively well-known plant varietals in English are *baby lima bean* and *butter lima bean*. Varietals are often trinomial in form.

In some parts of many folk botanical taxonomies there are six rather than five ranks. The additional rank occurs between life-forms and generics. Terms on this level are called *intermediates*. An example in English would be the term *pine* when used to include the *redwoods*, *spruces*, *firs*, and *pines*. (Here again we find polysemy, with *pine* having two meanings, one more inclusive, the other the "par excellence" or "focal" use for a more specific grouping.) An interesting thing about the intermediate level is that *most intermediate categories are not labelled*. For example, in English there is a recognized category of "trees with leaves" which contrasts with the intermediate level term *pine*, but there is no single term for this group. Such groupings are called *covert* categories (D'Andrade 1962; Berlin, Breedlove and Raven 1968).

Since covert categories have no single term to label them, special methods must be used to identify them. In a preliminary study of Tzeltal tree terms in 1962, I used the triads test to try to determine covert categories for a small sample of Tzeltal trees. However, the triads method requires too many judgments to be really useful with large numbers of terms. Even incomplete balanced block designs require too many judgments when the number of items is over fifty. Berlin, Breedlove, and Raven used an adaptation of the pile sort method (1974:59). The names of plants were written on slips of paper, and informants were asked to group into piles the plants that were "most like one another." Informants were first trained with a small sample of plant and animal names. Informants had no difficulty in sorting such a sample into plant and animal categories. Next, informants were given a set of plant names from the various life-forms. Again, informants had no difficulty in sorting the plants into their respective life-form categories. Once the idea of similarity sorting had been learned and demonstrated, informants were given names of generics from the same life-form. Informants again were able to do the task without difficulty. The resulting grouping produced covert categories at the intermediate rank.

Berlin, Breedlove, and Raven used a number of methods to determine the features used by informants to distinguish covert categories, including having a limited number of paired comparisons presented to informants and requesting them to state the ways in which the two plants were the same and the ways in which they were different. The results of these sorting and eliciting procedures are presented in detail in Berlin, Breedlove, and Raven's summary volume, *Principles of Tzeltal Plant Classification*. They found a total of fifty-three covert categories, ranging in size from two to six generic members.

Another method of identifying covert categories has been developed by Terence Hays, who worked with the Ndumba, an Eastern Highland people of Papua New Guinea. Using ten non-literate informants (five males and five females) Hays elicited an inventory of over 1,200 plant names, 970 of which all ten informants recognized. The average informant was found to know about 1,100 plant names. Using a standard series of queries (e.g. "Are there different kinds of ___?", "What kind of thing is ___?", "Is ___ a kind of ___?", "Are ___ and ___ the same?") the taxonomy for plants was worked out in detail. All the informants agreed on the five life-form terms. The greatest variation among informants occurred in the generic and species ranks. Hays used this variability in naming plants to identify covert categories. The basic idea is that to the extent that the same plant specimen elicits different names from different informants, these names are likely to belong to the same covert class. As Hays puts it:

> Assuming that my informants perceive their world and conceptualize it according to similar, though not identical informant processing rules (i.e., that there exists, in some sense, a "shared culture"), much of the variability in their statements and acts is likely to be patterned in discoverable ways. I suggest that one of the patterns in plant naming responses is that, far from indicating random guesses, the diverse names offered tended to form relatively small sets whose members tended to co-occur regularly. Multiple instances of such co-occurrences, I propose, may be taken as evidence of conceived similarity among the categories designated by the names such that their tokens were readily "confused" with each other . . . The categories designated by these co-occurring names, then, may be considered as conceptually grouped, whether the grouping itself is habitually named or not; when it is not, it may be referred to as a covert category. (1976:497)

Informants sometimes supported Hays' covert groupings with volunteered statements that the members of the groups "are brothers." A similar method, mentioned above, was used by Boster, Berlin, and O'Neill (1986) to identify covert classes of birds among the Aguaruna.

The diagram presented in Figure 5.1 portrays the ranks of a partial section of the folk taxonomy for *creatures* (or, in semi-technical terms, *animals*) in English. The dotted lines indicate that more terms would be included in the full taxonomy. The covert category for *wolf*, *dog*, *fox*, and *coyote* are usually called something like "animals related to the dog family." *Tigers* and *lions*, on the other hand, are *cats* – using the upper level meaning of the term. One can say "look at that cat" when referring to a tiger, but it would sound strange to say "look at that dog" when referring to a fox. Thus *cat* in its broad sense is a named rather than covert intermediate category.

The terms *Persian cat*, *Siamese cat*, *Manx cat*, etc., form a clear contrast set of secondary lexemes typical of folk specifics, as do *grey wolf* and *red wolf*. However, the folk specifics for kinds of *dogs* is not made up of secondary lexemes; *collie*, *poodle*, *terrier*, etc., are simple primary lexemes.

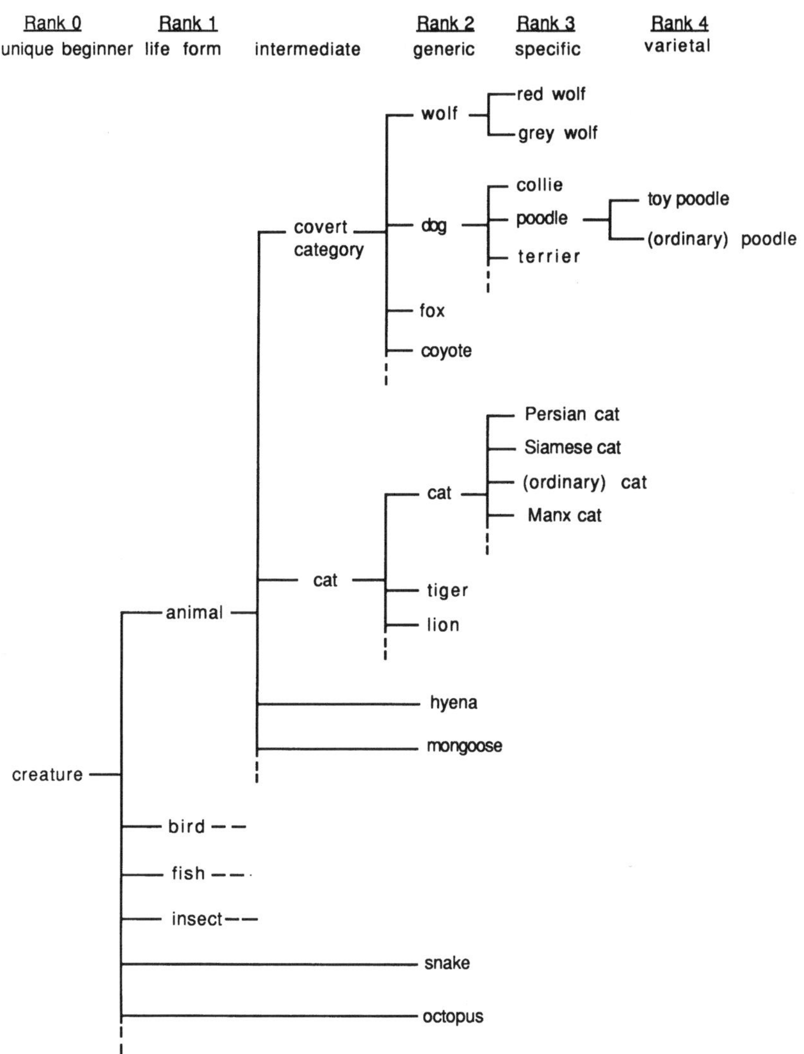

Figure 5.1 Partial taxonomy for *creatures* in English

Octopus and *snake* are generally considered non-affiliated generics; that is, generics which do not fall under any of the four life-forms. (One could argue that *octopus* and *snake* are really life-forms; there does not seem to be overwhelming evidence for either position.) In English a relatively large number of non-affiliated animal generics are found in the ocean or fresh water – *eels*, *coral*, *seahorses*, *clams*, *jelly fish*, *lobsters*,etc.

This small part of the *creature* or *animal* taxonomy displays some of the complexity of a folk rank system. One can see in this folk taxonomy the importance of the generics in folk biology; it is the generics which are the *basic level* of the category system, and which encode our intuitions about what constitutes *natural kinds* of objects. We can get along without life-form terms and even specifics tolerably well as long as the generics are present, as we do for the many forms of life which inhabit the ocean. Note that in the multidimensional scaling of animals presented in Chapter 4, all the terms which Henely selected for analysis were generics, since these were the "natural" objects to compare. The tighter clusters of animals in figure 4.3, such as the *mouse*, *rabbit*, *squirrel*, *beaver*, *rat*, *chipmunk* and *raccoon* cluster, generally correspond to covert categories – in this example the covert category of being "rodent-like."

One of the problems created by trying to place each term at a particular rank occurs when a general type of creature has specialized forms. The generic *cat*, for example, has a variety of coat colors and lengths. Then there are a number of specialized cats with distinctive colors and length of fur, such as the *Persian cat* and *Siamese cat*. The question is, at what rank should we place the ordinary house cat? In Figure 5.1 this problem is handled by creating a special term at the specific level for the "ordinary" cat contrasting directly with the specialized cats. The same kind of arrangement has been made in Figure 5.1 for the "ordinary" poodle. But it is not clear that this really corresponds to the way people think about these classes. Perhaps most people simply have a general construct for the generic cat along with constructs for the specialized forms, and the construct of an "ordinary" cat is created only at particular times by the complex operation of thinking of what remains when all the specialized cat forms are taken from the generic class of cats (see Hunn 1976 for further discussion of this issue).

The generality of the model of taxonomic ranks

The organization of plant and animal terms, worked out by Conklin, Berlin, and other ethnoscientists, has been generalized to domains outside biology. Cecil Brown, who had worked on folk botanical taxonomy among the Huastec of Mexico, was one of the first anthropologists to apply the taxonomic rank model to non-biological domains. With his associates, the taxonomic rank model was applied to "automobiles," "tools," "Finnish winter vehicles," and "Thai spirits/ghosts" (Brown *et al.* 1976). Other non-biological taxonomies have been described. Spradley (1970) elicited from tramps ("urban nomads") a taxonomy of prison *trustees*, a taxonomy of *flops* or "places to sleep," and a taxonomy of *time* referring to the lengths of jail sentences. Per Hage (1972) has described a taxonomy of *Munich beer*, and Charles Frake (1961) has described a taxonomy of illnesses among the Subanun. In general, Brown and his associates found that the non-biological domains were structured in much the same way as biological domains. They concluded:

(1) Non-biological taxonomies, like biological ones, rarely, if ever, exceed a maximum hierarchic depth of five levels.
(2) There are five taxonomic categories . . . [unique beginner, life-form, generic, specific, and varietal] Two of these categories, life-form and generic taxa, are as a rule labelled by primary lexemes, and two others, specific and varietal taxa, by secondary lexemes . . .
(3) The number of life-form taxa occurring in non-biological taxonomies is small [and does not] deviate significantly from the range for biological taxonomies. (1976:83)

Brown also finds "unaffiliated generics" in non-biological taxonomies, which, like the unaffiliated generics in biological taxonomies, often exhibit "morphological peculiarities."

Brown (1976) has also applied the taxonomic rank model to *partonomies.* A partonomy is based on the relation "X *is a part of* Y." A common example is the partonomy for the human body; the *finger nail* is a part of the *finger*, which is a part of the *hand*, which is a part of the *arm*, etc. Brown examined body part data from forty-one globally distributed languages. He found that body partonomies generally resembled folk taxonomies in having the usual five ranks from unique beginner to varietal, a small number of life-forms (typically "head," "body," "trunk," "arms," "legs") labelled by primary lexemes and a number of unaffiliated generics ("blood," "bone," "skin," etc.). The body partonomy appears to be somewhat different than plant and animal taxonomies in having a complex patterning of productive lexemes (e.g. *forearm*) and secondary lexemes (e.g. *toenail, fingernail*) across specifics and varietal levels.

Some critiques of the taxonomic rank model

The taxonomic rank model developed by Berlin and his associates has not been without criticism. Perhaps the most radical critique has been made by Robert Randall, who worked among the Samal, a fishing and horticultural people of the Philippines. Randall questions whether the taxonomic model has the kind of psychological reality it is assumed to have. Although informants will say that a *tree* is a kind of *plant*, and that an *oak* is a kind of *tree*, and that a *black oak* is a kind of *oak*, it may be the case that informants do not have the fact that *black oaks* are a kind of *plant* stored in memory. That is, it may be that what is structured in memory is a series of simple linkages, and it is only the anthropologist's queries which create the total structure. Randall gives as an example the results of queries that he asked Samal informants about marine life:

> In a subsequent economic and ecological study among the Samal, I found it comparatively easy to elicit marine food chains from fishermen. All I had to do was take a sufficiently large marine organism, such as *kiatan* ("shark"), and ask "What are all the things sharks eat?" Then, with ready answers such as *kaitan nahut* ("small sharks"), *panit* ("tuna"), . . . and the like, I was able to apply the "What-are-all-things- X-eat?" to the "sharks" prey. The questioning process was then continued recursively until answers

naming very small forms of marine life were given. Then, with such "primary consumers" as *daing nahut to'od* ("very small fish"), "producers" such as *lumut batu*("rock scum-algae"), and the "abiotic substance" *bohe"* ("water"), my informants reached the terminal consumable of the chain.

Although I elicited knowledge that was clearly stored in fishermen's memories, I do not think it correct to say that it was stored *directly.* My literate informants were much too surprised at my diagram for this to be old knowledge. Certainly, they "knew" all these facts about "sea life," but I doubt if they had even put them together in this way before. It had probably never occurred to them before that ultimately "sharks" depend for their food supply on the consumption of "water" by "rock scum-algae" . . . In this view, then, a folk taxonomy would be more like a previously undiscovered geometry theory than a basic axiom of geometry. (1976:545)

The kinds of taxonomic structures that Randall believes are stored in memory are what he calls "dwarf-trees," which are shallow, small, but well-organized sets of organisms, like the various types of *cats* in English which would include *tiger*, *lion*, *cheetah*, *leopard*, *lynx*, *ocelot*, (*house*) *cat*, etc. As part of each dwarf-tree, Randall hypothesizes that people store a configurational image – or prototype – of the various qualities of the group, such as whether it is cat-like, dog-like, has berries, or flowers, or whatever.

Some of Eugene Hunn's critique has already been presented. For Hunn, one problem with Berlin's taxonomic model is the fixity of the ranks. Hunn sees the taxonomic levels as continuous, able to grade from rank to rank. Another critical point that Hunn has been concerned with involves the character of life-forms. Hunn stresses that standard life-forms like *tree* and *grass* are not an especially important part of folk knowledge. Unlike generics they are typically composed of a relatively small number of abstract criterial features. Hunn calls such categories "deductive," and contrasts such life-forms with the concrete, inductively derived gestalt configuration of numerous features which comprise the generics – a kind of knowledge that cannot be obtained *a priori*, but only by extensive direct sensory experience (1976).

Among the Sahaptin of the Columbia River Basin Hunn found a plant taxonomy system which has few life-forms and few specifics; only 2% of all generics where further partitioned into specifics, and only *tree* and *grass* are found as standard morphologically based life-forms. The Sahaptin, who were primarily foragers prior to European contact, have extensive knowledge about their local plant and animal life, but this is not reflected in their taxonomies. Instead, aspects of Sahaptin knowledge about animals are encoded into non-taxonomic distinctions. For example, Sahaptin divide the animal world into "all the egg makers" versus "all the milk makers," The "egg makers" include birds, reptiles, fish, and insects, while the "milk makers" comprises the mammals. Hunn points out that the Saphaptin are the only people known to anthropologists outside of biologists to use the "milk-maker" criterion to define mammals as a distinct class. Cross-cutting this distinction is another dichotomy of "forage grass eaters" (herbivores) and "flesh eaters" (carnivores). A third set of cross-cutting distinctions involve locomotion and habitat; "flyers" such as birds and flying insects, "runners" such as deer and buffalo, "climbers" such as squirrels, "burrowers" such as ground squirrels and marmots, "head under water swimmers" such as fish, "head above water swimmers" such as beavers, turtles, and water striders, "creepers" such ants, bugs, spiders, and turtles, and "crawlers" such as snakes (Randall and Hunn 1984). These distinctions are cross-cutting and polylexemic, and so do not belong to a taxonomic system, but do code interesting observational attributes. Overall, the rich knowledge and sketchy taxonomy of the Sahaptin support Hunn's claim that taxonomy, *per se*, is not the center of biological folk knowledge.

Another controversial issue concerning the life-forms concerns the degree to which the criteria for defining these forms should be purely *morphological*. Morphological classes are based entirely on physical structure. *Functional* classes, on the other hand, are defined by the *use* or *function* of the object. Terms like *weed*, *flower*, *timber*, *vegetable*, and *herb* are functionals because they are primarily defined by the way the object is used or treated. Traditionally, anthropologists have excluded functionals from taxonomies, since they are not *kinds of things*, but rather *objects used in a certain way* (Wierzbicka 1984). Therefore, *weed*, *flower*, and *herb* are all excluded from the English plant taxonomy, leaving no life-form except perhaps the term *plant* in one of its many senses to refer to smallish, soft stem, "herbaceous" flora.

The problem is that not only does the removal of functional terms result in lexical gaps, but also that in many languages the life-forms have a mixture of morphological and functional features. For example, Randall finds than among the Samal there is a potential life-form, *kayu*, which is usually glossed as *tree*, but in fact seems to have as its focal meaning a plant that has wood that is good for cooking and making houses and canoe hulls (Randall and Hunn 1984). Situations of this kind appear to be relatively common and throw doubt on the degree to which life-forms are always purely botanical.

In contrast to Randall and Hunn, Brown (1977, 1979) claims that there *are* a small set of potentially universal botanical life-forms, although they may often be polysemous and have meanings that include functional features. For plants the potentially universal life-forms are *tree*, *grass*, *bush*, *vine*, *and herbaceous plant*. (Brown uses "herbaceous plant" to refer to the covert category of "small, soft stem" plants discussed above). Sometimes *herbaceous plant* and *grass* form a joint category, which Brown dubs a "*grerb*." For *creatures*, Brown finds *fish*, *bird*, *snake*, *worm/bug* (dubbed *wug*), and mammal-like *animal* are potential universals. Based on dictionaries, interviews with anthropologists, and work with native informants, Brown finds that these terms, or something close to them, occur around the world in unrelated languages. Not all these forms occur in every language, but they do show a patterned distribution. For example, if any life-form is labelled, it will be *tree*. If there are two forms, *grerb* will be the second. If there are three forms, either *bush* or *vine* will be labelled. (This kind of *implicational order*, in which terms appear in a certain order, has been extensively researched in the domain of color terms, and is discussed below.) The fact that these life-form terms sometimes contain functional features does not, in Brown's view, diminish the significance of the patterned distribution of these terms.

Other anthropologists have also discussed the ontological nature of folk taxonomies. Scott Atran (1985) has argued that humans respond in a special – probably genetically determined – way to plants and animals. According to Atran, folk taxonomies of plants and animals are not commensurate with taxonomies of artifacts like furniture and vehicles, since people recognize that plants and animals are partitioned into *natural kinds*. Thus, a table without legs and top is not really a table, but a tiger born without legs and stripes is still a tiger, because tigers are tigers by virtue of some natural essence, not because they have certain perceptual features. Atran also finds life-forms to be no more "artificial" or "special purpose" than higher order scientific groupings, such as phylum or class (1987). For Atran, the fact that folk biological life-forms do not correspond to the upper level categories of modern biology does not mean that these life-forms are not as universal, spontaneously obvious, and orderly as the generics.

These and other critiques of and refinements to the taxonomic model are discussed in detail in Berlin's *Ethnobiological Classification.* While there are a number of unresolved issues, there is now enough well-analyzed data to give a solid foundation to the study of folk biology. Berlin's *Ethnobiological Classification* summarizes over 300 folk biology studies, surveying a wide range of topics including the evolution of ethnobiological categories, sound symbolism in ethnobiological terminology, variability in ethnobiological knowledge, and cultural factors affecting the recognition of particular plants and animals. One of Berlin's general conclusions is of special interest:

> the ethnobiological data to be presented in the following sections will lend support to the claim that, while human beings are capable of recognizing many distinct patterns in nature's structure in general, in any local flora or fauna a single pattern stands out from all the rest. This overall pattern has been referred to by systematic biologists as the *natural system.* The natural system becomes manifest presumably because of the human ability to recognize and categorize groups of living beings that are similar to one another in varying degrees in their overall morphological structure, or morphological plan. This pattern-recognizing ability is probably innate. (1992:9)

Extended and focal ranges

One very general semantic phenomenon uncovered in the investigation of taxonomic systems is the *basic* (or *focal*) vs. *extended* range of terms. According to Berlin, Breedlove, and Raven "The basic range of a class includes all of its genuine referents; the extended range includes all those plants which habitually are seen as being more closely related to it than any other category." (1974:57). Typically, when an informant is confronted with an item from the extended range of a term, the informant will say "X *is like* Y." "A *panda* is like a *bear*," we say, and "a *hyena* is like a *dog*." Given that the natural world presents us with multifeature objects, and given that we create gestalt configurations of these features, the expansion of a term from its true referent to other objects which have many but not all of the features in the configuration is an efficient coding technique. According to Berlin, Breedlove, and Raven:

> General botanical collecting quickly revealed that the Tzeltal lacked legitimate plant names for much of the local flora. On the other hand, when presented with a particular plant specimen, informants rarely responded that the specimen had no name. Instead, they would systematically attempt to classify or relate the specimen under observation to one of the categories in their named taxonomy . . . these classificatory responses allowed for relatively accurate statements to be made as to the actual conceptual range of a plant category, for it provided information as to *focal* (*basic*) and *peripheral* (*extended*) ranges of each category. (1974:53)

The 471 generic names in the Tzeltal plant taxonomy refer to more than 1,750 distinct species. These 471 generics typically refer to only one or two focal specimens, while the extended ranges of these terms include a greater number of species.

The phenomena of *focal* and *extended* ranges of reference had been postulated for kin terms in 1964 in a classic paper by Floyd Lounsbury, "A Formal Account of the Crow- and Omaha-Type Kinship Terminologies" (1964). Crow- and Omaha-type terminologies are kin term systems in which there is *generational skewing* – that is, systems in which the same term is used for kin types in several different generations. In a simple Crow system, for example, where *father's sister* is called "aunt," *father's sister's daughter*, *father sister's daughter's daughter*, *father's sister's daughter's daughter's daughter*, etc., are also all called "aunt." Such systems occur primarily in matrilineal societies, where rights and duties descend through women. What happens in a Crow system is that since rights and duties descend through women, the daughter of an "aunt" is also, in a sense, conceived of as an "aunt," since she inherits her mother's position. Her daughter in turn is also an "aunt,"and so on through the generations. Lounsbury showed how a simple set of re-write rules could be used to describe such systems. In Lounsbury's treatment of Crow and Omaha systems, the *father's sister* is the focal referent of the term "aunt," while *father's sister's daughter*, *father's sister's daughter's daughter*, etc., are *extended* referents of the term created by application of special extension rules. Prior to Lounsbury's paper, it had been something of a dogma in social anthropology to deny that there were focal and extended senses of kin terms (although Malinowski had argued there were). Instead, the standard position had been that the entire range of a term determined the true meaning of that term. Behind this argument were some complex theoretical positions about the universality or non-universality of the nuclear family and the importance of kin groups versus dyadic family relations.[2]

Focal and extended ranges of color terms

In the late 1960s Brent Berlin and Paul Kay undertook a cross-cultural study of color terminology. The results are reported in their book, *Basic Color Terms.* Many of the concepts that had been developed in working with taxonomies of plants and animals were used in their investigation of the color domain. First, Berlin and Kay restricted their investigation to generic-like *basic color terms.* According to Berlin and Kay, *basic color terms* are:

1. Terms which are monolexemic; that is, terms whose meaning cannot be predicted from its parts. This criterion eliminates terms like *bluish, lemon-colored, dark brown,* and perhaps *blue-green.*
2. Terms which are not included by any other term; this principle eliminates terms like *crimson* and *scarlet,* which are kinds of *red.*
3. Terms whose application must not be restricted to a narrow class of objects, such as the term *blond,* which is restricted to hair and furniture.
4. Terms which are psychologically salient for informants, as measured by a tendency to occur at the beginnings of elicited lists of color terms and a general stability across informants and occasions of use. Examples of non-salient terms are *puce* and *magenta.*
5. Terms which have the same distributional potential as previously established basic terms. In English, for example, one can add *-ish* to basic color terms, creating forms such as *reddish, bluish,* etc. However, since *aguaish* and *fleshish* are strange or aberrant, they fail to pass this criterion.
6. Terms which have the name of an object characteristically having that color are suspect. For example *salmon, lime,* and *avocado* are suspect, and would have to pass the other criteria without doubt. *Orange* is an example which does pass the other criteria, and so is a basic term.
7. Recent loan words are suspect.
8. In cases in which the first criterion of *monolexemic* status is difficult to assess, morphological complexity is given weight as a secondary criterion. The English term *blue-green,* for example, could be argued to have a meaning not completely predictable from its constituents, but its morphological complexity eliminates it from the list of English basic level terms.

Using these criteria, there are eleven English basic level terms: *black, white, red, green, yellow, blue, brown, purple, pink, orange,* and *gray.*

[2] For a fine example of the anti-extensionist position, see Leach 1962.

Note that Berlin and Kay's strategy of eliminating non-basic terms grows out of the experience of determining *generics* in folk taxonomy. The assumption is that in every language there is a terminological level which names the perceptually salient objects or events – that names the things that obviously need names.

To investigate basic color terms, Berlin and Kay used as stimulus materials the Munsell array of 320 "chips." A Munsell color chip is a small rectangle of cardboard painted with a highly standardized color. The full Munsell Book of Color contains several thousand chips. Each page contains chips of a single *hue*. There are forty pages in the book, representing forty equally spaced hues, beginning with the red end of the spectrum and ending with the purple end of the spectrum. On each page the chips are arranged in eight rows with the lightest chips at the top of the page and the darkest chips at the bottom. This dimension is called *lightness*. The chips are also arranged by level of *saturation* across the page, with the most saturated chips at the far edge of the page and the least saturated towards the spine of the book. Saturation is hard to explain in words alone, although it is easy to demonstrate with a page of the Munsell book. For a chip to be highly saturated means that the color is "brilliant" or "vivid." Unsaturated chips are perceived as "dull" or "weak," and as the level of saturation decreases the chips finally become almost achromatic – white, gray, or black, depending on the level of brightness.

The array used by Berlin and Kay used only the most saturated chips for each hue and level of lightness. There are eight levels of lightness and forty hues, plus nine achromatic chips ranging from black through gray to white, making a total array of 329 chips. The chips were mounted on stiff cardboard and covered with clear acetate.

Berlin and Kay also used nine extra achromatic chips ranging from black through gray to white. Figure 5.2 presents the general setup of the array. Data was gathered in two stages. First, the basic color terms were worked out using the kinds of interviewing techniques which have been described in the last two chapters. Second, each subject was asked to select "all those chips you would under any conditions call *x*" (the extended use of the term), and "the best, most typical example of *x*" (the *focal* use of the term). The informants were native speakers of their languages who were living in the San Francisco Bay area (except for the Tzeltal informants). Twenty diverse languages were investigated.[3]

The focal choices for basic color terms for the twenty languages are presented in Figure 5.2. The focal choices have been normalized; that is, where more than one chip was chosen as a focal color, the chip mid-way between the chosen chips was selected to represent the focal point.

[3] The languages were Arabic, Bulgarian, Catalan, Cantonese, Mandarin, English, Hebrew, Hungarian, Ibibio (Nigeria), Indonesian, Japanese, Korean, Pomo (California), Spanish, Swahili, Tagalog (Philippines), Thai, Tzeltal, Urdu (India), and Vietnamese.

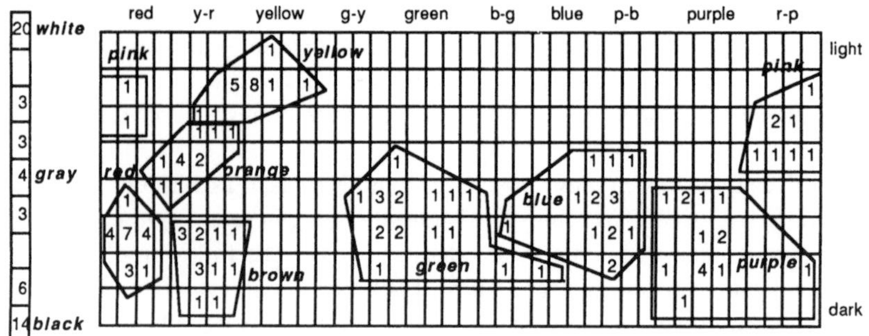

Figure 5.2 Normalized foci of basic color terms in twenty languages (adapted from Berlin and Kay 1969).
Numerals refer to the number of societies selecting that chip as the focal example of that color term.

The distribution of frequencies shown in Figure 5.2 make apparent the high degree to which different languages select similar areas of the color space for the focal points of basic color terms. *There is a high level of agreement across languages about where the best or most typical color chips are located.* This is especially true for "red" and "yellow." There is somewhat more dispersion for "green," "blue," and "purple," but the distributions are still impressively discontinuous. The focal points of basic level color terms are certainly not a random sampling of the color space.

While the focal colors were very similar across languages, the boundaries for the extended uses of color terms were found to be quite different across languages. Sometimes the extended use of a particular color term in one language will cover a large area of color space, while in another language which has a color term with an identical focal point, the term will cover only a small area spread in quite a different direction. It is also the case that the same informant, when asked to do repeated mappings, is very likely to be quite reliable about the focal placements, always choosing the same chips, but to be quite unreliable about the boundaries of terms, giving different boundaries each time. So informants, like languages, show a stable, agreed upon placement of focals, but considerable variability in the boundaries for the extensions of terms.

In plotting the distribution of basic level terms in color space, Berlin and Kay uncovered a surprising finding. First, not surprisingly, they found that the number of basic color terms varied – some languages had as few as two basic level color terms, while others had as many as eleven. What was surprising was that basic color terms appeared in a particular order. If a language had just *two* basic color terms, the focals for these terms were always "black" and "white." If a language had *three* basic color terms, the focals were always "black," "white," and "red." If a language had *four* basic color terms, the focals were always "black," "white," "red" and "green" *or* "black," "white," "red," and "yellow." That is, as new basic level color terms were added to a language, they appeared in a fixed order. Berlin and Kay found a total of seven ordered stages for focals:

Stage I: black, white
Stage II: black, white, red
Stage IIIa: black, white, red, yellow
Stage IIIb: black, white, red, green
Stage IV: black, white, red, yellow, green
Stage V: black, white, red, yellow, green, blue
Stage VI: black, white, red, yellow, green, blue, brown
Stage VII: black, white, red, yellow, green, blue, brown, purple, pink, orange, gray

This kind of ordering is called an "evolutionary sequence" because it predicts the sequence in which languages will develop new basic level terms. Thus if a language has a stage IV color term system, one can predict that when a new basic level color term enters the system, the focal for the new term will be blue. Further, there is a correlation between the number of basic level color terms and a society's level of technological development. All of the languages from highly industrialized societies are at stage VII, while all languages at stage III or lower are found in societies with small populations and limited technology.

Since languages have a larger number of color terms than just the basic level terms, it may seem that selecting just basic level terms for analysis is psychologically arbitrary. However, there is good evidence that the basic level terms are psychologically different than the non-basic terms. For example, Robert Boynton and Conrad Olson (1987) carried out a reaction time color naming experiment with English speaking Americans which showed that *respondents are quicker to use the eleven basic terms than non-basic terms*. In this experiment respondents were presented with 424 single chips from the Optical Society of America's collection of Uniform Color Scales. Upon presentation of a chip, respondents were asked to name the chip with a single color term as quickly as possible. Respondents' mean response time for the eleven basic level terms was approximately half a second faster than for non-basic terms. (Non-basic color terms used at least six times by one or more respondents were *tan*, *peach*, *olive*, *lavender*, *violet*, *lime*, *salmon*, *indigo*, *cyan*, *cream*, *magenta*, *turquoise*, *chartreuse*, *rust*, and *maroon*.)

Boynton and Olson not only found that respondents were faster in naming chips with basic level terms, they also found that respondents were more consistent in using basic level terms. That is, since each chip was presented twice to each respondent, that respondent's naming could be either consistent, with the same name being given both times, or inconsistent, with different names used on each presentation. Respondents were consistent more than 80% of the time when using basic level terms, but only 46% of the time when using non-basic terms.

Boynton and Olson further found that respondents show much more *consensus* using basic level terms compared to non-basic level terms. A chip was considered to have been labeled with consensus when *all* the respondents gave the same name to the chip. (There were seven respondents in total, but one of them used only basic level terms, and his results have been removed from the appropriate figures.) Approximately 30% of the chips labeled with basic level terms showed consensus. However, there were *no* chips labeled with non-basic names which showed consensus across all six respondents.

There was considerable critical reaction to Berlin and Kay's book. The major criticism was that the Berlin and Kay results could not be trusted because the informants were all bilinguals, living in an English speaking environment. The similarity in selection of focal chips for basic terms might, it was argued, be due to the informants all having learned the English color term system. Partially to answer this criticism, and partially to obtain larger samples of informants for each language, Berlin, Kay, and William Merrifield of the Summer Institute of Linguistics began in 1975 an intensive study of the color system of over 100 languages. Linguists from the Summer Institute systematically elicited color terms from 25 respondents in each of 130 languages in 18 countries. The field procedure began with having informants label each of 329 Munsell chips presented individually in random order. The next step was to present informants with a mounted fixed array and ask them to point out the best example of each color term elicited in the naming task. This procedure takes more time than the procedure used by Berlin and Kay in *Basic Color Terms* (approximately two hours per informant), but allows the elicitation of both basic and non-basic terms and a more natural determination of the boundaries of terms.

With the additional information generated by the new procedures and the larger number of informants for each language, the evolutionary stages were found to be more complex than indicated in *Basic Color Terms*. Earlier work by Eleanor Rosch (1972) with the Dani of Indonesian New Guinea had found that a stage I system did not actually divide the color space up into *white* vs. *black*. Although the focals were pure white vs. pure black, the extensions of these terms took into account something other than just the lightness or darkness of the chips. Roughly, the "black" term included both the "dark" and the "cold" colors (the blue-green area), while the "white" term included both the "light" and "warm" colors (red, yellow, and orange). These two terms covered 80% of all the chips, with the remaining 20% given non-basic term names.

While English does not contain any terms with extensions like the Dani terms, the later research of Berlin, Kay, and Merrifield (1985) found that this division of the color space into cool colors and warm colors was relatively common. Consider, for example, the stage III system of the Nafaanra of Ghana

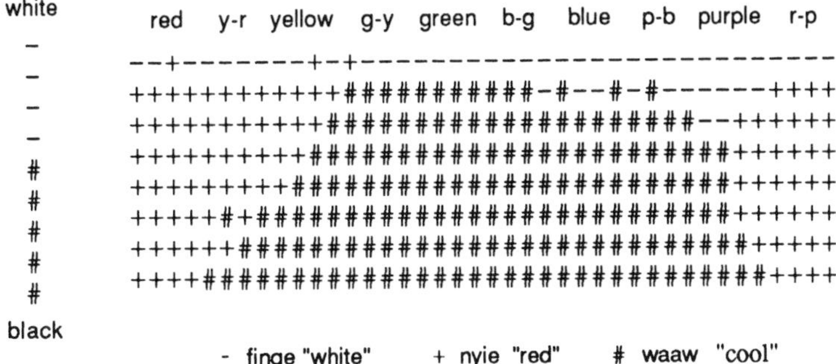

Figure 5.3 Modal color names for Nafaanra (Ghana) stage 2 (adapted from Berlin, Kay, and Merrifield 1985)

presented in Figure 5.3. The system has only three basic terms whose focals are black, white, and red. Figure 5.3 presents the full extensions of each of these terms, with the modal name given to each chip (i.e., the name used by the largest number of informants).

The term *waaw* is a good example of a "dark/cool" color term. It includes all the black chips, but also all the green, blue, and purple-blue chips except at their lightest levels. *Nyie*, whose focal point is a pure red, extends into orange and yellow and can be considered a "warm" term. If we put together the total range for *nyie* and *finge*, the combined total would have the extension typical of a "dark/cool" stage I term.

"Cool" and "warm" also occur in the mapping of Stage IIIa systems. The basic terms for Stage IIIa have as focal points black, white, red, and green. However, when the full ranges of the terms are examined, the term with the red focal point actually covers the "warm" part of the color space (red, yellow, orange), and the term with the green focal point covers the "cool" part of the color space (green, blue, and purple-blue). A Stage IIIa system is presented in Figure 5.4.

The larger sample of the World Color Sample has added complications to the understanding of the way in which color systems have evolved.[4] However, the major findings presented in *Basic Color Terms* have been strongly supported. The focal points for basic level terms collected for a world wide sample of language are found in the same small areas mapped in Figure 5.2 by Berlin and Kay. The focal points for basic terms tend to be highly shared, and to be differentiated in an evolutionary order. The various stages occur in unrelated

[4] More specifically, three additional varieties of Stage III systems and two additional varieties of Stage IV systems have been found. Also, there are cases in which the secondary hues *brown* and *purple* are encoded before the complete differentiation of Stage V has been achieved (Kay, Berlin, and Merrifield 1991).

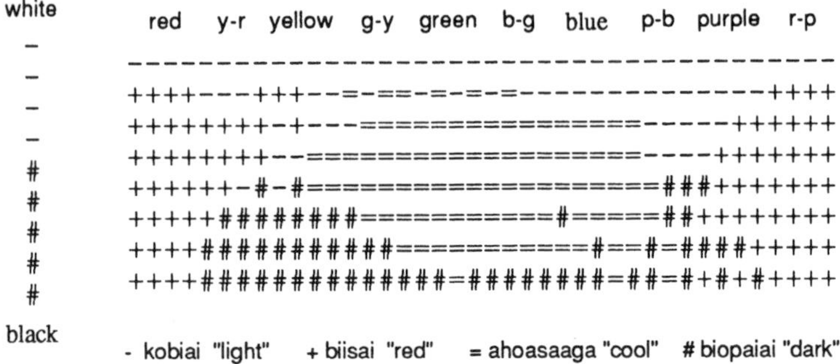

Figure 5.4 Modal color names for Mura Pirahã (Brazil) stage IIIa (adapted from Berlin, Kay, and Merrifield 1985)

languages and in geographically distant parts of the world. The findings reported in *Basic Color Terms* are clearly not the result of the bilingual acculturation of informants or of simple diffusion.

The use of more informants has also made possible the study of variation within a language community. One of the most interesting results has been the demonstration that very often when there is disagreement in a community on the basic level color terms, the disagreement is due to the fact that some of the sample have moved or are in the process of moving to the next evolutionary stage (for example, see Dougherty 1975; Kay 1975; Burgess, Kempton, and MacLaury 1985). In the case of the Aguaruna Berlin and Berlin (1975) found that thirty-four of their fifty-five informants had a basically stage IIIa system (with the exception that the focal point for the "cool" term was in blue rather than green), while five had a stage IV system and sixteen had a stage V system. In the Aguaruna case the aboriginal system had been influenced by loan terms from Spanish. The terms which were borrowed from Spanish were exactly those predicted by the normal evolutionary sequence ("yellow" was first added to make the stage IV system, and "green" was added to make the stage V system). Spanish terms for "purple," "brown," "grey," "orange," and "pink," representing more advanced evolutionary stages, have not yet been adopted.

While the evolutionary stages postulated by Berlin and Kay have stood up reasonably well, there has been the discovery of a new type of color system which does not fit in the Berlin and Kay sequence. This system, found among the Shuswap of Canada and a number of other tribal groups in the Pacific Northwest, has been explored in detail by Robert MacLaury (1987). What MacLaury has found is a system in which there is a composite category of *yellow and green*. The difficulty presented by the Shuswap system is that it cannot be accounted for by the theory presented by Kay and McDaniel (1978) to explain the evolutionary sequence presented in *Basic Color Terms*. The Kay and McDaniel theory links findings concerning the opponent process of color perception to the evolutionary sequence of color terms. The determination of opponent process in color vision is a result of relatively recent work in visual physiology. According to the theory proposed by a number of vision specialists, the three types of cones in the retina are synaptically paired into higher level "opponent process cells" such that input from one kind of cone increases the firing rate of these cells while input from a different kind of cone decreases their firing rate. Four kinds of opponent process cells have been found; these are labelled +red/–green, –red/+green, +yellow/–blue, and –yellow/+blue. The actual physiology is still not fully understood, and a number of psychological models have been proposed (De Valois and De Valois 1993). In the standard theory, pure yellow, for example, is perceived when the incoming light on the retina does not activate the red/green opponent cells, but does activate the +yellow/–blue cells. Color mixtures, like orange or purple, are the result of both the red/green and blue/yellow cells being activated to various degrees. The result of opponent processing is thought to produce four *pure* colors, red, green, yellow, and blue, and *blends* of these colors, such as orange, aqua, purple, etc.[5] Black and white are also pure sensations, and appear to use an achromatic opponent processing system.

According to Kay and McDaniel, the evolutionary sequences begin by dividing the color space into its most salient "pure" sensations; first the "light/dark" division, then the primary pure colors, beginning with red, followed by green and yellow, and then blue. After the primary colors have been differentiated, various blends of the primaries are recognized, such as purple, brown, pink, and gray. The problem with Shuswap is that the yellow-green term groups together hues which are separate in earlier systems. One possibility is that the yellow-green term is a result of the reorganization of a IIIa system, which has terms for white, red/yellow, green/blue, and black, in which the yellow has been incorporated into the range of the green/blue term. In fact, a composite term for yellow/green/blue does occur in at least three of the societies of the World Color Sample. The next stage would then separate blue from the yellow/green/blue term, leaving a yellow/green term. While this is a possibility, no physiological basis for such a reorganization is known.[6]

[5] A question immediately arises: do people *experience* the pure hues as *pure*? The issue is complex. Berlin and Kay's data is usually taken as evidence that they do, since red, green, yellow, and blue are found in the early stages of the evolutionary sequence. However, the hypothesis that people everywhere experience these four hues as pure does not explain the very early evolutionary stages, nor why the distribution of focals is just as restricted for the non-primary colors as for the primary hues. My own belief is that the major factor at work is the irregularity of the color space, which has an unusual shape with a number of "bumps" and "indentations" (D'Andrade and Egan 1974). I believe that this irregularity creates the observed sequence of color terms and the restriction of the focals to small areas, with successive splits of the color space being made according to a rough maximum distance principle.

[6] MacLaury has also directed attention to a number of languages in which there are terms which appear to code a particular degree of brightness without respect to hue (MacLaury 1992).

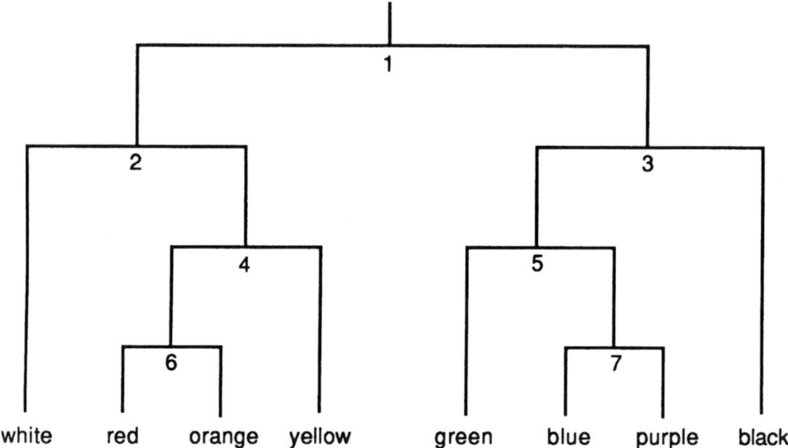

Figure 5.5 Cluster analysis of color chip sorting data (adapted from Boster 1986)

A simple but strong source of support for the Berlin and Kay general evolutionary theory has been provided by an experiment by James Boster (1986). In this experiment Boster selected a sample of eight color chips which were the typical focals for the colors red, orange, yellow, green, and blue, plus pure black and white. Using a sample of twenty-one young adults from the Berkeley area, Boster individually presented his respondents with the following instructions:

> What I would like you to do is sort these colors into two groups on the basis of which colors you think are most similar to each other . . . try to make two natural groupings. Imagine you speak a language which has two color words, how would you choose to divide up the colors and which colors would you put together in each group.

After the first sort, respondents were then asked to subdivide each of the two groups they had created. Respondents were then asked to subdivide again until all chips were separated. Results for all respondents were combined by calculating from each respondent's taxonomic tree how may splits separated each pair of terms, then averaging across respondents. A mean link cluster analysis was carried out on the resulting similarity scores and is presented in Figure 5.5. The numbers indicate the order in which the clusters are split; the first split (1) was between the "light/warm" color chips and the "dark/cool" color chips, the last split (7) was between *blue* and *purple* at the bottom of the tree.

The successive divisions of this tree reflect almost exactly the major Berlin and Kay evolutionary stages. The first split is between the "light/warm" colors and the "dark/cool" colors of stage I systems. The second split separates *white* off from the "warm" colors, *red* and *yellow*, typical of stage II systems. Stage

IIIa systems then make a split between *red* and *yellow* (4), while stage IIIb systems leave *red* and *yellow* undivided but split *black* from the "cool" *green* and *blue* colors (3). Stage IV systems make both split 3 and split 4. Stage V systems split *green* from *blue*, and stage VII systems split *purple* from the blue region. (Stage VI systems differentiate *brown* from *red* or *black* areas, but *brown* was not included in Boster's sample of colors.)

Overall, these results strongly support the idea that there is a relationship between the perceptual qualities of the color space and the evolutionary order of color terms. About this relationship Boster states:

> it is important to emphasize the task-dependent nature of this result. These results should not be interpreted as evidence that English speakers have proto-color categories in their heads, only that they will reconstruct them if faced with an appropriate task . . . the experimental results reported here do not prove that primitive color systems lurk in the deep recesses of our minds. Instead it appears that if an individual tackles a task analogous to the one that communities face in the course of color lexicon evolution, one of successively sub-dividing color categories, the individual will tend to solve the problem in much the same way that cultural communities do. This is probably no accident; communities are made up of individuals employing the same sorts of strategies tapped in these experiments. These results support the generalization that cultural universals result from pan-human communalities in individuals' responses to structure. In this case, that structure has its source in the physiology of human color vision. (1986:71)

The Roschian synthesis

Eleanor Rosch, a psychologist trained in Social Relations at Harvard, was involved in cross-cultural work on color and related nomenclature systems among the Dani, a highland people of New Guinea (1972). The Dani have only two color terms; a cool/dark term and a warm/light term. However, in testing the Dani on their memory for color, she found that they remembered best the color chips that corresponded to the focals of the basic color terms discovered by Berlin and Kay. These results, plus her discussion with Berlin about the psychological centrality of generic level terms in folk taxonomies, lead her to a radical reformulation of the feature model of folk categorization.

Rosch's reformulation (1978) was based on the notion that the generics, or following Berlin and Kay, the *basic level* terms, corresponded to *psychologically basic level objects*. These objects are perceived and remembered not as a list of features, but as a *gestalt* or *configurational whole*. She based her argument on two main propositions. The first proposition is that the category system of humans and animals is characterized by an attempt *to provide maximum information with the least cognitive effort*. The second proposition is that *the perceived world consists of structured information rather than a random or arbitrary collection of attributes (or features)*. Her examples are similar to those quoted above by Bruner, Goodnow, and Austin.

the perceived world is not an unstructured total set of equiprobable co-occurring attributes. Rather, the material objects of the world are perceived to possess high correlational structure. That is, given a knower who perceives the complex attributes of feathers, fur, and wings, it is an empirical fact provided by the perceived world that wings co-occur with feathers more than with fur. And . . . it is a fact of the perceived world that objects with the perceptual attributes of chairs are more likely to have functional sit-on-ableness than objects with the appearance of cats. In short, combinations of what we perceive as the attributes of real objects do not occur uniformly. (1978:28-29)

The conjunction of these two principles results in the formation of idealized or prototypical representations of those objects which correspond to the most commonly co-occurring sets of attributes or features.

With respect to taxonomic levels, or levels of inclusiveness, Rosch, following Berlin, argued that not all levels are equally informationally useful. The best level would be the most inclusive level at which the categories can mirror the structure of attributes perceived in the world.

To test these ideas, Rosch constructed a series of simple experiments. She used simple three level taxonomies. Two examples of these taxonomies are presented in Table 5.2. A total of nine such taxonomies were used; taxonomies for trees, birds, fish, fruit, musical instruments, tools, clothing, furniture, and vehicles.

To show that the basic level terms correspond to the most efficient information categories, Rosch investigated the distribution of attributes across the three levels for each taxonomy. The first test was to ask respondents to list all the attributes they could think of that were true of all of the items in each taxonomy. The general results were as expected. Few attributes were listed for the superordinate categories, a significantly greater number for basic level categories, and not significantly more attributes for the subordinate level than for the basic level. However, for the biological categories there was an exception to this general trend; the superordinate terms elicited as many attributes as the basic level terms. Rosch interpreted this result as due to the lack of salience of these categories for her respondents – unlike Tzeltal Indians, they did not know much more about *oaks* than they knew about *trees* in general.[7] In contrast, Brian Stross (1973) found that Tzeltal Indian children first learned the generic terms for plants. By the age of four the average Tzeltal child could correctly identify more than 100 botanical terms, the great majority of them generics. Tzeltal children later acquired life-forms, specifics, and even later varietals and intermediate botanical terms. Janet Dougherty Keller (1978), comparing Berkeley children with Tzeltal children, found that these American children

[7] Anna Wierzbicka (1984) has questioned whether Rosch's results are really due to a lack of cultural salience, or to the fact that the superordinates for the non-biological categories are not truly superordinates in the strict taxonomic sense of the term. However, Berlin and other ethnobiologists find a pattern similar to Rosch's using informants who are very knowledgeable about plants (see above).

Table 5.2. *Three level taxonomies*

Superordinate	Basic level	Dining room table
Furniture	Chair	Kitchen chair Living room chair
	Table	Kitchen table Dining room table
	Lamp	Floor lamp Desk lamp
Tree	Oak	White oak Red oak
	Maple	Silver maple Sugar maple
	Birch	River birch White birch

first acquired life-forms and intermediate level distinctions. Not until the age of eight did the average child know more than a dozen folk generic plants such as *eucalyptus*, *redwood* and *maple*. Dougherty suggests that a kind of *devolution* has occurred with modern urban folk who do not experience the kind of interaction with the natural environment which would give salience to generic forms, and so learn only the abstract features found at the life-form level.

Rosch also tested her respondents for attributes other than perceived attributes. She asked informants to describe in as much detail as possible the sequences of motor movements made when interacting with each object. Again the same pattern of results was found. There is not much we can say about what we do with a *tool*. There is a lot we can say about what we do with a *hammer*, but not much more that we can say about what we do with a *ball-peen hammer*. For a non-verbal test of this hypothesis Rosch had two dimensional silhouettes made of each of the items, and then measured the degree of similarity in shape by the proportion of overlap which occurred when silhouettes (normalized for size and orientation) were juxtaposed. Again the same pattern of results was found; when two objects from the same basic level term were juxtaposed (e.g. two *chairs*) there was a greater degree of overlap than when two kinds of furniture were juxtaposed (e.g. a *chair* and a *lamp*). A lesser gain in overlap was observed when two objects from subordinate levels were juxtaposed.

Concerning the psychological composition of the basic level objects, Rosch developed the notion of *prototypes*. As she states:

> In terms of the principles of categorization . . . cognitive economy dictates that categories tend to be viewed as being separate from each and as clear-cut as possible. One way to achieve this is by means of formal, necessary and sufficient criteria for category

Table 5.3. *Prototypicality (goodness of example) ratings for birds (adapted from Rosch 1975)*

Member	Mean	Member	Mean	Member	Mean
Robin	1.02	Hummingbird	1.76	Owl	2.96
Sparrow	1.18	Seagull	1.77	Pelican	2.98
Bluejay	1.29	Woodpecker	1.78	Goose	3.03
Bluebird	1.31	Pigeon	1.81	Vulture	3.06
Canary	1.42	Thrush	1.89	Stork	3.10
Blackbird	1.43	Falcon	1.96	Buzzard	3.14
Dove	1.46	Crow	1.97	Swan	3.16
Lark	1.47	Hawk	1.99	Flamingo	3.17
Swallow	1.52	Raven	2.01	Duck	3.24
Parakeet	1.53	Goldfinch	2.06	Peacock	3.31
Oriole	1.61	Parrot	2.07	Egret	3.39
Mockingbird	1.62	Sandpiper	2.40	Chicken	4.02
Wren	1.64	Pheasant	2.69	Turkey	4.09
Redbird	1.64	Catbird	2.72	Ostrich	4.12
Finch	1.66	Crane	2.77	Titmouse	4.35
Starling	1.72	Albatross	2.80	Emu	4.38
Eagle	1.75	Condor	2.83	Penguin	4.53
Cardinal	1.75	Toucan	2.95		

membership. The attempt to impose such criteria on categories marks virtually all definitions in the tradition of Western reason . . . *Another way to achieve separateness and clarity of actually continuous categories is by conceiving of each category in terms of its clear cases rather than its boundaries* . . . Categories can be viewed in terms of their clear cases if the perceiver places emphasis on the correlational structure of perceived attributes such that the categories are represented by their most structured attributes . . .

By prototypes of categories we have generally meant the clearest cases of membership defined operationally by people's judgments of goodness of membership in the category. (Italics added) (1978:35–36)

To get ratings of prototypicality, Rosch (1975) asked respondents (Berkeley undergraduates) to rate instances of different categories of objects on "the extent to which each instance represented their idea or image of the meaning of the category term." Table 5.3, presents prototypicality ratings for the category term *birds*. Respondents were asked to rate on a seven point scale how good an example of the category each instance was. A rating of "1" corresponded to a very good example, while a rating of "7" corresponded to a very poor example. Terms with high prototypicality ratings for the category term *birds* are *robin* and *sparrow*, while *emu* and *penguin* have low prototypicality ratings. In between are ratings for terms like *crow* and *parrot*.

Prototypicality ratings have been shown to be correlated with a wide range of cognitive effects. People are more apt spontaneously to list objects with high prototypicality ratings when asked to give examples of objects in a category

(Rosch, Simpson, and Miller 1976). Subjects can make judgments about whether an object belongs to a particular category much more rapidly for prototypic than non-prototypic objects (Rosch, Simpson, and Miller 1976). Young children learn category membership of prototypic objects before non-prototypic objects (Anglin 1976). Priming by use of the category name facilitates responses in a matching task to prototypic more than non-prototypic objects (Rosch, Simpson, and Miller 1976). People are much more likely to use "hedges" like "technically" and "actually" for non-prototypic objects in sentences like "A penguin is actually a bird" (Rosch 1976). It sounds odd to say "A robin is actually a bird" since a robin is a bird *par excellence*.

These psychological experiments give ample testimony to the psychological reality of prototypes. But what makes one object more prototypical than another? Why is a robin a prototypical bird while a penguin is not? James Boster (1988) investigated this question among residents of the San Francisco Bay area. He compared information on which birds people saw most frequently using the National Audubon Society's bird counts for communities in the San Francisco Bay area, information on which bird terms occurred most frequently in texts such as newspapers and books, and information on the biological taxonomic relations among these birds. He found that text frequency was only weakly correlated related to ratings of prototypicality ($r = .17$). The frequency with which different kinds of birds can be seen in the Bay area was moderately correlated with ratings of prototypicality ($r = .41$). However, ratings of prototypicality were strongly related to the taxonomic relations among birds. Boster measured the degree of taxonomic similarity of each bird to other birds by using a count of the number of species in the same scientific order and family. Thus a bird that came from a large order and family with respect to the number of species in that order and family would have a high similarity rating because it would be closely related to a large number of other species of birds. The r between this measure of taxonomic similarity and ratings of prototypicality was .70.

In general, the birds that are considered most prototypic are the *passerines*, the largest order of birds that includes the robin, sparrow, and bluejay. Except for the dove and the parakeet, the sixteen most typical birds are all passerines. These birds are closely related to each other and similar in shape and behavior. It is as if people *averaged* across the properties of all kinds of birds that they knew and developed a representation of a generalized profile of a bird. Since the family of passerines contains the greatest concentration of kinds of birds occurring in the area, the average bird is a passerine.

A similar pattern of results was obtained by Rosch and her associates. Rosch and Mervis (1975) found that the more prototypical members of categories shared more attributes with other members of the category than did less prototypic members. Using artificial stimuli (dot patterns, stick figures, letter strings) Rosch, Simpson, and Miller (1976) found that stimuli which had the greatest number of shared attributes were rated most typical, were most easily learned as members of a category, and were generated first when subjects were asked to produce members of the category.

In summary, the work by Rosch and others on prototypes and basic level objects generalizes and synthesizes the findings of the research on folk taxonomies. Field research on folk taxonomies found that there were cognitive differences between different hierarchical levels. Upper level terms such as the life-forms and intermediates are typically composed of a relatively small number of features, often relatively formal and schematic in character. This can be understood as an efficient means of making broad distinctions – simplification by reduction in the number of attributes. Such a strategy is most effective in a world which is structured into broad and distinct kinds of things – trees vs. bushes vs. grass. Taxonomic generics, on the other hand, are composed of a large number of attributes formed or "chunked" in configurational gestalts. These are what Rosch calls "basic level objects." Such a cognitive strategy is most effective in a world in which objects are composed of a large number of attributes, and these attributes are at least partially correlated with each other. Patterns of attributes can be discovered by the human ability to form configurational gestalts – even though many objects may not fit the patterns perfectly. These patterns are then used to classify particular objects into kinds of things. Finally, basic level objects which have the greatest number of attributes shared by other members of the same superordinate category are considered to be the best examples of that category and often serve as the cognitive representation of that category.

It is as if the human cognitive system were a structure seeking device. At the appropriate level of detail, it finds which attributes of a class of instances are most strongly correlated, and creates generic or basic level objects by forming a gestalt configuration of these attributes. As a result, the cultural and individual systems of thought are made up of more than just a list of features or attributes varying in salience. Features are grouped together into object-like things, making for greater cognitive efficiency in categorization. Once formed, these objects can then be extended to cover instances which have some commonality with the prototypic examples of the category.

Sometimes the attributes of the basic level objects are physically salient features, sometimes they are features which become salient because of the way humans interact with these objects, and sometimes these features become salient only because of cultural meanings which are imposed on these objects, like the "holy" nature of the bible compared to the ordinary secular nature of most books. These kinds of mental objects can be quite abstractly relational, as, for example, the "demotion" of an army *corporal* to a *private*. Humans have a remarkable ability to treat events and relations as if they were objects. Cultural systems of meaning build on and enhance this ability.

Thus the work on taxonomies shifted cognitive anthropology from an exclusive interest in features to an interest in configurations of features which create psychological objects. It is not that features had become irrelevant. But the new interest in the way a combination of features forms an object gave rise to the idea that some combinations of features have greater salience than others. The prototype, as such a combination, was a psychological entity of a new type.

6 The growth of schema theory

The development of prototype theory and related ideas about basic level objects moved the focus of cognitive research from simple features to a more complex type of category structure. However, the trend towards greater complexity did not stop with the development of a theory of prototypes. In the mid-1970s it became apparent across the fields of linguistics, anthropology, psychology, and artificial intelligence that human cognition utilizes structures even more complex than prototypes. There was considerable variation in the names given for these more complex structures. "Frame," "scene," "scenario," and "script" have all had some terminological currency. While this variability in labeling has not fully settled down, some consensus has developed on the use of the term *schema*.[1]

George Mandler, a cognitive psychologist, describes a schema as a "bounded, distinct, and unitary representation." He points out that the term goes back at least to Kant, who described the schema of a dog as a mental pattern that "can delineate the figure of a four-footed animal in a general manner, without limitation to any single determinate figure as experience, or any possible image that I can represent *in concreto*" (Kant, [1781] 1929).

Mandler describes schemas as "organizing experience." He says:

> activation of parts of a schema implies the activation of the whole, distinct from other structures and other schemas. Schemas are built up in the course of interaction with the environment.
>
> The schema that is developed as a result of prior experiences with a particular kind of event is not a carbon copy of that event; schemas are abstract representations of environmental regularities. We comprehend events in terms of the schemas they activate.
>
> Schemas are also processing mechanisms; they are active in selecting evidence, in parsing the data provided by our environment, and in providing appropriate general or specific hypotheses. Most, if not all, of the activation processes occur automatically and without awareness on the part of the perceiver-comprehender. (1984:55–56)

1 There have been a number of comprehensive reviews of the schema concept, as well as extensive discussions of the utility and limitations of schema theory. See, for example, Casson 1983; M. Minsky 1975; Rumelhart 1980; Mandler 1984; Quinn and Holland 1987; Singer and Salovery 1991.

The need to postulate the existence of complex cognitive structures arose as researchers began investigating more complex kinds of cognitive processing. Prototype and feature models were sufficient provided the analysis was limited to a relatively restricted domain, such as plants or kin terms. However, when faced with the analysis of real discourse, new analytic concepts were needed. Charles Fillmore, in an influential paper written in 1975, argued as follows:

> It seems to me that what is needed in discourse analysis is a way of discussing the development, on the part of the interpreter, of an image or scene or picture of the world as that gets built up and filled out between the beginning and the end of text-interpretation experience. One way of talking about it is this: *the first part of a text creates or "activates" a kind of schematic or outline scene, with many positions left blank, so to speak*; later parts of the text fill in the blanks (or some of them, anyway), introduce new scenes, combine scenes through links of history or causation or reasoning, and so on. In other words, a person, in interpreting a text, mentally creates a partially specified world; as he continues with the text, the details of this world get filled in; and in the process, expectations get up which later on are fulfilled or thwarted, and so on. *What is important is that the ultimate nature of this text-internal world will often depend on aspects of scenes that are never identified explicitly in the text.*[2] (Italics added) (1975:125)

For illustration, Fillmore contrasts the "text coherent relations" involved in the English verb *to write* and the Japanese term *kaku*. These two terms are frequently acceptable translations of each other, but in fact there are differences in the two schemas. Both schemas include a scene in which somebody guides a pointed trace-leaving implement across a surface. Such a scene invokes a *writer*, an *implement*, a *surface* on which traces are left, and a *product*. However, the Japanese schema leaves the nature of the resulting trace more or less unspecified. To a question in Japanese "What did you *kaku*?" one can answer by identifying a word or sentence or character or even a sketch or doodle. The English verb *write*, unlike *kaku*, restrictively invokes the notion of *language*; the result of the act of *writing* cannot be a picture or doodle, but has to be something in some language.

Note that the schema invoked by the English term *writing* does not specify the particular instrument used – it could be pencil, or pen, or piece of chalk, a typewriter – anything capable of leaving a trace. The surface can be paper, or a black-board, or stretch of sandy beach, a computer screen, or even the the sky. The thing written can be in any script and in any language and vary from a single letter of the alphabet to a massive monograph.

Such a scene is highly *schematic* – it leaves unspecified a number of "slots" which can be filled in by context or by additional information from the speaker. Furthermore, what is filled in for one slot may affect what can be filled in for other slots; if for the *writing* schema, if the thing written on is the sky, then the thing doing the writing would be an airplane. To the extent that no slot

2 A more extended presentation of these ideas can be found in Fillmore 1977.

information is available, hearers tend to fill the slots with their normal expectations, sometimes called "default values." For me, normal default values for *writing* invoke someone writing a message in English on a piece of white paper with a pen. This is my "prototype" of *writing*.

Note that a prototype is not the same as a schema; a schema is an organized framework of objects and relations which has yet to be filled in with concrete detail, while a prototype consists of a specified set of expectations. The filling in of the slots of a schema with an individual's standard default values creates a *prototype*. A prototype is a highly typical *instantiation* (i.e., an instance of a) schema (Langacker 1987).

An important aspect of the organization of schemas is that simpler schemas can be "embedded" within more complex schemas. Or, to put it another way, schemas[3] can be hierarchically structured. The *writing* schema contains within it a number of sub-schemas; the schema for a writing implement, a writing surface, a language, and an entity that is trying to communicate. Further, each of these sub-schemas is composed of sub-sub schemas; there are schemas for *pens*, *paper*, *English*, *authors*, etc.

There are a number of advantages to the use of the schema concept. First, it becomes possible to relate terms from different domains to each other. That is, the *writing* schema relates *pencils*, *pens*, *chalk*, *typewriters*, etc., to *paper*, *blackboards*, *newspapers*, *manuscripts*, etc., to *English*, *French*, *Arabic*, etc., to *authors*, *correspondents*, *pen-pals*, *memos*, etc. Understanding the full schema allows a fuller explication of the semantics of these terms.

Second, there are often terms which identify ways in which the full schema fails or is only partially satisfactory. The term *scrawl* refers to a failure to make one's writing on something fully legible, the term *illiterate* refers to someone who is not able to utilize the *writing* schema because they cannot read or write effectively. Such terms can only be defined and understood through a comprehension of the full schema and what can go wrong within it.

A nice example of this point has been made by Dorothy Holland and Debra Skinner in a study of the American collegiate schema for *romance*. They describe the "taken-for-granted world of male/female relations" from the perspective of a woman as follows:

> a male earns the admiration and affection of a female by treating her well. Intimacy is a result of this process. The female allows herself to become emotionally closer, perhaps as a friend, perhaps as a lover, perhaps as a fiancee, to those attractive males who make a sufficient effort to win her affection. Besides closeness and intimacy, the process of forming a relationship also has to do with prestige. When a male is attracted

[3] "Schemata" and "schemas" are both used as the plural of schema. "Schemata" sounds somewhat more erudite and impressive than "schemas," but the usual process in English is that as foreign terms become an ordinary part of the language they come to use ordinary English pluralization. The assumption here is that "schema" has become a standard part of the language of the cognitive sciences.

> to a female and tries to earn her affection by good treatment, her attractiveness is validated and she gains prestige in her social group. For his part, the male gains prestige among his peers when he receives admiration and affection from and gains intimacy with females.
>
> Normally, prestigious males are attracted to and establish close relations with prestigious females, and vice versa. Sometimes, however, a male can succeed in winning the affection of a female whose prestige is higher than his own. However, the more attractive she is, the more he must compensate for his lack of prestige by spectacular efforts to treat her well. Correspondingly, females sometimes do form close relationships with males who have higher prestige than they do. When the male is more attractive or has higher prestige than the female, she often must compensate by giving her affection to him without his doing anything to earn it. (1987:101-102)

Within this simplified and idealized world, one set of problematic males is termed *jerks*, *nerds*, *turkeys*, and *asses*. These are men who are both unattractive and insensitive. Because of their insensitivity, they both fail to please women and fail to realize that they are not attractive, often acting as if relationships were closer than the women want. These men are too dumb to "take a hint," and therefore have to be rejected in such direct ways that the women have to be repeatedly unpleasant, which is often personally stressful for the women. To understand what one of Holland's informants means when she calls a man a *jerk* requires understanding the *romance* schema.

Stories and other kinds of discourse also require understanding the schemas which have been invoked. Consider the following short story:

> John wanted to do well on the exam, but his pen ran out of ink and his pencil broke. He tried to find a pencil sharpener, but there wasn't one in the room. Finally he borrowed a pen from another student. By then he was so far behind he had to rush, and the teacher took off points for poor penmanship.

Nowhere in the text is the link between writing implements and the act of writing actually stated, nor that what is marked on a surface should be an alphabetic script. To understand this story, one has to understand the *writing* schema because without it one would not understand that John's running out of ink results in his not being able to write.

The fact that much of human discourse makes reference to unstated schemas and cannot be understood without knowledge of these schemas became increasingly apparent throughout the late 1970s as researchers in artificial intelligence tried to create computer programs which could understand stories and other kinds of text. It was found that for a computer program to have the ability to paraphrase a story, or answer questions about a story, much more was required than simply knowing grammar and being able to look up the dictionary meanings of words. The computer program had to have an explicit formulation of the schemas referenced in the text and to be able to integrate it with the information from the text. Even a very short story, such as the example above, often requires knowledge of a number of schemas. John's story, for example, also requires knowledge of *school* and *exam-taking* schemas, as well as knowledge of the sub-schemas for *pencils* and *pens*.[4]

One interesting by-product of the work on schemas in psychology and artificial intelligence was the careful formulation of particular pieces of American culture. Cultural schemas for restaurants, doctor–patient office visits, chess gambits, social contracts, American–Russian nuclear confrontation, the evaporation of water, story grammars, and birthday parties were all used in psychology experiments and artificial intelligence simulations. Use of these examples required a formulation of the descriptive content of these cultural schemas in enough detail to judge the success of the simulation or the experimental manipulation. The result was a limited but carefully stated account of small pieces of western culture.

The germ schema

In my own work in the early 1970s I had begun to encounter difficulty with further analyses of American beliefs about illness. Consideration of these difficulties led me to the conclusion that something like schema theory[5] was necessary for an adequate description of cultural knowledge.

The problem in the analysis of the American beliefs about illness came about as the result of pondering a simple question: "How did American informants answer all those questions?" Recall from Chapter 4 that respondents were asked to judge whether the sentences constructed by filling thirty illness terms (*chicken pox*, *malaria*, etc.) into thirty belief-frames (*You can catch ___ from other people*, *You never really get over ___*, etc.) were true or false (See Table 4.5). This required each respondent to make 900 judgments. After the intial study with Quinn, Nerlove and Romney was published, I began to wonder how our respondents had been able to do this. Did they know as individual entities each of the 900 belief-frame and illness combinations? This seemed unlikely, since some of the combinations (*Runny nose is a sign of poison ivy. Most people catch dental cavities in bad weather*) appeared to be entirely novel to the respondents, and they said that they had never thought about whether these statements were true or false before. What they said they did, and what seemed most plausible, was to figure out the answer to these unusual statements from other things they already knew.

[4] The classic work on the relation of schemas to story understanding is Schank and Abelson's book, *Scripts, Plans, Goals, and Understanding*. In anthropology see Agar 1980.

[5] The term "schema theory" is a little grandiose. As Jean Mandler says "The use of *schema theory* has become widespread in psychological research. The phrase itself is perhaps misleading, since no one has yet developed a coherent schema theory for any domain. A more accurate phrase might be *schema framework*, since the principles subsumed under this view of the mind consist of very general beliefs about how this form of organization works" (1984:1).

But if they figured out the answer to these unusual statements from other things they knew, what were these things and how did they do the "figuring out"? One answer to how they did the "figuring out" might be that the properties involved in the belief-frames were *logically* related to each other. For example, from Table 4.5 it can be worked out that every disease which *you can catch from other people* is a disease which is *caused by germs*. Also, every disease which is *caused by germs* is *not* a disease which *runs in the family*. So, if one knows that a particular disease can be *caught from other people*, one also knows this disease is *caused by germs* and that it does not *run in the family*.

Logical relationships of this type could greatly reduce the amount that one has to know to answer all 900 questions. In order to discover all the logical relationships between the 30 belief-frames, a computer program was written to test for such relationships (D'Andrade 1976). Out of the 435 pairs of belief-frames, 119 were found to have significant logical relationships.[6] Many of these relationships were redundant. For example, every disease which is a *children's* disease is also a disease which is *contagious*, and every disease which is *contagious* is also a disease which is *caused by germs*. As a logical consequence of these two relationships every disease which is *a children's disease* is also *caused by germs*. Or, in more formal terms, if A is a subset of B, and B is a subset of C, then it necessarily follows that A is a subset of C.

Removing all the logically redundant relationships left thirty-one basic relationships. A graph of these thirty-one relationships is presented in Figure 6.1. The belief-frames are represented in capital letters; for example, RUNDOWN (SIGN OF) stands for the belief-frame "Feeling generally rundown is a sign of __." (The complete list of belief-frames is given in Table 4.4.) The arrows between boxes indicate that one set of diseases is a subset of the other; for example, the arrow pointing from the set of diseases characterized by being "rundown" to the set of diseases which "spread through your whole system" indicates that all the diseases listed under being "rundown" are also diseases which "spread through your whole system."

There are three main clusters of disease properties. The first cluster includes properties of being *serious*, *fatal*, *crippling*, *affecting the heart*, and not being a disease that is *gotten by almost everyone*. The second cluster contains the properties of being *caused by germs*, being *contagious*, causing *fever*, getting *better by itself*, *signaled by a runny nose*, coming with a *sore throat*, being *contracted in bad weather*, being *caused by lack of resistance*, which can be treated *with miracle drugs*, and not a disease which is *crippling* or which you *never get over*. This grouping contains a sub-cluster of *children's diseases*, which are

6 The computer program did not require that the pair of belief-frames have a perfect logical relationship; up to three exceptions were permitted. For example, every disease which *brings on fever* is also a disease which *is caused by germs* with the exception of *appendicitis*. The program would classify this pair of belief-frames as having a subset/superset relationship despite the one exception.

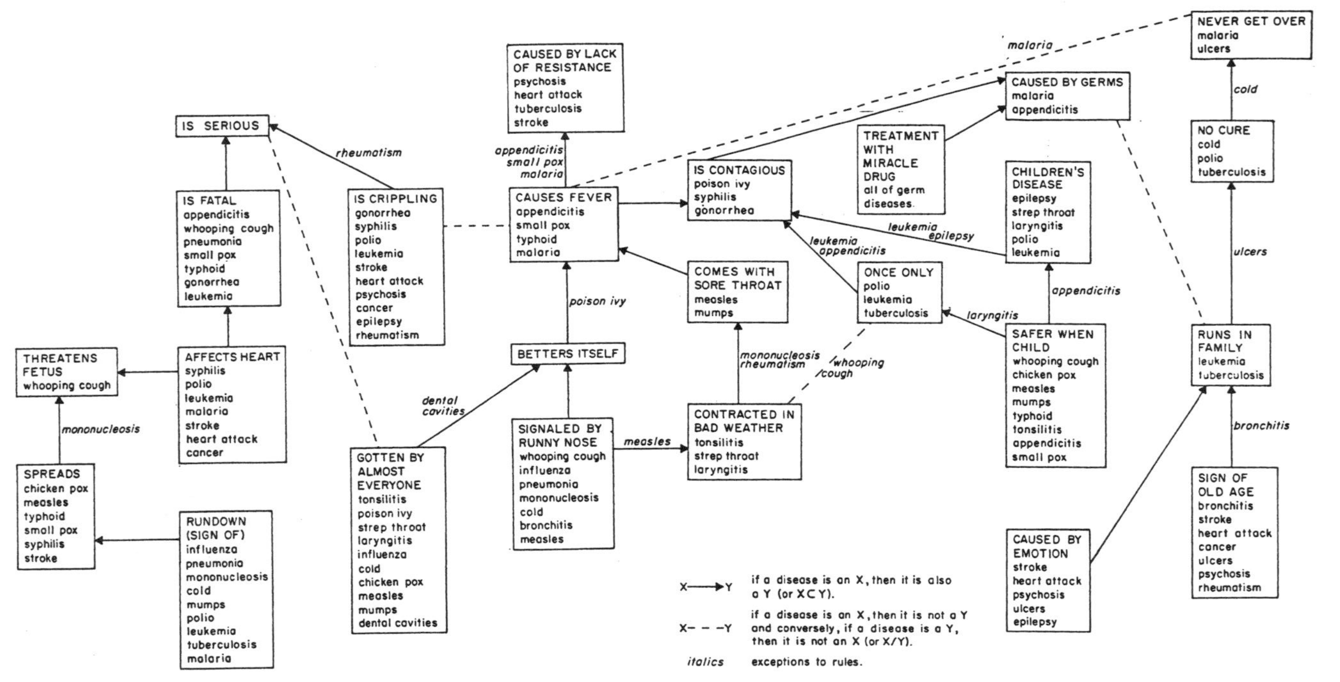

Figure 6.1 Logical relations among American disease properties

safer to get when a child, and which one gets *once only*. The third cluster consists of diseases which one *never gets over*, which have *no cure*, which *run in the family*, are a *sign of old age*, and which are *caused by emotion*.

The properties within each of these clusters have the capacity to generate inferences; following the arrows between properties in Figure 6.1 shows that if a disease is *safer to get when you are a child* you can infer that it is also a disease which one can get *once only* (with the exception of laryngitis, which one can get many times), is a *children's disease* (with the exception of appendicitis), *is contagious*, and is *caused by germs*.

While I was pleased at the large number of inferences which could be generated by the graph in Figure 6.1, I was disappointed by the failure of the graph to give anything like a representation of the way Americans actually understand illness. Treating myself as an informant, I could explicate *why* many of the these properties were linked to each other, but nothing in the graph contained this information. For example, because of the ideas I have about *germs* I could understand why germ diseases were *contagious*. Germs are, as we all know, very small cellular disease causing creatures which can travel from one person to another through various kinds of contact or through the air, making the disease *contagious*. But this basic idea about germs is nowhere represented in the graph. Similarly, it is generally understood that a particular kind of germ, once it invades the body, usually stimulates the immune system to create antibodies, and that these antibodies can destroy future invasions of the same kind of germ. Because this is part of the understanding of germs, one can understand why many diseases which one can get *once only* are also *germ* diseases. But this crucial idea is nowhere represented in the graph.

More generally, the kind of analysis presented in Figure 6.1 fails to give an adequate representation of American beliefs about illness because it does not explicate the *schemas* Americans use to understand illness. To understand American beliefs about *colds*, *measles*, *polio*, etc, requires an understanding of the *germ* schema and this cannot be obtained from an analysis of the properties of diseases alone. The answer to the question about how respondents were able to answer novel questions appears to be that they made use of complex schemas to compute their way through new terrain.

The *germ* schema held by most Americans is a simplified version of the findings of scientific medicine. When pressed for more details about germs, respondents typically say that they are not doctors, and if you want to know all about germs go to a doctor or a book on medicine. Most of the schemas by which Americans understand illness seem to be derived from scientific medicine, rather than coming from an independent folk tradition.

However, not all the ideas that Americans have about illness come from science. For example, there is an interesting "unscientific" idea that most Americans hold about colds and other respiratory illnesses. It is widely believed that being exposed to cold weather can lower one's resistance to germs, making it more likely that one will catch a cold in cold weather. However, medical research on the effect of temperature and humidity has consistently found that weather conditions have no effect on resistance to catching a cold. To determine this, volunteer subjects have been exposed to a standard cold virus and then subjected to various conditions of cold and damp. In no case did this research show any effect of cold and damp on the likelihood that the subjects would come down with a cold. It appears that colds are more frequent in winter than summer because people close windows and other sources of ventilation in winter to keep warm and prevent colds, thereby increasing greatly the "germ count" in the air. Thus the belief that getting cold causes *colds* indirectly creates the conditions which support the belief (Douglas, Lindgre, and Couch 1968; Andrews 1978).

From the clusters in Figure 6.1 and from what respondents said about their answers to the frame/disease questions, it is clear that a number of schemas are used to answer these questions. Respondents have complex schemas about the function of the heart, the circulation of blood and the formation of blood clots, and stroke. They also have complex schemas about the way cancer spreads, the effects of aging on the joints and muscles of the body, and some relatively loose conceptions about the way in which emotion and genetics interact with disease processes. Further, besides schema based knowledge, respondents also have a relatively large amount of particular knowledge about specific diseases; for example, that syphilis and gonorrhea are transmitted by sexual intercourse, that mumps is a children's disease, etc. Particular knowledge about specific diseases is then integrated with more schematic kinds of knowledge to make up a general folk theory of illness which gives informants the ability to answer a great number of questions about diseases and their properties. To understand folk beliefs about illness, more is required than just an analysis of the properties of illnesses. Knowledge of relevant cultural schemas is also needed.

Cultural schemas

The idea that the investigation of cultural understandings involves more than the features of particular terms or the taxonomic relations between terms was not restricted just to researchers concerned with cognition. David Schneider (1965), an anthropologist interested in kinship and cultural symbols, made this point in a critique of Goodenough's feature analysis of Yankee kinship terminology. Schneider's book, *American Kinship: A Cultural Account*, attempts to lay out the interrelated cultural schemas by which Americans understand kinship and the family. These schemas involve the notions of *blood* and *marriage*, *conjugal love* and *erotic love*, the *family* and *inlaws*, etc. According to Schneider:

The symbols of American kinship consist of the unity of flesh and blood, in the fact that the child looks like the parents or takes after a grandparent, and in the affirmation that blood is thicker than water – one meaning of this is reiterated in the statement: "A house is not a home." The symbols of American kinship affirm that the union of a husband and wife is a spiritual union as it is a union of the flesh, and that it is a personal union, and that out of that union a new person is formed. The word for such a spiritual union is love. Love brings opposites together into a single unit, while it holds together those things which are moving apart – the child and its parents, or brothers and sisters growing up, finding mates of their own, and founding their own families. The symbols of American kinship consist of motherly love and brotherly love and conjugal love and paternal love, and filial feelings of loyalty and respect. (1968:49)

While Schneider uses the term *symbol* rather than *schema* as his major analytic tool, it is clear that what is actually being presented is a very general and abstract account which relates *love*, *sex*, and *birth* as parts of the general American conception of the *family* – that is, the cultural schema for *family*. It is through this schema that Schneider defines such as *father*, *relative*, *in-law*, *home*, etc. A number of these terms are polysemous, and Schneider also shows how different senses of a term depend on the particular schemas being employed.

Another example of the need to invoke schemas in order to carry out a satisfactory analysis of a cultural category can be found in Michael Moffatt's (n.d.) study of American *friendship*. In carrying out ethnographic research on the life of college students in a large Eastern university, Moffatt found that *friendship* was a social institution of great importance for most American undergraduates. While undergraduates treat *friendship* as an unproblematic, natural tendency to establish relationships with the people one likes, Moffatt found the cultural assumptions underlying this concept actually involve some very abstract cultural notions.

It is not that American respondents cannot define what a friend is – they say with considerable unanimity that a friend is someone whom one enjoys being with, whom is "close," who one can be "open" with, whom one is "comfortable" with, and whom you do not have to hide your "true feelings" from, etc. The analytic problem is to discover what makes a person someone with whom one can be "close," "open," etc. According to Moffatt, "a true friend is someone who is close to one's real self." For these undergraduates the *real self*, Moffatt finds, is an internal place, where what happens is natural, unique, and the center of human agency. This *real self* naturally cares for others and needs others. The *real self* is naturally spontaneous, unlike the *social self*, which consists of the roles and masks one has to wear in the "real world." The *social self* must be controlled, orderly, and on-stage. For undergraduates, a large part of the "real world" is work, with requirements of punctuality and high standards.

Since what most people see is one's *social self*, they do not know the private truths of the *real self*. It is the private truths of the *real self* that one shares with friends; friends are those who can be trusted not to use these secrets against one. One does not have to "play games" with *true friends*.

Once *true friendship* is linked with the *real self* certain implications follow. Friendship becomes almost impossible to institutionalize or formally ritualize because by definition social institutions and rituals are part of the activity of the *public self*. One cannot say *a priori* what a friend should do to become a friend, or what should count as friendship behavior, because if it is to be a relationship between *real selves*, then it should be expressed by spontaneous, unique, free actions without social constraints. This also makes it difficult to determine exactly who one's *true friends* are, since public social actions are an uncertain index of what the other person really feels or thinks. It makes friendship intrinsically dyadic, since relations through other people should not constrain whom one will be friends with. It also makes friendship intrinsically unique, and therefore not a relationship that has to follow any normative pattern. And it makes it a joint choice, since it must be a *reciprocal* relationship between *real selves*. Friends should do things for each other, but should not be too instrumental, since that puts a social weight on the relationship, removing it from the spontaneous expressive action of *true friendship*. As Moffatt puts it:

> American friendliness thus bridges or mediates the opposition which contemporary American culture itself posits between the real inner self and more problematic social identities. It is a small, routine daily ritual, and involves assertion of the self and of the values of the self in even the most hostile and anti-individualistic of settings. It is the way Americans remember, and periodically "express," what they are *really* like, even when functioning with their unfortunately necessary social masks on: authentic, individualistic persons who are open, given the right conditions and free choice, to egalitarian friendships with *anyone*. (n.d.: 24)

These ethnographic examples of schemas – the *germs*, *romance*, the *American family*, and the *real self* – are culturally shared mental constructs. These schemas as cognitive objects should be clearly distinguished from the *institutionalized behavior* to which they are related. The institution of the *American family*, for example, with its social roles and their behavioral norms, is not the same as the ideas or schemas that people use to represent, understand, and evaluate the behavior of family life. The way in which houses are furnished and lived in as homes, the conventional exchanges around the dinner table, the use of various kin terms, etc., are often symbolic as *indices* and *icons* of the family schema (to use Pierce's terminology) which "point to" the family schema in different ways, but are not the schema itself, which is a cognitive entity.

Image schemas

There are as many kinds of schemas as there are kinds of things; there are event schemas, orientational schemas, narrative schemas, propositional schemas, metaphoric schemas, image schemas, etc. George Lakoff, in *Women, Fire*, and

Dangerous Things, describes a number of these kinds of schemas. One of the most basic of these is the *image* schema; that is, a schema which forms a perceptual abstraction. A good example is the *container* schema. This is an abstract perceptual object which contains an *interior, boundary, and exterior.* For a container everything is either inside or outside. The most common example of a container is our own body, which, according to Mark Johnson (1987), serves as the pre-verbal kinesthetic basis for our understanding of this schema. The *container* schema is used for a great variety of objects; one walks *out* of a room, puts milk *in* a glass, falls *out* of love, puts ideas *into* words, falls *into* a trap, etc.

Abstract image schemas are characteristic of the grammatical elements in a language. Leonard Talmy has pointed out that grammatical particles, such as inflections for number or tense, or prepositions, or deictic elements like *this* and *that*, are abstractly *topological* in character (1978). Talmy uses the term *topological* because the notions used by grammatical elements are like forms of the rubber-sheet geometry of mathematical topology. That is, "spaces" are partitioned into regions without any consideration of actual magnitude, shape, or kind of material. According to Talmy, grammatical elements never specify color, or speed, or kind of substance, or quantified magnitude, or other sensorimotor characteristics. Such characteristics are specified by the open classes of non-grammatical elements such as nouns and verbs.

For example, consider Talmy's analysis of the sentence *A rustler lassoed the steers*. The grammatical elements include:

(1) *-ed*: "occurring at a time before that of the present communication"
(2) *the*: "already has identifiability for the addressee"
(3) *A* "not before in discussion or otherwise readily identifiable for addressee"
(4) *-s*: "multiplex object"
(5) *A . . .*: "uniplex object"
(6) the category of "verb" for *lasso*: "eventhood"
(7) the category of "noun" for *rustler/steer*: "objecthood"
(8) the relations of "subject"/"object" for *rustler/steer*: "agent/patient"
(9) active voice: "point of view of the agent"
(10) intonation, word-order, state of auxiliaries: "the speaker 'knows' the situation to be true and asserts it"

The lexical (non-grammatical) items can be characterized in the following way:

(1) *rustler*: property ownership, illegality, mode of activity
(2) *steer*: appearance, physical makeup, relation to animal kingdom
(3) *lasso*: certain materials (a body and a lasso) in certain configurations, movement sequences of materials' parts, concomitant mental intentions, directings, etc.

About this analysis, Talmy says

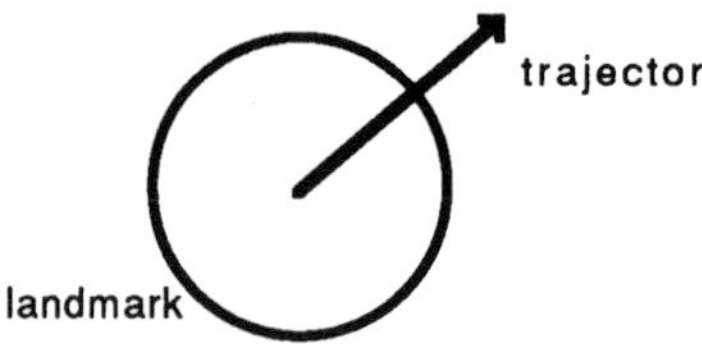

Figure 6.2 Prototypic sense of *out*

In surveying the lists, we can see these differences emerge: The grammatical elements are more numerous and their specifications seem simpler and more structural. Together, their specifications seem to determine the main organizational and communicational delineations of the cognitive representation evoked by the sentence. The lexical elements are fewer in number, but their specifications are more complex and seem to comprise most of the content of the cognitive representation. The lexical specifications are complex in three ways: compared to a grammatical specification, each has a) more total information, b) greater intricacy of information, and c) more different types of information together. (1978:3)

Here again we see the contrast between the human ability to be schematic and the ability to form complex feature gestalts into basic level objects. The difference Talmy finds between lexical and grammatical elements is reminiscent of the difference between *generic* and *life-form* terms in folk taxonomies. Two different cognitive capacities appear to be involved to different degrees throughout language. One capacity is *abstraction*, the ability to find patterned commonalities among varying materials. Using this capacity, highly schematic terms, such as grammatical elements or life-forms, can be learned and communicated. The other is a capacity to chunk together details into a complex composite image. Using this capacity, basic level terms such as *rustler* and *lasso* can be constructed which are defined by a relatively large number of physical and functional features.

English prepositions are a rich source of abstract image schemas. The highly abstract image schemas involved in the polysemous meanings of the English preposition *out* have been analyzed by Sue Linder (1982). This analysis uses the concepts of a *trajector* and a *landmark* developed by Ronald Langacker (1987). The trajector is the primary entity that makes the movement, while the landmark is a secondary entity which serves as a reference mark for the trajector. Figure 6.2 summarizes diagrammatically the prototypic sense of *out*.

In Figure 6.2 the movement of the trajector over time is represented by an arrow. In prototypical *out* a physical object moves through space from within a container to the outside of this container, as in (1)a:

(1)a Squeeze some toothpaste out.

This sense of *out* is extended from the domain of physical space into many other domains. For example:

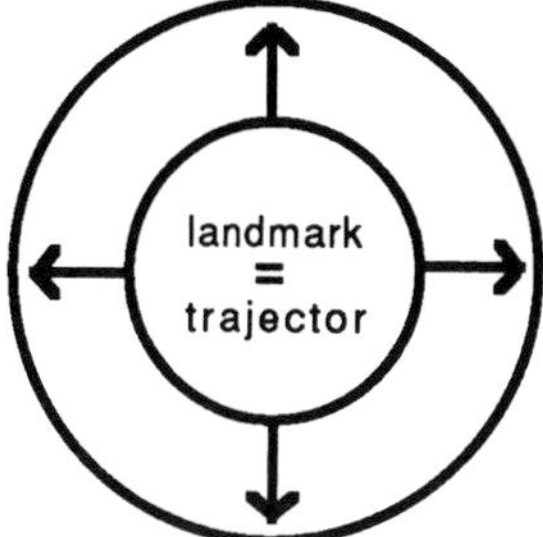

Figure 6.3 Secondary sense of *out*

(1)b He rented out his house.
(1)c He weaseled out.
(1)d His shirt brings out the blue in his eyes.

In (1)b the landmark encodes the metaphoric "neighborhood" defined by possession; in (1)c by a situation of obligation; and in (1)d by a perceptual state.

The second major schema for *out*, presented in Figure 6.3, neutralizes the distinction between the landmark and the trajector, encoding a reflexive trajectory of expansion and separation. Again the prototypical example is the movement of a physical object through space with a verb of motion:

(2)a Roll out the red carpet.

An extension of this schema to encode an "abstract" domain is given in (2)b. Also common are extensions in which the landmark/trajector "moves up to" some metaphoric or actual "boundary" or "fills" some "canonical form" as in (2)c through (2)g:

(2)b The company is branching out into new areas.
(2)c Fill out the form.
(2)d She really fills out the dress.
(2)e Write out your ideas.
(2)f Round out the meal.
(2)g Argue it out.

The third major schema identifies the landmark with the trajector's initial location and encodes the trajector's path away from this location, as diagrammed in Figure 6.4. Examples of this schema:

(3)a They started out for Alaska.
(3)b He set out on his long journey.

In her dissertation, Linder also analyzed the different senses of the preposition *up* and found a similar linked series of image schemas. Claudia Brugman (1981) carried out a similar analysis of *over*, finding nearly one hundred uses.

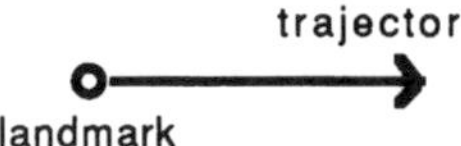

Figure 6.4 Tertiary sense of *out*

An extended discussion of the way in which the different senses of such prepositions form complex chains and structures is presented in Lakoff's *Women, Fire, and Dangerous Things* (pp. 418-461).

An extensive analysis of the schematic aspects of language has been made by Ronald Langacker in his two volume work, *Foundations of Cognitive Grammar.* For Langacker, a language does not consist of rules in the sense of some general algorithm which states like a computer program what can be done at each step. Rather, the regularities of language are the result of the operation of multilevel schematic patterning. Langacker's position is a major revision of much of present day theoretical linguistics, explicitly grounding linguistic theory in clearly formulated cognitive processes. Using a cognitive framework, Langacker is able to give a semantic account of a wide range of phenomena in the grammar of natural languages.

Schemas as processors

So far, only the representational aspects of schemas have been discussed. The development of the schema concept includes the idea that a schema is more than just a representation; it is also a *processor* of a special kind. Psychologists have been especially interested in the processing side of the schema concept because their experimental data shows that well-formed, salient mental representations involve strong expectations about what goes with what along with a powerful tendency to group together such parts into a gestalt whole (Neisser 1967; Rumelhart 1980). From this perspective schemas are a kind of mental recognition "device" which *creates* a complex interpretation from minimal inputs; it is not just a "picture" in the mind.

Despite its great potential schema theory proved surprisingly difficult to simulate. One test of how clearly one understands some process is to see if one can create a reasonable computer simulation of that process. The verdict of those most involved in developing schema theory was that none of the attempts at concrete specification through computer simulation adequately captured the characteristics that schemas were supposed to have (Rumelhart, Smolensky, McClelland and Hinton 1986). This was puzzling because ordinary computer programs in standard computer languages had been successful in a number of areas of artificial intelligence, such as playing chess and solving logic problems.

The normal computer program uses a *serial symbolic processing model.* The serial symbolic processing model has been the standard model in artificial intelligence and much of cognitive psychology since the 1950s, and has almost

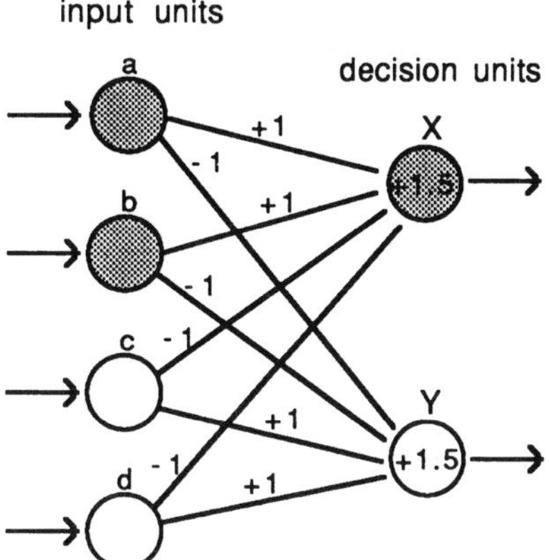

Figure 6.5 Perceptron with two output units
Decision unit X is activated when input units a and b are active; decision unit Y is activated when input units c and d are active

achieved the status of common sense. In this model, symbols are the basic objects of the computer/mind. The senses/input devices bring in information about the outside world which is encoded in symbols/binary bits so that a representation of the world can be created. Once this representation has been formed, the mind/computer manipulates these symbols/bits using the rules of logic (as in a syllogism) or in a heuristic search (as in searching for the best move in a chess game). The rules are applied serially, forming a chain of steps through which a decision is reached.

The serial symbolic processing model is not the only computer model of how the mind might work. Beginning with work by Warren McCullock and Walter Pitts in the 1940s, and continuing with work by Donald Hebb and Frank Rosenblatt, models for the way in which a network of neurons could learn to associate events and to recognize patterns were developed using a very different kind of architecture (Quinlan 1991). In the 1950s, when modern computers became available, this model was simulated in computer programs. The best known of the early computer models is Frank Rosenblatt's *perceptron*.

The perceptron is a very simple device, consisting of a set of input or sensory units with fixed connections to a second layer of output or decision units. Each of the connections has a certain *weight* – the weight determines the degree of *activation* or *excitation* passed along that connection to the output or decision unit. When the sum of the activation of an output unit by all the connecting input units exceeds a certain threshold level, the output unit "fires." In figure 6.5, a perceptron is diagrammed which will identify two different patterns; one pattern in which input units a and b are activated, the other pattern in which

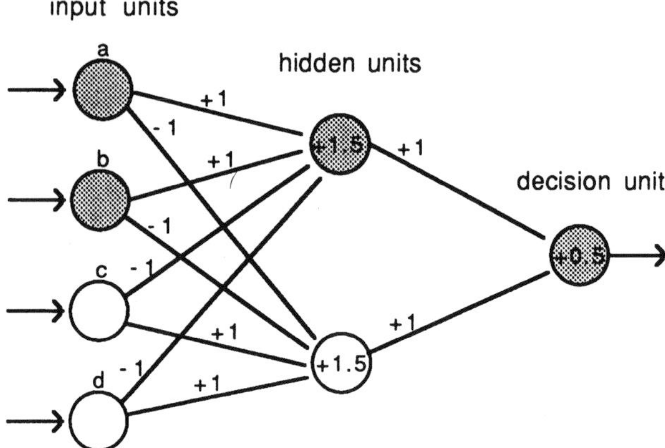

Figure 6.6 Connectionist network with one decision unit
This unit is activated when input units a and b are active *or* when input units c and d are active *but not both.*

input units c and d are activated. The weights of each connection are indicated by +1 or –1 and the threshold levels by numbers within the unit.

Using a procedure developed by Rosenblatt a perceptron can be trained to discriminate between a variety of different patterns. This is done by inputting a particular pattern and if the network responds with the wrong output unit then the weights of all those input units which activate the correct input are increased while the weights of all those input units which activate incorrect units are decreased.

Perceptrons can only identify certain kinds of patterns. They cannot be trained to discriminate between an odd versus an even number of points, or between connected lines and disconnected lines, or to recognize the logical pattern of *exclusive or.* For example, the perceptron in Figure 6.5 cannot be trained to discriminate when input units a and b are active *or* when input units c and b are active *but not both.* In part because of these problems, perceptrons lost out to serial symbol processing systems as the architecture of choice for cognitive modeling in the 1960s and 1970s. However, it was recognized by the 1980s that the limitations of the perceptron with respect to pattern recognition could be overcome by adding a series of intermediate or *hidden* units between the input and output units. The name "perceptron" was dropped and the new device with intermediate units came to be called a "parallel distributed processing network" or "connectionist network." (The term "neural net" is also used.)

Figure 6.6 gives a diagram of a connectionist network for learning an "exclusive or" pattern. The decision unit will "fire" if either units a and b are activated, or if units b and c are activated, but not both. Using this simple three layer architecture, connectionist networks have been trained to do a great variety of pattern recognition tasks, such as discriminating underwater explosive mines from rocks based on sonar signals, outputting the proper pronunciation of words from standard written English input, learning the correct relationship between semantic interpretations and grammatical forms of English sentences, and learning the proper past tense form for English "regular" and "irregular" verbs.[7]

While connectionist models gained popularity, the standard serial symbolic processing model had begun to appear problematic. Again and again researchers found that serial symbolic processing programs are very context bound and "brittle" – if the input is altered very slightly or the task is changed somewhat, the whole program is likely to crash. Furthermore, despite the great speed and power of serial symbolic processing models when dealing with logic and math, it was found that these models are very slow and ineffective in doing certain kinds of things. For example, in the world of robotics, where a machine has to learn to perceive and navigate in a real world of physical objects, attempts to develop ambulatory robots using serial symbolic programing have been generally unsuccessful. One strange six legged robot vehicle which appeared in a 1988 TV show on robotics, given the task of climbing over a barrier, took over half an hour to figure out how to get two legs up on the barrier and never did figure how to climb all the way over it. Yet simple minded little ants can do this type of task in seconds. The ant's success must be the result of its possession of a well-constructed neural network which does lots of simple little computations in parallel. Certainly it is not because of the speed of the ant's brain impulses, which are many thousands of times slower than the electronic impulses inside the computer of the robot vehicle.

Connectionist models respond to stimuli in a very "human" fashion. Psychologists who had been working in cognition found that connectionist networks were excellent models for how the processes of schematization might actually work in the brain. First, connectionist networks have a great capacity for "filling in" missing inputs with default values. If parts of a pattern or configuration are missing, the network is not only likely to respond with the right output, but also to activate those hidden units which would normally be activated by the *complete* input pattern. Second, connectionist networks can be trained to learn very abstract and subtle characteristics of stimuli – in fact, a connectionist network typically carries out a kind of cluster analysis or multidimensional scaling of the input stimuli, finding underlying structures. Third, connectionist networks are sensitive to context – able, for example, to change the pronunciation of a particular alphabetic letter as the letters surrounding that letter change. Fourth, connectionist networks are able to *blend* interpretations into a reasonable synthesis when presented with parts of different patterns.

[7] See Quinlan 1991 for a review of connectionist models in psychology.

There are a number of other advantages that connectionist models have over serial symbolic processing models in simulating human cognition. Connectionist models show "graceful degradation" when parts of a network are destroyed (like humans when they lose brains cells due to the effects of alcohol or injury) rather than the complete "crash" which typically occurs if even a small part of a serial symbolic processing program is destroyed. Connectionist models of memory are naturally content addressable,[8] and generalization in response occurs automatically to similar stimuli. Priming effects also occur naturally in connectionist nets. How distinct a particular pattern of stimuli is depends on the kind of stimuli to which the network has previously been exposed – good recognition depends on being trained with good examples. Finally, connectionist nets display the kind of distortion that occurs in memory and perception when a weak anomalous input pattern is interpreted as a different but related pattern which has strong internal and external connections.

All of these properties – being able to fill in missing values with default values, learning underlying structure, context sensitivity, blending of interpretations, graceful degradation, content addressable memory, generalization, priming, memory distortion, stimulus averaging, etc. – make connectionist networks a remarkable mechanical model of how schema processing might work in the human brain. Furthermore, there is little doubt that the brain, with its ten billion or so neurons, *is* a massively parallel connectionist network.

The mechanics of what happens in a connectionist model and what happens in a serial symbolic processing model are quite different. In a serial symbolic processing model the input from whatever sensors is recoded into symbols. In a connectionist model the input is transformed into weighted connections between neuron-like units. In a serial symbolic processing model sensory input is recoded into symbols. In a connectionist model thinking consists primarily of pattern recognition; learning "what goes with what" by association.

It is important to recognize that proponents of connectionist models do not deny that some kind of serial symbolic processing occurs in the brain (some such thing is happening now as you read these sentences), and that proponents of serial symbolic processing models do not deny that some kind of parallel distributed process occurs in the brain (some such thing is happening each time

[8] The property of content addressability involves the way in which a memory system locates items already in memory. Consider a memory system which has a hundred "faces" in memory. When the perceptual system "sees" a face, the memory system is searched to discover if this face is already in memory. But how can this be done? One way is to search every face in memory to see if it matches the face seen by the perceptual system. This would do the job, but it would take a very long time if there were a lot of faces in memory. A faster method is to use the very features of the perceived face to tell the memory searching process where to look for the face – e.g. "look in the memory space reserved for faces with a big nose, little chin, wide forehead, etc." This is called a "content addressable system" because the content of the item tells the memory search processes where to go to see if an item is already in memory. Connectionist nets do this quite efficiently (see Quinlan 1991:50–51).

you recognize one of the written words in this sentence).[9] According to Rumelhart, Smolensky, McClelland, and Hinton: "processes that happen very quickly – say less than .25 to .5 seconds – occur essentially in parallel and should be described in terms of parallel models. Processes that take longer, we believe, have a serial component and can more readily be described in terms of sequential information processing models" (1986:56).

The issue is the degree to which normal human cognitive processing can be understood as *primarily* a parallel distributed process versus *primarily* as a serial symbolic process. As an example, consider chess playing. Serial symbolic processing proponents point to the fact that they have been able to create chess playing programs which compete successfully with master chess players, indicating the dominance of serial processing in at least some kinds of human cognition. Connectionists respond by saying that chess playing programs do not reason like humans and that human chess playing is more strongly dependent on recognizing patterns and less dependent on step-by-step reasoning than most people realize. To make this point, Hubert Dreyfus (1987) set up a demonstration in which an international master played and won five-second-a-move chess against a somewhat weaker player while rapidly adding numbers presented audibly at the rate of one number per second. Since a human adding digits cannot at the same time engage in deep multimove strategy, the superiority of the international master in this instance must rest on his ability to recognize chess patterns "automatically".

It has been estimated that a master level chess player can recognize something like 50,000 different chess board configurations. The serial reasoning component of human chess playing, on the other hand, has been found to be surprisingly minor and not to vary much by level of skill (DeGroot 1965; Eisenstadt and Kareev 1977). Obviously, say the proponents of connectionism, much of the intellectual skill of chess playing is pattern recognition, which is the sort of thing a serial symbolic processing device does very poorly but a connectionist device does quite efficiently (However, as yet, no connectionist program plays chess).

Modifications of schema theory and limitations of connectionist models

It is interesting that the connectionist model, originally thought of by some as a simulation of schema theory, has begun to modify the basic concept of a

[9] There is a problem in talking about serial symbolic processing and parallel distributed (connectionist) processing as two distinct types of cognitive process in that most cognitive scientists agree that at the implementational level, the brain functions as a massively parallel connectionist system. Most cognitive scientists also agree that the brain has a special architecture that somehow organizes various connectionist networks in ways that result in serial symbolic processing. The brain is basically connectionist, yet able to do serial symbolic processing. How this is accomplished is not yet well understood.

schema. In a paper reflecting on the impact of connectionist models on cognitive science, Donald Norman states:

What about the schema, the omnipresent, powerful tool of modern cognitive theory? Well, . . . the schema still exists, but in a somewhat different form than that which schema theorists have thought of it . . . Schemas are not fixed structures. Schemas are flexible configurations, mirroring the regularities of experience, providing automatic completion of missing components, automatically generalizing from the past, but also continually in modification, continually adapting to reflect the current state of affairs. Schemas are not fixed, immutable data structures. Schemas are flexible interpretive states that reflect the mixture of past experience and present circumstances.

Because the schema is in reality the theorist's interpretation of the system configuration, and because the system configures itself differently according to the sum of all the numerous influences upon it, each new invocation of a schema may differ from the previous invocations. Thus, the system behaves as if there were prototypical schemas, but where the prototype is constructed anew for each occasion by combining past experiences with biases and activation levels resulting from the current experience and the context in which it occurs. (1986:536).

Norman stresses the flexibility and plasticity of schemas, but it should also be noted that connectionist networks can be constructed which are very inflexible and rigid. Networks can range from very easy to very hard to change with experience and from very biased towards one interpretation to very balanced in choice. One can create networks which form *preemptive* and *coercive* schemas, just as one can create networks which form flexible and accommodating schemas (Hutchins 1991).

Norman's comments make clear that the distinction between a schema and a non-schema is a matter of degree rather than an all-or-none affair. In another place I described the situation as follows:

To say that something is a "schema" is a shorthand way of saying that a distinct and strongly interconnected pattern of interpretive elements can be activated by minimal inputs. A schema is an interpretation which is frequent, well organized, memorable, which can be made from minimal cues, contains one or more prototypic instantiations, is resistant to change, etc. While it would be more accurate to speak always of *interpretations with such and such a degree of schematicity*, the convention of calling highly schematic interpretations "schemas" remains in effect in the cognitive literature. (1992:29)

The point is that many of the objects and categories found in any culture will be "weak" schemas, lacking the power that well-formed schemas have, such as the power to create illusory correlations or organize memory or enable reasoning.

It would be a mistake to leave the impression that connectionist models are a completely satisfactory implementation of schema theory. There are a number of things that connectionist models seem – at least at this point in time – unable to do. For example, connectionist models are said to be unable to learn *matching* or *oddity* as such. In an oddity problem an animal will be given three stimuli, two of which are the same, one of which is different. If the animal selects the different stimulus object the animal is rewarded. Once the animal has learned a specific problem, the task is changed and three new objects, two identical and one different, are introduced. Again the animal is rewarded for selecting the different object. After repeated trials with many different stimulus objects, some animals will "catch on," and immediately select the different object when a new set of objects is presented.

Not all animals can learn this type of problem. Corvids – ravens, crows, jays, and magpies – can learn the oddity or matching problem relatively quickly, but pigeons cannot (Mackintosh 1988). Nor can current connectionist networks (Quinlan 1991:264). Like pigeons they learn to solve each of the tasks with time, but they do not improve across tasks. They seem unable to form an upper level schema of "oddity." Since humans and crows obviously can form an "oddity" schema, how do they do it? Is it just a more complex type of connectionist net, or is there a new kind of neural architecture at work here?

Connectionist networks are also said to be unable or to have great difficulty in discriminating between an instance and a variable, or between a type and a token (Norman 1986:540). Given the information "John lost a dollar" and "Helen needs a dollar" a connectionist system is not good at representing John's dollar as a specific instance of a general category that is needed by Helen. There are many speculations about how connectionist networks might be augmented so that they could carry out such tasks. However, as yet no proposal has general acceptance. In any case, the failure of connectionism to give a complete account of how schemas operate is not a great drawback to the use of schema theory. We can still use psychological knowledge about schemas even if no complete connectionist account yet exists.

The implications of schema-connectionist theory for the study of culture

For anthropologists interested in culture, what are the implications of recognizing the importance of connectionist models in human cognition?

The first implication concerns *rules*. Culture is often said to consist of *rules* – rules for how to form the English plural, rules for proxemics, rewrite rules for kinship terminologies, rules for games, moral rules, etc. These rules are said to be *implicit* because ordinary people cannot tell you what they are. A connectionist network, when it has learnt to produce a certain output from a particular input, looks as if it were following rules in the sense that the relation between the output and the input can be *described* by a set of formal rules. However, as David Rumelhart and other connectionists have pointed out, there are no rules – explicit or implicit – *in* a connectionist network, only a set of weights and connections (Rumelhart and McClelland 1986).

The point is that anthropologists and other social scientists sometimes ascribe *rules* to the actor when it is only the actor's *behavior* that is being described. In many cases in which behavior is described as following rules, there may be in fact no *rules* inside the actor – only networks of certain kinds. For example, the *behavior* of a person reading a list of English words may be said to follow the rules that relate the written forms of English to the spoken forms of English. However, these rules may correspond to nothing in the person's psyche – the person reading the list may not be aware of any of these rules, unable to state such rules, and even on an unconscious level there may be no representation of the rules. The only thing *in* the actor may be a network of differentially interconnected elements.

Connectionist based learning contrasts with learning brought about by serial symbolic processing rules; that is, rules which are symbolically encoded propositions to which the actor is directly responding such as the rule "drive on the right." First, serial symbolic processing learning is typically *quicker* than connectionist based learning. One can learn a verbally stated rule like "drive on the right" in a few minutes, while connectionist based learning typically takes hundreds or thousands of encounters. Also it is generally easy to *change* serial symbolic processing based behavior. For example, one can tell an American "this is England, drive on the left" and they can change their behavior immediately. Behavior based on connectionist learning, however, requires many encounters to shift from one output to another.

Another important difference between these two kinds of learning is that connectionist based learning, while slower to master and harder to change than serial symbolic processing based learning, is typically much more *automatic* and *rapid* in execution than rule based behavior – one does not need to think of the rule and then to decide to act on the rule; rather, one simply reacts to the situation "without thought" as the network "fires" – as in the case of a master chess player adding numbers in his head while playing a five-second-a-move game.

George Mandler has divided *memory* into two different kinds, which he terms *automatic* and *non-automatic*. Automatic memory is fast, involuntary, and does not require a conscious attempt at retrieval, while non-automatic memory is relatively slow and requires conscious intentional processing. Mandler notes that "automatic retrievals appear to be confined to previously organized, well-bounded, and unitary objects and events, typically involving a single organized schema. Non-automatic retrievals, on the other hand, typically involve relations among two or more such structures" (1985:93–94). The distinction here parallels the difference between the response of a simple connectionist network and a serial processing system which retrieves the memory of relations among two or more schemas.

In many cases "rule following behavior" may be the result of *both* connectionist networks and verbally statable, declarative knowledge. Or there can be cases in which the verbal rule conflicts with the connectionist network. Again take the example of driving. When Americans go to England, they are aware that the rule changes, and that one should drive on the left. That rule is verbally statable, declarative knowledge about where one should drive and is easy to change as one's location changes. This permits a rapid shift in behavior. But problems can occur when actually driving. When there is an emergency, for example, such as a car approaching head-on, there is a tendency to respond with one's well-learned automatic connectionist network and pull to the *right*, not the left, forgetting the verbal *rule*, and causing an accident. A connectionist network based on many thousands of driving experiences produces the powerful automatic expectation that one should be to the right of an approaching car, along with an almost automatic response based on this expectation. This network is not rapidly modifiable the way verbally based declarative knowledge is. The driver has both kinds of knowledge – verbal rule knowledge and connectionist knowledge – but they are learned differently, affected differently by external factors, and have different psychological and behavioral outcomes.

Just how much of culture consists of connectionist learning and how much consists of verbal rule learning is hard to say. Many of the regularities found in language, in social interaction, in crafts and artistic skills are likely to be connectionist based; these things are typically learned with a minimal use of stated rules and a maximal dependence on numerous encounters with specific instances. Other parts of culture, such as school learning and formal systems of ethics, law, and etiquette are more likely to involve verbal rules. However, many if not most kinds of cultural learning probably involve both verbal rules and connectionist networks in complex amalgams – such a mixture has the potential advantage of being quicker to master than pure connectionist learning, yet to be more rapid and effortless in performance than pure serial symbolic processing learning. In any case, the notion that culture consists of rules, propositions, or other types of verbal declarative knowledge needs to be modified to include connectionist-like types of learning in which there may be regularity in behavior but no direct representation of the rules in symbols.

Maurice Bloch, a British social anthropologist who has worked among the Zafimaniry on Madagascar, makes this point in his Frazer lecture in which he describes a Malagasy farmer making the decision that a particular piece of forest would make a good field (1992). In the symbolic processing model, such a task would be extremely complex, involving the integration of many kinds of information about vegetation, slope, surrounding countryside, hydrology, soil, etc. However, an average Malagasy farmer can do this task in seconds. Bloch argues that the task seems so difficult because we use a folk model of psychological processing which is based on language-like serial symbolic processing. Bloch goes on to argue that connectionism is an alternative theory of thought which explains how such commonplace feats can be done. He concludes:

> Since much of culture consists of the performance of these familiar procedures and understandings connectionism may explain what a great deal of culture in the mind-brain is like. It also explains why this type of culture cannot be either linguistic or "language-like." Making the culture efficient requires the construction of connected domain-relevant networks, which by their very nature cannot be stored or accessed through sentential logical forms such as govern natural language. (1992:192)

A second implication of connectionist models for the way we think about culture involves the relation between the structures in the mind and the structures that are in the external world. Since the 1950s, most anthropologists have defined culture as a purely *mental* phenomena – consisting of meanings, understandings, knowledge, values, beliefs, etc. The structures that exist in the physical world as objects or events – the patterned sounds of language (including ordinary talk and specialized narratives), role behavior, the countless pieces of material culture, the enactments of ritual – are all thought to be produced by the structures in the mind, and thus considered to be more or less a *reflection* of these mental cultural structures.

There are problems with this reflection metaphor. How do mental structures ever get learned? To the extent that connectionist networks are involved in learning, mental structure is strongly influenced by physical structure. That is, a connectionist network will typically learn structure if there is clear structure present in the input. This means that many of the structures that develop in the mind will be to some extent a *reflection* of the structures in the external physical world. So with respect to connectionist based learning, there is likely to be a reversal of "what is a reflection of what."

The circular cause and effect relationship between external and internal structures occurs not only with respect to learning, but also with respect to understanding. On one hand, the external forms which are physical representations depend on a cognitive system to give these representations meaning. On the other hand, the cognitive system cannot express and communicate meanings without the external physical forms of talk, writing, ritual, etc., to convey these meanings.

It is not that one can not define *culture* so that it consists of just mental structures. One can – and in fact, since the 1950s, with some exceptions, anthropologists generally have. The point is that such a definition legitimizes the study of mental structures but leaves unlegitimized the study of external structures. One solution to this definitional problem, developed by Ed Hutchins, is to shift the whole ontological basis of the concept and define culture as *process* rather than *content* and consider both mental structures and physical structures as a result or residue of the process of cultural transmission and adaptation (Hutchins 1994). At this point my own solution is to use the term *culture* to characterize the entire content of a group's heritage, corresponding to Tylor's earlier use of the term, and to try to be specific when talking about things cultural, specifying *cultural schemas* or *understandings* as against *material culture*, *cultural practices*, *cultural talk*, etc.

Another important implication of connectionist models has been discussed by Naomi Quinn and Claudia Strauss (n.d.). Recent discussions of cultural theory have criticized an older position which treated culture as *unified*, *uncontested*, and *unchanging*. Quinn and Strauss point out that it is equally wrong to describe culture as if it were totally diverse, never accepted, and never the same. The problem is to construct a theory which can explain how culture can be both – partially shared and partially diverse, partially contested and partially accepted, partially changing and partially permanent. To do this, Quinn and Strauss argue, requires a psychological theory which explains how people learn from experience, and this entails examining socialization experiences in greater detail to discover what learners *internalize*. They go on to argue that connectionist/schema theory offers such an account. They give examples of the way in which cultural schemas for things like *self-reliance* are learned so that such schemas become, for some people, strong values and motives, while for others they are only cliches.

In this paper Quinn and Strauss compare cultural schema theory with Bourdieu's conception of *habitus*. Bourdieu (1977, 1990) is concerned with developing an alternative to two extremes of social theory; one in which action is the mechanical enactment of learned cultural rules or unconscious structures, the other in which action is purely self-interested, unconstrained by culturally conditioned values or other mental structures:

> Bourdieu's alternative is not to say that sometimes humans enact learned structures and sometimes we are "free." Instead, he argues, we are *always* constrained by the dispositions learned from our experiences, but our habitual responses rest on knowledge that is not learned from or cognitively represented as rules. Our internalized (in his words "incorporated" or "embodied") knowledge is looser and fuzzier than rules. This form of internalization enables people to react flexibly to new contexts instead of enacting the same structures over and over again. This imprecise knowledge Bourdieu calls *habitus*. (n.d.)

Quinn and Strauss point out the similarity between Bourdieu's concept of *habitus* and the connectionist concept of a schema – that both are flexible, implicit recognition procedures, not rules, which are not necessarily consciously known. They also point out some of the differences between the concepts; for example, Bourdieu stresses the fact that people are unconscious of their habitus, while schema based learning *can* be conscious:

> Learning by modeling, which may occur largely out of awareness, is not forever after barred from awareness. While it is true and significant that such knowledge *tends* to remain backgrounded in consciousness, it is entirely possible to foreground and describe it: Novelists and the authors of joking "how to" texts (how to dress like a preppy, act like a real man, be a Southerner, etc.), among others, recognize and verbalize this typically unspoken knowledge all the time. Nor is this ability limited to "advanced" societies. (n.d.)

Quinn and Strauss also describe other differences between *habitus* and *schema*; habitus is always widely shared, has no clear relation to motivation and emotion, and seems to be learned automatically, without reference to the learner's motivational state. Schemas, on the other hand, may or may not be widely shared and can be strongly influenced by emotion and motivation.

Quinn and Strauss stress that the learning of schemas is not like loading in a set of instructions in a computer:

> Connectionist models give us another way of thinking about internalization: not as loading in a set of instructions, but as gradually building up associative links among repeated or salient aspects of our experience. The understandings that are built up through this process tend to be stable in persons and durable historically. Depending on the cultural inputs from which they are learned, they may tend to be shared across persons and thematized across cultural contexts. Finally, if these associations are learned along with strong emotional reactions, they may acquire powerful motivational force. This model makes it clear that all of these centripetal cultural effects are a contingent product of interaction between minds and a world shaped a certain way – not an inevitable functional requirement of social systems (to put it in the theoretical terms of the 1950s and 1960s) or of human needs to find meaning through socially given symbol systems (in the terms of the symbolist anthropology of the 1970s). Thus, it follows that it is equally possible for cultural inputs to result in understandings that vary across individuals and contexts and are learned without the emotional associations that give them motivational force. Furthermore, with changes in the circumstances under which people grow up, understandings can undergo historical change and with intentional effort, people can change their own habitual responses. (n.d.)

The final point to be considered here involves the often asserted idea that *symbols determine how we experience the world.* For example, Marshall Sahlins quotes Leslie White as follows: "Thus [with symbols] man built a new world in which to live. . . . Between man and nature hung the *veil* of culture, and he could see nothing save through this medium . . . permeating everything was the essence of words." (Sahlins 1978:105). Sahlins (1978) himself makes similar claims. Indeed, in anthropology, the idea that language or other symbol systems determine how the world is experienced is not unusual. It is explicit in the Sapir Whorf hypothesis and is a general presupposition in much symbolist, structuralist, and interpretativist anthropology.

Once one accepts the metaphor of cultural symbols forming a kind of veil between the human eye and the external world, one has accepted a large part of *epistemological relativism* – the claim that there is no principled way for people of different cultures to come to an agreement about matters of truth. That is, since there is no way of knowing anything outside of what comes through the veil of cultural symbols, there is no way of knowing how distorted one's own perceptions are – in short, no true external standards are available to the veil wrapped human, making objectivity and science impossible.

This metaphor of cultural symbols as a veil comes from the idea that language and other symbol systems *determine* what we experience. From the connectionist viewpoint, the veil story is incorrect. Since connectionist networks are very sensitive to input structures, one expects that mental structures will have some correspondence to physical structures – both the physical structures that are part of the natural world, like trees and pain, and the behavioral structures that are part of the cultural process, like speech and ritual. *In the connectionist model "words" do not "encode" experience.* Rather, words signify schemas, which means that the units activated by a particular speech sound also activate a larger pattern of connections which are the active schema for a particular experience. The sounds of words are like "pointers" to patterns of experience – indices to internal mental structures, not "veils" between reality and experience.

From the connectionist position, one would expect that the distinctions in a language would be likely to reflect salient differences in the way the world is experienced, since such differences are most easily learned. And indeed, this is what the research on taxonomies and classification systems, described above, has found. But this does not imply that individual or cultural meaning systems are *nothing but* a reflection of our naive perceptions of the external world. Claudia Strauss (1992a:9) has called the notion that humans simply reproduce the cultural forms they encounter the "fax theory of cultural transmission." The kinds of discriminations that are taught, the influence of one schema on another, the influence of motivation and emotion on learning, and the influence of others on what one thinks all have the capacity of creating great cultural and individual variation.

Thus a theory of culture which incorporates what is known about connectionist based learning would reject both the extreme idealism of the metaphor of culture as an *all encompassing veil* and the extreme objectivism of the metaphor of culture as a *simple reflection* of the naively perceived external world. By changing the model of human cognition and meaning from a system containing *only* symbolic serial processing to a system containing both symbolic serial processing *and* connectionist parallel distributed processing, a number of things about human culture look different. First, culture is no longer seen as consisting *only* of symbolic objects, such as rules and propositions. Instead, culture includes not only rules and propositions, but also connectionist based procedural learning which differs in important ways from true rule based learning. Second, it becomes clear that encounters with a structured environment are a major factor in the transmission of culture, both with respect to learning and to the production of representations. Third, the theoretical dilemma of describing culture as either uniform, rigid, coercive internal structures or as entirely plastic, negotiable, shifting external structures is resolvable. And last, the notion that culture is a veil which continuously distorts what can be truly known of the external world changes from a plausible metaphor to an incomplete account of a much more complex process.

7 Models and theories

The development of schema theory and its embodiment in connectionist networks brought about a real theoretical advance in the cognitive sciences. An important property of a schema is that it is an abstract organ zation of experience. It constructs the objects of recognition; sometimes obvious objects, like *cats*, sometimes non-obvious objects, like the *real self*. But cognitive organization is not restricted to the formation of objects. There are other kinds of cognitive organization which link together objects but are not themselves objects. *Lists*, such as the alphabet or the days of the week are a good example of a very simple kind of organization of objects by serial ordination. *Taxonomies* are an example of a different kind of organization; the objects in a taxonomy are related through the single relationship of inclusion. A *componential paradigm* is another example; here objects are related through the sharing and contrasting of features.

Propositions are another means of relating objects.[1] In a proposition something is said about something: "Sunday was rainy." A proposition combines some number of separate schemas into a more complex organization.[2] One has a schema for *cat*, for *on*, and for *mat*. The proposition "the cat is on the mat" integrates these three schemas into a new complex entity – the cat-on-mat event.

There are sharp limits to the number of elements humans can cognitively integrate into a schema even if they are organized propositionally:

> This is the farmer sewing his corn
> that kept the cock that crowed in the morn
> that waked the priest all shaven and shorn
> that married the man all tattered and torn

[1] The term *objects* as used here includes physical things (tables), events (walking), and relations (inequality).

[2] Ronald Langacker's *Foundations of Cognitive Grammar* provides a detailed analysis of the schematic construction of sentences. A proposition is generally defined as the sense of a sentence that makes a truth claim; while not exactly the same thing, both should have the similar types of cognitive organization.

that kissed the maiden all forlorn
that milked the cow with the crumpled horn
that kicked the dog
that worried the cat
that killed the rat
that ate the malt
that lay in the house
that Jack built

is too much for most people to integrate into a single representation. As always, the seven chunk limit of short-term memory is a strong constraint on any kind of human information processing. Recall of this nursery rhyme is typically done by learning a sequence of associative links (dogs chase cats, cats kill rats, rats eat malt, etc.), not by "reading-off" from a mental picture or schema of the whole shebang.

Propositions are culturally codified in *slogans*, *cliches*, *wise words*, *maxims*, and other kinds of formulaic sayings: "A stitch in time saves nine," "Look before you leap," "You can't take it with you," "The grass is always greener on the other side of the fence," "Make love not war," "Misery loves company," etc. Geoffrey White (1987) has examined a selection of such sayings and found that while they appear to stand alone they actually rest on large and complex bodies of shared implicit cultural understandings. A good proverb appeals by selection to one of these common bodies of understandings in such a way as to create strong normative implications for action. Propositions too can be organized into even larger units such as stories, poetry, syllogisms, arguments, and theories. Complex relations can also be represented by drawings, maps, scale models, etc., which combine graphic symbols rather than verbal symbols into multi-schematic configurations.

Models

The idea of cognitive models was introduced by Kenneth Craik in the 1940s in his book, *The Nature of Explanation*. Craik stressed the use of models in thinking:

> If the organism carries a "small-scale model" of external reality and of its own possible actions within its head, it is able to try out various alternatives, conclude which is the best of them, react to future situations before they arise, utilize the knowledge of past events in dealing with the present and future, and in every way to react in a much fuller, safer, and more competent manner to the emergencies which face it. (1943:13)

A model consists of an interrelated set of elements which fit together to represent something. Typically one uses a model to reason with or calculate from by mentally manipulating the parts of the model in order to solve some problem. Every schema serves as a simple model in the sense that it is a representation of some object of event. For example, seeing a grocery store clerk hand a bag of apples to a shopper and accept money, the *commercial transaction* schema, described in Chapter 3, would serve as a probable model for what has been seen. However, many models are not schemas themselves, although they are composed of schemas. Models are not schemas when the collection of elements is too large and complex to hold in short-term memory (by definition, a schema, as a "bounded, distinct, and unitary representation," must fit into short-term memory). Examples of model which are not themselves schemas are discussed below.

A number of examples of cultural models are presented in Holland and Quinn, *Cultural Models in Language and Thought.* An extensive review of the use of cultural models in anthropology is presented in a chapter by Quinn and Holland (1987).

The Caroline Islands navigation model

One of the best systematic descriptions of the use of a cultural model is found in Thomas Gladwin's book, *East is a Big Bird.* Gladwin gives a detailed account of the physical and conceptual technology used by the navigators of Micronesia, who sailed great distances across the Pacific, accurately locating tiny islands in a world that is less than two-tenths of 1% land. Micronesian navigators regularly traveled between islands as distant as 450 miles, and shorter trips of 150 miles or so were made routinely. While in Polynesia and other areas of the Pacific, traditional techniques have been lost, in some areas of Micronesia the traditional methods are still taught and used.

Gladwin's major informant, Hipour, was a navigator from Puluwat, one of the central Caroline Islands. The Micronesian navigator's technology includes a special kind of star compass, the categorization of different kinds of ocean currents, and an unusual orientational model involving the use of a reference island by which the progress of the outrigger toward the target island can be measured.

Since the publication of *East is a Big Bird* further ethnographic studies of Micronesian and Polynesian navigation have been carried out by David Lewis (1972) and Ben Finney (1979). A complete presentation of what is now known about the Micronesian system of navigation would require at least a full length monograph. However, the main outline of one part of this system, the reference island model, can be presented briefly. The description given here follows a synthesis developed by Edwin Hutchins (1983, 1994).

For the Micronesian navigator the horizon of the ocean is marked by the positions at which a number of stars – Vega, Aldebaran, Altair, etc. – rise and set (Goodenough 1953). While the sun and the moon will rise and set at different compass points along the horizon over the year, from any latitude the stars rise and set at exactly the same compass points throughout the year. For example, in the Carolines, Altair rises at a point almost due east on the horizon in the east and travels across the night sky to set at a point almost due west. Thus Altair's path makes a *star track* which acts to mark two positional points on the circumference of the horizon. Other stars which also rise at the same position as Altair are then joined together to form a *linear constellation.* A system of star tracks makes an excellent compass in tropical latitudes where the north star and southern cross remain close to the horizon and where stars rise and cross the sky from east to west in almost vertical paths. Even if the stars that make up a particular star track are not near the horizon, the navigator can estimate from their position in the sky and their relation to other stars where they would have risen on the horizon and where they will set. Similarly, during the day the navigator can use the sun to estimate the position of various star tracks since he knows at any time of year which star track the sun is in.

The complete Micronesian star compass contains sixteen star tracks creating thirty-two horizon positions. The star track directions needed to sail from one island to another are well known to the expert navigator, having been handed down from navigator to apprentice for many generations. But to get from one island to another, besides knowing star track directions, a navigator must know the distance between the islands and be able to estimate how far his ship has traveled. This is an important judgment. If ocean currents and winds shift the direction of the outrigger even slightly from the direction intended by the navigator, the ship may pass the target island without sighting it. And if the navigator fails to realize that he has traveled the approximate distance to the island and continues to sail onward in the same direction he is likely to become lost in the vast Pacific. To keep this from happening the navigator must be able to estimate when he has reached the approximate distance to the target island. Then, if he has reached this distance and no island can be sighted, the navigator can turn and begin to search the nearby region for the island.

The problem, therefore, is to have a system by which distances can be estimated. The standard way this is done in western navigation is to estimate the speed at which the ship has been traveling and multiply the speed by the time traveled (distance = rate × time). If the ship has been traveling at different speeds, one must keep a record of how long the ship has been traveling at each speed and add together the distances (distance = [rate1 × time1] + [rate2 × time2] + . . .).

In Micronesia and Polynesia a completely different system of estimating distance has evolved which does not require the arithmetic and account keeping skills needed for western navigation. This system makes use of a *reference island* in estimating distances. For most pairs of islands navigators know of a reference island which lies fifty miles or so off the direct course between the islands and which is approximately equidistant from both the starting island and the destination island. In those rare cases in which there is no such island, a fictitious island is created.

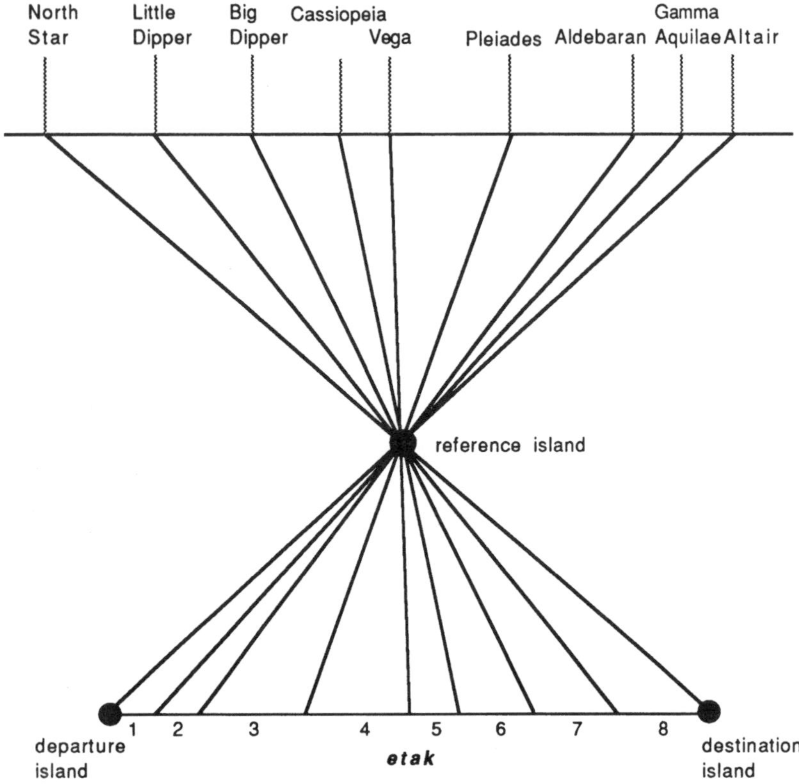

Figure 7.1 Star tracks – etic construction

The navigator cannot see the reference island during the trip. The use of the reference island is purely conceptual. What the navigator knows is the star course directions of the reference island. Consider the map given in Figure 7.1. As the outrigger moves from the departure island to the destination island, the star course directions to the reference island shift. The reference island is under the star Altair as the outrigger leaves the starting island. As the outrigger moves toward the destination island, the star course direction to the reference island will shift to Gamma Aquilae, then Aldebaran, then the Pleiades, then Vega, etc. Finally, when the outrigger reaches the destination island, the reference island will be under the North Star.

In this example, the shift of the reference island through different star tracks divides the journey into eight unequal segments. Each segment is called an *etak*. However, Hutchins has argued, the Carolinian navigator does picture his position with the kind of birds-eye view map illustrated in Figure 7.1. Instead of imagining the canoe traveling through one *etak* after another, what the

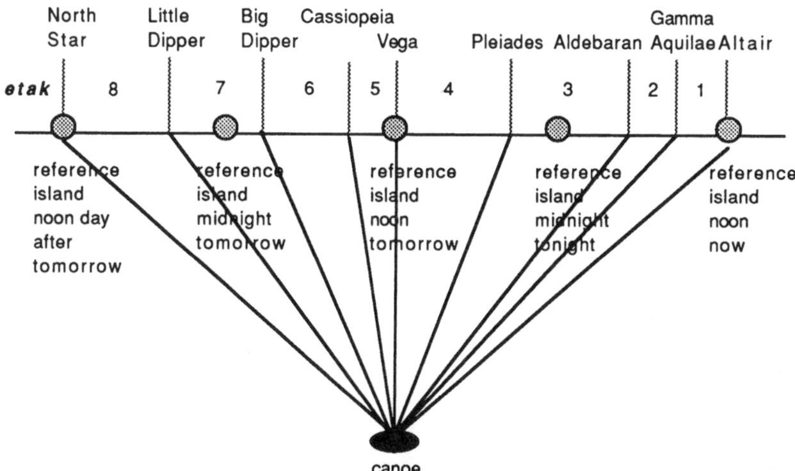

Figure 7.2 Star tracks – emic construction

navigator does is to visualize the canoe as the stationary center of the world. Seeing himself as stationary, the navigator pictures the world slipping by on either side of the canoe. In our example, the navigator would imagine the reference island at the start of the trip in front of the canoe under Altair. Then as the trip progresses, the navigator visualizes the reference island moving along the horizon until at the about the half-way point of the trip it would be to the immediate left side of the canoe under Vega. At the end of the trip the reference island would be pictured as if it had fallen to the rear of the canoe under the North Star as pictured in Figure 7.2. Thus the navigator continuously uses the imagined movement of the reference island along the horizon as an indicator of where he is.

The idea that the canoe is stationary and the islands are moving may seem strange at first, but actually it accords with the way things look when at sea. As one sails, the position of the stars and the sun do not change. What the sailor sees is a world in which the water around the canoe is moving back behind the canoe while the sun and stars stay fixed. The islands around the canoe, could they be seen, would also move on the horizon from front to back against the fixed framework of the sun and stars.

The mental construction of the reference island and *etak* segments does not guarantee that the navigator is where he thinks he is. What the *etak* segments do is give the navigator a way to *transform continuously* estimates of speed and time into estimates of position. Without using clocks or written records or the multiplication and addition of numbers, the *etak* schema makes it possible for the Caroline Island navigator to estimate continuously his relative position between the departure and the destination island.

Two basic elements in Caroline Island navigation are the star track schema and the reference island schema. Integrating these two schemas together makes it possible to create a model which produces the *etak* segments. With this model the navigator has at his disposal a conceptual scheme which allows him to estimate continuously where he is and how far he still has to go.

If, upon reaching the last *etak*, the navigator cannot see the destination island, or any of the shore bird life that indicates the nearby presence of the destination island, the navigator knows he has a problem – either he has underestimated the distance he has traveled, or he has strayed from the trip line. In either case, he knows corrective action has to be taken, and can bring to bear whatever other kinds of information he has about the way the trip has gone and the immediate appearance of the ocean to make a guess about the best course of action.

There is much more to the Caroline Island navigation system then presented here. However, what should be clear is, as Gladwin states:

> the contribution of etak is not to generate new primary information, but to provide a framework into which the navigator's knowledge of rate, time, geography, and astronomy can be integrated to provide a conveniently expressed and comprehended statement of distance travelled. It also helps keep his attention focused on these key variables which are central to the entire navigation process. It is a useful and deliberate logical tool for bringing together raw information and converting it into a solution of an essential navigational question: "How far away is our destination." (1970:186)

Together the star track compass, the reference island, and the *etak* segments create a multischematic model by which the navigator can estimate his position. This is an *explicit* model. The experts not only use the model, they also formulate in words and sand table arrangements the parts of the model and how the parts fit together to teach this model to students. Despite its explicit nature, however, everything about the model is not stated; Gladwin describes the situation as follows:

> Although Hipour and other navigators refer explicitly to a moving island when talking about *etak* or tacking, the larger logical context in which this concept operates is not described by them in words. This does not mean it is not real to them; it means only that they share and take for granted all the cognitive antecedents of saying that an island "moves." They find no need and therefore have had no practice in explaining this to someone like myself who starts out thinking of a voyage as a process in which everything is fixed except the voyager. The situation I suspect would be similar if an American, accomplished in interpreting the stylized symbols and distortions of a highway map, were asked to explain to our old friend the man from Mars what he really means when he points to the map and says, "We are here." (1970:181)

Cultural models were discussed by Clifford Geertz in the 1960s in his paper "Religion as a Cultural System," and reprinted in his book *The Interpretation of Cultures*. Unfortunately, Geertz limited cultural models to perceptible embodiments – external physical structures – and excluded internal, mental constructions. Geertz argued that anthropologists should not try to find out what is in people's heads, but rather should study public, out-there-in-the-world-for-all-to-see physical representations. For Geertz the kind of approach taken by cognitive anthropologists is "a mentalistic world of introspective psychology, or worse, speculative philosophy" where one wanders "forever in a haze of 'Cognitions,' 'Affections,' 'Conations' and other elusive entities" (1973:91).

The danger of getting lost amid elusive mental entities is real; just trying to develop a consistent and coherent vocabulary of cognitive structures is a difficult task, as much of this book makes apparent. But, in fact, there is no effective alternative. The physical embodiments of most cultural models do not lie in the perceptible world in a clump like Crown Jewels in the Tower. What the ethnographer sees and hears at different times and places are little bits of this and that, all of which must be put together into a coherent framework. And, given the impressive ability of humans to construct *something* out of almost anything, the question of psychological reality immediately arises – how do we know that the model constructed by the ethnographer is, in fact, a model for the native? Geertz, for example, developed a cultural model of Balinese personhood based on such observable cultural forms as naming practices, titles, and kinship terms, concluding that the Balinese have a "depersonalizing conception of personhood" (1973:391). But the reality of this model has been strongly challenged by another ethnographer of Bali, Unni Wikan (1987, 1989), who argues on the basis of intimate conversations she had with Balinese people about interpersonal loss and threat that the Balinese have a very vivid *personal* sense of themselves and others, but they mask their personal feelings behind a surface of aestheticism, grace, and gaiety in order not to offend and not to display vulnerability.

Such a discrepancy highlights the fact that the "depersonalizing conception of personhood" Geertz postulated is not a simple observable fact. It is an induction from many cultural practices to a *mental state* – a "conception." Geertz did not observe a model of Balinese personhood, he created a *theory* about the cognitive model Balinese use to represent personhood. The theory does not account for Wikan's data. If one accepts Wikan's data then one must either reject Geertz's theory or modify it so that it can account for the way the Balinese discuss their intimate affairs.

One can never be sure from observation *alone* what the native representation or cultural model is. Consider the *etak* model. Although one can directly observe the practice of navigation, could the entire model ever be constructed from the observation of practice alone? Even in the case of an explicated model such as this, where navigators explain the model to students, it is hard to be sure that one has it right. Gladwin, who wanted to understand the *cognitive* model used in Micronesian navigation, says:

> I arrived, through my own style of induction, at a description of the Puluwat navigator's cognitive map, the only description I could conjure up which would account for all the different things that a number of different people said in the course of trying to explain to me what *etak* was all about . . . Having arrived at this construct I explained it carefully to Hipour, as was my custom whenever I felt I had mastered a particular topic. He agreed in broad outline but made one modification, one which in itself encouraged me to believe he understood what I was saying. Later in talking with other people, and in particular when it came time for me to learn about navigation when tacking, I found my perception of the system could be used without leading to any more misunderstandings. In other words it made sense out of everything which followed, both familiar and new. It is for this reason in particular that I am satisfied the cognitive map I constructed is real. (1970:181)

The modification that Hipour made to Gladwin's description of the immobile canoe and the moving islands was to add that this was true only as long as the canoe was on course. If the canoe moves off course because of a storm or to chase fish, the canoe is then pictured as moving and the movement of the reference island ceases (1970:183).

Here Gladwin lays out two techniques for checking on the reality of a postulated cognitive model; first, describe the model to expert informants for their comment, and second, collect new kinds of data to see if the model still stands up. The natives learned the model; so can the ethnographer.

The model of the mind

A basic cultural model in all cultures is the representation of what happens inside people – in their minds, or psyches – that results in their doing what they do. The model of the mind described here is common among western cultures, and probably shares most of its parts and organization with a more general, universal model (D'Andrade 1987a). This model can be called a *folk model* because it contrasts in a number of ways with the expert model(s) of the mind found in psychology and philosophy.

There is some question about the naming of this model. Anna Wierzbicka (1992) points out that *mind* as a folk concept is focused primarily on thinking and does not include emotions, desires, or intentions. However, in Webster's *New International Dictionary* the term *mind* has a variety of related meanings; for philosophy and psychology *mind* is explicitly defined as "the agent in knowing, feeling, or taking any action." Furthermore, there is general agreement that thoughts, feelings, desires, perceptions, and intentions are *mental* states and processes, and according to Webster *mental* means "pertaining to the mind." But Wierzbicka is right; the default sense of *mind* centers on thought. The difficulty here is that upper level taxonomic terms (*animal*, *bush*, *mind*) are typically more ambiguous then basic level terms (*horse*, *lilac*, *think*), for all the information processing reasons discussed in Chapter 5.[3] Thus, despite the awkwardness of using the term *mind* in a special sense, *model of the mind* seems to be the most informative title. The alternatives – *model of the psyche* or *model of the person* – both sound odd; *psyche* is a word not in common use, while *person* includes not only *mind* but *body* and *social status*.

Like the *etak*, the model of the mind is used to navigate one's way through the world using unseen reference points, where the unseen reference points are the mental states of other persons. The problem is to predict and understand the actions and reactions of others. Consider the following simple experiment: a child is presented with a scenario in which a little girl named Sally puts a marble in her marble bag and then leaves the room. Then another little girl, Ann, comes into the room and takes the marble out of the bag and puts it in a box. The child is then asked where Sally will look for the marble when she returns. Children under four typically say that Sally will look in the box, while four year olds say that Sally will look in the marble bag (Wellman 1990).

What is it that the four year old knows and the three year old does not? Presumably the four year old realizes that Sally did not *see* the marble taken out of the bag and put in the box, therefore Sally could not *know* that the marble would be in the box, not the bag, therefore Sally would *believe* the marble was still in the bag, therefore when Sally *wanted* to get the marble she would go to where she *believed* the marble was, therefore Sally would look in the marble bag, not the box.

What the four year old has done here is to use a model of what happens inside people. In this model certain events in the environment affect things inside the person, and because of the way these things have affected the person, the person will be likely to act in certain ways. The three year old either does not know people look for things where they believe they are or does not realize that Sally will still *believe* the marble is in the bag and therefore look for the marble in the bag. From the adult viewpoint, the three year old's model of the mind is defective.[4]

3 It is probably because of the fact that upper level terms are not so firmly fixed by the structure of the world that cultures vary in such interesting ways with respect to terms like *mind*. Wierzbicka, for example, shows interesting relations to national character in the contrasts to be found between the Russian term *dusa*, the English terms *mind* and *soul*, and the German term *Seele* (1992:31-63).

4 For a thorough examination of exactly what the child knows about the mind, see Wellman 1990. The current evidence indicates that the three year old's problem is not a failure to understand the relationship between belief and desire, but rather a failure to understand that Sally cannot know the marble was moved. A good summary of the child's understanding of epistomology is found in Flavell 1988.

The five major parts of the model of the mind are distinctly lexicalized in English verbs and nouns: nominal headings for these five classes are *perception*, *thought*, *feeling*, *wish*, and *intention*. Basic level verbs for each of these parts are:[5]

1. Perceptions
   a. simple state – *see, hear, smell, taste*
   b. achieved state – *spot, sight, notice, perceive, sense*
   c. simple process – *look, observe, watch, listen, touch, remember*
2 Thoughts
   a. simple state – *believe, know, doubt, suspect*
   b. achieved state – *understand, realize, infer, conclude, forget*
   c. simple process – *reason, think about, expect*
   d. accomplished process – *infer, learn, find out, discover, guess*
3. Feelings/emotions
   a. simple state – *love, like, fear, hate, blame, approve, pity, itch, lust*
   b. achieved state – *forgive, surprise, be scared, be angered*
   c. simple process – *enjoy, mourn, feel sad, feel tired, ache*
4. Wishes
   a. simple state – *want to, desire, like to, feel like, need*
   b. achieved state – *choose, select*
   c. simple process – *wish, hope*
5. Intentions
   a. simple state – *intend to, aim to, mean to, plan to*
   b. achieved state – *decide to, resolve to*

It is interesting that the English verbs for five of the six categories contain both *process* and *state* verbs (Vendler 1967). A process is something that consists of repetitive actions; one can ". . . ing" a process verb to form the progressive tense. Thus we can say John is *looking*, *reasoning*, *mourning*, etc., just as we can say John is *walking*, *talking*, *eating*, etc., because a process is involved. However, it is odd to say that John is *believing*, or *liking*, or *needing* something. These verbs are usually conceived of as states of mind, not processes. Because they are relatively permanent states of mind, one can say of a sleeping person while she is sleeping that she *believes*, *likes*, or *needs* something, but usually not that she is *reasoning about* or *enjoying* or *expecting* something (however, she may be *dreaming* about something).

These grammatical distinctions are very tricky. If one says "I am smelling a rose," *smelling* is being treated as a process and one can imagine taking lots of big sniffs at the rose. If one says "I smell a rose," one means that one is in a mental state in which some rose has a smell. Part of the difficulty is that when we think about perceptions, we imagine to ourselves a process, but when we

[5] The model here is changed slightly from the model presented in *Cultural Models in Language and Thought*. "Resolutions" are not treated here as a major part of the model, and "feelings" have been expanded to cover body sensations.

use perception verbs, we characterize ourselves as in a state. We say "I see a rose," not "I am seeing a rose." The last sounds like either a philosopher or some man who is dating a very special woman.

The fact that English verbs for mental events can be either process verbs or state verbs indicates that the folk model conceptualizes the mind as both a *processor* and a *container.* As a processor the mind engages in the processes of *looking*, *reasoning*, *enjoying*, and *wanting;* as a container the mind holds what it *sees*, *believes*, *loves* and *wishes*. The same mental event can be either a *state* or a *process;* the choice appears to depend on whether one is focusing on the ongoing activity or on the enduring result. Intentions, however, have only state verbs; perhaps because intentions are one-time things they cannot be iterated, and hence they cannot be spoken of in a progressive tense.

There is another grammatical contrast in English verbs based on whether an event is defined throughout the total time involved or only by some climax or terminal point. *Realizing* something is an *achieved state*; no matter how long one has been pondering, *realization* does not come until the instant one *realizes* it. The concept here is defined by its end point. Similarly, *figuring out* something is an *accomplished process* which does not happen until it is *figured out*. One can ask "How long did it take to *realize/figure out* that?" but not "How long did it take to *believe/think about* that?" Achieved states and accomplished processes are defined by their climax, while simple states and process are homogeneous throughout. This contrast treats the mind as something which can be constant through periods of time, but can also come to sudden end points where an abrupt change takes place (Vendler 1967).

The six major classes of mental events are not independent of each other. There is a major direction of causation which runs from *perception* to *thought* to *feeling* to *wish* to *intention* to *action*. This is easiest to describe by running the causal chain backward:

action:	Why did James yell at Harry?
intention:	He was trying to get his attention.
	Why was he trying to get Harry's attention?
wish:	Because he wanted to distract him from his game and make him lose.
	Why did he want to distract Harry from his game and make him lose?
feeling:	Because it makes him mad to see Harry win.
	Why does it make him mad to see Harry win?
thought	Because he thinks Harry is too conceited.
	Why does he think Harry is conceited?
perception	Because he has heard Harry boasting all over the place about how great he is.

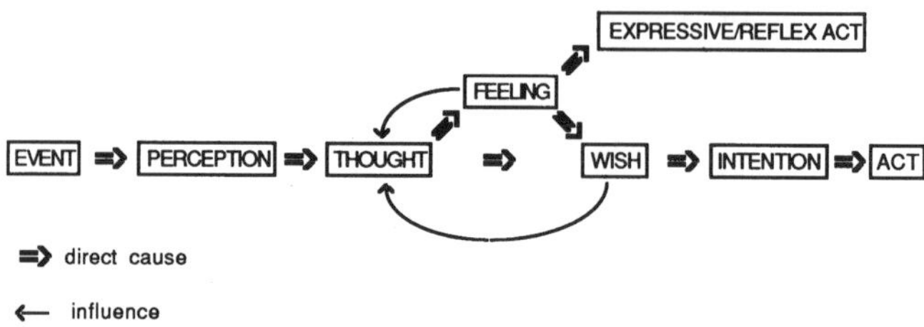

Figure 7.3 Some causal relations in mental processes in the folk model

In this example the action – yelling – is intended. But not all actions in the folk model are intended. There is a category of reflex actions, like sneezing, and a category of expressive actions, like smiling and crying, which are not under voluntary control (although one can smile and some people can even cry "on purpose"). Reflex and expressive actions are thought to be caused by a salient feeling or emotion – James might be yelling because something fell on his foot.

The diagram in Figure 7.3 presents the default situation; given no other information it is assumed that causation runs as pictured by the double arrows. To illustrate the alternative pathways from thought to wish, consider the possibility that James wants to make Harry lose the game not because he is angry at Harry, but just because he thinks it would be a good thing if Harry learned to lose. In such a case, James' wish is not due to some feeling, but to a belief about what is right.

Not all mental events follow this diagram. Sometimes, for instance, one may have a thought, or a feeling, or a wish "for no reason" which means that there is no belief or perception which accounts for why we feel something or want something. But when strong and persistent feelings and desires occur "without reason," they are considered "abnormal."

Under certain conditions parts of the chain presented in Figure 7.3 are skipped. If a person sees that they are about to be hit by a car, for example, they may leap out of the way without even thinking about it or feeling anything or experiencing any kind of wish. Such an act is intentional, however, not just a reflex – one meant to get out of the way. Anscombe (1963), an English natural language philosopher, calls this "intention in action."

The chain of causation in Figure 7.3 also leaves out certain kinds of within-category causation; in the folk model thoughts can cause other thoughts, feelings can give rise to other feelings, and wishes can lead to other wishes. Another important addition to the default chain of causation, indicated in Figure 7.3 with curved single line arrows, is that sometimes causation runs "backwards." That is, sometimes desires and feelings can influence what one thinks about things. This reversal of the normal causal order is generally thought to be bad – one's beliefs should not be influenced by desires and feelings. Those people whose thoughts are often influenced by their desires and feelings are considered foolish. No matter how much one wants to win the lottery, it would be *weak minded* to think that one's chances are better than anyone else's.

The folk model also contains the idea that under some conditions desires and feelings can even influence perception. But here the mechanism is complex – some unusual physical crisis, such as a high fever, or drugs, or some unspecified "mental breakdown" causes the normally tight link between the real world and perception to be broken, resulting in hallucinations. Once the link between the real world and perception is broken, then what one wishes or how one feels can easily affect the content of the hallucination. This also happens in the natural process of dreaming.

Another major characteristic of the folk model is that most of the things that happen in the mind are thought to be *conscious*. Or, to put it another way, according to the model, what happens in the mind are various events which can be perceived just as external events can. Unlike the psychodynamic model of the mind which holds that thoughts, desires, and even intentions can be unconscious, the folk model allows only for a certain haziness. In the folk model you might be angry at someone and not really recognize your anger, but if you talked about how you felt about that person, you would probably realize you were angry. And you might want to hurt that person but deny that you really did, but at the back of your mind you would really know it. In the folk model there does not appear to be a real unconscious, only a kind of myopia about certain mental states.

The conscious, perceiving center of awareness and agency is the *self*. However, in the folk model the self is a composite entity; it is composed of both a conscious, aware *perceiver* and a thing that is perceived as doing the perceiving. William James called the *perceiver* the "I" and the entity perceived the "me." The *perceiving self* not only observes things in the world, it also perceives that it is perceiving – that is, it is *conscious*. The *perceiving self* has a continuing identity through time; it knows that it is the same *perceiving self* that it was aware of across previous observations – it observes that it is the same observer that was observing before.

Most people have a single, continuing *perceiving self* throughout their life. Each *perceiving self* is separate and distinct; the *perceiving self* which is *me* can never be *you*. The *perceiving self* is also unique, since no other *perceiving self* can have the same perceptions, thoughts, and memories.

The other half of the self is the *perceived self*. The two halves are inseparable; there cannot be a perceived self with a perceiving self, and there cannot be a perceiving self that has nothing about itself to perceive.

The perceived self in the folk model has an onion-like character with many layers which can be peeled away. That is, one can say "I want a cigarette"; here the center of awareness and agency includes the desire. Or, one can say "I'm going crazy for a cigarette." Here the desire is treated as outside the self; acting on the self. "The thought struck me" and "I was overcome by my feelings" are other examples of phrases where the process of thinking and the process of feeling are treated as outside the self. However, intentions are *always* within the self – an intention *is* the self deciding to act.

For most people, their body is an important part of their *perceived self*, but there are people who say that they feel that their actual body is not really their self – that they are really a woman, not a man, or really young, not the old person you see. Also the *perceiving self* sometimes notices inconsistencies in what it thinks, likes, wants, feels, etc. These inconsistencies can lead to a sense of being "divided," "fragmented," etc., and sometimes thoughts and feelings are said to be experienced as "not really me" as if the *perceiving self* was experiencing someone else. However, the normal-expectation is that one's body, one's past actions, one's perceptions, thoughts, feelings, desires, and intentions are part of oneself. The *real self*, discussed in Chapter 6, is that part of the *perceived self* which is not divided or fragmented, but which is a natural and spontaneous source of thought, feeling, and desire.

The *perceived self* cannot only contract, it can expand. Certain things and certain people can become a part of the self in the sense that the things that happen to these things and people are experienced as happening to the *perceived self* – my child is hurt and I feel the hurt, my country is insulted and I feel insulted, my car is admired and I feel good. This expansion of the self is linguistically coded in the first person plural pronoun forms *we*, *us*, and *our* in which some aspect of identity is shared.

The total self is thought to be able to control actions – most of what one does one intends to do, so one *could* have decided to do differently. However, although one is not able to control what one feels or desires, because one can control what one thinks, one can (sometimes) affect what one feels or wants by not thinking of the things that give rise to these feelings or wants. Thought is also important in creating the objects of desire; generally speaking one can only want what one can think of (however, sometimes one wants something without knowing what one wants).

It is interesting that the folk model acknowledges that many events can happen which are not predicted on the basis of the model. In hypnosis, one can be induced to "not see" what is in front of ones eye's, and to "see things" that are not there. In depression, one has feelings of despair that have no rational source. However, such events do not challenge the truth of the model. Instead such events are defined as "abnormal"; the sort of thing that happens in "depression" or "addiction" or "compulsion" or "fever" or "hypnosis" or "mental breakdown." By defining what it fails to explain as abnormal, the folk model protects itself from falsification. The folk model may have a good deal of truth to it, but it is not science.

The folk model of the mind is quite complex. A number of additional propositions about this model are presented in my paper in *Cultural Models in Language and Thought*. However, the major outlines of the model should be clear. Like the model used in Caroline navigation, the folk model of the mind has a number of parts which are interrelated, and it is the relationships among these parts that are used in figuring out why it is that someone did something, or what it is that someone is likely to do given that something happened. We use what we know about the past history of someone's beliefs, feeling, and desires to understand and predict that person's actions, filling in the missing gaps with a wealth of specific propositions about how the mind works.

The data for this description of the folk model comes from a variety of sources. I have used my own intuitions, work in the philosophy of mind, and interviews with informants to formulate the model. Some of these interview materials are presented in the paper in *Cultural Models in Language and Thought*. Overall, I feel relatively sure that the major categories of perception, thought, feeling, wish, and intention correspond to psychologically salient schemas of ordinary Americans (although the distinction between wish and feeling is not as clearly worked out as I think it could be). I feel less secure about causative relations between the categories, the nature of consciousness, the way in which the objects of feeling and desire relate to thought, and the expansive and contractive nature of the self. The problem here is not so much in finding answers once a question arises; it is in trying to formulate the right questions.

A question arises concerning the truth of the folk model. One explanation for why we have the folk model that we do might be that this is simply the way the mind works, and by introspection we directly "see" how it works. If true, there is little left for psychology to do except add embellishments to the already existing model. Another position is that the folk model is quite wrong and that introspection is untrustworthy. This is the position of most psychologists, who believe that the folk model will eventually be replaced by a scientific model. A more radical position is held by philosophers like Paul and Patricia Churchland who believe that the upper level folk model will be replaced by a lower level neurological model of brain processes (Paul Churchland 1979). This seems unlikely; Robert McCauley (1986), a philosopher of science, has pointed out that the history of science reveals *no* case in which a lower level theory has replaced or eliminated an upper level theory. A third position is that the folk model of the mind described here is purely a construction of western culture and that models of the mind of non-western cultures would be quite different.

There is some evidence that while non-western models of the mind are not identical to the western model, they are quite similar to it. Wierzbicka says:

> Findings of cross-linguistic semantic investigations show that much of the folk model presented above ("our own folk psychology"; cf. D'Andrade 1987[a]) corresponds in fact to the folk model operating in any other culture of the world: despite the very considerable differences between different folk psychologies that have been described in the literature, the idea of a "person" who "thinks," "wants," "feels," and "knows" (as well as "says" and "does" various things) appears to be universal. The fact that all languages appear to have words for all these concepts (though not for "believe" or "desire," as distinct from "think" and "want") provides evidence for the universality of this model. (1993:212-213)

Catherine Lutz (1985) has summarized the ethnopsychological knowledge of the people of Ifaluk, a small atoll located in the Western Caroline Islands. The general framework of both models is similar, with a division of internal states into thoughts, feelings, and desires. However, on Ifaluk the distinctions are made less sharply, and one of the two major terms used to describe mental states covers both thought and emotion, rather like the way the English word *feel* can be used both to refer to emotions ("I feel sad") and to thoughts ("I feel you should stay home"). The people of Ifaluk also differ from the western folk model in locating mental processes primarily in the gut and in being more consistent in making the distinction between emotions and physical sensations; thus they distinguish with separate words the physical sensations of hunger, pain, and sexual arousal from the emotions that follow from these physical states.

Another study of a non-western model of the mind has been carried out by Steven Parish (1991), who worked among the Newar of Nepal. The Newar also have a similar framework of verbs of perception, thought, feeling, and desire. According to the Newar, mental states and processes reside primarily in the heart. Parish stresses that for the Newar, mind, self, and emotions are *sacred* and *moral*. Just as there are gods in the outer world, so too is there in everyone's heart a god. For Hindu informants, the heart god is called Narayana or Bhagaban, an avatar of Vishnu. It is the power of the god that makes it possible to recall and visualize things when one's eyes are shut. The heart god does more than explain behavior; it represents and invokes the moral order within. One informant said: "You think of the god who dwells in the heart and [you] act. Don't do wrong acts. If you do something wrong this Narayana who dwells in the heart will curse you. The Narayana who dwells in the heart will curse you. Curse, meaning rebuke". (1991:319).

The Newar model of the mind includes the description of two emotions, *lajya* and *pastae*, which have strong moral connotations. *Lajya* involves a kind of moral shame or embarrassment, felt when one is caught in a lie or seen doing something improper. *Pastae* is similar to *lajya*, but is felt after something wrong is done, usually harm to another. It seems to be a kind of guilt, or strong moral remorse. Along with these moral emotions, the Newar have a rich variety of ideas about self-control, the control of desire, and the painfulness of giving in to improper desires. Among the Newar, workings of the mind are directly related to the Hindu religious system, and this gives their model a special quality. As Parish says:

> To point out that models found in different cultures make similar assumptions about the categories or organization of mental experience is not to say that the ways in which these assumptions are fleshed out, represented, and reconstructed in particular cultures do not make a difference. They do . . . Newar concepts of a psychologically active and morally sensitive "heart," their vision of a moral god animating and inhabiting this heart-mind, and their cultural experience of moral emotions, all help articulate a concept of the moral person. These ideas build on, and elaborate, the notion that "self" can passively experience – and yet actively evaluate – thoughts and feelings originated by other parts of the self. This "self" integrates a capacity for self-knowledge and self-control (however problematic) with sensitivity to moral emotions . . . Newar concepts of mind help Newars know that "the person" is constituted as a moral being, with an "inner" life that participates in the moral and sacred. (1991:345–346)

Comparing the Caroline navigation model and the western model of the mind, it is apparent that the two models are quite different in the ways they are learned and the ways in which they are embodied. The navigation model is learned by explicit instruction and demonstration, and many of its parts, such as the star tracks and the reference island, consist of physical objects. The model of the mind is not learned by direct instruction; I doubt that any child is ever told "Desires are often caused by feelings, and are not subject to control by the self." Much of the folk model of the mind is deeply embodied in the lexicon of natural language, so that in learning the language the child learns the great distinctions between perception, cognition, affect, motivation, and intention. Also, as the philosopher Zeno Vendler (1972) has pointed out,[6] there is a close correspondence between the kinds of speech acts found in natural language and these same categories. Only the speech act category of *declarations* is unmatched by a specific mental process/state.[7]

Speech act categories		*Mental processes*
Representatives	<==>	Thoughts
I hereby state, claim, deduce...		I think, believe, infer . . .
Directives	<==>	Wishes
I hereby order, request, invite...		I want, need, wish for . . .
Commissives	<==>	Intentions
I hereby promise, vow, commit . . .		I intend to, aim to, plan to . . .
Expressives	<==>	Feelings
I hereby apologize, commend . . .		I feel sorry that, proud of . . .

6 For a review of different classifications of speech acts, see D'Andrade and Wish 1985.

7 A *declaration* is a speech act in which some entity is brought into existence by being declared – "I pronounce you husband and wife," "I christen thee 'James'," etc.

What this correspondence does is give an external structure by which internal mental states can be identified. That is, what are wishes? Wishes are what directives express. Thoughts are what representatives express. Intentions are what commissives express. And feelings are what expressives express. To learn to use these speech act categories is to learn the identity of the mental processes which they express.

Stories about people are another way in which the model of the mind is physically embodied; the basic schema which has been worked out for narratives by Jean Mandler (1984) and others specifically contains the links between the perception of some event (called the *setting*), the desire or feeling aroused because of that event (called the *reaction*), and the action taken (called the *attempt*).

In fact, the model of the mind is so deeply embedded in everything we say that most of the time we do not explicitly reference large parts of the model because everyone knows these parts and can fill in the gaps. We say "Jean's mother fainted and she called the paramedics." We do not need to say that Jean *saw* her mother faint, that she *realized* that she had fainted, that she reacted with *fear* for her mother's health, that she *wanted to* do something to help her mother, that she *knew* that the paramedics could help her mother, and that she called the paramedics with the *intention* of helping her mother, because we can fill in all that. The model of the mind is *intersubjectively shared* by all competent members of our culture; that is, we know that others know the model, and we know that they know that we know the model. Because the model is intersubjectively shared, we do not need to state the obvious.

The Caroline navigation model is an expert's model. It is not shared with everyone. Gladwin does not tell us whether or not most crew members know the model well enough to develop intersubjectivity about the model with their navigator; it seems likely that they do. But still the number who know the model is small. The navigator's model is more like the model of the mind held by a trained psychiatrist. Both are learned late in life with considerable difficulty, requiring lengthy direct verbal instruction, but unlearnable without a great deal of practice doing the real thing.

Despite these many differences, the navigation model and the folk model of the mind are alike in certain crucial respects. Both are used to figure things out. The way the parts of the model are put together is believed in both cases to be the same as the way the world is put together, so that by relating the parts to each other one can figure out how things in the world are likely to be related to each other. Also, both are *multischematic*; that is, both models are composed of a number of separate schemas. In the case of the navigation model the results of using the star track schema, the reference island schema, and the *etak* schema are integrated together into a constantly changing image in which the reference island moves from *etak* to *etak*. It is this output which is the final result of the model. In the case of the model of the mind, there are separate schemas for events, perceptions, thoughts, feelings, desires, intentions, and actions. Given

Table 7.1. *Characteristics of marriage commonly expressed in metaphor*

1. Sharedness
We are together in this.
I felt like marriage was just a partnership.
2. Lastingness
It was stuck together pretty good.
We feel pretty confident about being able to continue that way.
3. Mutual benefit
That was something we got out of marriage
Our marriage is a very good thing for both of us.
4. Compatibility
The best thing about Bill is that he fits me so well.
Both of our weaknesses were such that the other person could fill in.
5. Difficulty
That was one of the hard barriers to get over.
The first year we were married was really a trial.
6. Effort
She works harder at our marriage than I do.
We had to fight our way back almost to the beginning.
7. Success or failure
We know that it was working.
The marriage may be doomed.
8. Risk
There are so many odds against marriage.
The marriage was in trouble.

some input – some specific information about some of these states, such as "Her mother fainted and she called the paramedics" – the causal chain can be used to produce any of a number of outputs; what the actor wanted, or how she probably felt, or what she must have known.

The American model of marriage

These two models contrast with a third ethnographic example, the American model of marriage, studied by Naomi Quinn (1987). Quinn carried out extensive non-directive interviews with a small sample of American husbands and wives from North Carolina. Husbands and wives were interviewed separately and asked to talk about their marriages. About fifteen hours of tape recorded interview were obtained from each informant. Working from the transcriptions of the interviews, Quinn used a number of techniques to formulate her informants' model of marriage, including the semantic analysis of key words, like *commitment*, *love*, and *fulfillment*, the categorization of metaphors, and the analysis of the informants' reasoning about marriage.

Eight major characteristics, expressed in a rich variety of metaphors, were used by informants to talk about marriage. Examples of each of these characteristics are presented in Table 7.1. It is striking that in many hundreds of metaphoric characterizations of marriage, these eight classes account for *all* instances. Putting together these characterizations of marriage with the stories and other talk of informants, Quinn outlines the following model:

In Americans' model of it, marriage is expected to be *shared*, *mutually beneficial*, and *lasting* . . . this particular constellation of expectations derives from the mapping of our cultural conception of love onto the institution of marriage and the consequent structuring of marital expectations in terms of the motivational structure of love. Because people want to be with the person they love, they want and expect marriage to be *shared;* because they want to fulfill the loved person's needs and have their own needs fulfilled by that person, they want and expect marriage to be *beneficial* to both spouses in the sense of mutually fulfilling; and because they do not want to lose the person they love, but want that person to go on loving them forever, people want and expect their marriages to be *lasting*.

The remainder of the cultural model of marriage reflected in the metaphors for *compatibility*, *difficulty*, *effort*, *success* or *failure*, and *risk*, derives from a contradiction that arises inevitably between the expectation of *mutual benefit* and that of *lastingness*. Fulfillment of the spouses' needs, the expected benefit of marriage, is understood in terms of the *mutual benefit* expected of all voluntary relationships. Just as in other such relationships, if one individual or the other is not benefiting from this one – not experiencing fulfillment – he or she is free to leave it. However, another understanding . . ., one special to marriage, is that it is not supposed to end. (Italics added) (1991:66–67)

Thus the three central characteristics of *sharedness*, *mutual benefit*, and *lastingness* are based on the expectable outcome of a love-based relationship, while the characteristics of *compatibility*, *difficulty*, *effort*, *success* or *failure*, and *risk* are expected outcomes of the fact that marriage is a voluntary relationship plus the fact that it is hard to maintain a high level of mutual benefit in any relationship.

This model of marriage contains not only the standard American understandings of what marriage is – a love-based relationship in which people share their lives with the hope that the relationship will be a lasting one despite the difficulties of trying to maintain mutual benefit – but also a guide or map to what has happened, is happening, and may happen in the future to oneself and one's spouse.

The following is a quote from one of Quinn's informants.

I think during some of Tom's and I – during some of the most difficult passages that we had when we have really despaired in a sense and thought, "This – we are going to be driven apart by all our problems," including, you know, our problems with each other, and one of the things we have both thought is that, "If I know Tom as well as I know him and love him as much as I love him and still have this much trouble being married to him, what in the world chance would I have of finding anybody else who would be any easier to be married to and I wouldn't know that person any better when I got – married him than I knew Tom."(1987:173-174)[8]

[8] The following analysis of Nan's statements is taken from Quinn 1987.

Here we see a part of the model in action. The informant, called Nan, begins with an introductory scenario. The scenario consists of past situations in which both spouses have had the despairing thought that "we are going to be driven apart by all our problems." Nan assumes the hearer understands that being "driven apart" would destroy the sharedness of a marriage, and therefore destroy the marriage. About this thought Nan and her husband have a complex reaction. Broken into its parts and unstated assumptions, it can be paraphrased as follows:

(1) I know and love my spouse [which would make you think there would be so much mutual benefit that it would be easy to be with each other]
(2) [yet] I have trouble being married to him [not because of something particular about him, but because there are always compatibility problems in marriage]
(3) [and since I don't right now have a deep acquaintance with someone else who might be a substitute for my current spouse] the someone else would be someone I do not know any better than I knew my spouse when we first got married
(4) therefore, I have no real chance of finding someone else who would be easier to be married to
(5) [and therefore I should stay in the marriage]

Here the model forms a framework within which the argument is made. The assumptions that love should lead to *mutual benefit*, that a marriage can not be a marriage without a *shared* life (not being "driven apart"), that there are always problems of *compatibility*, are part of the standard model. Nan uses these assumptions in her reasoning, putting them together with the idea that *mutual benefit* requires knowing a lot about each other, to reach the conclusion that the problems would be as bad or worse with anyone else so she and her husband should stay married.

Of course, Nan could use the same model of marriage to come to very different conclusions. If she thought that the problems of compatibility were due to some special fault of her husband, and that there was nothing she could do to make the marriage mutually beneficial, then she might conclude that their problems with each other would eventually drive them apart, and that the marriage would not be lasting, and that therefore she should get out of it now. Given the American model of marriage, a crucial determination concerns whether or not the difficulties experienced are based on an incompatibility that makes an acceptable level of mutual benefit impossible. We know Nan's evaluation on this point not because she states it explicitly, but because she makes the assumption that no one other than Tom would be easier to be married to. That is, if something particular to Tom was to blame, then there would be other men who would be easier to be married to. Since she tells us that she believes there are not, we know she is letting us know she does not believe that Tom is the source of the problem.

In carrying out her analyses, Quinn found that her informants bring a number of models beside the model of marriage to bear in understanding their marital situations. A well-elaborated model of *utilitarian exchange* is used to understand mutual benefit and compatibility.Three distinct models of *personhood* are used by Quinn's informants – the person as *human being* (with the rights of a human being), the person as an *occupant of social roles* (daughter, teacher, etc.), and the person as a *possessor of attributes* (hardworking, generous, etc.) (Quinn 1992). The overall picture is of a complex system of interrelated models, some which are hierarchically organized in part-whole relationships, others which are loosely associated as participants in the same body of problems and decisions.

The model of marriage and the model of the mind are similar in that both models are learned informally, without direct instruction. It seems to be a characteristic of informally learned models that people are much better at *using* such models than describing them. Informants usually can give a partial account of the model, especially if asked a specific question about how a piece of the model works. But they typically cannot provide an over-all account of the model; the model seems more like a set of *procedures* they know how to use than like *declarative* knowledge they can state.

To date, no anthropologist has taken an inventory of all the models used in any one culture. This is probably too large a task ever to be practical. However, it might be possible to determine the basic models used in a culture that concerned a single domain, such as human relationships, or recreation, or sailing. The problem with such a cognitive ethnography is that, at present, working out just a single model takes a large amount of time. I estimate that most of the cultural models described in *Cultural Models in Language and Thought* took over a year of research and analysis. Most of these models were taken from American culture, in which the anthropologist has the advantage of already knowing the language and understanding the culture. It would probably take two or three times as much time to carry out the equivalent analyses in a different language.

The idea that no ethnographic endeavor should take more than a year or so of research is based on the practical requirements of academic life. Cognitive ethnography is hard to do; it requires systematic data collection and intensive analysis. However, because the work is potentially cumulative, the task of describing a culture can be done by many people sharing each other's results. In time, there will be cognitive ethnographies of whole domains from a variety of cultures, but they will be multiperson projects containing work done over many years.

Cultural theories

A cultural theory consists of an interrelated set of propositions which describe the nature of some general phenomena. Several things distinguish cultural models from cultural theories. First, the propositions of a cultural theory are statements which are made by the natives, unlike the propositions of many cultural models, which are typically assertions by the analyst of the way people represent something based on the way they reason or their understanding about it, or which is implicit in what they say about it. While the knowledge which makes up a cultural model often is procedural in character, a cultural theory is made up primarily of declarative knowledge, which means that one can ask directly about the phenomena in question and receive direct answers. Also, cultural theories are often about very general and abstract topics, like the origin of life or the character of the supernatural, and the propositions which describe this topic may be only loosely related to each other.

Most standard ethnographies contain a number of descriptions of cultural theories. Religion and the supernatural are especially fertile fields for cultural theories, which can range from the formal doctrines of the immaculate conception or the trinity to informal theories about channeling spirits or folk beliefs about the nature of heaven. One of the classic works in anthropology, Evans-Pritchard's *Azande Witchcraft*, contains an extensive analysis of witchcraft as a cultural theory. Perhaps religious and supernatural matters are so often found in the form of cultural theories rather than cultural models because the only way this kind of phenomena can be learned is by direct verbal statement.

While the general propositions of a cultural theory are relatively easy to discover, since people know them and use them, working out with precision what people believe can be quite tricky. A major problem is determining which theory takes precedence when theories conflict. For example, in a national survey, 89% supported the statement

> I believe in free speech for all no matter what their views might be.

However, when asked

> Should a community allow the American Nazi party to use its town hall to hold a public meeting?
> __ Yes
> __ No

only 18% said yes (McClosky and Brill 1983). The problem here is to understand why the strongly supported right to free speech should be limited in this particular context. It is likely that the conflicting theory in this case involves the notion that one should not give aid to those doing undesirable things. That is, the use of community property may imply that the community is lending aid to or sponsoring Nazis. One would need further research to discover exactly why the consideration of giving assistance to those having undesirable views weighs so heavily against the right of free speech. The general point is that to understand a cultural theory requires more than just a formulation of its general principles; it also requires understanding what the theory is applied to and how it relates to other theories.

The cultural theory of conventionality

There is an interesting controversy between Richard Shweder and Elliot Turiel concerning cultural theories of morality. Turiel, a psychologist, has developed a theory of morality which holds that children come to learn that some rules are *conventional*, and that such rules are understood to be arbitrary, relative, and alterable, involving less serious issues (like chewing gum in school, calling the judge "your honor," etc.). Children also learn that some other rules are *moral*, which means that the rules involve more serious issues relating to harm, justice, rights, and the allocation of resources, and that such rules are seen as rational, universal, and unalterable.

Turiel holds that these two theories – a theory about morality and theory about conventionality – are found universally (Turiel, Killen, and Helwig 1987). Shweder, in a study with Manamohan Mahapatra and Joan Miller (1990), attempted to find out whether or not these two contrasting theories are also found in India. They studied a sample of Indian children and adults from a temple town in Orissa to see if they showed the same learning pattern as American children and adults from Hyde Park, Chicago, with respect to these two theories. Comparable questions were asked of respondents from both cultures concerning thirty-nine practices (e.g. one of your family eats a dog regularly for dinner, a brother and a sister decide to get married and have children, a father told his son to steal flowers from his neighbor's garden, etc.). The questions were:

1. Is (*the behavior under consideration*) wrong?
2. How serious is the violation?
   (a) not a violation
   (b) a minor offense
   (c) a somewhat serious offense
   (d) a very serious violation
3. Is it a sin?
4. What if no one knew this had been done. It was done in private or secretly. Would it be wrong then?
5. Would it be best if everyone in the world followed (*the rule endorsed by the informant*)? [UNIVERSAL VS. RELATIVE]
6. In (*name of a relevant society*) people do (*the opposite of the practice endorsed by the informant*) all the time. Would (*name of relevant society*) be a better place if they stopped doing that? [UNIVERSAL VS. RELATIVE]
7. What if most people in (*name of informant's society*) wanted to (*change the practice*). Would it be okay to change it? [UNALTERABLE VS. ALTERABLE]
8. Do you think a person who does (*the practice under consideration*) should be stopped from doing that or punished in some way?

Table 7.2. *Percentage of moral and conventional responses for two cultural practices by culture and age group*

	Practice	
	Twenty-five year old son addresses father by first name	Family member eats beef regularly
Brahman children		
Moral	75	77
Conventional	6	0
Brahman adults		
Moral	87	82
Conventional	0	0
American children		
Moral	85	90
Conventional	10	5
American adults		
Moral	20	44
Conventional	30	20

Note: moral = universal and unalterable
conventional = relative and alterable

In Table 7.2 are results for two illustrative practices adapted from Shweder, Mahapatra, and Miller's data.

The percentages do not add to 100 because some respondents show neither a purely moral or purely conventional pattern of response. The small sample of practices presented in Table 7.2 reflects the general trend found for all thirty-nine practices; Indians generally do not consider their cultural practices to be conventions, while Americans consider *some* of their practices conventional. Around 20% of Indian children and adults seem to think that it might be all right for people in *other* societies to do certain things differently concerning food, clothes, and forms of address. However, they do not think it would be all right for *their* society to change these practices.

From these results it would seem that Indian culture lacks a theory of conventionality. Shweder, Mahapatra, and Miller argue that Indian culture has a duty-based approach to human relations which assumes that social arrangements have moral significance and that a differentiated, hierarchical social structure is part of the natural order of things. Within this framework, cultural practices are seen as god given, following moral law, leaving little room for a theory of conventionality containing ideas about how cultural differences come about by history and chance or how cultural practices change because of fad and fashion.

However, the question of conventionality in India is not entirely closed. Turiel, Killen, and Helwig argue that Shweder *et al*'s method of defining conventionality may bias the results; for example, 44% of his sample of

American adults seem to think it best that everybody in the world eat beef, and that it would not be permissible to change this. By Shweder *et al*'s definition, this makes eating beef a *moral* practice. But it seems more likely that many Americans simply believe that eating beef is good for you – the universality and unalterability of the goodness of beef eating come from its putative nutritional status, not the morality of eating it. Perhaps by redefining how *conventionality* is determined and selecting other practices, one might find more evidence for an Indian theory of conventionality. However, one can guess from Shweder's results that even if a theory of conventionality were found in India, it would be limited in its range of application.

This example of research on theories of conventionality and morality illustrates how complex the determination of cultural theories can be. In this example we see that the questions used and the range of things asked about need to be selected with care, and that even the best research does not get absolute answers.

The theory of essences

It is a common belief, found in many western cultures, that certain things are the way they are because of some *essence*. Thus, tigers are said to have a certain essence which makes them tigers, which is not the same thing as the various properties tigers have, like stripes, tails, whiskers, claws, etc. One can bleach the stripes, clip the tail, whiskers and claws, yet the creature still has the essential property of being a tiger. Slightly differing doctrines of essence have been propounded by Aristotle, Aquinas, and various Scholastics: the general doctrine has been attacked by Locke and other empiricists, as Bertrand Russell outlines in his *History of Western Philosophy.*

There is disagreement about the source of this cultural theory. One position holds that over many hundreds of thousands of generations, humans and their primate ancestors have interacted with plants and animals, with the result that the recognition that plants and animals are segregated into natural kinds has become innate in the sense that humans learn that plants and animals form natural kinds with a special ease and readiness. Scott Atran says:

> Humans, let us suppose, are endowed with highly articulated cognitive faculties for "fast-mapping" the world they evolved in, and for which their minds were selected. The "automatic" taxonomic ordering of phenomenal species, like the spontaneous relational ordering of colors, would then be a likely product of one such faculty.(1990:65)

> Humans appear to be inherently disposed to classify living kinds according to presumptions about their underlying physical natures. Cross-cultural evidence indicates that people everywhere spontaneously organize living kinds into rigidly ranked taxonomic types despite wide morphological variation among those exemplars presumed to have the nature of their type. (1990:70–71)

Another view is that the universal and rapid learning of natural kinds is based on the fact that natural kinds have very special structures with many co-occurring attributes; this is the position Rosch has taken, described above in Chapter 5. A third position is that the notion of essences and natural kinds is based neither on an innate mental structure nor the structure of the world, but solely on culture, and that while most societies do have some kind of taxonomic system for plants and animals, the universal presence of plant and animal taxonomies does not prove that most societies have a true theory of essences and natural kinds.

The evidence for a universal theory of essences is not at this point compelling. However, this area of cognitive anthropology is not well explored, and it may be that even where evidence of a formulated *theory* of essences is lacking, it can be shown that people have *models* of plants and animals that implicitly contain the ideas of essence and natural kind.

An ethnographic study of beliefs about essence on West Fatuna, Vanuatu, by Janet Keller and F. K. Lehman (1993), has explored the meaning of two terms, *hkano* and *ata*, which are glossed "material essence" and "efficacious image." These terms are part of a traditional cosmology, and are important in understanding how magic works. Basically, the underlying theory seems to be that certain things have both a material essence and an efficacious image. The material essence of a human is the physical body, of a canoe its main hull, and of a song its verses. The efficacious image of human is the person's shadow, of a canoe the outrigger, of a song its chorus. The connection between the efficacious image and the material essence allows magic to be done; things done to the efficacious image produce effects on the material essence.

According to Keller and Lehman, the ideas embedded in the meanings of *hkano* and *ata* are not discussed or argued about; they are simply presupposed as fundamental concepts about the nature of reality and used in doing magic. The theory is tacit or implicit and is not stated as declarative knowledge. The whole system appears to work on the cognitive level as a model rather than as a theory. This particular model does not address the issues of essence that Atran is concerned with – issues which have to do with basic fixity of natural kinds, not with mystical connections between "stuff" and "image." The people on West Fatuna may also have the conception that some things are natural kinds which retain their essence however their physical shapes are transformed, but *hkana* and *ata* are silent on this.

An extension of the notion of essence and natural kinds has been discussed by Pascal Boyer, a cognitive anthropologist who has worked among the Fang of Cameroon, West Africa. Boyer (1993) presents the hypothesis that humans extend the idea of natural kinds from plants, animals, and certain substances (gold, iron, water, etc.) to domains in which it is not really applicable. These extensions create *pseudo-natural* kinds. For example, among the Fang, witches, traditional healers, people with special skills in oratory, and people who are especially successful at business are thought to have a special invisible organ called an *evur*, which confers upon them their special abilities. What makes one really a healer, or witch, or orator, is not the particular behaviors that one performs. It is some magical essence, here reified into the belief in a physically real but invisible substance. Like the "giraffenss" of a giraffe, the "*evur*-ness" of certain kinds of powerful people lies not in any perceptible characteristic, but in something unseen. But unlike giraffes, which *do* form a "natural kind" (which we can explain through the operation of DNA), the Fang category of having an *evur* is not a natural kind.

An important point about natural kinds is that one can make strong inductive generalizations about them. If one encounters four *aye-ayes* and they are all smaller than a cat, have five fingers, sharp nails, round eyes, large ears, and are solitary, nocturnal bug-eaters, one can pretty safely assume that other *aye-ayes* are the same. An obvious example of the generalization of the doctrine of essence to pseudo-natural kinds is the notion that humans come from different *races*, and that, since *races* are natural kinds, one can generalize from skin color to character. That is, if *races* are natural kinds, then if most of the "Asians" one knows are smart and hard-working, then "that is the way those people are," and it is part of their natural substance to be that way (rather than a result of culture or social circumstances). Despite years of proselytizing, anthropology has been unable to convince the American public that races are *not* natural kinds. Boyer's hypothesis is that this extreme readiness to inappropriate generalization is the result of a deeply embedded cognitive model – sometimes expressed verbally as a theory – of essences and natural kinds which is appropriate to oaks and rabbits but not to skin color and orators.

The discussion of essences makes clear that the distinction between a *theory* and a *model* is complex. A culture may have a *model* of essence embedded in notions about plants and other things, and at the same time, a *theory* of essence propounded by its philosophers. The distinction here concerns the difference between that which is explicitly verbally formulated versus that which is known implicitly. This distinction was discussed in Chapter 6 with respect to parallel distributed processing in contrast to symbolic serial processing, where it was argued that parallel distributed processing is more automatic and rapid in execution than serial symbolic processing. Given that a primary function of models is to make possible calculations of what will happen, parallel distributed processing is a more efficient form of embodiment for a model than serial symbolic processing. However, because parallel distributed knowledge is implicit, it is hard to criticize and modify. Cultural theories, on the other hand, are too slow to think *with*, but easy to think *about*. Thus the basic models of a culture, which are almost always learned through parallel distributed processing, are protected from conscious, rational, critique. This makes for stability, but makes it difficult to change even very change-worthy models, such as the current model of race as a natural kind.

An ontology of cultural forms

Over the past six chapters, a number of cognitive forms or structures have been presented. Below is a summary outline of these forms.

Properties

Criterial attribute – a property which an object or class of objects has that distinguishes it from other objects or classes of objects. For example, *maleness* is a criterial attribute of the class of stallions, distinguishing stallions from mares.

Dimension – a property which forms a continuum along which objects or classes of objects can be placed. For example *maturity* is a dimension along which stallions, colts, and foals can be placed.

Objects

Schema – the organization of cognitive elements into an abstract mental object capable of being held in working memory with default values or open slots which can be variously filled in with appropriate specifics. For example, most Americans have a well-formed schema for a *commercial transaction* in which a buyer and seller exchange money for the rights over some object.

Prototype – a typical example of a type of object capable of being held in working memory, often with many properties "chunked" together to form a rich, specific image. For example, a *robin* is a prototypic bird, a *penguin* is not. A prototype is the instantiation of a schema; thus a *robin* is an instantiation of the *bird* schema.

Symbol – a word, phrase, or picture, or other physical representation, used to denote things in the world, and which has a meaning or sense (the schema to which symbol signifies). A symbol is a physical thing – the sounds which compose a word, the marks which compose a picture. The physical symbol is represented in the mind by a distinct schema which identifies that particular sound or set of marks. The schema which represents the sound of a word and the schema which represents the thing in the world referred to by that word are entirely different, although tightly connected in that the schema which represents the sound of a word signifies (has as its meaning) the schema which represents the thing in the world.

Configurations of objects

Taxonomy – a set of schemas which form a hierarchy of abstraction such that the actual things represented by the lower level schemas are subsets of the things represented by the upper level schemas and the schemas at each level partition the things represented into mutually exclusive classes. Typically, each schema is represented by a separate lexeme, although on occasion "covert" classes may be encountered which lack a single term. The English taxonomy of *plants* is a standard ethnographic example of a taxonomy.

Model – a schema or interrelated set of cognitive schemas used to represent something, to reason with or to calculate from by mentally manipulating the parts of the model to solve some problem. A single schema may serve as a model – the *commercial transaction* schema, for example, or a number of interrelated schemas may be used to construct the model, as in the *Caroline Island model of navigation*. Typically, cultural models are not formulated as explicit declarative knowledge (as in a *theory*), but are implicit knowledge, based on schemas embedded in words but not formulated as explicit propositions.

Proposition – a proposition is the sense of something said about something (typically a sentence) and involves the integration of a relatively small number of separate schemas into a more complex schema; a proposition asserts the relation between this integrated schema and the world; for example, *dinosaurs may have been warm blooded*.

Theory – an interrelated set of propositions which describe the nature of some phenomena. Cultural theories are explicit formulations in language; for example, the theory of the *evolution of species*, or the Aristotelian theory of *essences*.

I do not expect that this particular classification of cognitive forms will endure for long. Not only are young sciences marked by continuous change in terminology, they are also notorious for their shifting ontologies. But it is important to be clear about terminology; otherwise one wanders in metaphysical fogs.

Some of the contrasts found in this classification have major psychological implications. One of these is the *schema/symbol* contrast. The idea that *words carry meaning* has been a long-term source of confusion in the cognitive sciences. Even the standard definitions of the terms *word* and *symbol* reflect this confusion; is a "word" or "symbol" the "physical thing" or its "meaning'? The metaphor *words carry meaning* treats mental schemas as if they were the shadows of physical artifacts- as if there could be no "meanings" without words. By distinguishing *schema* from *symbol* each can be treated as independent phenomena in their own right.

Another important aspect in this ontology is the contrast between knowledge which is implicit, unverbalized, rapid, and automatic, versus knowledge which is explicit, verbalized, slow, and deliberate. Each has its strengths and weakness; I have tried to describe in the last two chapters current thinking about how these two kinds of knowledge are formed by different cognitive mechanisms (parallel distributed processing versus symbolic serial processing), and how they relate to the kinds of things people do with their knowledge (rapidly compute an expected outcome versus formulate a consistent and coherent doctrine, for example).

Finally, the distinction between a *prototype* and a *schema* concerns the contrast between cognitive structures that are content rich (like the cognitive representation of a typical *rose*) and cognitive structures that are abstract (like the cognitive representation of a *container*). While this distinction is a matter of "more or less" rather than "all or none," nevertheless it appears that natural language makes differential use of this capacity, with basic level nouns and verbs serving as prototypes which carry rich informational content while grammatical elements such as tense, aspect, and number serve as schemas which carry more abstract and relational information.

8 Cultural representations and psychological processes

Cognitive representations – properties, prototypes, schemas, models, theories – make up the stuff of culture in the mind. These representations are adaptive in simply being representations; that is, in providing maps o: the world. Such a function is not trivial, since effective action requires an understanding of how the world is organized. But cultural representations do more than provide maps. This chapter will consider evidence that under certain conditions cultural representations have significant effects on perception, memory, and reasoning. The argument here is not that of extreme cultural constructionism, which argues that everything is determined by culture, nor that of psychological reductionism, which argues that all culture is determined by the nature of the human psyche. The position taken here is that of interactionism, which hypothesizes that culture and psychology mutually affect each other. The problem, as Richard Shweder (1993:500) says, is to determine "how culture and psyche make each other up."

Perception

One of the earliest hypotheses about the cognitive effects of cultural representations was the hypothesis that cultural categories influence how people think. If this is true, then natural language, as the great matrix of cultural categories, should be an important determinant of thought. In the anthropological literature this has been called the Sapir–Whorf hypothesis, named after Edward Sapir, a famous anthropological linguist who did pioneering work on American Indian languages in the 1920s, and Benjamin Whorf, a linguist and autodidact who wrote about the the effects of language on thought in the 1940s. In fact, neither Sapir (1921) nor Whorf (1956) were very specific about exactly *what* would be effected by natural language categories; each speaks in general terms of how language affects the *organization of thought*.[1]

[1] A good review of past research on the Sapir–Whorf hypothesis can be found in McNeill 1987:173–198.

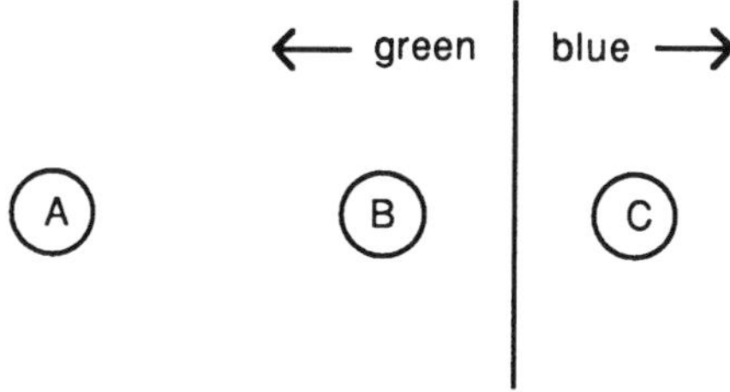

Figure 8.1 Perceptual distances between three color chips

One specification of the Sapir–Whorf hypothesis is that natural language categories affect *perception*. For example, if a language lacks color terms which differentiate *green* from *blue*, according to the Sapir–Whorf hypothesis, native speakers of this language should not perceive the difference between green and blue objects as saliently as speakers of a language which does contain this distinction.

Exactly this hypothesis has been tested by Paul Kay and Willet Kempton (1984) using native speakers of English and Tarahumara, an Uto-Aztecan language of northern Mexico. Tarahumara has only one term, *siyóname*, for both green and blue. Using a series of Munsell color chips graded from pure green to pure blue, native Tarahumara and English speaking respondents were asked to judge, for every triad of chips, *which chip was the most different in color.* Consider the three chips A, B, and C illustrated in Figure 8.1. The color boundary for the English terms *green* and *blue* passes between chips B and C. In English, one would describe chip A as "green," chip C as "blue," and chip B as "a green color which has some blue in it." When English speakers were asked to select the chip which is most different, they selected chip C – the one that they call *blue*, leaving the other two which are called *green*. Native speakers of Tarahumara, in contrast, choose chip A as the most different, since A is, according to vision experts, the most different.

One would feel even more confident of the effect of name category boundaries on perception if some condition could be found which would block English speakers from thinking of the color names of the chips, and if, under this condition, English speakers would also perceive A as the most different of the three chips. In fact, Kay and Kempton were able to create just such a experiment. They placed the three chips A, B, and C in a container with a sliding top that permitted the respondent to see alternately either of two pairs of the three chips, but never all three at once. Respondents were then asked which was bigger: the difference in greenness between chips A and B or the difference in blueness between chips C and B.

Kay and Kempton say that their respondents did not experience these instructions as hard to understand. In this experiment, English speaking respondents reverse their judgment, saying that A and B are further apart than B and C. What seems to have happened here is that when *pairs* of chips, rather than *triads*, are judged, name differences in color are not salient. In this case the A and B pair of chips are alike in both being more or less green, and the B and C pair of chips are alike in both being more or less blue, so that the contrastive judgment that "these two are green, that one is blue" does not arise. When name differences are not salient, informants judge accurately the purely perceptual differences between chips.

There are three take-home lessons to be learned from this neat experiment. First, how people label things can affect the perception of similarities between these things. Second, the effect will only occur if the names or labels are salient at the time the judgment is made. Third, the Sapir–Whorf effect on perception is not very large or powerful – it only occurs when dealing with judgments that are difficult to make on perceptual grounds alone. For the effect to work, Kay and Kempton had to select triads of chips so that the perceptual distance between chips A and B were nearly equal to the distance between chips B and C. The effect will not work if the perceptual differences are large. In general, naive perception can be influenced by cultural schemas, but not much.

Memory

The effects of cultural representations on long-term memory are complex. Memory is affected by a great variety of conditions, such as the well-formedness of relevant schemas, the degree of attention, the number of similar past experiences, and the strength of emotional involvement in the event. One simple general rule is that, all things being equal, an event which can be encoded by a well-formed schema will be better remembered than an event for which no such schema is available. A well-known example of this rule is found in the superior memory of master chess players who can remember entire chess games with ease. Good chess players know a large number of chess pattern schemas which make it possible to remember whole games without great effort. It is important to note that master chess players do not have better memories for just anything associated with chess; for example, if chess pieces are randomly placed on a board, rather than forming a meaningful pattern (such as a pattern that might result from the playing of a game) then master chess players are no better at remembering the positions than novice chess players (Chase and Simon 1973).

The obvious extension to anthropology is the generalization that events which can be encoded by cultural schemas will be better remembered than events which cannot. The assumption here is that while a few individuals might have idiosyncratically well-formed schemas for particular events which lack cultural schemas, most would not, so that across a sample of individuals and a sample of events, events coded by cultural schemas would be better remembered than events which cannot be coded by cultural schemas. Since culture is a great storehouse of schemas, and natural language contains the "names" of these schemas, one would then expect that events which can be encoded by single lexical terms would be better remembered than things which require long, complex descriptions.

In anthropology, most experimental work on memory has been done with color. Work with color has a number of advantages for anthropologists: materials can easily be taken into the field and manipulated experimentally; there are interesting cultural differences in color naming; and the relation between color names and specific chips can be mapped with a high degree of reliability. One of the first systematic studies of cultural differences in color naming was carried out by Eric Lenneberg, a psychologist, and John Roberts, an anthropologist, comparing English and Zuni (1956).

The classic study of color and memory was carried out by Roger Brown and Eric Lenneberg (1954), who wanted to test the Whorfian hypothesis that the color lexicon was related to accuracy of memory. Brown and Lenneberg showed subjects color chips for a few seconds, then the chips were removed and after a short wait subjects were asked to locate the same color chips in an array of 120 Munsell chips mounted on a card. The 120 chips were high saturation chips selected from twenty alternate hues and six levels of brightness. Brown and Lenneberg found that color chips which are most *codable* – that is, which have *short*, *reliable*, and *well-agreed-upon* names – are most accurately remembered.[2] Brown and Lenneberg argued that such chips are more accurately remembered because, in trying to recall the color chips, subjects retrieve the names they gave to chips, and the more accurately the chips are named, the better they are remembered.

However, the relation between accuracy of memory and codability turned out to be unstable. Lenneberg (1961) found that when a different kind of array of color chips was used, the relation between codabililty and memory disappeared. This array, called the Farnsworth–Munsell array, is used in tests of color blindness, and contains a single row of chips all at the same level of saturation and brightness, varying only in hue. In this array there are no true red, yellow, orange, or purple colors, so that the normal color lexicon does not accurately describe the colors.

In the 1960s a measure was developed by Volney Stefflre (Lantz and Stefflre 1964) which successfully predicted memory accuracy in both types of arrays. This measure, called *communication accuracy*, is calculated by asking one group of individuals to write descriptions of each chip "in such a way that another person will be able to pick it out." Another group of individuals is then asked to take each description and pick out the chip to which this description best applies. The degree of communication accuracy is computed for each chip

[2] Brown and Lenneberg (1954) found these three variables highly intercorrelated.

by calculating the percentage of descriptions of that chip which the decoders correctly identified. Stefflre found communication accuracy to be strongly related to accuracy of memory for both the original array used by Brown and Lenneberg and for the Farnsworth–Munsell array.

Communication accuracy makes a good predictor of accuracy in memory because, Stefflre argued, it reproduces the general problem of memory. In recognizing the correct chip, the individual communicates with himself or herself across time, recalling the description of the to-be-remembered chip from memory. This communication process is approximated by having individuals communicate with each other, with the expectation that items accurately communicated interpersonally will also be accurately communicated intrapersonally.

In another study comparing different languages Stefflre, Castillo, and Morley (1966) found that communication accuracy was strongly related to accuracy of memory for the Farnsworth–Munsell array using Spanish and Yucatec speakers (rank correlations of .45 for Yucatec and .59 for Spanish). The chips which were easy to communicate differed considerably in the two languages; the rank correlation across chips between Yucatec and Spanish for communication accuracy was only .11. The chips which were easy to remember also differed greatly; the rank correlation across chips between Yucatec and Spanish for memory accuracy was -.06.

One might have thought that this series of experiments would have firmly established the effect of language categories on memory. However, a strong anti-relativist, anti-Whorfian view of the world had begun to develop in anthropology and psychology, beginning with Berlin and Kay's work on basic color terms. The general hypothesis that memory for colors depends on language specific coding was challenged by Eleanor Rosch. Using Berlin and Kay's work on basic color terms, Rosch (1973) argued that focal color chips – the best examples of the basic level color terms – should be more memorable in any language, even languages which lack some of the basic level terms, because focal chips have *inherently greater perceptual salience*. Rosch's work with the Dani of New Guinea had given her an unusual opportunity to test the effect of language on memory because the Dani have only two basic level color terms; a dark/cool color term and a light/warm color term (see Chapter 5). Using a procedure modeled after the Brown and Lenneberg experiments, she found that Dani speakers, while lacking basic level terms for red, orange, yellow, blue, green, etc., remembered the focal color chips for these colors more accurately than non-focals (26% to 7%). A comparison sample of Americans showed the same result; while Americans have generally better memories for color chips than the Dani, they also remember focal chips better than non-focals (66% to 36%).

Rosch's study came as something of a shock to many anthropologists and psychologists who had generally underemphasized the effect of real-world structure on cognition. However, Rosch's research left the issue of the relation of language to memory ambiguous. On the basis of her data, it might be argued that the previous results of Roberts, Lenneberg, Brown, and Stefflre are due to a confounding of perceptual salience effects with language effects. But, one could equally well argue that both effects occur independently. Or, one could even argue that focals are for some reason better coded linguistically (even among the Dani, who do not use basic level color terms to code the focals, but who may use derived terms, like "grass-color" or "sky-color") and that the better memory for focals is primarily due to their linguistic coding, not their perceptual salience. To resolve these issues John Lucy and Richard Shweder (1979) undertook a series of experiments contrasting the effect of *focality* and *codability* on memory accuracy.

Lucy and Shweder began by reexamining the array of color chips used by Rosch. This array was similar to the Brown and Lenneberg array, consisting of high saturation Munsell color chips from twenty alternate hues for eight brightness levels, making a total of 160 chips. Lucy and Shweder found that *focal* test chips (the test chips are the chips that are presented to the subjects to remember and try to locate in the array) were easier to locate than the *non-focal* test chips in a direct matching task ("find the chip in the array which matches this test chip"), apparently because the non-focal chips were perceptually closer to their neighbors than the focal chips. Lucy and Shweder point out that this perceptual *discriminability* factor is not the same as Rosch's *salience* factor; salience is supposedly an inherent property of a color, not something which is dependent on how similar or different the surrounding chips are. To put it another way, in a six chip array with five red chips and one pale chartreuse chip, the pale chartreuse chip will be easier to remember not because it is intrinsically easy to code, but because it is easy to distinguish from the other chips.

In order to control for bias in discriminability, Lucy and Shweder removed from the array chips which had been confused with the non-focal target chips in the direct matching task. Forty chips were removed, and the resulting 120 chip array was randomly reordered into an eight-by-fifteen grid. The new array was found to show no significant difference between focals and non-focals in either number of mistakes or response times in the matching task.

Using this new array, twenty-four University of Chicago students were presented with a test color chip for five seconds, then after a thirty second delay asked to locate the test chip in the array.[3] Lucy and Shweder found a slight but non-significant advantage for focal chips over non-focals, with subjects remembering 62.5% of the focals correctly and 53.7% of the non-focals correctly. This contrasted with Rosch's results, in which approximately 65.6% of

3 There was also a very long-term delay condition, in which subjects were asked to wait for thirty minutes before being presented with the array and asked to find the test chip. The results for this condition are very similar to the results for the thirty second delay period, and are not reported here.

Table 8.1. *Basic descriptions used to identify test chips in the Lucy Shweder experiment*

Modifier	Head term	Modifier	Head term
—	Red	—	Purple
		Dark	Purple
—	Pink	Reddish	Purple
—	Orange	Dark	Blue
Yellowish	Orange	Greenish	Blue
		Light	Blue
—	Brown	Medium	Blue
		Royal	blue
—	Maroon		
		—	Turquoise
—	Flesh		
		Avocado	Green
—	Peach	Blue	Green
		Bright	Green
—	Yellow	Brownish	Green
		Dark	Green
—	Lavender	Light	Green
		Olive	Green
—	Violet	Pastel	Green
		Yellowish	Green

the focals but only 35.9% of the non-focals were remembered correctly. Lucy and Shweder attributed this difference to the fact that Rosch's array was biased in favor of focals, as demonstrated by the matching task.

While communication accuracy gives a good prediction of which items in an array will be most accurately remembered, it is not, by itself, informative about which schemas and which verbal terms are involved. To find out something about the specific relation between English color terms and memory, Lucy and Shweder developed a new measure, which they call *group communication accuracy.* First they gathered a collection of phrases used by university students to describe the test chips. These phrases were then analyzed to determine the *head* term and *modifiers* (e.g., in "light pea-soup green," *green* is the head term and *light* and *pea-soup* are modifiers). The frequency of each of the head terms and modifiers were then calculated, and any head term plus modifier combination which occurred in more than 14% of the descriptions for a chip was considered to be a *basic description* of that chip. The basic descriptions for the test chips are presented in Table 8.1.

One can see from the listing of descriptions in Table 8.1 that more is involved in describing colors than just Berlin and Kay's eleven basic color terms. Many descriptions have modifiers – *light, dark, pastel, reddish,* etc. – and almost half the descriptions are based on non-basic color terms – *maroon, lavender, violet, peach, flesh,* etc. The lexicon from which American–English color descriptions are generated is relatively complex, and is surprisingly unstudied.

Once the basic descriptions for each chip had been selected, ten university students were asked to pick out the best example of each description from the array. The measure of *group communication accuracy* was the number of times subjects correctly selected the original test chip as the best example of the basic description. This measure was found to be highly related to memory, correlating .59 with the number of correct identifications in the memory task. Thus, how well the basic descriptions of a color chip pick out that chip from an array predicts how well that chip will be remembered.

What does all this experimental work tell us? First, we find that there is a relation between language and memory, but that this relationship is not simple. It is not just a matter of having one or another kind of lexicon that makes memory better or worse. The lexicon permits the rememberer to construct descriptions of what is to be remembered, and it is the *interaction* of these descriptions with the things to be remembered that influences memory. If the lexicon makes it easy to construct descriptions which select out the correct objects without confusing them with other potential objects, memory is likely to be good. But if the constructed descriptions do not select out the correct object, memory is likely to be bad. Whether a description is "good" or "bad" will depend on the interaction between the lexicon and the objects, and in many cases cannot be predicted from either alone.

There is a *coda* to the story about memory and color chips. Recall that Lucy and Shweder found only a 9% difference between the memory for focal versus non-focal color chips. Linda Garro, a cognitive anthropologist, in replicating Lucy and Shweder's experiment (1986b), found much greater advantage for focal color chips, with 82% of the focals remembered correctly, compared to only 62% of Lucy and Shweder's subjects. The major difference between her experimental conditions and Lucy and Shweder's experimental conditions was that Lucy and Shweder permitted conversation during the filler period between seeing the test chip and trying to locate the chip in the array. Garro speculated one of the major memory strategies is to try to maintain a visual image of the color in working memory, and that conversation interferes with this strategy.

Lucy and Shweder (1987) then repeated their experiment under two different conditions; in one condition subjects were permitted to converse during the filler period, and in the other they were asked to remain silent. They found that under the *no-conversation* condition subjects remembered approximately 80% of the focals and 51% of the non-focal correctly, while under the *conversation-permitted* condition, subjects remembered only 65% of the focals and 51% of the non-focals correctly.

Lucy and Shweder also asked their subjects about the strategies they used to remember the colors. Verbal labeling was the most frequently mentioned strategy, but visualization was used slightly more under the *no-conversation* condition. Overall, it is reasonable to conclude that if one is trying to remember colors by visualization, then focal colors are easier to hold in mind than non-focals.

Looking at the history of research on color and memory in anthropology, it is apparent that the story becomes more complex as it grows longer. Under some conditions there will be better memory for colors which have short single words, but not under other conditions. How well one can identify a color in words will correlate with how easy that color is to remember, but some colors are naturally easier to remember visually if one is not distracted. Overall, it can be said that neither the perceptual structure of colors nor language *determines* memory for colors, but that both *influence* color memory.

The effect of language on the recall of color chips is a relatively simple example of the relation between cultural schemas and memory. However, it only examines this relationship for one kind of memory – what Endel Tulving (1983) calls *episodic memory* rather than *semantic memory.* This distinction concerns the contrast between the memory of "personal happenings and doings" as against general "knowledge of the world." Semantic memory contains items like "6 × 6 = 36," "Sacramento is the capital of California," "an oak is a kind of tree," etc., while episodic memory contains items such as the name of one's first grade teacher, where one was when one first heard that Jack Kennedy was shot, and the color of that last color chip. There is debate about whether these two types of memory are really separate systems, but the usefulness of the distinction in classifying different types of knowledge is generally acknowledged (Mandler 1985).

Episodic memory forms an important part of one's personal identity, but much of one's *reality* – how one understands the world to be – is based on semantic memory. A nice study of semantic memory is reported in a paper by Hamilton and Fagot (1988). Hamilton and Fagot are social psychologists, interested in stress and gender. They asked a large sample of male and female undergraduates at the University of Oregon to list the daily events they found stressful, to rate how stressful the events were, and describe how they attempted to cope with these events. They found that men and women recalled different events as stressful. The pattern of differences corresponded to previous research and general cultural notions about gender differences, with women recalling more concern with destructive criticism, unfriendly people, prejudicial behavior, being kept waiting, peer pressure, lying, lack of punctuality, appearance, and dissatisfaction with weight.

To check this memory based data against a less memory-fragile set of data, Hamilton had a second sample of men and women make ratings over an eight week period of stresses encountered in the last twenty-four hours. Under these conditions she found that, with the exception of the problem of weight, men and women did *not* experience different events as stressful, *nor* did they evaluate the stressfulness of specific events differently, *nor* did they differ in the types of coping strategies they used. The difference between the two conditions appears to be the result of a bias effect which occurs when people are asked to assess from long-term memory the frequency with which events of various kinds have happened to them.

In Chapter 4 the bias in memory based ratings was discussed. The phenomenon here is similar; people are biased towards recalling as going together things which they associate as going together.[4] American women believe themselves to be very concerned with interpersonal issues, and hence they are more likely to recall events of this kind. In fact, in the undergraduate world, men and women live in very similar social settings under similar social demands. The women recall responding to destructive criticism more frequently and with more stress because it is easier to bring to mind instances of schema congruent events – "I am the sort of person (a woman) who is bothered by this kind of thing." Here cultural representations have a great effect on memory; American undergraduates appear to have memories that are systematically biased to fit the cultural images of their gender.

In general, complex schemas, because they are made up of a number of cognitive elements organized together, have a great influence on memory. Since one is more likely to remember elements as going together if there is some associative link between them, one is likely to remember the parts of a schema as going together, whether or not they actually do so. Given complex cultural schemas for different types of things – males and females, paperback novels, WASPs, mosques, New England colleges, etc. – one is very likely to find that one's semantic memory corresponds to the cultural schema – for instance, that males tend to have all those attributes that men are thought to have, etc. The associative effect biases our memories, and gives each of us the comforting illusion that the world *is* pretty much the way we think it is, which is also pretty much the way our culture says it is.

This is not to say that one will not notice exceptions. Indeed, it has been found that memory for *individual* exceptions to schemas is relatively good (Hamilton 1988). I can recall a number of things about individual women which are not what one might expect on the basis of gender, including a number of individual women who were not at all sensitive to interpersonal issues. But if asked to recall *generally* what women are like, I consistently produce a memory based over-all assessment that women are more sensitive to interpersonal issues than men.

Because memory is so often incorrect, there is a tendency to dismiss all memory based assessments as unreliable. Such a dismissal would have a devastating effect on the conduct of anthropological research, since, by necessity, a great deal of ethnographic information is based on informants' accounts of events rather than direct observation. A number of studies of informant accuracy have been carried out; these studies have typically found little

4 There is a large literature supporting this proposition; see, for example, Chapman 1967; Chapman and Chapman 1969; and Shweder 1982.

correspondence between what people remember as happening and what actually happened. Russ Bernard, Peter Killworth, David Kronenfeld, and Lee Sailer (1985), in a review paper treating the issue of informant accuracy, estimate that episodic memory based inaccuracies are so common that about half of what informants tell us is wrong. However, this is not necessarily as devastating as it might seem. Linton Freeman, Kim Romney, and Sue Freeman (1987) have carried out a study of informant memory which not only illustrates the ways in which memory is biased, but also shows how these biases can be used to obtain accurate data.

The Freeman, Romney, and Freeman study used attendance data for participation in an informal seminar of the Irvine Mathematical Social Science Program during the spring quarter of 1985. The seminar met in a large lounge in which participants sat in a circular pattern, with everyone visible to everyone else. Attendance was recorded for nine consecutive sessions. The ninth and final session was used as the memory target session. All participants were interviewed five days after the final session and asked if they had been at the ninth meeting, and if so, who else had attended. All those who had attended (17 persons) remembered attending; their error rate was 52% – on the average they forgot about 6 of the 16 other people that were there, and recalled the presence of 1.5 persons who, in fact, were not there.

Based on a survey of the literature on memory, Freeman *et al.* hypothesize that memory recall of an event will depend on two major factors; first, how well organized the person's schema is for that kind of event, and secondly, how typical the event to be remembered is. The better organized the schema, the better over-all memory will be, and the more typical an event, the more likely it is that it will be remembered. However, the more typical an event, the more likely it will be recalled falsely as occurring because it will be "filled-in" by the schema rather than actual perception.

Freeman *et al.* divided the seminar participants into two groups; an "ingroup" of faculty and graduate students who all have space together on one floor of the Social Science Building, and an "outgroup" of faculty and students whose offices are elsewhere. This spatial division corresponds to a clear social reality in which certain people are face-to-face colleagues, teaching similar courses and involved together in a variety of day-to-day concerns. Freeman *et al.* expected that the ingroup would have a much better formed schema for the membership of the seminar, and thus to remember more of the participants for the final session. This, in fact, was the case; ingroup members forgot on the average the attendance of 4.7 persons, while outgroup members forgot 8.1 persons. However, the ingroup produced more false recalls, having an average of 2.8 false recalls per informant, while the outgroup only produced 0.4 false recalls per informant. Not surprisingly, those who attended most of the nine sessions were forgotten least often and were most likely to be the subject to false recalls.

Freeman *et al.* show that, using just the three most productive informants (those who produced the most names), and simply counting the number of times a person's name is recalled, one can accurately identify all of the ten most active participants of the seminar. The correlation between the number of times a name is recalled by the ten most productive informants and the attendance of that person across the nine sessions is .88. What this means is that the memory of those with well-formed cognitive structures reflects long-term patterns quite well, although they are more likely to distort what happened at an actual event, adding in those who are usually there and forgetting those who are not regular attendees.

The results from the least productive participants are quite different. Pooling the memory data of the five least productive informants predicts all the participants who were *actually* at the ninth session with only one false recall. Because the low-knowledge informants had little cognitive structure to work with, their memory is not productive but it is not biased. While each non-productive informant provides meager information, pooled together in sufficient numbers they provide a good picture of what actually happened. Thus, while memory is often both scanty and biased, biased memory can be used to uncover the long-term patterning of events, and scanty memories, when pooled, can be used to recover what actually happened at specific moments.

It would be nice if human memories were *only* biased by the accumulation of actual experiences. However, there is considerable evidence that memory can just as easily be biased by verbally learned stereotypes as by long-term experience, as described above. To return to the issue of women and interpersonal sensitivity, one can only say that the problem is confounded. It may be that women are more stressed by interpersonal events than men, and undergraduate women recalled more stress because in the past they had experienced more stress, although while in college they were not actually experiencing more stress. Or it may be that the memory distortions of undergraduate women are biased by expectancies generated by a self-concept which emphasizes concern with relationships, while males have self-concepts which deny such concerns. Here, one can really say, more research is needed.

Reasoning

In the previous chapter it was argued that cultural models are used to reason with or calculate from. In this chapter it will be argued that the relation between reasoning and cultural models is a two way street; that the ability to reason works to form cultural models, while at the same time cultural models *make possible* complex reasoning. Or, to put it another way, because we can reason we need cultural models, *and* because we have have such models, we can reason.

One of the major studies of reasoning in a non-western society was carried out by Edwin Hutchins in the 1970, and described in his book, *Culture and*

Inference. Hutchins worked with Trobriand Islanders, the people studied by Malinowski in 1915–1916 and 1917–1918. In the 1940s, based on Malinowski's published linguistic materials, Dorothy Lee, an anthropological linguist, argued that Trobriand Islanders, unlike Europeans, do not have concepts of causality or intention (1940, 1949). For a number of years the Trobrianders were considered a possible exception to any claim that there is a pan-human logic by which humans reason.

To study reasoning ethnographically requires a setting in which people reason out loud. It is likely that in all cultures there are particular settings in which people argue with each other. In the Trobriands, there are village law courts for land disputes, held by the native chiefs, to which conflicting parties bring their disputes. Each side presents its claims and the local chief then gives his decision. Such an institution offers a good location for the study of reasoning. Hutchins tape recorded a number of land tenure cases in the Trobriand language, then transcribed the cases and carried out a line by line analysis of the reasoning used.

One of the first things that Hutchins found was that to understand reasoning about land tenure he had to understand the Trobriand model of land tenure. The Trobriand Islanders are a gardening people who use a slash and burn technique which leaves much of the land fallow at any one time. Basically, land is owned by matrilineal descent groups, called *dala*, whose claim to the land is based on a mythological account of their ancestors' association with the land. The relationship of the land to the *dala* is immutable and non-transferable. On occasion there are disputes about which *dala* owns a particular piece of land, and in such cases adjudication requires knowledge of sacred lore. More frequently, legal problems concern issues of who has the right to *use* the land. When a man holds the *use right* to a particular plot, he has the right to garden the plot himself or to let someone else garden the plot for a portion of the harvest. In such a case the person sharecropping has no permanent rights in that plot, and once the gardening season has ended, permission to garden that plot must be renegotiated.

Use right is an enduring relation between a man and land, but can be transferred by a proper formal transfer. To add further complexities, having the use right does not *necessarily* mean that one has the right to transfer this right to another person. To transfer the use right one must engage in a formal prestation, called *pokala*. Typically, this is done by presenting a gift of bananas, fish, and yams to the person who has the right of allocation. If the person doing the *pokala* comes from a different *dala*, use rights may be given but the *right of allocation* stays with the people of the owning *dala*. If the person with the use right dies, one of his or her heirs may give a "warming-up" prestation to maintain the use right. If the person from the owning *dala* wishes to retrieve the use right to their land, he must present the person who holds the use right with valuables, which "bring back" the use rights. Finally, the allocation right – the right to "bring back" a particular plot, may be passed on to one's heirs.

These different patterns of rights give rise to complex webs of relationships between persons with respect to the land. Such relations easily become confused and entangled, so that sorting out who really has what rights is sometimes a difficult task. Consider the case of Kailimila versus Motabasi, heard before the Tukwaukwa village court on July 26, 1976. Both men had considerable power and prestige. They were matrilineal parallel cousins, offspring of two sisters. The case arose when Motabasi sent a young man to begin gardening the plot in dispute. Kailimila, hearing of this, and intending to garden the plot himself, brought the case to court.

Based on the available evidence, Hutchins' reconstruction of the case is that the original use rights and allocation rights were held by an older brother of Motabasi. This older brother died, giving the use right and allocation right to the garden to his sister, Ilawokuva. Ilawokuva held the rights for several gardening seasons. Solobuwa, an important man from another *dala* then gave *pokala* to Ilawokuva, and Ilawokuva gave him the use right (but, since he was from a different *dala*, not the allocation right) to the garden. Solobuwa grew old, and his younger brother, Monilobu, gave a "warming-up" prestation of one arm of bananas so that he could maintain the use right to the garden.

Motabasi, who had been away in Port Moresby during part of this time, had been visiting during the time Monilobu gave the "warming-up" prestation, and saw the giving of the bananas. However, Motabasi did not know that the use rights to the garden had already been given to Solobuwa. Motabasi thought that this was an original *pokala*, and he felt that a single arm of bananas was not enough of a gift, and he advised Ilawokuva not to give the garden to Monilobu.

At a later time, Kailimila gave *pokala* to Ilawokuva, who told Kailimila that when Solobuwa died, Kailimila could retrieve the garden, thus bequeathing to him the right of allocation. But Kailimila did not know that the use right had passed by virtue of the "warming-up" ceremony to Solobuwa's brother, Monilobu. Kailimila and Monilobu then had an altercation about the use of the garden, and a court case was heard, which Monilobu won. However, as part of this case, it was acknowledged that the right of allocation was Kailimila's. Kailimila was instructed by the court that if he wanted to have the use right returned to him, he must make a sufficient prestation to Monilobu. Kailimila later did so, and recovered the use right.

At this point Motabasi returned to the area and began gardening for Ilawokuva, his sister. After gardening for her for fifteen years, she gave him the rights to three gardens. Meanwhile, Kailimila used the disputed garden for a number of years, and then had other men garden for him. Motabasi was away during part of this time, and when he returned he sent a younger man to start gardening the plot. Kailimila heard about this, and brought the case to court.

The court hearing was long and complex. Both litigants gave their own account of what they believed had happened. Motabasi was hampered by the fact that he was away for long periods of time, and did not know a number of crucial events. What he tried to do in his presentation was make a credible case for his having the rights to the garden. A summary of his argument goes as follows:

(1) My sister Ilawokuva had the rights to the garden, given to her by our older brother when he died.
(2) Because my sister had no one to garden for her, I gardened for her.
(3) This work for her was my *pokala* for the gardens she gave me.
(4) The disputed plot is one of these gardens she gave me.
(5) Although Monilobu gave one arm of bananas to my sister, and she said let us eat this *pokala*, I told her "O sister, land is very dear. Let him bring a bit more."
(6) Kailimila and his brothers did not garden for Ilawokuva, they gardened for their own mother. But *their* mother did not have the rights to the garden.
(7) If their mother had held the garden, I would give them their land.
(8) Because the garden was held by my sister, Ilawokuva, the garden is mine.

Given that Hutchins' translation is reasonably accurate, it is clear that Lee's claim that Trobriander's lack any notion of intention or cause is quite wrong. For example, points (2) and (8) are explicit causal claims. The Trobriand term Motabasi uses here is *pela*, which Hutchins translates as "reason, goal, end." Intentions are also expressed throughout Motabasi's statement, but like most people, Motabasi usually leaves it up to the hearer to infer intentions from the actions when the inference is obvious. For example, Motabasi says that he gardened for his sister as *pokala*, and she bequeathed to him her gardens. He does not explicitly say that in doing the *pokala* it was his *intention* to obtain the rights to his sister's gardens because everybody understands that one does *pokala* because one intends to acquire garden rights.

In the next part of the case Kailimila recounted the history of the plot – Ilawokuva's giving use rights to Solobuwa, how these use rights were transferred to Solobuwa's younger brother Monilobu, Kailimila's court case with Monilobu, the instruction by the court that he, Kailimila, must give a return payment to Monilobu, and how he gave a return payment and started gardening the plot. A number of witnesses were called and supported the history given by Kailimila. This strongly undercut Motabasi's case. After a summing up, a verdict was delivered by the chief that the garden was Kailimila's.

In carrying out an analysis of the logic of the various arguments, Hutchins found that Trobrianders use many of the standard forms of the sentential calculus. Logical connectives corresponding to *if–then*, *only–if*, and disjunctive *either–or* are found in the Trobriand language. Logical forms of inference, such as *modus ponens* (if p then q, p, therefore q) and *modus tollens* (if p then q, not q, therefore *not* p) are found throughout. These logical forms map on to the contingencies of land tenure. To know the rules of Trobriand land tenure is to know that *if* the rights to a garden go to someone *then* they must have given *pokala* to the previous holder of the rights. Because everyone knows this, when Motabasi says that the one arm of bananas given by Monilobu was not sufficient for *pokala*, he has invoked the *modus tollens* inference that therefore Monilobu did not receive the rights to the garden. Spelled out more fully, the reasoning goes as follows:

(a) if the rights to a garden go to someone (p) then they must have given *pokala* to the previous holder of the rights (q)
(b) Monilobu's gift of one arm of bananas to Ilawokuva was not sufficient for *pokola* (*not q*)
(c) therefore the rights to garden did not go to Monilobu (*not p*)

Another example of Motabasi's use of the *modus tollens* form is found in the rhetorical counterfactual he uses concerning Kailimila's mother. The logical form goes as follows:

(a) if their mother had held the rights in the garden, I would give them their land
(b) [unstated but obvious – I am not giving them the land]
(c) [implied inference – because their mother did not hold the land]

This a nice example of the way in which people leave unstated a good deal of their reasoning, assuming that others will fill in the unstated parts. The subtlety in this example is in the making of a point by leaving it up to the hearer to draw the concluding inference.

Hutchins also found that the Trobrianders make frequent use of *plausible inference*.[5] One form of plausible inference is:

(a) if p then q
(b) q
(c) therefore p is more likely

To conclude from a) and b) that p is *true* would be a logical fallacy. For example, given:

(a) If John was born in San Diego then John was born in California.
(b) John was born in California.
(c) Therefore John was born in San Diego.

Clearly, the fact that John was born in California does not prove that John was born in San Diego – he could have been born in Los Angeles, for instance. But knowing he was born in California makes it somewhat more plausible that he was born in San Diego than if all we know is that he was born somewhere in the western world. A good example of plausible inference is presented by Motabasi when he argues that his gardening for his sister constituted giving

[5] For a detailed theory of plausible reasoning, see Collins and Michalski 1989.

pokala for the garden in question, which makes it plausible that she gave him the garden. The logical schema is:

(a) If you have obtained the rights to a garden from someone, then you must have given *pokala* to that person.
(b) I gave *pokala* to my sister.
(c) Therefore it is plausible that she gave me the rights to garden.

Motobasi and the court all realize that a plausible inference is not a strict proof, but it is the best Motabasi has to offer – his unsupported testimony that his sister verbally gave him the right to the garden carries little weight in court dispute. Despite Motabasi's logical dexterity, the facts were against him, and he lost the case and his temper.

In *Culture and Inference* Hutchins gives a clear demonstration not only that Trobrianders can and do reason effectively, but also that reasoning is bound up with cultural models. The schema for the transfer of gardening rights contains a variety of contingencies. It is these contingencies that Trobriand Islanders use in their reasoning. Their reasoning cannot be understood without also understanding these contingencies. Without an understanding of these contingencies – i.e., understanding the model – it is impossible to see that Trobrianders *are* reasoning in their talk about land tenure. And once the model is understood, it is impossible *not* to realize that Trobrianders reason just as other people do. Hutchins states:

> The analysis of litigation has shown that a model of folk logic developed from purely western sources is quite adequate as an account of the spontaneous reasoning of Trobriand Islanders. It is not straight Aristotelian logic, because it contains plausible as well as strong inferences, but then so does our own reasoning . . . The clear difference between cultures with respect to reasoning is in the representation of the world which is thought about rather than in the processes employed doing the thinking. It is clear that Trobrianders cut the world into a different set of categories from those we entertain, and that those categories are linked together into unfamiliar structures. But the same types of logical relations underlie the connections of propositions in our conceptions and theirs, and the inferences that are apparent in their reasoning appear to be the same as the inferences we make. (1980:127-128)

Hutchins' study of the Trobriand Islanders has thrown serious doubt on the claim that different cultures have different kinds of reasoning.[6] Reasoning capacity appears to be a human universal. It is an important universal – reasoning is a crucial cognitive process in dealing with the world. Unfortunately, the process of reasoning is not well understood psychologically. Lance Ripps, a cognitive psychologist, says:

[6] James F. Hamill, in his book, *Ethnologic*, argues that particular semantic complexities in the meaning of logical connectives of different languages make for culturally specific logics; however Hamill also holds that the "structure of categorical reasoning is the same regardless of language or culture" (1990:103).

Reasoning infiltrates other forms of thought. Perceiving, for example, includes reasoning if, as is commonly assumed, perceptions result from inductive combination of sensory and memory information. Categorizing includes reasoning in exactly the same way. Comprehending includes reasoning since it involves filling in missing information and predicting new information as we read or listen. Problem-solving, decision-making, learning, and social understanding all obviously include reasoning. In fact, when we conceive of reasoning in this very general way, it seems to encompass almost any process of forming or adjusting beliefs and is nearly synonymous with cognition itself.

By contrast, the psychology of reasoning has been something of a research backwater. Although the topic has been part of experimental psychology since the turn of the century, it has played only a minor role in work on mental processes. A glance at the Standard References on this topic may convince you that research on deductive reasoning is preoccupied with a couple of clever brain teasers invented by Peter Wason and with the categorical syllogisms invented by Aristotle (but now considered by most logicians little more than a historical curiosity with the much more powerful systems of modern logic). Similarly, most research on inductive reasoning seems to busy itself with the way people learn arbitrary sets of geometric shapes, random dot patterns, or schematic faces. The "long and dull history" of other areas of experimental psychology appears lively and eventful by comparison. (1990:321–322)

Logic and the psychology of reasoning

One view, held by a number of cognitive scientists, is that humans have an inbuilt capacity to do *logic*, and it is the use of this capacity which we call reasoning (for example, see Braine, Reiser, and Rumain (1984) and Adams (1980)) . To be able to reason by logic is to be able to make inferences on the basis of the *form* of the argument alone. Logic is basically a matter of consistency; if you say that if *p* is true then *q* is true, and then you say that *p* is true, to be consistent you must then say that *q* is true. In logic, the content of the propositions is irrelevant and is replaced by *p*'s and *q*'s. If the logical form is correct, then the inference will be correct, no matter what is being said. Thus, if humans use logic to reason, then the *content* of the problem should not affect the reasoning. However, the content of many "logic" problems has been found to have drastic effect on the ability to reason.

Perhaps the most famous example is the Wason problem, developed by an English psychologist in the 1960s (Wason 1968). One version of this problem is:

All labels made at Pica's Custom Label Factory have either the letter A or the letter E printed on the front of the label, and have either the number 2 or the number 3 printed on the back side. The machine never makes a mistake about this – it always puts the letter A or E on the front, and the number 2 or 3 on the back.

As part of your job as a label checker at Pica's, you have the task of making sure that *if a label has an E printed on the front, it has a 2 printed on the back.* You have to check this because sometimes the machine makes a mistake and breaks this rule.

Which of the labels below would you have to turn over to make sure that the label has been printed following the rule? Mark an X under the labels you would have to turn over.

A	3	2	E
____	____	____	____

About 80% of undergraduates fail to solve this problem. The correct solution is to turn over the E label and the 3 label. Typically, subjects fail to select the 3 label, choosing instead the 2 label. Subjects who have gotten the problem wrong sometimes refuse to believe that they have made a mistake. They say they have followed the rule in turning over the label with a 2 on it because the rule *says* to check on labels with a 2 on them (although it does not). When shown that one *must* turn over the label with a 3 on it because, if that label had an A on its front, it would break the rule, and when further shown that a label with a 2 on it need not be turned over because no matter what is on the other side it will not break the rule, many subjects still remain stubbornly unconvinced, lost in a confusion of 2s and 3s, As and Es.

The Wason problem generated a number of studies to investigate what makes it so difficult. An early study by Johnson-Laird, Legrenzi, and Legrenzi (1972) discovered that if the problem is translated into the right realistic form, subjects can generally solve it. The realistic form they developed uses a rule about letters and stamps ("if a letter is sealed, then it has a 5 penny stamp on it"), to which over 90% of their English subjects gave the right answer. Since the realism of this form depends on an acquaintanceship with the British postal service which American undergraduates lack, for use in classroom demonstrations I developed a realistic form involving signing receipts at a store:

As part of your job as an assistant at Sears, you have the task of checking sales receipts to make sure that any sale of $100 or over has been approved by the sales manager. The amount of the sale is written on the front of the form, while the section manager's approval is initialled on the back of the form.

Which of the forms would you have to turn over to make sure that the sales clerk had been following the rule? Mark an X under the forms you would have to turn over.

1 chair $170	approved ____	1 lamp $15	approved [initialled]
____	____	____	____

Over 70% of American undergraduates get the correct answer to this form of the Wason task – everyone sees that the $170 receipt must be turned over, and there seems to be no difficulty in recognizing that the receipt which is *not* signed on the back, rather than the one that is, must be turned over. A number of other realistic versions of the Wason test have been developed, including one which uses a rule about age of drinking (Cox and Griggs 1982) and others which involve various kinds of social permission (Cheng and Holyoak 1985). Most of these forms are relatively easy for undergraduate subjects to solve.

There are a number of hypotheses about why the Wason task should be difficult in the Label Factory form yet easy in various realistic forms. It has been argued that because subjects have more experience with the conditions described by the realistic forms that they are more likely to understand the problem and realize which cards must be turned over. Another hypothesis holds that the realistic forms which are easy to solve all have some kind of social contract implicit in them, and that these forms are easy to solve because humans have evolved a special innate algorithm to detect people who cheat on social contracts (Cosmides 1989).

All forms of the Wason test have exactly the same logical structure: The rule stated has the form:

If *p* (on the front) then *q* (on the back)

The cards have *p*, *not p*, *q*, and *not q* printed on them. To test to see if the proposition is true, one must check the *p* card to make sure *q* is on the other side, and one must check the *not q* card to make sure that *not p* is on the other side.

For almost all forms of the Wason test, subjects realize that they must turn over the *p* card. But when taking the Label Factory form of the test, subjects fail to realize that they must turn over the *not q* card to make sure that *not p* is on the other side. In logic, this is a failure to infer the *contrapositive* – the contrapositive of "if *p* then *q*" is "if *not q* then *not p*." This is equivalent to failing a *modus tollens* problem.

A simple hypothesis about why arbitrary forms of the Wason problem are difficult is that people have difficulty with *any* arbitrary *modus tollens* problem. To test this hypothesis, I developed a standard type of verbal reasoning task with the following format (D'Andrade 1989):

Please circle the correct answer to each of the questions below:

1. GIVEN: If James is a watchman then James likes candy.
   SUPPOSE: We find out that James *is* a watchman.
   THEN:
   (a) It must be the case that James likes candy.
   (b) Maybe James likes candy and maybe he doesn't.
   (c) It must be the case that James does not like candy.

2. GIVEN: If Jim cut himself then Jim would be bleeding.
   SUPPOSE: We find out that Jim *did not* cut himself.
   THEN:
   (a) It must be the case that Jim is bleeding.
   (b) Maybe Jim is bleeding and maybe he isn't.
   (c) It must be the case Jim is not bleeding.
3. GIVEN: If this rock is a garnet then it is a semi-precious stone.
   SUPPOSE: This rock is *not* a semi-precious stone.
   THEN:
   (a) It must be the case that this rock is a garnet.
   (b) Maybe this rock is a garnet and maybe it isn't.
   (c) It must be the case that this rock is not a garnet.
4. GIVEN: If it is raining then the roof is wet.
   SUPPOSE: The roof *is* wet.
   THEN:
   (a) It must be the case that it is raining.
   (b) Maybe it is raining and maybe it isn't.
   (c) It must be the case that it is not raining.

The four logical forms in the test above are:

Modus ponens (Problem 1 above with arbitrary content)
  if *p* then *q*
  p
  therefore *q*
Modus tollens (Problem 3 above with realistic content)
  if *p* then *q*
  not q
  therefore *not p*
Affirmation of the consequent (Problem 4 above with realistic content)
  if *p* then *q*
  q
  therefore maybe *p* and maybe *not p*
Denial of the antecedent (Problem 2 above with realistic content)
  if *p* then *q*
  not p
  therefore maybe *q* and maybe *not q*

Using this format, a series of questionnaires with different problems were given to different samples of undergraduates. Each questionnaire had a variety of logical problems, some with arbitrary content ("If James is a watchman then James likes candy") and some with realistic content ("If this rock is a garnet then it is a semi-precious stone"). In any one questionnaire each premise occurred only once, but across questionnaires the same premise might be used in different logical problems. Thus "If James is a watchman then James likes candy" was used on one questionnaire in a *modus ponens* problem and in another questionnaire in a *modus tollens* problem.

Table 8.2. *Results of if–then tests*

	% Correct	Sample size
Modus ponens (If *p* then *q*. *p*. Therefore *q*.)		
Arbitrary content		
If James is a watchman then James likes candy.	96	50
If Jones is an artist then Smith is a baker.	91	60
If Roger is a musician then Roger is a Bavarian.	89	30
If A is true then B is true.	87	29
Affirmation of the Consequent (If *p* then *q*. *q*. Therefore maybe *p*, maybe not *p*.)		
Arbitrary content		
If Howard is in France then George is in Italy.	82	30
If Oscar is a card player then Oscar is left handed.	83	35
If X is true then Y is true.	80	29
Denial of the antecedent (If *p* then *q*. Not *p*. Therefore maybe *q*, maybe not *q*.)		
Realistic content		
If Jim cut himself then Jim would be bleeding.	82	50
If it is raining then the roof is wet.	80	29
Arbitrary content		
If P is true then Q is true. (P is not true.)	81	24
If M is true then N is true. (M is false.)	70	24
If Sally is a manager then Sally is a blond.	69	35
Modus tollens (If *p* then *q*. Not *q*. Therefore not *p*.)		
Realistic content		
If this rock is a garnet then this rock is a semi-precious stone.	96	50
If Tom was born in San Diego then Tom is a native Californian.	86	35
If Janet lives in San Cristobal then Janet lives in Mexico.	80	50
If Bill cut himself then Bill would be bleeding.	77	35
If it is raining then the roof is wet.	68	33
If John bought a present then John spent some money	65	60
Arbitrary content		
If Janet went to town then Janet brought home some bread.	**57**	60
If Roger drank Pepsi then Tom sat down.	**53**	60
If Roger is a musician then Roger is a Bavarian.	**52**	50
If James is a watchman then James likes candy.	**51**	35
If D is true then E is true. (E is false.)	**45**	33
If Harold is a politician then Harold is from New York.	**40**	35
If J is true then K is true (not K is true.)	**33**	34

These results show that American college students can solve *modus ponens*, affirmation of the consequent, and denial of the antecedent problems whether the content is arbitrary or realistic. However, as predicted, students are poor at solving *modus tollens* when the content is arbitrary (see the bold type percentages in Table 8.2), yet are relatively good at solving *modus tollens* problems when the underlying relationships and objects constitute a realistic schema.

What is it, then, that makes *modus tollens* difficult? I believe *tollens* is more difficult than the three other logical problems because it requires the reasoner to *reverse* perspective and imagine what might be the case if *not q* is true. This is not difficult to do when the relationship between *p* and *q* is based on a well-understood schema. "If this rock is a garnet then this rock is a semi-precious

	is a garnet	is not a garnet
is semi-precious	many cases	many cases
is not semi-precious	no cases	many cases

Figure 8.2 The contingency between being a garnet and being a semi-precious stone

stone" uses a standard cultural schema – that garnets have the property of being semi-precious stones (in fact, this is the only thing many people know about garnets). So, if this rock is *not* a semi-precious stone, what follows? Well, it follows this rock *could not* be a garnet because garnets *are* semi-precious stones. One immediately sees the contrapositive because one has a full representation of the relationship. A full representation of the idea that a garnet is a semi-precious stone contains the representation of a certain *contingency* – a contingency created by the relationship that *x* has some particular property *y*. This contingency is that of all the garnets in the world, there are not any which are not semi-precious stones. One can illustrate this contingency with a simple two-by-two table (Figure 8.2).

People can view a contingency like this from different perspectives. Starting with garnets (going down the first column in Figure 8.2), one can say that garnets are *all* semi-precious stones because there are not any garnets which are *not* semi-precious stones. Starting with things that are *not* semi-precious stones (going across the bottom row of Figure 8.2), one can say that none of *them* are garnets.

To really understand – to fully represent – a contingency is to be able to take either of these two perspectives. When given a problem about a rock which might be a garnet, one knows if it is a garnet it is a semi-precious stone, and if it is not a semi-precious stone, it is not a garnet. This is not done by logical inference, but simply by knowing the contingency pictured in Figure 8.2.

There are a great number of relationships which can create the kind of contingency table illustrated in Figure 8.2. Relations of spatial inclusion (San Diego is in California), class inclusion (marsupials are mammals), class membership (Aristotle was mortal), having a property (cats are fickle), and causality (getting cut causes bleeding) are common kinds of relationships which all produce this kind of zero-cell contingency.

Reasoning is done by mentally manipulating what one knows about contingency relationships in order to come to conclusions about what must be the case, or what is likely to be the case. If there were no contingencies between *x* and *y* – no constraints on what can never happen, or what always happens, or what is likely to happen with respect to *x* and *y* – there would be no way to say anything about *y* from what one knows about *x*. But if there are contingencies between *x* and *y*, then from knowing something about *x* one can know something about *y*.

Every "if *p* then *q*" creates the kind of zero-cell contingency illustrated in Figure 8.2. The English words "if . . . then" mean that this sort of contingency exists between whatever is said in the first part of the sentence and whatever is said in the second part of the sentence. This contingency is *contentless* unless one already has a schema for the relationship. If one knows some schema which makes a relationship between *p* and *q* – say the causal relationship between getting cut and bleeding – the statement "if cut then bleeding" instantiates this causal relationship, even though it is not explicitly stated, and the contingency is understood in terms of this relationship. But when no relationship is known except the bare bones provided by "if . . . then . . ." the reasoner must try to hold on to the contingency without support. If the inference is an easy one, the reasoner will be able to carry out the mental steps to get from *x* to *y*. But if the reasoning is complex, involving various shifts and reversals, most reasoners cannot. When someone is told "if James is a watchman then James likes candy" no relationship of cause, or inclusion, or anything else has been stated which would make it possible to understand the contingency mapped by the terms "if . . . then . . .". When further told "James does not like candy," this fact is not seen as bearing on what was already asserted because a well-formed representation is not in place which would make it possible to trace a pathway from "does not like candy" to the zero cell and recognize that James, then, could not be a watchman.

This argument rests on the assumption that changing perspective makes demands on the cognitive processing system. *Modus tollens* puts a greater cognitive load on working memory than any of the other three logical forms. This idea that failure to solve *modus tollens* is caused by loss of the full representation of the contingency between *p* and *q* which, in turn, is caused by the fragility of such representations when the contingency has no specific content, is similar to Cox and Griggs" hypothesis that realistic content serves a memory cue for tasks like the Wason problem: "performance . . . is significantly facilitated only when presentation of the task allows the subject to recall past experience with the content of the problem, the relationship expressed, and a counter example to the rule governing the relationship" (1982:497). However, the emphasis here is on the presence of a *cultural* schema by which the subject can represent the contingency between *p* and *q* rather than on any *specific* past experiences with such contingencies. In the problem about garnets and semi-precious stones, for example, it is doubtful that the good performance on this problem is due to much *real* experience with garnets and semi-precious stones. It seems more likely that the good performance is due to the culturally well-defined schema for the *relationship* between being a garnet and being a semi-precious stone. (A similar argument has been developed by Richard Nisbett (1993) and his associates.)

It is interesting that when students explain their mistakes on the realistic *modus tollens* problems, they often say they got the wrong answer because they added more to the state of affairs than was given in the problem. One person, for example, explained that it *might* be raining even if the roof is *not* wet (given that "If it is raining then the roof is wet") because there *might* be a tree over the roof which would keep the rain off. It was pointed out to the student that since the problem explicitly asks one to assume that *if* it rains the roof *will* get wet, one must also assume that there is no tree blocking the rain. The student immediately saw that this was the case and groaned. The rapid and vivid perception of the mistake made here contrasts with the difficulty of getting subjects to see why they should turn over the label with a 3 on it. Perhaps it is easier to see that one has added something extra than it is to see that something is missing – it is harder to see what is not there. In any case, the student's *reasoning* was not at fault; what was incorrect was the way the problem was *represented*.[7]

If the findings presented here that people cannot do complex problems like *modus tollens* with arbitrary content are generally true, then so-called *formal* reasoning – which by definition is reasoning without respect to content – must be limited to the simple logical operations which people can do regardless of content, such as *modus ponens*. Other common forms which people are able to do regardless of content, or by virtue of form alone, are:

p or *q*
not p
therefore *q*

not not p
therefore *p*
(see Braine, Reiser, and Rumain 1984).

Thus, human reasoning involves at least two different cognitive processes; the first is a tendency towards consistency based on form alone, operating primarily on a few very simple logical arguments, such as *modus ponens*. The second process involves the mental manipulation of specific representations, in which plausible and deductive inferences are made by tracing out contingencies.

Although people are not very good at using what are called "abstract" schemas, like *modus tollens*, it is possible to train people to use some abstract schemas effectively..Two senses of the term *abstract* need to be distinguished.

[7] This appears to have been the problem of Luria's Uzbekistan informants, replicated by Cole and Scribner with the Vai of Liberia. A common "failing" of unschooled people is that they rerepresent the premises of some logic problem in a way that makes more sense to them, and then reason in a perfectly adequate way about this new representation. For a review of this issue see Scribner 1977.

One kind of abstraction can be seen in the playing of chess; a good chess player knows a variety of abstract patterns or configurations. These patterns are abstract in the sense that they involve higher order relations, but they remain patterns of *chess*. I call this "content based abstraction" (D'Andrade 1981).

A second sense of "abstraction" refers to the recoding of content into a different kind of model or symbol system. For example, when the Label Factory problem is recoded into *p*'s and *q*'s, the content of the problem, involving labels, letters, and numbers, disappears. Similarly, algebra problems about, for example, how far a boat has travelled under various conditions, involve recoding the problem into *x*'s and *y*'s. I call this "formal language abstraction" because, to be solved, the problem must be recoded into a different language. There are a number of such formal languages, such as algebra, calculus, the sentential calculus, and the first order predicate calculus, as well as the specific mathematical equations of statistics and economics.

Both kinds of abstraction are difficult for people, but formal language abstraction seems especially difficult. The major difficulty seems to be not in learning the manipulation of the formal symbols, but rather in learning how to apply these symbols across many different domains. Richard Nisbett, a cognitive social psychologist, has found that people *can* learn to apply abstract statistical rules, and even formal logic, if taught with a variety of good examples, although he notes that people do better with the more pragmatic types of rules (such as *cost-benefit* rules, or the *law of large numbers*, as contrasted with *modus tollens*) (1993).

The position argued above about how people reason is similar to the position taken by Johnson-Laird (1983) concerning the importance of mental models in reasoning. However, emphasis is placed here on the importance of having an already available well-structured schema which can be used as the template for a specific representation of a particular state of affairs. More generally, what we find is that the ability to reason is very strongly influenced by the presence of cultural models. When we have good models, we can reason adroitly. When the representations are incomplete or not well learned, we reason poorly. Thus, to the extent that a culture has good cultural models (*good* in the sense that the schema captures the real world contingencies and is well learned), a member of that culture will be able to reason well about the objects and events referred to by these models. Trobrianders reason skillfully about land tenure because they have learned the complex model of ownership which is a part of Trobriand culture, not because they are smarter than other people.

Distributed cognition, artifacts and representational structure

Cultural models are not the only models people use in reasoning; idiosyncratic models can also be used. But there are major limitations on idiosyncratic models; one must create the model for oneself, and this seems hard for humans.

Watching psychological experiments carried out during the 1970s by Marc Eisenstadt and Yakov Kareev (1975) on learning of board games, I was impressed with the difficulty students had in learning new representations on their own. Typically, students would play game after game of gomoku or some other board game against a computer program and make the same mistakes over and over – despite the use of clever computer programs which allowed the students to "look ahead" for what might happen, or to "look back" at how they had gotten themselves in the trouble. In Eisenstadt's and Kareev's experiments, students won only 20% of their games against the computer.

In contrast to the students, the experimenters were all very good at these games, and most of them could almost always beat the computer. When I inquired about this, I received various explanations, such as "students are dumb," or "playing against computers throws people off." What Eisenstadt and Kareev suggested to me was that the experimenters all knew the "winning patterns," while the students did not. And how did the group of experimenters learn the winning patterns? They learned from each other, or from texts. Content based abstraction is usually easy to learn if someone points it out, but hard to achieve on one's own.

The simple point is that most people are smart because someone taught them the right models. Our folk model of "smartness" makes intelligence an individual thing, a result of being able to learn quickly and having a high IQ. The position taken here is that the folk model stresses the wrong thing; it is not that quick learning and a high IQ have *no* effect, but rather that this effect is very small compared to the effect of being taught versus not being taught.

Since so much of our intelligence and ability comes from having good cultural models, and these cultural models are held by a group which maintains the existence of these cultural models by teaching them to others, one can speak of cognition as *socially distributed.* The individual is only a part of the general process by which models are invented, elaborated, taught, replaced, and forgotten. Further, a major fact about any society is that there is a division of labor with respect to *cognition.* The cognitive division of labor has not been investigated extensively by anthropologists, although John Roberts (1964) presented an innovative account of this phenomena, and Marc Swartz has developed a theory of culture that explicitly recognizes the distributative character of cultural knowledge (Swartz 1991). Recently Edwin Hutchins has undertaken a series of studies investigating the social distribution of cognition.

One example of the way in which the social distribution of cognition affects decision making involves the degree of independence between decision making units. The units may be people, or teams of people, or even different networks within the same brain. In his book, *Cognition in the Wild*, Hutchins has demonstrated with a series of computer simulations that if the amount of influential communication between the decision makers is very large, then it will be very likely that the decision makers will reach a consensus, but it is also much more likely the decision will be a poor one. When the amount of influential communication is low, the problem of reaching a consensus is greater but the probability of reaching the right decision is also greater.

Hutchins uses Issac Asimov's novel *Foundation's Edge*, a story in the far future about Gaia, the original earth planet on which all life forms are now in total psychic communication with each other at all times, to illustrate the problem. Hutchins points out that the problem with a Gaia-like system is that if for any reason the total system begins to move towards a bad decision, the weight of the later evidence encountered by single individuals is so greatly overbalanced by the weight of everyone else's opinion that discrepancies which point to a different decision get ignored. Hutchins calls this an example of *confirmation bias*: "the propensity to affirm prior interpretations and to discount, ignore, or re-interpret evidence counter to an already formed interpretation."

Culturally institutionalized solutions to prevent confirmation bias caused by too much intercommunication can be observed in cultural rules such as the rule that jurors may not discuss a case with each other until all the evidence has been heard. Many of the institutions within the world of science appear to be adaptations to prevent confirmation bias, such as the blind review of articles and grants so the judges will not be influenced by their prior opinions about the author. The stereotype of the scientist as cold, dispassionate, and objective, is, as we all know well, far from the fact. Most scientists possess deep prejudices about how the world is which they defend passionately. The objectivity of science comes about not because the individual scientists are without confirmation bias, but by having a large number of decision makers who are independent of each other, and by having some agreed upon rules about the kinds of data needed to confirm or disconfirm a theory.

Diversity of opinion brings another problem to the fore; that is, how to make a decision when there is disagreement. Hutchins points out that a social system can solve this problem by giving one person the authority to make the final decision, or by having various kinds of voting schemes. According to Hutchins there is a fundamental tension between the problem of casting a wide net for all kinds of information, which will often make for diversity of opinion as different individuals encounter different information, versus reaching a decision, which involves the problem of obtaining consensus or using authority. Hutchins says:

> In the simulations presented here, the effects of group level cognitive properties are not produced solely by structure internal to individuals, nor are they produced solely by structure external to individuals. Rather, the cognitive properties of groups are produced by an interaction between structures internal to individuals and structures external to individuals. All human societies face cognitive tasks that are beyond the capabilities of any individual member. For example, even the simplest culture contains more information than could be learned by any individual in a lifetime, so the tasks of learning,

remembering, and transmitting cultural information are inevitably distributed. The performance of cognitive tasks that exceed individual abilities is always shaped by a social organization of distributed cognition. (1994)

Another kind of distributed structure that Hutchins has investigated is the structure of "cognitive artifacts." In *Cognition in the Wild* Hutchins presents an ethnographic account of how such artifacts are used in navigation in the American Navy. The Navy has a set of complex procedures for determining the position of a ship as it cruises off-shore or comes into a harbor. These procedures make use of a variety of cognitive artifacts distributed across a team of individuals.

The basic technique is to find three landmarks on the coast that correspond to two identifiable points on a chart, then to determine the angles of the lines of sight from the ship to the landmarks, and then to compute the point of intersection of the three lines on the chart. The intersection of the lines indicates the position of the ship. A variety of distinct physical structures are used in this process. The general notion of a physical structure was discussed at the end of Chapter 6, where the argument was made that there is a complex relation between mental structures and external physical structures with respect to communication and learning; simply put, the argument is that since minds cannot communicate by telepathy, there must be some structured physical medium by which communication takes place through which new mental structures – models, taxonomies, theories, etc. – are learned. Spoken language is one kind of physical structure, which, although evanescent, is our principal medium for communication. However, spoken language is not permanent; many cognitive artifacts are made of more durable stuff.

A *cognitive artifact* is a physical structure which helps humans perform some cognitive operation. Cognitive artifacts range from complex machines such as computers to simple devices such paper and pencil. In the navigation of a ship near shore, one important device is the pelorus. The pelorus combines a telescopic sight, called an *alidade*, with a gyrocompass and scale. There are two pelorus operators in the navigation team, and it is their job to locate landmarks and measure their direction from the ship. The landmarks are selected by another member of the navigation team, the bearing recorder, who chooses landmarks from a chart in the pilot house. The chart landmarks have special names – "Dive Tower," "Hotel Del," "Point Loma" – and the names of the selected landmarks are called by phone to the pelorus operators. It is their job to locate the landmarks along the shore, to point the alidade at the landmark until it is lined up with a vertical hairline, and then read off where the hairline crosses the compass scale. The number that is read from the scale gives the direction in degree from true north of the landmark from the ship.

The alidade is a physical structure that makes possible a particular kind of computation – the determination of an angle to a distant point. This is a relatively simple kind of cognitive operation, but one which humans are not good at judging unaided. Two important structures in the alidade are the hairline sight and the compass scale. For the computation of the angle, the hair line must cross both the landmark and the compass scale. The compass scale consists of tick marks with numbers written every ten degrees, and the pelorus operator counts the number of tick marks from the number on the right to get the proper number of degrees.

Once the pelorus operator has determined the number of degrees to a particular landmark, and announced the number at the bearing recorder's command to "mark," the number is written down in a log book by the bearing recorder along with the time in hours and minutes. Three bearings are taken for each "fix," two from one pelorus operation and one from the other. The plotter, using a one-armed protractor called a *hoey*, marks a line on the chart from the landmark towards the approximate position of the ship by aligning the hoey on the chart so that the angle of the line drawn corresponds to the number of degrees of the sighted landmark from true north. As each of the three bearings are given to the plotter, lines are drawn on the chart. If the bearings have been taken with absolute accuracy, the three lines will intersect at a point. If there is some inaccuracy in the bearings – as there almost always is – the three lines will make a small triangle, and the location of the ship on the chart is somewhere within this triangle. The speed of the ship is calculated from the distance and time passed since the last plot, and the position of the ship at the next plot is estimated. Information about the speed and location of the ship is continuously passed to the pilot, making possible appropriate course corrections.

This is a "bare bones" account of one cycle in the navigation process, described in much greater detail in Hutchins' book. A major point that Hutchins makes is that a great number of physical structures are being used in this process and that these structures are placed in *coordination* with one another. By means of such coordinations, the *propagation of representational states* from one medium to another is effected until the final representation is achieved. In the case of navigation, the representational state is the position of the ship relative to the shore, and the information about this representational state is propagated from hairline sights that are coordinated with marked scales into numbers spoken as words, and then these spoken numbers are transformed into marks written on paper and angles on a protractor which are coordinated with north–south directions on the chart and transformed into lines on the chart where finally the intersection of lines represents the position of the ship.

A general point that Hutchins makes is that human intelligence is deeply bound up in the use of external structures of a great variety of kinds. A mathematician sitting at a table and writing equations may be taken as the example of totally internalized thought, but as Hutchins points out, even the lone mathematician uses external structures. The mathematician uses symbols which have a visual form which can be written down and manipulated in the mind. Furthermore, the two dimensions of the piece of paper serve as a coordinating structure to display the "before and after" sequencing of thought, in English corresponding to the sequence of symbols from top to bottom and left to right, as well as serving as a permanent memory of that thought.

Of course, the doing of mathematics is more than just shuffling marks. Real mathematicians have understandings about relationships among abstract entities, and these entities are more than uninterpreted scratchings on a piece of paper. The entities are abstract things such as space, lines, points, quantities, equivalences, changes, changes in changes, etc. It is the relations between these abstract things that mathematics is about, and it is these relations that mathematicians discover. However, while mathematicians may reason about these relations in pure form, they are given an immense assistance in such thinking by having physical symbols to stand as markers of these relationships along with the two dimensional organization of these symbols on paper to correspond to the flow of thought.

Given the intimate relationship between mental and physical structures, it is not surprising that Hutchins finds the definition of culture as a purely mental organization to be counterproductive. Definitions are supposed to "carve nature at the joints." But looking at the world of navigation, the ideas – the cognitive models – are not separate from the physical structures which embody them. Clearly, a better definition of *culture* is needed. As discussed in Chapter 6, my solution is to define *culture* as the entire social heritage of a group, including material culture and external structures, learned actions, and mental representations of many kinds, and in context to try to be specific about the kind of culture I am talking about.

Consensus and cognition

James Boster, in working on Jivaro folk botany, obtained a striking result involving consensus (1985). In a study of informant variability in plant naming, Boster set up experimental gardens planted with different varieties of manioc. Informants were then asked to name each of the varieties. The modal name (the most frequently given name) for each variety was determined. Boster then retested six informants and calculated a reliability score for each informant: the percentage of plants given the same name on both trials. What Boster discovered was that there was almost a perfect correlation between percentage of modal names used by an informant and the informant's reliability; informants who used more modal names were more likely to give the same names to plants on both trips ($r = .92$). Correlations this high between clearly different measures are unusual in the social sciences, indicating the operation of strong causal forces.

Boster's finding has been confirmed and extended in a series of studies by Kim Romney, Sue Weller, Linda Garro, and others. The core finding is that individual cognition is related to cultural consensus; those who agree with the cultural consensus are more reliable (i.e., give the same response on the second presentation of a task), more consistent (i.e., in a ranking task, if A is said to be greater than B, and B is said to be greater than C, then A is said to be greater than C), have faster reaction times, and, other things being equal, are also likely to be better educated, more experienced, and more intelligent.[8] This pattern of relationships has been found in a wide variety of cultural domains, including color (Boynton and Olson 1987), beliefs about disease (Weller 1984; Garro 1986a, 1988), plant taxonomies (Boster 1985), and American parental sanctions for rule breaking (Weller, Romney, and Orr 1986).

The relation between reliability and consensus found in this and in other studies raises a number of cognitive issues. Why *should* the Jivaro informant who uses the modal terms for plants be more reliable? Why is not the correlation reversed – why are not those who use idiosyncratic names more reliable, consistent, intelligent, and so on? The answer to this question appears to involve the process of learning. It is a common finding that when people do some simple naming task, like naming color chips, the color chips with the best agreed upon names are also the color chips which are most reliably named (the same name will be given on subsequent trials), and also the chips which are most quickly named. This is what Boynton and Olson (1987) and Brown and Lenneberg (1954) found in their studies of color naming.

The usual explanation for this is that people are more reliable and faster at doing those things for which they have better training. One gets good training – consistent, clear, instruction – about the greenness of grass, but much less clear instruction about the color of water in swimming pools. High cultural consensus is likely to be the result of consistent training, and consistent training creates consistent responses. Further, since this knowledge is well learned, the informant can produce it without hesitation, resulting in faster reaction times.

This is a reasonable explanation for why somebody labels one color chip more reliably and faster than another, but it does not explain why some *individuals* are, with respect to some particular domain, such as plant names, generally more reliable in their responses. Boster, for example, developed two different experimental gardens, one with a small number of easy to identify manioc plants, the other with a larger number of more difficult to identify manioc plants. He found that informants who gave more modal names in the easy garden were also very likely to give more modal names in the hard garden ($r = .62$). Thus knowing the "right" name for manioc plants is a general ability of Jivaro individuals. Of course, if we assume that some Jivaro have *generally* better training in manioc plant names, then we would also expect them to be *generally* better in both gardens. The better training might be the result of more extensive experience, or greater aptitude, or better teachers, or any

[8] See a special issue of the *American Behaviorist*: 31:2 (1987), edited by James Boster, devoted exclusively to the study of intracultural variation.

combination of these. Also the greater amount of communication with others that goes with greater experience and training would constantly push the learner towards the use of modal terms and propositions because these are least likely to be misunderstood by others.

This pattern of results might be argued to be the result of simple conformity – those who conform most are closest to the cultural consensus, and they are most reliable because they know they are doing the right thing, and so feel sure of themselves and do not change their minds and answer promptly. To see if the consensus effect could be found in a domain in which there are no clear right or wrong answers, and hence no obvious effect of conformity, I examined already published results of word association tests (D'Andrade 1987b). In doing word associations one is supposed to respond to a stimulus word – "cat" – with the first word that comes to mind – "dog" – and whatever one says is acceptable. I found a study conducted by three psychologists (Moran, Mefferd, and Kimble 1964) which also contained a reliability test. Moran *et al* gave word association tests to seventy-nine normal and seventy-nine schizophrenic subjects on four successive days, using a list of 125 words. After each set of twenty-five words, subjects were retested on the same words with instructions to give the same responses they had given the first time. Subjects were also given the vocabulary section of the Wexler–Bellvue IQ test and their education level was assessed.

From their word association data, Moran *et al.* constructed a measure of modality, termed *commonality*, by assigning a value for each response produced by a given subject which corresponds to the percentage of times that response was given by the total sample. The commonality score for each subject is the sum of these values. This measure of commonality correlated .90 with commonality scored according to the standard norms for the 100 Kent–Rosanoff list. The other variables coded by Moran *et al.* were *blank* responses (number of times the subject fails to respond within twenty seconds), *distant* responses (number of times the subject gives a response that has no apparent semantic relation to the stimulus word), *speed* of response (average reaction time between presentation of the stimulus word and the subject's response), *reliability* (number of times the subject gave exactly the same associations to the same stimulus word), and *education* (number of years of formal schooling).

The results are exactly what would be expected on the basis of the linkage between training and consensus. Those subjects who most frequently gave modal word associations (measured here by *commonality*) were more *reliable* ($r = .58$), gave *faster* responses ($r = .45$), were less likely to give *distant* associations ($r = -.66$), and were less likely to draw *blanks* ($r = -.33$). The subjects who gave more modal associations also had higher IQs ($r = .42$) and were somewhat better educated ($r = .29$). Not surprisingly, the schizophrenics produced fewer *modal* associations, were less *reliable*, and were more likely than the normals to give *distant* associations and draw *blanks*.

It might seem strange that in a word association test those who give the most modal answers are also the most reliable, fastest, smartest, and best educated. After all, there is no obvious knowledge involved in producing word association. However, for there to be an association there must be some connection between the test word and the response. Common word associations are derived from a relatively small set of semantic relationships, such as *opposition* (light/dark), *superordination* (carrot/vegetable), *subordination* (jewel/diamond), *coordination* (man/woman), *verb/object* relations (milk/drink), and so on. Those who are most expert in the use of language (as measured by the Wexler–Bellvue vocabulary test) and who have the most education would tend to be most knowledgeable about such semantic relationships, and would be most likely to produce associations generated by these relationships, and to do so rapidly. Since there is nothing else to constrain word associations, the modal or most frequent association is likely to be that association which is generated by the most semantically relevant relationship, and hence is the "best" answer. So even when there are no right or wrong answers, and no pressure of conformity, and not even an obvious kind of knowledge involved, the same pattern is found; those who are closest to the cultural consensus are more reliable, faster in their answers, more intelligent, better educated, and more likely to be normal. The consensus effect is quite robust.

These results concerning consensus are relevant to methodological issues concerning anthropological field work. There is a general belief among anthropologists that a small number of knowledgeable informants is sufficient to obtain an adequate cultural account. To many social scientists this seems a naive approach to sampling, since there is a general bias in the social sciences towards the belief that accuracy requires large numbers. However, if experienced and knowledgeable informants really are a good mirror of the cultural consensus, then a small number of good informants might be enough. The question is – how can one find out how many is enough?

This question can be answered by a formal model of cultural competence developed by Romney, Weller, and Batchelder (1986). The model assumes that the level of agreement between informants is due to their joint agreement with the cultural consensus, and that the probability an informant will answer a given question correctly is a result of that informant's competence with respect to that domain of knowledge. A third assumption is that there is a correct answer for every question; i.e., whatever the cultural reality is, it is the same for all informants. If these assumptions have been met the matrix of informant intercorrelations will contain only one major factor, indicating there is enough agreement on what is correct for everyone to be more or less similar to each other.

The data for the consensus model consists of the responses of each informant on each question or task. A computer program, developed by Steve Borgati as part of a general package of statistical programs, can be used to analyze such data.[9] From the raw data the program produces two major outputs; the first is each informant's level of competence (the probability of that informant's knowing the correct answer to any question); the second is the correct answer for each question and its associated confidence level. Many kinds of data have been analyzed with the model, including folk medical beliefs, occupational prestige, causes of death, and hot–cold concepts of illness (See Romney, Batchelder, and Weller 1987). It has been found that in the domains examined, a relatively small number of informants (twenty to forty) is more than sufficient to determine at high levels of confidence the "correct" cultural response. Typically average levels of informant competence run higher than .5, indicating that the average informant knows the correct answer to somewhat more than 50% of all the questions. When competence levels rise to .7, Romney, Weller, and Batchelder were able to show that sixteen informants is sufficient for almost all purposes, and that with competence levels of .9, seven informants is enough.

Summary

There are two sides to the issue of cultural variation. On one side is the need for a division of labor in who knows what, both because there is too much to be known for any one person to know it, and because independence in who knows what makes for less confirmation bias and potentially better decision making. The difficulties in cultural transmission and formation of various kinds of subgroups also create variation within a culture. These forces for dispersal are opposed by forces which create consensus, such as the need to communicate effectively and share expertise. The result is that the cultural heritage tends to divide into two parts – one part a high consensus code which everyone is expected to share, the other a proliferating number of distributed knowledge systems. The issue is not "how shared is culture," but rather how to understand both distributed and high consensus aspects of cultural knowledge.

In the earlier part of this chapter some of the complex ways in which cultural representations affect perception, memory, and reasoning were outlined. Considering these representations as part of *culture*, one can reasonably say that "culture influences perception, memory, and reasoning." This is old news. Many anthropologists believe culture does just about everything, so the claim that one needs well-formed cultural models to do *modus tollens* is not likely to cause excitement. But culture does not really do *everything*. The effect of culture is greatly exaggerated by many anthropologists. So far as we know, no cultural particulars are needed for humans everywhere to do *modus ponens*, or remember the color of apples, or perceive that a hawk is different than a handsaw.

9 Steve Borgati, Anthropac 4.0. Columbia, North Carolina: Analytic Technologies, 1993.

Where culture seems to have its greatest effect is on semantic memory and complex reasoning. Here, the evidence, while scanty, indicates that cultural models and other types of cultural representations have a large impact. Our cleverness as a species is primarily a matter of being able to learn representations. We are not too good at inventing new representations – the people who do this are our culture heroes – but we learn quickly, and we have good memories. Once we learn the representations, we can reason adroitly and calculate outcomes. Part of the price we pay for these representations is memory bias, since we are likely to remember the world as we represent it, but this is made up for both by the increment in reasoning power and the greater memory power for events which fit these representations. Our need for these representations makes us dependent on others and on the cultural heritage which they can teach us.

9 Cognitive processes and personality

One of the basic undertakings for cognitive anthropology is to work out how representational aspects of culture affect the individual. In the last chapter a sketch of how cultural schemas affect perception, memory, and reasoning was presented. In this chapter, the relation between cultural schemas and the personality will be explored. By *personality* I mean primarily the emotional and motivational aspects of human behavior. The general argument is that it is through linkages with emotion and motivation that cultural schemas affect human action.

Emotion

In the western folk model of the mind, emotion contrasts sharply with cognition. In the folk model emotions are *feelings* which have little to do with what one thinks. Feelings include localized physical sensations like hunger and pain, as well as unlocalized sensations like anger and joy. According to the folk model, one can direct one's thoughts but one cannot control one's feelings, which are a natural consequence of events. And feelings can be so strong they prevent clear thinking and lead to irrational action. In the folk model, thought and feeling are often cast as opposing forces.

This view of emotion and thought has changed radically over the past thirty years in both psychology and anthropology. A series of experiments in psychology carried out by Stanley Schacter and Jerome Singer in the early 1960s, now described in almost every introductory psychology textbook, are the canonical reference for this change. In one experiment, Schacter and Singer (1962) gave experimental subjects injections of adrenalin. One group of subjects was informed correctly about the effects of the drug – "effects last only 15 or 20 minutes. Probably your hands will start to shake, your heart will start to pound, and your face may get warm and flushed." The other group was misled into thinking the drug was just a vitamin compound which might effect vision. After the drug injection, subjects were put in a waiting room. Half of the subjects from each group found a high spirited person in their waiting room who played with paper airplanes, practiced basketball with a crumbled paper and the wastebasket, and encouraged the subject to join the fun. The other half of the subjects in each group were asked to fill out a long, infuriating questionaire. Present in their waiting room was a person answering the same questionaire who acted very angry and agitated, and who finally ripped up the questionaire and stamped out of the room. Throughout the waiting room period subjects were observed through a one way mirror and their emotional behavior recorded. Subjects also filled out a mood questionnaire after the waiting period was over.

The results were that subjects who did not know about the effects of the drug were strongly affected by the experimental conditions, displaying much more anger in the anger-arousing condition, and much more happiness in the euphoria-arousing condition, than subjects who knew about the effects of the drug. A separate experimental group who were given a saline solution injection were not as strongly affected by either emotion arousing condition as those who received adrenaline. These results have been taken to show that physiological arousal (the presence of adrenaline) is a precondition for emotion, but *which* emotion will be experienced depends on the way the arousal is interpreted. If the arousal is interpreted to be the result of a drug, neither anger nor happiness will be induced by the external circumstances. If subjects do not know that their physiological reactions are due to a drug, they interpret their arousal as due to either happiness or anger, depending on the circumstances. According to this theory, the meaning of the arousing situation is blended into emotional experience, and *it is arousal and meaning together that make up the experience of emotion.*

The idea that the sensate side of emotion is limited to just arousal (i.e., the sensations produced by the autonomic nervous system) has been controversial. Most psychologists of emotion believe that the sensate side of emotion includes more than just the physical sensations caused by the reaction of the sympathetic and parasympathetic nervous system; however, just how much more varies from theorist to theorist. For Nico Frija there are just two kinds of response; an evaluative response (good–bad) and arousal. For Oatley and Johnson-Laird there are five primary sensations; joy, fear, sadness, anger, and disgust. Paul Ekman, who bases his typology on universal facial expressions, postulates seven basic emotions; joy, surprise, sadness, fear, anger, disgust, and contempt. Carol Izard proposes ten primary emotions; joy, surprise, interest, distress (sadness?), fear, anger, disgust, contempt, shame, and guilt. (See D'Andrade 1993 for a review of the basic emotions controversy.).

There are a number of considerations that affect exactly which emotions are considered basic. For example, the discovery of endorphins has strengthened the claim that some part of happiness involves a central, brain based sensation, not reduceable to just autonomic arousal. As more and more neurotransmitters are discovered, like dopamine and serotonin, and their effects on emotion are worked out, it should be possible to understand more about the brain structures that are involved in emotional experience.

Another consideration relevant to the determination of basic emotions involves the ability of observers to tell which emotions other people are experiencing. One might expect that any basic emotion would be readily identifiable. Somewhat surprisingly, when asked to judge which emotions other people are experiencing from photos, audiotapes, or videotapes, people are only able to assess reliably two dimensions; degree of arousal and happiness/unhappiness (D'Andrade 1993; Smith and Ellsworth 1985). However, observers have been trained to code reliably all of Ekman's universal facial expressions based on the analysis of the movement of facial muscles. It is likely that most normal judgments about the emotions of others are based on some knowledge of both the situation that aroused the emotion and subsequent actions carried out in response to the situation, and this makes judgment based on facial expression and tone of voice alone difficult.

At this point, the only consensus about basic emotions is that the number of unique, emotion related sensations is limited, and that emotional experience consists of a synthesis of these sensations with a cognitive appraisal of the situation. Such a synthesis is obvious in an emotion like jealousy, in which there *must* be an appraisal that someone else has something that one wants and cannot have, as well as some bad feeling towards the person who possesses the desired object. One could not have a feeling of jealousy without such an appraisal – to say that one feels jealous means that such an appraisal has been made and one has a bad feeling about it. Even for "simple" emotions like sadness, or anger, or fear, some appraisal seems to be a part of the definition of the emotion – sadness implies an appraisal that some kind of loss had happened, anger implies an appraisal that something frustrating or unfair has happened and that the responsible agent should be attacked, fear implies an appraisal that danger is present and that one should flee. According to the folk model, one can feel joy for no particular reason, but this would be likely to be associated with an appraisal that the world is a good place.

This leads to an interesting issue. Once appraisal is recognized as an important part of emotion, then does the appraisal have to be *exactly* the same for people to feel the same emotion? Given slightly different appraisals involved in the English terms *pine for*, *miss*, *homesick for*, *long for*, and *nostalgic about*, are these different varieties of a basic emotion of sadness, or are they distinct emotions? Or, as Wierzbicka has asked (1992), if the French term *dégôut* has more physical emphasis on a bad taste in the mouth than the English term *disgust*, which term is the right one to stand for the universal basic emotion of disgust postulated by Ekman?

Wierzbicka has attempted to provide a framework by which the meaning of emotion terms in different languages can be compared. She uses a terminology of probable semantic universals which include *I*, *you*, *someone*, *something*, *this*, *say*, *want*, *feel*, *think*, *know*, *where*, *good*, *bad*, *because*, *if*, *can*, *like*, *the same*, *kind of*, *after*, *do*, *happen*, and *all*. Emotion terms are then defined in this language. For example:

X is *homesick* =>

X thinks something like this:
  I am far away from home
  when I was there, I felt something good
  I want to be there now
  If I were there now, I would feel something good
  I cannot be there now
because of this, X feels something bad (Wierzbicka 1992:122)

English *homesick* is similar to, but is not the same as the Polish term *teskni*.

X *teskni* do Y =>

X thinks something like this:
  I am far away from Y
  when I was with Y I felt something good
  I want to be with Y now
  if I were with Y now I would feel something good
  I cannot be with Y now
because of this, X feels something bad (Wierzbicka 1992:121)

From these two definitions, it can be seen that the Polish term, unlike *homesick*, refers to a person. Unlike the term *miss*, the Polish term implies pain and necessarily involves a separation by distance. Neither *longing* nor *pining* are restricted to separation by distance (one can long to have a vacation, and pine for a dead pet). According to Wierzbicka, there is no exact translation for *teski*. About this situation she says:

> Does this mean that native speakers of English do not know (never experience) the feeling in question? Not necessarily. Individual speakers of English have no doubt experienced this feeling. But the Anglo-Saxon culture as a whole has not found this feeling worthy of a special name.
>
> Nor does the fact that a language has not encoded a particular emotion in a separate word mean that the speakers of this language cannot perceive that emotion as a distinct, recognizable feeling or that they cannot talk about it. Both everyday speech and psychologically sensitive literature are full of attempts, often highly successful, to convey feelings for which there is no simple word. (Wierzbicka 1992:123)

In Wierzbicka's universal language, there are only two kinds of "feelings." One either "feels something good" or "feels something bad." All the differentiation between different emotions is in the appraisal – "X thinks something like this . . ." However, this is not really sufficient. Consider Wierzbicka's definition for *homesick*. The appraisal is that one is away from home, where one felt good, and one wants to be there now, but because one cannot be there, one *feels something bad.* This "bad" feeling is not specified, but we infer that the feeling is some kind of sadness because we know that loss causes sadness, and being away from home is a kind of loss. But what if the "bad" feeling a person had under these same circumstances was acute fear? Imagine a child's frightened reaction to being away from home. That would be a very different emotion than *homesickness.* Yet the child's situation would fit Wierzbicka's definition. Wierzbicka avoids specifying kinds of feeling, and thereby escapes the controversy about basic emotions. However, this avoidance is only partially successful. Wierzbicka is able to avoid giving any labels to what is felt except "something good" or "something bad" because there are such tight links between what we feel and the conditions which arouse the feeling that an emotion can usually be specified by detailing the appraisal that gave rise to it. This does not really dispose of the problem of identifying basic emotions, however; it merely hides it.

The issue of exactly how variable the emotion vocabularies of different cultures are is currently a matter of contention. Clearly, one can make reasonable translations. Wierzbicka (1992) presents translations for Japanese *amae*, Ilongot *liget*, Javanese *sungkan*, Ifaluk *fago*, Hawaiian *aloha*, Tahitian *arofa*, Utku Eskimo *iva*, Australian Pintupi *watjilpa*, Czech *litost*, and Russian *zalost'*. While one might quibble over whether these definitions escape from the problem of basic emotions, there is little doubt that these definitions effectively capture the meaning that ethnographers have described for these emotions. So the issue of variability is not translatability. The real issue seems to be something like the following: because people in other cultures *describe* certain experiences differently than we do, does that make their experience different?

To answer this question, it is necessary to analyze further the relation between appraisal and emotion. In the terms of this book, an appraisal is the activation of a schema. Consider the emotion of fear. An infant has, in some form, an innate set of simple schemas which, when activated, trigger various fear responses – the sensation of fear, the facial expression of fear, the autonomic reactions to fear, etc. The feeling of falling, being hurt, being abandoned, loud noises, etc., are examples of stimuli which trigger these fear responses. Over time these schemas are integrated together to form a general "danger to the self" schema, which when activated, arouses fear reactions. Eventually, very abstract kinds of "danger to the self" will arouse fear, such as the threat of financial ruin or threat to the lives of family members, as well as more concrete dangers, such as the threat of being hit by an automobile or the threat to life involved in a medical operation.[1]

One way that the cultural heritage effects the emotion of fear is by

[1] See Lazarus 1991 for a comprehensive review of the role of appraisal in emotion. For a more psychoanalytic view see Rosenblatt 1985.

shaping what is defined as a threat. If one's soul is thought to leave the body when one sneezes, and sometimes not return, resulting in death, then sneezing is likely to be frightening. Cultural definitions of *kinds of danger*, or *kinds of loss*, or *kinds of reward*, etc., affect the appraisal system. Of course, cultural definitions are not always effective – people can refuse to believe that smoking endangers their health, or that condoms are necessary for safe sex, and so experience no fright because they do not believe. For this kind of cultural shaping of emotion to work, people must really believe the *X is a kind of Y* linkage. However, while it is likely the number and types of linkages would affect how frequently and strongly an emotion was felt, it would not seem to have any necessary effect on the *experience* of emotion itself.

Following a general Whorfian hypothesis, it has often been suggested that the way in which emotions are *defined* might affect the very way emotion is experienced. Robert Levy, a psychiatrist turned anthropologist who worked in Tahiti, suggests that a culture may *hypocognize* an emotion. According to Levy (1984), a culturally hypocognized emotion is "underschematized" – it is only sketchily defined and is unelaborated in cultural models. For example, in Tahiti, the emotion of sadness is hypocognized. Levy found no unambiguous terms representing sadness or loneliness in Tahiti. When Tahitians were in a situation Levy judged would lead to sadness, they would use terms to describe their situation which can best be glossed as "feeling troubled," "feeling heavy," and "not feeling a sense of inner push" (Levy 1973). These terms are both vague and without any sense of some external, social cause for the emotion. In general, Tahitian culture holds the irrevocable loss of others to be a minor matter, something which can be managed through immediate replacement by other persons.

What, then, happens to the experience of emotion in Tahiti? Levy says:

> One of the consequences of hypocognition is that the felt disturbance, the "troubled feelings," can be interpreted both by the one who experiences them and by others around him as something other than "emotion." Thus, the troubled feelings that persist too long after the death of a loved one or those that occur after some loss that Tahitian ideology holds to be trivial and easily replaceable are in the village often interpreted as illness or the harmful effects of a spirit. In many cases connections between the feelings of disturbance with . . . the eliciting event are not in any way recognized. A young man whose transient woman has just left him, taking their baby with her to a distant island, may look sluggish and despondent and, diagnosing himself as physically ill owing to some extraneous cause, seek some herbal medicine. If the bad feelings persist, he may go to a spirit doctor who will help him identify and treat the spirit that is possessing him . . . Note that for the young Tahitian there are two kinds of knowing involved: that covert knowing, which recognized certain events as a loss and which produced a felt organismic response, and a later overt knowing, which is associated with a culturally patterned evaluation of, and response to, the feeling. (Levy 1984:220)

Levy presents a clear paradigm concerning the relation between a *primary appraisal* and a *secondary appraisal.* The primary appraisal is innate and gives rise to a "felt organismic response." Levy hypothesizes that the modification of primary appraisal can occur as a result of early socialization, and the effect of such socialization is typically a shift in sensitivity or reactivity to the appraisal. For example, a child who has only one mothering person is more likely to experience the inevitable temporary separations from that person as very dangerous compared to a child who has numerous mothers. Someone raised as a one-mother child would therefore be more likely, as an adult, to react to the appraisal of potential loss very strongly, and to experience more intense and devastating episodes of sadness than someone raised with numerous mothers.

The *major* effect of culture on the experience of emotion appears to occur as a result of the secondary appraisal system. Where, as in the case of sadness in Tahiti, an emotion is unspecified by any secondary cultural appraisal, the person will *not* have the fully conscious experience of the emotion. Instead, the unexplicated feeling is likely to be experienced as a physical, somatic reaction. A similar outcome occurs among the Utka Eskimos with respect to anger, as described by Jean Briggs in her book, *Never in Anger.* The Utka Eskimos have no specific terms for anger. Angry behavior is described with the same word that is used for immature behavior, and is something expected only of children and foreigners. The Utka do not express anger openly, and, according to Briggs, they do not feel *anger* as such, but they do get physically "heated up" and have hostile thoughts for the same sorts of reasons people in other cultures do. Occasionally, they perform hostile acts. Here the conscious experience of an emotion is affected by not only the lack of a secondary explication of what is felt, but also by an explicit ideology that strongly devalues the entire action program associated with that particular emotion.

While the cultural hypocognization of an emotion seems to result in a lack of conscious experience of that emotion, a high degree of cultural elaboration of an emotion seems not only to make that emotion salient as a conscious experience, but also to shape its experience in various ways. There are a number of ethnographic examples of this; one of the best documented is the Samoan cultural complex centered on the term *alofa*. The term has the general meaning of *love*, but includes *compassion*, *empathy*, and *pity.* In the hierarchical cluster analysis of Samoan emotions terms, presented in Figure 9.1, one branch of the positive emotion centers on *alofa.*[2] The other emotions immediately included with *alofa* are feeling generous, agreeable, humble, forgiving, and peaceful. The overall sense of this cluster is nicely captured in the following scenario:

[2] The Samoan data was collected by Eleanor Gerber (1985), who asked informants to make similarity judgments among a selection of emotion terms.

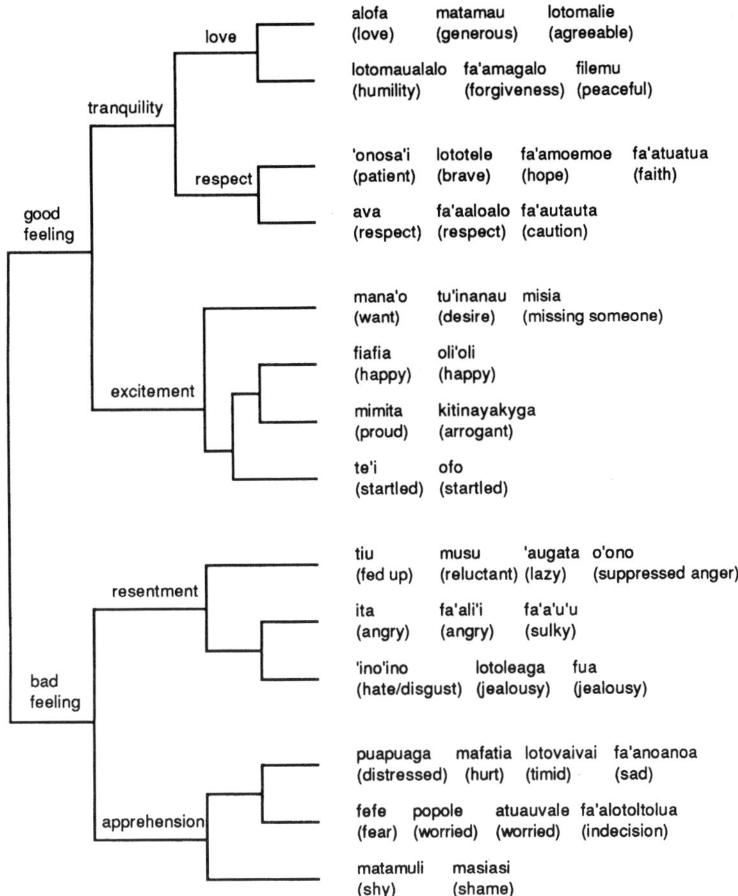

Figure 9.1 Hierarchical cluster analysis of Samoan emotion terms (after Gerber 1985)

The scenario frequently invoked to illustrate this sense of *alofa* as a minimal behavioral requirement is as follows: an old person, often portrayed as a stranger, is seen walking along the road, carrying a heavy burden. It is hot, and perhaps the elder seems ill or tired. The appropriate response in this instance is a feeling of *alofa*, which implies helpful or giving actions such as taking over the burden or providing a cool drink and a place to rest. (Gerber 1985:145)

Bradd Shore, an anthropologist who has worked in Samoa, points out that *alofa* is expressed by a subordinate towards an authority figure; it is the *proper* response to authority (Shore 1993). According to Shore, a brother should feel *alofa* for his sister, since a brother should respect a sister. Traditionally, sisters, and especially elder sisters, outrank brothers within the family, and a sister has the power to curse her brothers with sterility if they do not honor her. The *alofa* a brother should have for a sister, like the *alofa* felt towards parents, older people, and authorities, is an appropriate, respectful, accepting, feeling; a loving acceptance of duty. The primary behavioral expression of *alofa* is giving and helping, and the fulfilment of an obligation. The child expresses *alofa* for the parents by cooking for them and serving them food; the parents express *alofa* by giving to their children and by disciplining them.

The physical expression of affection is not included in the expression of *alofa*; smiles and embraces are part of the excitement cluster, not the tranquility cluster. The emotions of the excitement cluster – wanting something, being happy, feeling proud, or being startled – in contrast to the *alofa* related emotions, are feelings marked by high arousal and personal satisfactions. Unlike these selfish feelings, *alofa* is tranquil and other-oriented.

Not too surprisingly, Samoans do not always respond with *alofa* to the demands of their parents and other authorities. In fact, the Samoan emotion lexicon contains a rich set of terms for varieties of duty-caused anger – the resentment cluster includes terms for being fed-up, reluctant, lazy, and full of suppressed anger. However, there is no socially acceptable way of *directly* expressing anger towards parents and authorities; the marginally acceptable response is a muted "reluctance" (Gerber 1985). [3]

Samoan *alofa* contrasts in many ways with American *love*, with its passionate intensity, possessiveness, physical expression, and idealization. Based on the theory presented here, the differences are the results of secondary appraisals of a primary appraisal involving interpersonal attachment. That is, at the root of both there is an affective interpersonal attachment system that is common to most primates. However, as Bradd Shore says:

> Though "love" is in some sense based on the attachment system, it is simplistic and misleading to reduce the former to the latter or simply identify the two. Attachment is not synonymous with "love" in any of its numerous forms. Attachment theorists are quick to stress that observable behavior and complex emotions may involve a number of component behavioral systems. Moreover there is considerable uncertainty as to where the attachment system ends and other systems such as reproductive drives or a caretaking system begin . . . Yet I think the attachment system (whether understood as a single global system with multiple realizations or a functionally delimited system that interacts with other behavioral systems) provides a good candidate for a common biological context within which operate the emotional complexes that get conceptualized as love. (Shore 1993:11)

The argument here is that secondary appraisals based on cultural models have a large effect on the total gestalt that makes up the conscious experience

[3] Gerber, in her paper "Rage and Obligation," discusses how the controversy between Derek Freeman and Margaret Mead about Samoan character results from each seeing only one side of Samoan emotional life; Mead the *alofa* side, Freeman the angry side.

of an emotion. This does not mean that sometimes Americans do not feel *alofa*, or that Samoans do not sometimes feel *love*. Perhaps it is easier for Americans to feel *love* than *alofa* (especially when they are teenagers). And perhaps the total gestalt of *alofa*, with its full complement of feelings of peace, empathy, and humility, is felt only by some Samoans and other Pacific peoples. But perhaps not. Emotional experience is very complex. The techniques for surveying emotions are underdeveloped, and much work is needed before questions like these have answers.

Given the strong effect of secondary appraisal on the conscious experience of emotion, the question arises as to whether or not emotions *work* the same way when they are experienced differently. Michelle Rosaldo, who worked among the Philippine Ilongot, has argued that the Ilongot, who do not conceptualize themselves as having "an autonomous inner life," do not suffer from repressed anger the way westerners do (Rosaldo 1984). According to the Ilongot, anger can be dissolved and forgotten easily. Ilongot ethnopsychology has no place for submerged energies – they do not explain violent actions as the result of a history of frustrations buried in an unconscious mind. Rosaldo holds that because of the way the Ilongot conceptualize anger they are able to forget anger in a way we cannot, and therefore are not bothered by repressed angers.

Melford Spiro, using the published ethnographic materials of Michelle and Renato Rosaldo, rejects this argument. Spiro (1984) points out that although Michelle Rosaldo points to instances in which Ilogonts seem to have "forgotten" their animosities, one can observe the exact same "forgetting" of anger in western culture. Certainly the issue of whether repression occurs in either culture cannot be decided on the basis of *conscious* experience. Nor would it be surprising if Ilongot repressed angry feelings, since they believe anger to be extremely destructive and say that anger towards kinfolk is frightening. Furthermore, the Ilongot are vigorous headhunters, and the pattern of hostile emotion displayed by the Ilongot when headhunting is what would be expected from a people with considerable repressed anger. Rather than serving as an example of a culture in which differences in secondary appraisals bring about differences in the way emotions work, the Ilongot can just as easily be used to demonstrate the reverse; that secondary appraisals affect the conscious experience of emotions but do *not* affect the psychological operation of emotions with respect to repression and other psychological defenses.

Internalization

Through secondary appraisals and the cultural shaping of emotion, the beliefs and values of a culture may be *internalized*. The term *internalization* is common in psychological anthropology, where it refers to the process by which cultural representations become a part of the individual; that is, become what is right and true. Spiro distinguishes four different levels of internalization

(Spiro 1987) . At the first and lowest level, the individual is acquainted with some part of the cultural system of representations without assenting to its descriptive or normative claims. The individual may be indifferent to, or even reject, these claims.

At the second level of internalization, cultural representations are acquired as *cliches*; the individual honors the descriptive or normative claims more in the breach than in the observance. Spiro uses the example of people who say they believe Jesus died for their sins, but who have no sense of sin. "When a cultural system is acquired at this level, it is, as Edward Sapir put it, 'spurious'." (Spiro n.d.a)

At the third level, individuals hold their beliefs to be true, correct, or right. At this level, cultural representations structure the behavioral environment of social actors and guide their actions. When the proposition that Jesus died for man's sins is acquired at this level, the individual feels a sense of sin and is concerned to perform the actions necessary to achieve redemption. At this level, cultural representations can be said to be *internalized.*

At the final level, the system of cultural representations is not only internalized, it is highly salient. The cultural system not only guides but *instigates* action, and the entire system is invested with emotion. Thus, believing that Jesus died for man's sins, the believer is filled with anxiety about his own sins, and driven to try to atone for these sins in prayer and deeds, and filled with relief and joy at evidence of being saved.

Up to this point in this book, cultural models and other kinds of cultural representations have been treated as items to be "known" – things which one can use to distinguish one thing from another, or which can be used in reasoning, or which can help memory, etc. The relation of cultural models to *action* has not been an issue. On the purely cognitive level, one knows things at various levels of expertise, but the problem of "belief" does not arise. However, when relating the cognitive system to emotion, motivation, and action, this issue comes to the fore.

To return to the Samoan representation, *alofa*, Gerber points out that:

> The behavioral dispositions consonant with these feelings may be seen as a connecting link between the upper-level values of a society and their day-to-day expression in people's behavior. By defining "right" feelings in a consonant manner, adherence to the value of mutual aid and hierarchy is not only made surer; it is rendered less painful. A Samoan gives, therefore, not only because he or she has been trained to view giving as morally correct *but also because his or her training has created a disposition to feel such an act as "natural," seeming to rise out of the very depths of his or her being.* Similarly, acceptance of hierarchical relations is given an emotional underpinning that is likely to reduce tendencies to chafe under associated societal strictures. (Italics added) (Gerber 1985:153).

Emotion has this sort of extra effect on internalization because emotion is a very special kind of informational system.

What do emotions do? I have argued in other papers that emotions are a special kind of informational system which is complementary to the cognitive system and which evolved along with it. This hypothesis is supported by the observation that species which are highly intelligent are also likely to be highly emotional. One reason that the two systems might have evolved together is that the cognitive system is specialized to give an account of the external world rather than an account of how well one is doing in that world. The emotional and physical sensation systems give an account of how things are going for the self – the physical sensation system tells about how the body is doing, the emotion system tells how well one is doing in relation to the world. Feelings and emotions permit delay, but work against forgetting how one is doing. If the delay is too great, and one's relation to the world or one's body is of the wrong kind, feelings and emotions will interrupt old plans and prompt remedial action. However, one can continue to use the cognitive system at the same time one is experiencing strong feelings or emotions. According to this model, emotions and cognitions together form a highly adaptive representational system. (D'Andrade 1993:19-20)

Through the use of the secondary appraisal system, and by linking through subsumption (X is a kind of Y) primary appraisals to various cultural conditions, parts of the cultural cognitive system influence the operation of the emotional system, and thus are internalized. This cultural shaping of the emotions gives certain cultural representations emotional *force*, in that individuals experience the truth and rightness of certain ideas as emotions *within* themselves – as something internal to themselves. This is what Gerber says happens to Samoans; the moral dictates to be obedient and dutiful are experienced (sometimes) as a loving feeling.

Motivation

One major idea about people is that human behavior is motivated. In the folk model, this idea is formulated in terms of *wants* or *desires*; people do what they do because, directly or indirectly, it satisfies some *wish*. Hunger, pain, and sexual desire are the easy examples – it is not difficult to identify the conditions that produce these desires, and also not difficult to identify the desire itself, typically reflected in a conscious wish. Other kinds of motives can be more difficult to identify. Interpersonal attachment and self-esteem are examples where the conditions that create the wish and the nature of the conscious experience of the wish are difficult to specify.

One general method of identifying motives is by their goals; if someone pursues a goal for its own sake, that goal can be taken to represent a motive (McClelland 1951). For example, a person who persistently strives to outdo others, even when there is no extrinsic reward for doing so, can be characterized as someone with a strong competitive motive. In the 1930s and 1940s, Henry Murray, a major figure in the study of personality, began to develop a taxonomy of motives based on his reading of the psychological literature and his clinical experience. After a number of personality assessment studies he identified twenty-two major human motives, each of which is defined by the goal towards which the person strives. These are:

Need abasement: to submit passively, to accept injury, punishment.
Need achievement: to accomplish something difficult, attain a high standard.
Need acquisition: to gain possessions and property.
Need affiliation: to cooperate, to please others, to win friends.
Need aggression: to attack, punish, revenge an injury, overcome opposition.
Need autonomy: to be free, to resist coercion, to be unattached.
Need cognizance: to explore, ask questions, seek knowledge.
Need contrarience: to act differently, to be unique, take opposite views.
Need defendence: to defend the self against attack.
Need deference: to admire and support a superior, to yield eagerly to influence.
Need dominance: to influence or direct others, to get others to cooperate.
Need exhibition: to make an impression, to be seen and heard.
Need harmavoidance: to avoid pain, injury, to take precautionary measures.
Need infavoidance: to avoid humiliation.
Need nurturance: to help, feed, protect, comfort, take care of others.
Need order: to put things in order, achieve organization and precision.
Need play: to act for "fun," take a playful attitude.
Need rejection: to exclude, expel, be indifferent to negatively regarded others.
Need sentience: to seek and enjoy sensuous impressions.
Need sex: to seek an erotic relationship, to have intercourse.
Need succorance: to be nursed, supported, protected, loved, indulged.[4]

Murray was quite successful in his assessment project. As he describes in his book, *Explorations in Personality*, he had subjects come to his clinic and be interviewed by a number of psychologists in a variety of settings, including a group meeting, a simulated therapy session, and both directive and not-directive interviews. There was good agreement by the assessors concerning the degree of strength of each of the Murray needs for the sample of subjects. Thus, reliable assessment could be carried out using humans as the assessors. However, the interview technique did not provide an *instrument* by which these motives could be reliably assessed. As a method of assessing motives, Murray developed the Thematic Apperception Test, in which subjects are asked to tell imaginative stories about the figures in a series of drawings. These stories are then coded and scored for various kinds of imagery and fantasy. Reliable coding systems have been developed for the assessment of a number of motives, such as achievement, affiliation, and power (McClelland, Atkinson, Clark, and Lowell 1953).

[4] The definitions of these needs is abstracted from Murray 1938.

In the 1950s and 1960s the identification of motivation was a central ethnographic project for the anthropologists interested in culture and personality. The standard account was that through socialization the individual develops a series of central motives and conflicts, and that an interesting variety of cultural institutions can be understood as expressions of such motives and conflicts.[5] The theory had much to support it – animal learning experiments, human clinical data, and a variety of cross-cultural correlations between child training practices and cultural institutions like initiation ceremonies, witchcraft, and beliefs about supernaturals.[6] However, a major problem was that there was no satisfactory method by which motives could be assessed in the field. During the 1960s the reliability of the TAT became suspect among psychologists, and the Rorschach even more so.[7] Furthermore, these tests gave at best only an overall measure of the general level of motivation for an individual or group; they did not provide information about why *particular* actions were taken. The Ilongot are head hunters; a psychological anthropologist would like to understand what motivates this behavior. But the psychometric arsenal does not contain any standard instruments for determining the motive(s) involved when X does Y.

Recently an approach to the investigation of human motivation has been developed within cognitive anthropology that promises to have some utility for anthropologists. Some results of this approach have been presented in *Human Motives and Cultural Models*, edited by D'Andrade and Strauss. The basic idea is that some cultural schemas function as goals for individuals. For example, *achievement* refers to a complex cultural schema doing something which meets a recognized standard of excellence. Some people have strong achievement needs; they consistently and persistently undertake tasks at which they have a chance to meet standards of excellence (McClelland, Atkinson, Clark, and Lowell1953). For this motive to work, the individual must have a well-formed schema by which potential achievement can be recognized. Normally, such a schema is learned as part of the individual's cultural heritage.

In this case the achievement schema is more than just a recognition device; it has the power of instigating action. One can say a schema has *motivational force* for an individual in the same way one can speak of a request as having *directive force*.[8] An appropriate request does more than just describe what somebody wants; it has the pragmatic effect of instigating the other person to action. In a similar manner, a schema can serve as more than a recognition device; its activation can be an instigation to action.

On purely theoretical grounds, one would expect that some schemas would

5 For example, see Kardiner and Linton 1949.

6 For example, see Whiting and Child 1953.

7 Walter Mischel's book, *Personality and Assessment*, written in 1968, delivered a major blow to the then standard practices of personality assessment.

8 For a well worked out taxonomy of kinds of speech acts see Searle 1975.

serve as goals simply because one of the main purposes of human cognition is to relate the individual to the environment through behavior. One needs to *know* in order to be able to *do*. The point of most *knowing* is to make possible *doing*.

The goal functions of schemas are related to the way schemas form hierarchies. Schemas form hierarchies in a variety of ways. One schema may include another schema, or have a *kind of* relation to another schema, or be related as a causal or logical antecedent to another schema. The hierarchy consists of *passing on* an interpretation from a lower level schema to a higher level schema, until the more or less final, top level interpretation of what is happening is created. The role of top level schemas will usually be to determine action, since that is the basic function of interpretations.

As a rough approximation, schemas can be ranked by hierarchical position into three classes. At the top of the interpretive system are schemas which function as a person's most general goals, called *master motives*. They include things like *love* and *security* and *play* which instigate action relatively autonomously. In the middle range of the hierarchy are schemas for things like *marriage*, *my job*, etc. These middle range schemas contain whole clusters of powerful goals, but are not fully autonomous in the sense that one's marriage, or one's job are means to more ultimate goals like love and providing for oneself. At the bottom of the hierarchy are schemas for things like *writing memos*, *going to the bank*, *finding a birthday present*, etc. These schemas are entirely dependent on higher level schemas for their motivation force; one goes to the bank not for the sake of just going to the bank, but because it is part of some larger schema or plan perhaps relating to purchases and savings, which in turn may be part of a larger schema having to do with providing for oneself.

This formulation of motives as schemas within a hierarchy makes possible the resolution of a number of problems that have plagued the analysis of motivation. The standard conception of motivation treats motives as a free-floating energy source. For example, one might explain the fact that a particular individual gets into many angry conflicts with his boss as due to that individual's *hostility* – even though this individual does not get into fights when drinking in bars. Another person, who never gets into fights with his boss, but often gets into fights in bars, might be assessed as equally hostile. This is the problem of *situational variability* – because people display great situational variability in behavior, it has been hard to argue that there are any general motives; if motives are general, why are not the behaviors associated with these motives general?

The problem of situational variability is more explicable from the goal-schema perspective than from the motive-as-energy perspective. The man who is aggressive towards his boss but not his drinking companions may have a high level schema about bad authority and self-protection which activates sub-goals of argument and resistance. The man who is aggressive towards his drinking companions but not towards his boss, on the other hand, might have a high level schema about competition, macho-ness, and self-esteem which activates subgoals of physical confrontation and self-arrogation. Schemas are context-dependent interpretive devices, connected together in hierarchical networks. To describe a man as having a top level schema in which he sees himself as threatened by bad authority which will destroy his autonomy and gender identity, and then to go on to detail the particular events which are likely to trigger this interpretation and the way in which middle level goal-schemas of involving argument and confrontation are embedded in this hierarchy, results in a picture of the kind of organized complexity that is so typical of human behavior.

Another advantage of the goal-schema perspective involves the problem of determining *kinds* of motives. Henry Murray's attempt to make an encompassing list of all human motives has often been criticized; every theorist of motivation adds to or subtracts from or redefines the list. There does not seem to be a principled method of determining exactly how many kinds of motives people have. The answer to the question from the goal-schema perspective is relatively simple: there is no one list of motives. There are as many motives as there are relatively autonomous goals. Given the normal external conditions of human life, and the normal experience of living in a human body, one can assume that certain things are likely to be universal goals, such as being healthy, having some protection from the attacks of others, maintaining relationships, etc. However, the specifics of life in particular societies and cultures brings about differentiation into specific goals; to earn money, to take a head, to accumulate yams, etc. Instead of seeing every action as the outcome of a limited number of universal motives, action is seen as the outcome of a hierarchical *network* of goal-schemas.

A third advantage of the goal-schema perspective is that it is a *relatively* straightforward task for an ethnographer to determine whether or not a particular schema has motivational force. For example, Claudia Strauss, in her paper "What Makes Tony Run" in *Human Motives and Cultural Models,* describes how she investigated the motivational force of the American cultural model of "getting ahead." Using in-depth interviews with a small sample of male Rhode Island blue-collar workers, she found that all of these men had a well-formulated model of success. Her informants repeated with apparent conviction the standard American idea about success; that if you work hard enough, you can achieve anything you want. They also recognized that Americans are judged by this success standard, and felt somewhat defensive about their own lack of occupational achievement. However, Strauss found that all but one of her informants did not seem strongly motivated by the success model; that in fact they had consistently made choices and pursued objectives that prevented or hindered them from achieving occupational mobility. Strauss also found that the success model was held as "a relatively isolated, compact package of ideas only weakly linked to a larger picture of reality or sense of the self" (1992b:205). In the terms used in the last chapter, Strauss' informants held the standard

American propositional *theory* of success, but did not hold the model as a central schema within the hierarchical network of schemas.

For Strauss' informants, the model that did have motivational force was the *breadwinner* model. In this model the interests of the family come ahead of individual achievement, and the primary responsibility for the support of the family belongs to the husband/father. What the breadwinner should be able to do is provide for the basic needs of the family in an uncertain and undependable occupational world. Unlike the success model, the breadwinner model is seen as a basic fact of existence; men *are* responsible for the support of their families, jobs *are* often hard to get and hard to keep, security *is* better than risk. As Strauss says "In talking about choices faced by breadwinners, they tended to speak not of what people *should* do, but of what they have no choice but to do" (1992b:217). Of course, their sense of "no-choice" is not really because they had *no* choice – they could have left their wives and kids, or taken higher risks by setting up their own businesses, etc. But within *their* interpretative framework, there was no other choice for *them*. The motivational force of the breadwinner model is also increased by its connection to feelings of self-esteem; to know oneself to be a good breadwinner is a source of real satisfaction for these men.

One way that anthropology has dealt with the problem of the relation of motivation to action is simply to say that "action is culturally constituted." It is clear, for example, that the Yanomano Indians of Amazonia are very aggressive. The Semai of Malaysia, on the other hand, are pervasively non-aggressive. Rather than develop a psychological account, an easy escape is just to assert that these differences are culturally determined – as if somehow the culture, by itself, makes them do it. However, this is unsatisfactory, since culture, whether defined as mental representation or public discourse, by itself obviously can not make anybody do anything.

Perhaps as a result of the intellectual vacuity of the "culture makes them do it" position, a number of anthropologists have turned against the notion that culture has any causal properties at all. According to this position, culture is "negotiable" and "contestable" – that is, entirely uninternalized, a set of cliches to be used as tokens in the real wars of self-interest. This seesaw between culture as completely and unproblematically internalized and culture as entirely negotiable and contested results from an attempt to have a cultural theory without any psychology – a cultural theory with empty people.

It is important to note that determining whether or not a cultural model has motivational force is something that can be done by an ordinary ethnographer without special training in projective tests. In the papers in *Cultural Models and Human Motives* a variety of domains were investigated, including romance, marriage, gender, child training, success, and emotion. Although most of the work was done with American informants, work by other anthropologists indicates that assessment of motivational force can also be carried out in non-western cultures. For example, Spiro's (1982) study of Burmese supernaturalism found that most Burmese men, while knowledgeable about *nirvana*, and while holding that it is what all should aspire to, did not in fact pursue *nirvana* as a goal. They did, however, pursue goals such *goun*, roughly translated as "prestige," with considerable energy, and were willing to go to extraordinary lengths to *avoid* the loss of *goun*, which is called a "destruction of face" (Spiro n.d.b). Similar examples can be found across a wide range of ethnographic studies; obligation in Japan (Benedict 1946), shame among the Swahili (Swartz 1991), the acquisition of cattle among the Nuer (Evans-Pritchard 1940), etc.

Given that cultural schemas come to act as important goals for individuals, the issue immediately arises as to how this comes about. Richard Shweder (1992) points out that the motivational force of some goals can be a simple result of what people understand to be the realistic facts of life. For example, Americans believe children can easily be hurt by a number of common objects, such as hot stoves and razors and poisons. This understanding of the world creates a great number of specific goals connected to the more general goal of protecting children from harm. Or, if one is taught and believes that powerful malevolent witches exist, then a set of goals concerning protection from witchcraft will be created as a natural consequence of this belief. (The question then arises – why *do* people believe in witches? Shweder points out that we, the anthropologists, do not really know that there are no witches, and that it would be arrogant always to assume that those we study are irrational when their version of reality conflicts with ours.) However one feels about this, it is clear that some goals come to have motivational force because particular cultural models define the world in certain ways, resulting in certain middle level goals (e.g. fighting witchcraft) being seen as the natural means to higher level goals (e.g. protection from harm).

Naomi Quinn, in a study of the motivational force of the American model of marriage (1992), also asks how cultural schemas come to act as important goals for individuals. She finds that, for her informants, goals embedded in the model of marriage can be recruited into the person's model of the *self*. Quinn found three major sub-schemas in the American model of the self. The first is the "human equality" schema, which contains a network of notions about how every person has equal rights. The second is the "self as occupant of roles," in which one's self, by virtue of holding a certain role, has certain duties and privileges. The third is the "self as possessor of attributes," in which one comes to see oneself as *brave* or *clever* or *resourceful*.

One of Quinn's informants, whose husband wanted her to do the housework although they both worked, felt strongly conflicted because she felt that, as a person, she was not being treated fairly. She usually gave in to her husband's requests, however, probably because of her childhood experience in a broken home and her determination to be the kind of person (unlike her mother) who could make a marriage work. The conflict experienced by this informant appears to be a result of the way two different models of the self – the self as having equal rights and the self as the possessor of attributes – are related to the model of marriage. The "marriage requires effort" element of the model has become a powerful goal for this informant because it has become a sub-goal of a self-esteem goal contingent on being the kind of person who has a successful marriage. However, this sub-goal conflicts with her maintenance of the "equal rights" sub-goal, which is also related to her sense of self-worth. Quinn says:

> Now we re-encounter the question left hanging at the very beginning of this paper: How is it that goals embedded in upper-level schemas, such as human equality, marital success, wifely commitment . . . have the motivational force that they do? It is because these schemas and these goals have become, in each case, the woman's understanding of herself – and because these self-understandings cast her as a natural being and a moral actor . . .
>
> Far from sharing the kind of global cultural understanding of themselves as women and wives that the academic literature on gender identity often assumes, . . . different women give . . . quite different renditions of what it means to be a wife. Rather than reflecting some large whole in which each wife's conception represents a piece, these are alternative definitions of the wifely role, having no necessary connection to one another . . . A better way to think about these women's differing views of wifehood is to imagine that they have each drawn, selectively, from a cultural repository of complexly interrelated but separable schemas available to them for conceptualizing this role. From this pool of possibilities, each has taken that cultural understanding of her wifely role that holds force for her . . .
>
> Again, and importantly, it is not simply the abstract moral rectitude or inherent naturalness invested in these cultural ideas about human fairness, wifely obligations, and women's proclivities, that make these ideas compelling for these women. In each case, the ideas in conflict have become the woman's understandings of herself as a moral actor and a natural being, human and female. (1992:118–120).

From the interview data, Quinn speculates about the socialization and enculturation experiences reported by her informants that led them to associate rewarding feelings with certain understandings of the good and the natural self. However, as Quinn notes, such retrospective data is limited and subject to all the biases of memory. Dorothy Holland (1992) in a study of how women learn to become experts in the world of *romance*, was able to observe the socialization of motivation process more directly (see above in Chapter 6). Holland studied twenty-two women at two different universities to investigate how women's peer groups affected their career choices. Although not the direct topic of investigation, Holland found that many of these women spent much of their time and energy working on romantic relationships. She was able to follow her informants developing ideas and motivations over the year and a half of her study, participating with them in their peer activities. As Holland puts it, "the cultural idea of romance acquired motivating force as the women developed mastery of it and their mastery, in turn, depended upon their development of a concept of themselves as actors in the world of romance" (1992:61–62).

Holland found that her women informants varied considerably with respect to the amount of time they spent on romantic activities and the degree to which they had an identity as a participant in the world of romance. Although most women in these colleges are normally considered to be interested in romance and are treated as if they were potentially involved in romantic relationships, the women's actual participation in the world of romance varied greatly. Some resisted identification as romantic participants, some rejected parts of the model of romance, and some developed strategies for avoiding romantic experiences. Others were more involved in romantic liaisons, and some clearly became active experts at the "game" of romance.

Holland found that active involvement and identification with the cultural system of romance developed side by side with increasing expertise in romance. She says:

> The research suggests, in other words, that involvement – the salience of and identification with the cultural system of romance – co-developed along with expertise. If the woman had not developed a clear identification of herself in the world of romance – an image of herself that mattered to her – then romance was not likely to be very salient for her and she was not likely to be very expert in conducting romantic relationships. Similarily, if for some reason she had not been able to develop expertise then she was unlikely to have formed much of a romantic identification. Salience, identification, and expertise appear to develop together as an interrelated process – a process that was continually supported and shaped in the context of social interaction (1992:79).

Holland traces out in particular case histories how different women came to identify or not identify with being an agent in the world of romance, and some of the unanticipated costs of this identification (Holland and Eisenhart 1990). A variety of circumstances and personal experiences seem to affect the likelihood that this identification will be made and the model of romance will come to have significant motivational force, including such things as the degree of success experienced in initial romantic encounters, the degree to which the woman's friends are also involved in the romances, and the degree to which the woman was unable to find a promising career path through academic work.

Quinn's study of conflicting motives in marriage and Holland's study of romance both indicate that identification plays an important role in the development of motivational force. Some goals come to be experienced as right and natural – as a good and true part of the self. Strauss' working-class men show the same pattern. Of course, not all goals are integrated into self-schemas; people sometimes pursue objectives which they cannot integrate into their self-schema, and develop various psychological defenses against the recognition of such goals. Americans, for example, have difficulty recognizing their own strivings for positions of power. The typical defense against seeing oneself as "power-hungry" is to try to believe (and convince others) that it is not that one wants the position for the power that it brings, but rather what one really wants is to keep certain other people who would misuse it from gaining this power.

It is important to stress that the position presented here about motivation does not conflict with the idea that humans are motivated by psychobiological drives, or by strong emotions such as anger, shame and fear. According to the theory presented here, drives and affects have powerful effects when they activate goals, but unless channeled into a network of goal-schemas, create only diffuse and usually unpleasant internal states.

Humans are complex creatures. There are a great number of things which can affect the motivational state of an individual; tissue needs, the drives of sex and aggression, a variety of emotions ranging from stark fear to mild curiosity, universal needs having to do with self-preservation, relatedness to others, self-esteem, etc. There is no one kind of "motivational energy." Rather, there are complicated interactions between the body, the world, and the psychological self, which use quite different physiological and neural pathways. For the anthropologist, what can be observed is that whatever these sources of motivational energy are, these energies have become organized into a network of goal-schemas, such that various cultural models (and idiosyncratic models) have assessable degrees of motivational force.

In fact, the metaphor that things like hunger, sex, anger, and self-esteem are a *general* source of "energy" is probably relatively misleading, because it leads to various implications that are probably not true, such as:

> Without such energies, the person could not do anything.
> The greater the amount of energy, the more vigorously the person will do something.

The energy for human behavior is actually found in the various metabolic processes by which sugars get converted into energy. The brain and sensory systems might more profitably be thought of as a "control" system, in which tiny amounts of energy (neural activation) are able to reset the "switches" of the upper–level directive system. Of course, all such metaphors are dangerous, and the brain is only *somewhat* like an electronic guidance system. The argument here is that human motivation is *more* like an electronic guidance system than it is like a furnace or battery. Human action is more directly understood by identifying the conceptual network of things toward which the creature strives than by identifying energy sources (Rosenblatt and Thickstun 1977).

Consider an example of someone who is very competitive. Assume that this person constantly treats situations as if they were contests in which there is a winner and loser. Also assume that this person is emotionally aroused by competitive situations, and finds winning very satisfying and losing very frustrating. We would say that the goal of beating others in competition had strong motivational force for this person. If this person were to undergo a lengthy psychoanalysis, he or she would probably discover this need to compete had complex roots in past experiences with parents and siblings, in various school and sports settings, etc., each with complex and strong emotions and significant meanings. One could imagine that in the course of these experiences the competition schema had come to absorb more and more "energy." This energy can be conceptualized as "greater connectionist weights," or as an increase in "cathexis," or as a greater "redintegration of affect," or as stronger "habits of the heart," or as an increase in "motivational force." The term does not matter greatly; the idea is that the goal has gained causal efficacy.

A number of critics of the goal-schema approach have argued that it cannot be the schema *itself* that has "force" or "power," because schemas are not things that can have such causal properties, being only "ideas" or "interpretations" or "templates" or "representations." The schema, they say, can only be a way of *directing* the energy towards completion; it can not be the source of energy. A better motivational analysis would search for the elements that are linked to this schema, such as various anxieties or gratifications, that are the true energy sources.

I agree that schemas do not have, by themselves, any force or power, and that they are not the source of whatever energy is needed to instigate action. And certainly it would be good to know in this hypothetical instance the various anxieties and gratifications that are linked to the competition schema. In the usual case, there would be a large number of different sources of gratification and anxiety that are associated with competition in various ways, and the entire network of linkages to "energy sources" would be very complex. Tracing out the network would perhaps give a "deeper" analysis, but might not give any increase in predictive power concerning what this person is likely to do and what is likely to instigate him or her to do it. The empirical issue here is about the nature of motivation. Are goals powered by a small number of energies, or are goals powered by a large number of linkages to a great variety of "arousing" experiences? In both cases the "energy" ultimately comes from somewhere other than goals, but in the first case one gains much by deeper analysis, in the second case one gains much less.

My own assumption is that the usual situation is the second case. I believe most upper level goals for most people are multiply determined, and that the idea that there are just a small number of basic or ultimate energy sources is wrong. In the usual case, individuals learn to want to do things that are normal cultural goals by the ordinary experience of seeing admired others do these things, receiving approval for doing them oneself, and experiencing a variety of intrinsic gratifications by doing them and as a result of doing them.

A striking study of the ordinary way in which the internalization of cultural models takes place was carried out by Yasuko Minoura, a social psychologist at Tokyo University (Minoura 1992). Minoura investigated the factors that lead children, raised in Japan and then brought to the United States by their parents as a result of an overseas business assignment, to reject the Japanese model of proper interpersonal behavior and accept the American model. In the Japanese model, for example, being sensitive to the needs of others, not boasting or acting self-assertively, communicating wants indirectly, not saying "no" directly, and conforming to group standards are "normal" ways of acting, while in the American model, being self-assertive, direct in one's expression, and "going one's own way" are normal ways of acting.

Minoura observed the children in school, talked with them at recess and lunchtime, and went to their homes for intensive interviews. For these children, the culture inside the house was Japanese, but outside was American. Most of the children not only attended a local American school but also went to a Japanese school for supplementary education on Saturdays. In her interviews with the children and their parents, Minoura focused on two issues: whether or not the child had an accurate perception of differences between American and Japanese models of interpersonal behavior and whether or not the child displayed the behavior and feelings appropriate to the Japanese model or the American model.

Minoura found that she could typologize the children into five levels of increasing degree of internalization of the American model. At the first level were children who did not perceive differences between Japanese and American ways of behaving, and whose ways of thinking, feeling, and behaving were very Japanese. The second level consists of children who have an articulate perception of Japanese–American differences, but who do not practice or like the American way. As one young girl said "Americans don't admit their faults even if they are responsible for them. They attack mercilessly when someone else makes a mistake. Really horrible! I don't like that." The third level consists of those who have two sets of cultural models, one Japanese, one American, and switch according to the demands of the situation. The fourth level consists of those children who primarily use the American model, but who do not show a clear emotional attachment to this model. The fifth level consists of children who believe the American way is the only way, and can be said to have internalized the American model.

All of the Japanese children at the fifth level came to the United States before the age of nine. Along with her assessment of the level of internalization of the American model of interpersonal behavior, Minoura also obtained data on a number of other variables. The correlation of these variables with the level of internalization of the American model of interpersonal behavior is presented in Table 9.1. A multiple regression analysis indicates that the strongest independent predictors of the child's internalization of the American model are the child's proficiency in English (.58), density of interaction with Americans (.41), age of entry (.37), and length of stay (.37).

What these data and correlations show is that the internalization of a basic cultural model, such as the model for interpersonal behavior, is generally the

Table 9.1. *Correlation of selected variables with internalization of the American model of interpersonal behavior for seventy-two Japanese children growing up in Los Angeles (adapted from Minoura 1992)*

.76	Proficiency in English
.76	Preference for American school versus Japanese school
.69	Degree of English usage among siblings
.64	Density of interaction with American peers
.61	Length of stay
–.60	Age of entry
.54	White American inclusion in Japanese child's peer network after school
.35	Mother's proficiency in English
.34	Extroverted behavior tendency
.26	Father's contact with Americans in company he works for

result of the amount of interaction the child has with those who use the model. Being proficient in English, having many Americans in one's peer network, and living in the United States for a longer period are all conditions which make for more frequent and more effectively intense interaction. The age at which the child is exposed to those practicing the model is also important; as mentioned, those who came to the United States before nine are considerably more likely to internalize the American model. Of course, more is actually happening to the child than just "interaction." The Japanese child who interacts frequently with American children not only is exposed to more aspects of the American model, but is also likely to have received more rewards for using the model and the rewards are more likely to have come from those who have achieved a greater significance to the child.

Minoura also interviewed fifty-four of the Japanese children after they had returned to Japan. She found that children who returned after the age of eleven or so had difficulty shedding the American model and returning to the Japanese way. Many of them maintained a stubborn attachment to the American model. Minoura speculates that this may be due to a kind of critical period in which the "cultural meaning system of interpersonal relationships appears to become a salient part of the self-identity to which they are emotionally attached" (Minoura 1992:327).

Coda

This review and discussion of the process of internalization presents another example, like reasoning, of the way in which cultural schemas and psychological processes interact to "make each other up." Our emotional experience and our goals are made up, in part, by cultural schemas. Our personalities are thus partially formed by cultural representations. But, just as our personalities are partially created by cultural representations, it is the capacity to feel and desire that gives these representations life. Unless they are internalized in the emotional or motivational system of individuals, cultural schemas are nothing more than cliches and dead tropes. Even the ordinary, instrumental aspects of culture – how to spell *cat*, how to dig a well, how to greet a stranger, etc., are maintained only because they are linked to goals and emotions that insure their continued use.

While the psychological processes by which cultural schemas become subsumed in emotional appraisals, or become part of the secondary emotional appraisals, or become relatively autonomous goals, are not as well understood as one might wish, neither are these processes a total mystery. The material in this chapter is a review of some of what is known or thought about these processes.

Much of the current work on *power and discourse* in anthropology is concerned with problems related to the psychological force of cultural models – debates over what is natural and right. In modern pluralistic societies the cultural heritage contains many alternative and even conflicting cultural models about how things are and how one should act. For example, currently there is great strife in America around the issue of gender and gender relations, marked at the extremes by the debates of feminists, Christian fundamentalists, pro- and anti-abortionists, etc. In this kind of situation, cultural models become part of social conflict, and social processes by which laws are constructed, norms are established, and deviance is controlled – or fails to be controlled – interact with heated ideological debate over cultural models.

In a democratic society conflict resolution can occur by debate and the power of consensus rather than only by violence and fear. The implication here is that, to the degree a society does resolve conflict by democratic means, the general psychological force of a cultural model can decide social outcomes. The power to chop off heads is one thing, the psychological power of a cultural model is another. Both are real and both need to be understood in any study of conflict and social process.

It is to be hoped – to put it in academic fashion – that at some point anthropologists and other social scientists will come to see that a reasonable theory of power, or of any other social process, needs *some* psychological theory. A theory of power has to have some explication of the kinds of events that "make" people do things, and this *always* involves postulating a psychological theory. The great social theorists of the past – Marx, Durkheim, Weber – created complex *ad hoc* psychologies because no reasonably sound body of theory and research was available to them. Unfortunately, this tradition of inventing a psychology for each social and cultural theory has continued into the present, as the psychologies developed by structuralists, interpretativists, and post-modernists attest.

Much work remains to be done on the processes by which cultural schemas are incorporated or not incorporated into individual personalities. Little research has been done on the degree to which social influences are necessary to maintain the psychological force of cultural schemas. Our prevailing individualistic tradition tends to keep us from noticing how important the social milieu is in maintaining our internal guidance systems. It may well be the case that most goals lose their motivational force without the support of significant others. Similarly, study of the role of ritual in integrating emotional and motivational systems with cultural schemas offers a rich field of exploration. A church needs the assembly and the ritual as well as the belief.

A last chapter note: many of the ideas in this chapter were put forward in Geertz's great essay, "Religion as a Cultural System," first published in 1966.[9] In this article, Geertz says:

> a religion is: (1) a system of symbols which acts to (2) establish powerful, pervasive, and long-lasting moods and motivations in men by (3) formulating conceptions of a general order of existence and (4) clothing these conceptions with such an aura of factuality that (5) the moods and motivations seem uniquely realistic. (1973:90)

What happened in anthropology was that all of culture came to be treated as if it were a religion. Of course, it is not, but it does consist, among other things, of a *number* of systems of symbols, *some* of which are internalized so that powerful motivations and emotions are established in *many* individuals. Geertz was not interested in tracing out the specific psychological processes involved in internalization, perhaps because he thought that the "factuality" invoked by "conceptions of existence" could explain motivations and emotions without recourse to further psychological theory. However, I would argue, any cultural theorist interested in action needs a psychological theory of internalization. Otherwise, one cannot understand why a system of symbols may act to establish motivations for some folk, but not others.

[9] Reprinted in *The Interpretation of Cultures*, New York: Basic Books, 1973.

10 Summing up

Chapter 9 completes a general account of the development of cognitive anthropology. This account is not a full history; a number of areas of research in cognitive anthropology have not been discussed or have been mentioned only in passing. For example, research on narrative and discourse analysis has not been described here (Labov and Fanshel 1977; Colby and Colby 1981; Agar 1980a). Also undescribed is work in the 1960s and early 1970s on decision making (see Quinn 1975 for a review of this field). A related line of research being carried out by the soviet activity school and those interested in situated cognition has also not been discussed (Cole 1989; Lave 1988; Suchman 1987). The large amount of research on metaphor has been discussed here only briefly.

The account presented in this book is biased by my own interests and perspectives. But whatever the incompleteness of this history, it should at least serve as enough of a sample to give the reader a general understanding of the general enterprise and make possible an appraisal of the contribution of this enterprise to anthropology and the social sciences.

A bird's eye view

A bird's eye view of the thirty-five years of work gives a picture in which there are four major periods. The first period is an introductory phase in which the agenda of the field was formulated. The general movement towards more study of symbolic systems in anthropology, plus the advances in linguistics, led to a formulation by Ward Goodenough and others of *culture as knowledge*. Associated with this definition was a clear research goal – to determine the content and organization of such knowledge. Anthony Wallace's notion of the individual *mazeway* and the associated construct of *revitalization movements* was an early working out of the implications of a "culture as knowledge" position (Wallace 1960). It is interesting that Wallace immediately saw and discussed the *problem of sharing* issue which arises once culture is defined as knowledge, as well as the concomitant problem of how social action can be coordinated in a world with little sharing.

The second phase initiated detailed research in the analysis of cultural knowledge. This research, described in Chapter 2 through Chapter 5, began by using methods that already existed. The methods of componential analysis, developed in linguistics for the analysis of phonemic systems, was adapted by Lounsbury and Goodenough to the analysis of kinship terminologies. The development of methods to analyze taxonomic relations was adapted by Conklin and Frake from biology, with an explicit label as *ethnobotany.* The basic theoretical model of this period is centered on analyses of words, from which the organization of cultural categories could be discovered. With the linguistic emphasis went a great concern with the development of rigorous methods. The expansion of the study of categories through techniques borrowed from psychology involving similarity judgments and scaling methods continued this trend towards the development of an explicit methodology to discover underlying cultural categories.

This second period is marked by little psychological theorizing about categorization, although there was work which was related to other psychological issues. Wallace published his study of the relation between the limitations of short-term memory and the size of kinship terminologies; Romney and I and others investigated the psychological reality of different analyses of underlying cultural categories; Roberts, Brown, Lenneberg, Stefflre, and others did research on the relation between memory and naming in the domain of color; and Shweder and I investigated the effect of cultural categories on memory in the construction of personality traits. However, this psychologizing was external to the theory of cultural categories and word meaning *per se*. No particular psychological theory was invoked in the analysis of categories; it was not understood that any was needed.

This second period of research extended from the late 1950s to the early 1970s. This was a time in which anthropology and the social sciences in general were strongly oriented towards method, formalization, and quantification. Most of the development occurred at five universities – Yale, Pennsylvania, Stanford, Berkeley, and Irvine. A number of contributors received their graduate training at the Harvard department of Social Relations. By my estimate, nearly a third of the people who have done significant work in cognitive anthropology were trained by or strongly influenced by A. Kimball Romney, who received his degree from Social Relations, then went to Stanford and later Irvine. During this period a fair number of training grants were available from NIMH for graduate students, and these programs were generally supportive of work in cognitive anthropology. Anthropology expanded rapidly during this period, a number of new specialities developed, and cognitive anthropology fit well into this pattern of specialized growth.

The internal intellectual debate during this period centered on the question of whether this new approach should be considered simply a kind of ethnography – sometimes called *ethnoscience*, or *ethnolinguistics*, or in other contexts, *the new ethnography* – or should be a branch, however distant, of psychological anthropology. For example, there was a controversy around whether or not the attempt to ascertain the psychological reality of a componential analysis was either logically possible or empirically feasible. On the other side, many of the anthropologists who were attracted to this new approach were interested because of its psychological applications. Certainly that was the attraction for me; semantics offered a way into the mind.

The external debate at this time between cognitive anthropology and other approaches to the study of culture was concerned with issues of method as well as an ontological debate about the locus of culture. Geertz had made clear his disapproval of the formalizing and quantitative aspects of this new approach, and used his formidable persuasive skills to argue the case against the "cognitive fallacy" that "culture consists of mental phenomena" (1973:12). It is probably the case that the mainstream of anthropology was more or less convinced by Geertz's arguments; it was felt without much explicit discussion that there *is* something public about culture, and that placing meaning *too* deeply in the mind would lead to imperialist claims by psychologists. As a number of discussions in the pages above indicate, this debate is not yet finished, although there does seem to be some general agreement that culture has *both* a public and private aspect.

This second period of work produced an extensive body of work that showed how features and taxonomic relations could be analyzed. A large range of domains were investigated; kin, plants, animals, character terms, diseases, colors, etc. The general theoretical vocabulary for semantic analysis was clarified and extended, and methods from psychology were integrated with the more standard linguistic techniques.

The third period of development, beginning in the mid-1970s, was initiated by Eleanor Rosch, who introduced a *psychological* theory about categories. No longer were all categories on an equal footing; some linguistic categories were linked to prototypes – a purely psychological entity – and it was the prototype that gave basic level categories their salience and power to affect memory and reasoning. By the early 1980s schema theory had replaced the prototype model in anthropology. Finally, by the mid-1980s, the possibility of implementing schemas in connectionist networks was widely realized, resulting in an even more abstract psychological theory about the nature of mental representations.

Schema theory and connectionist networks created a new class of mental entities. Prior to the development of schema theory, the major things in the mind, at least in anthropology, were symbols – words or other kinds of signifiers – and features, which are the perceptual qualities that connect linguistic forms to the world. With schemas and connectionist networks the strong dependence of thought upon language was broken. Connectionist networks put together schematic clusters of features into complex objects without any necessary linguistic base. Along with this divorce from strict semantic analysis went an increase in interest in mental processes such as reasoning, metaphor, and memory. In anthropology this period was marked by a focus on cultural models and their function in inference and metaphor, as exemplified by Holland and Quinn's volume, *Cultural Models in Language and Thought*, and George Lakoff's *Women, Fire, and Dangerous Things*, both published in 1987.

One by-product of the work in cognitive anthropology over these first three periods was the breaking up of culture into parts. It was not that earlier anthropologists did not think that culture had parts, but there had been little clarity about what these parts might be or how they could be identified. In contrast to culture, social structure had a clear ontology of parts – roles, statuses, institutions, groups, classes, etc. Possible terms for a "part of a culture" were rarely used and sounded awkward. The term *trait* had been strongly discredited in cultural anthropology since Malinowski. As Kroeber and Kluckhohn said in *Culture: A Critical Review of Concepts and Definitions*:

> Most anthropologists would agree that no constant elemental units like atoms, cells, or genes have as yet been satisfactorily established with culture in general. Many would insist that within one aspect of culture, namely language, such constant elemental units have been isolated: phonemes, and morphemes. It is arguable whether such units are, in principle, discoverable in sectors of culture less automatic than speech and less closely tied (in some ways) to biological fact. (Kroeber and Kluckhohn 1963:319)

This lexical gap was more than just an oddity of vocabulary. Behind it lay a lack of conceptualization about exactly what was being studied. If culture was meaning and symbol, but not in anyone's mind, how could one do more than interpret whatever one considered symbolic – a ritual, a cockfight, kinship terminology, or whatever? And what sense did it make to count interpretations?

However, if culture is placed in the mind, then the organization and limitations of the mind can be used to find cognitively formed units – features, prototypes, schemas, propositions, theories, etc. This makes possible a *particulate* theory of culture; that is, a theory about the "pieces" of culture, their composition and relations to other things. Once such pieces or units are defined, new questions arise. How shared are these units? How are they distributed across persons? Which ones are internalized? Again, it is not that these questions were not asked before, but with a new vocabulary these issues arose with greater force. Models of cultural consensus and distributed cognition began to occupy more attention in the later part of the 1980s. This work was done almost entirely by cognitive anthropologists because the questions concerning consensus and distribution did not even make sense within much of the mainstream framework of cultural anthropology. One has to have a notion of separable units before the study of their distribution has any meaning.

The fourth phase of cognitive anthropology is too new and unformed to be definitively described. There appears to be a trend toward the study of how cultural schemas are related to action. This brings to the front issues about emotion and motivation, along with a general concern about internalization and socialization. At the same time, there is growing involvement in issues concerned with the way cognitive structure is related to the physical structure of artifacts and the behavioral structure of groups. The overall view is one in which culture is seen to be particulate, socially distributed, variably internalized, and variably embodied in external forms.

None of these four periods – defining the agenda, the early work in semantics and scaling, the formulation of schema theory and cultural models, and the latest concern with action – are completed episodes. Work is still being done in all of these areas. What can be hoped for is a general consolidation of method and theory; unfortunately anthropology is a somewhat erratic discipline in which old and good problems often get dropped in favor of the latest fashions. However, the basic problem of cognitive anthropology – how cultural knowledge is organized in the mind – will remain a good problem until it is fully solved, no matter what discipline works on it.

The historical context

As discussed in Chapter 1, in the mid-1950s the focus in anthropology shifted from the study of social institutions to the study of symbolic systems. In the mainstream of cultural anthropology there were two general positions that dominated much of the 1960s and 1970s. One of these was structuralism, primarily as created by Claude Levi-Strauss. For Levi-Strauss, the unconscious structures of the human mind were expressed in a variety of cultural materials; in myths, kinship systems, masks, funeral practices, etc. A number of anthropologists took up the structuralist agenda and began to look for structuralist oppositions and transformations in the cultural materials they were investigating. Since these structures were thought to be imposed on cultural materials by an unconscious mind, there was no point in finding out what the natives consciously thought about these materials, and no way to validate one's interpretations about the content of these structures.

The alternative approach was that of symbolic anthropology, as shaped by Victor Turner, David Schneider, Clifford Geertz, and others. This approach, later called interpretative anthropology by Geertz, stressed the distinction between action as behavior and action as symbol. While Turner tended to restrict his study of symbolic action to ritual, Geertz and Schneider treated all cultural practices as part of the symbolic system. The metaphor of culture as text expressed this constant dualism; one could read from any set of cultural practices a cultural meaning. However, again there was no method of validation; since the meanings were not in anyone's mind, even an unconscious one, no method of verification was possible.

Both structuralism and symbolic/interpretative anthropology are now abandoned agendas. I believe that the abandonment was due not just to shifts in intellectual fashions, but to the problem that comes with an inherently unverifiable approach. No one could build on what was done before, because building requires criticism, modifications, and selection of what is sound from what is unsound, and this is not possible in a world where there is no way of knowing what is better and what is worse.

One of the things that both structuralism and symbolic/interpretive anthropology had as a basic assumption was the idea that culture is *a* structure, or system – some kind of unified thing. Geertz's defense of this during the *Culture Theory* conference in 1980 was quite passionate, although the printed text does not convey this very well. "As I've said before, the elements of a culture are not like a pile of sand and not like a spider's web. It's more like an octopus, a rather badly integrated creature – what passes for a brains keeps it together, more or less, in one ungainly whole" (Shweder and LeVine 1984:19).

The various definitions of culture across the last hundred years have often stressed that culture is "a complex whole," "integrated," "structured," "patterned," etc. This is an article of faith, since no one ever offered an empirical demonstration of any culture's structure. What could be demonstrated was that any one piece of culture was very likely to be connected in *some* way to some other piece. But a world in which everything is somehow related to something else does not make a *structure* or even a *system*, and certainly not "one ungainly whole."

During the early years of cognitive anthropology there was an idea that there might be a *grammar* for each culture. The idea of a single grammar from which all cultural behaviors could be generated did not last very long; the particularities of any domain quickly led away from anything so grandiose. Work across a wide variety of cultural domains in a number of cultures has found that cultural models are independent of each other. The empirical fact is that culture looks more like the collected denizens of a tide pool than a single octopus. Empirical work on plant taxonomies, color terms, models of the mind, navigation, land tenure schemas, kin terms, etc., reveals a world of independent mental representations. Each cultural model is "thing-like," but all the models together do not form any kind of thing.

There are theories about culture which make sense out of this situation. If culture is seen as socially inherited solutions to life's problems (how to form families, obtain food and shelter, raise children, fight enemies, cure disease, control disputes, etc.) then the forces that make for system or structure are the constraints and interdependencies found within these problem-domains. The cultural solutions to life's problems *do* form systems of various sorts; systems of social relationships, systems of economic exchange, systems of government, etc., but these systems (each made up of a complex of cultural models, roles, activities, etc.) are as various as the problems are. There is no *one* problem of human life to which culture is a solution.

Once the idea that culture is *a thing* disappears, part of the impetus to study culture *for its own sake* disappears. Radcliffe-Brown said, years ago, "You cannot have a science of culture. You can study culture only as a characteristic of a social system." (1957:106). Of course, one can study in a scientific way the elements of culture, but to find out why cultural elements exist and how they fit together one has to step *outside* the concept of culture and look for whatever it is that creates and organizes these elements, such as the problem of biological reproduction, or the problem of getting food out of the environment, or human cognitive limitations, or personality needs, or whatever.

These notions return to earlier ideas in anthropology. The early work of Malinowski used a rough functionalism based on human needs as a theoretical underpinning to explain the way in which cultural institutions were organized into systems. Malinowski's functionalism was later eclipsed by Radcliffe-Brown's notion of social structure, which held that the social system was a system of real relationships between individuals which brought about the mutual adjustment of interests of members of the society. Culture, for Radcliffe-Brown, was the heritage of learned ways of feeling, thinking, and behaving that solve the requirements of mutual social adjustment. Work by Meyer Fortes and Evans-Pritchard continued this tradition, but placed more emphasis on the role of political and jural interests. However, in part influenced by Levi-Strauss, over time British social anthropology moved away from an interest in systems which organize cultural beliefs and practices to the study of abstract structures *per se*. Robin Fox's *Kinship and Marriage* is a fine exposition of such structures. But the only problem these different structures seem to be a solution to is the problem of seeing how many ways people can organize marriage and descent – as Fox himself noted (1968).

In turning to the study of culture, with the hope that culture would prove to have the secret of order within it, anthropology committed itself to a task that could not be done. Today, the trend is to reject the notion of culture, substituting the term *discourse* when referring to symbols and meanings. For example:

> Although only beginning to find its way into anthropological writing, discourse in this much wider Foucaultian sense is being adopted to do the theoretical work of refiguring two terms that it replaces: culture and ideology. For many, the . . . term "culture" has become problematic for several reasons. First, built into it is a distinction between a realm of ideas, even if public rather than in people's heads, and material realities and social practices, a distinction some users of discourse would like to problematize. Second, the term seems to connote a certain coherence, uniformity, and timelessness in the meaning systems of a given group, and to operate rather like the earlier concept of "race" in identifying fundamentally different, essentialized, and homogeneous social units (as when we speak about "a culture"). Because of these associations, invoking culture tends to divert us from looking for contests for meaning and at rhetoric and

power, contradictions, and multiple discourses . . . It also falsely fixes the boundaries between groups in an absolute and artificial way. (Lutz and Abu-Lughod 1990:9)

The current post-modernist position presented above comes at too great a cost; it is a theory in which there is only one real system, the power system. Further, it does not investigate the "on-the-ground" social processes by which power is used and maintained, but rather focuses on *interpretations* of discourse to discover how power maintains its hegemony. Without a theory of social process or a psychological theory of how meanings come to have power, post-modernism serves mainly as an ethical vocabulary for the indentification of social evils.

Rejecting the notion that culture is a single structure does not imply that there is no reason to investigate culture. If one is interested in society, culture needs to be investigated because the way society works is deeply affected by what is learned as the cultural heritage. Another reason to study culture is that one can not understand individual humans without understanding their culture. The individual psyche appears to consist of several interrelated systems. The cognitive system – reasoning, memory, and perception – are all tightly linked together by the requirements of problem solving. Similarly, personality is a system because of the requirements involved in doing what personality does (which is to guide us around in such a way as to insure that we maintain a good relation to our social and physical environment). This requires not only a problem solving system, but also an emotional system to let us know how we are doing and a motivational system to provide a structure of goals so that we are directed to do what needs to be done.

Much of the material in this book has been about the way in which cultural materials are organized by the needs of this human psychological system – schemas as models by which things can be figured out, as objects to reason with, as ways of organizing memory, as a goal system for directing behavior, as extending the appraisal system for emotions, etc. Here culture and psyche make each other up – parts of culture are organized together to make up the functioning of the cognitive system and the personality system. In my opinion, the interpretative and symbolic anthropologists were most successful, and certainly most interesting, exactly when they were doing *cultural psychology* – talking about the self, identity, emotions, primordial sentiments, the need for meaning, etc. They denied that they were doing psychology, but what else was it?

Final comment

Overall, one of the main accomplishments of cognitive anthropology has been to provide detailed and reliable descriptions of cultural representations. This was the original goal of ethnoscience, and it has continued to be a central part of the agenda. Another major accomplishment has been to provide a bridge between culture and the functioning of the psyche. The earlier culture and personality approach demonstrated the way socialization experiences influence personality systems which in turn influence cultural practices and beliefs; cognitive anthropology has demonstrated that the psyche is influenced by the representations it learns as part of the human cultural heritage. Cognitive anthropology has also tried to show that the cultural heritage itself is influenced by the inherent capacities and limitations of the human cognitive system – that the influence between cultural representation and cognitive process is reciprocal.

What will happen next in the development of cognitive anthropology is unclear. Whatever the new directions, it is nice to look back at what has been done and realize that when this work was started we did not know how to do lots of the things we can do now. The things we know how to do – to work out a taxonomy, or scale terms in a domain, or find prototypic objects, or work out a cultural model, or show how reasoning or memory or other psychological processes are affected by cultural representations, or investigate the way in which cultural knowledge is distributed – are modest accomplishments. Though modest, if these accomplishments can be built on, the venture will have proven worthwhile.

References

Adams, Marilyn J. 1980 Inductive Deductions and Deductive Inductions. In *Attention and Performance*, Volume VIII, R. S. Nickerson, ed. Hillsdale: Erlbaum.

Agar, Michael H. 1980a Background Knowledge and Themes: Problems in the Analysis of Life History Narrative. *American Ethnologist* 7:223–239.

1980b *The Professional Stranger: An Informal Introduction to Ethnography*. New York: Academic Press.

Aldenderfer, M. A., and R. K. Blashfield 1984 *Cluster Analysis*. Beverly Hills: Sage Publications.

Andrews, Christopher H. 1978 The Common Cold. *Scientific American*, March (39–45).

Anglin, J. 1976 Les premiers termes de référence de l'enfant. In *La Memoire Sémantique*, S. Ehrlich and E. Tulving, eds. Paris, Bulletin de Psychologie.

Anscombe, G. 1963 *Intention*. Ithaca: Cornell University Press.

Atran, Scott 1985 The Nature of Folk-Botanical Life Forms. *American Anthropologist* 87:2:298–315.

1987 Ordinary Constraints on the Semantics of Living Kinds: A Commonsense Alternative to Recent Treatments of Natural-Object Terms. *Mind and Nature* 2:1:27–63.

1990 *Cognitive Foundations of Natural History*. Cambridge: Cambridge University Press.

Baars, Bernard J. 1986 *The Cognitive Revolution in Psychology*. New York: Guilford Press.

Baddelely, Alan 1990 *Human Memory: Theory and Practice*. Needham Heights MA: Allyn and Bacon.

Banfield, Edward 1958 *The Moral Basis of a Backward Society*. Glencoe: The Free Press.

Beattie, J. H. M. 1955 Contemporary Trends in British Social Anthropology. *Sociologus* 5:1–14.

Bellah, Robert 1952 *Apache Kinship Systems*. Cambridge: Harvard University Press.

Benedict, Ruth F. 1934 *Patterns of Culture*. Boston: Houghton Mifflin.

1946 *The Chrysanthemum and the Sword*. Boston: Houghton Mifflin.

Berlin, Brent O. 1976 The Concept of Rank in Ethnobiological Classification: Some Evidence from Aguaruna Folk Botany. *American Ethnologist* 3:3:381–399.

1992 *Ethnobiological Classification.* Princeton: Princeton University Press.

Berlin, Brent O., and Elois Ann Berlin 1975 Aguaruna Color Categorie. *American Ethnologist* 2:1:61–87.

Berlin, Brent O., Dennis Breedlove, and Peter Raven 1968 Covert Categories and Folk Taxonomies. *American Anthropologist* 70:290–299.

1973 General Principles of Classification and Nomenclature in Folk Biology. *American Anthropologist* 75:214–242.

1974 *Principles of Tzeltal Plant Classification.* New York: Academic Press.

1976 The Concept of Rank in Ethnobiological Classification: Some Evidence from Aguaruna Folk Botany. *American Ethnologist* 3:3:381–399.

Berlin, Brent O., and Paul D. Kay 1969 *Basic Color Terms.* Berkeley: University of California Press.

Berlin, Brent O., Paul D. Kay, and William Merrifield 1985 Color Terms, Recent Evidence. Paper delivered at the Annual Meetings of the American Anthropological Association, November 6, 1985.

Bernard, H. R., P. D. Killworth, D. Kronenfeld, and L. Sailer 1985 On the Validity of Retrospective Data: The Problem of Informant Accuracy. *Annual Reviews in Anthropology.* Palo Alto: Stanford University Press.

Black, Mary 1987 Eliciting Folk Taxonomy in Ojibwa. In *Cognitive Anthropology*, S. A. Tyler, ed. Prospect Heights, IL: Waveland Press.

Black, Mary, and D. Metzger 1965 Ethnographic Description and the Study of Law, *American Anthropologist.* 6:2:141–165.

Bloch, Maurice 1992 Language, Anthropology and Cognitive Science. *Man* (N.S.) 26:183–198.

Bock, Phillip K. 1980 *Continuities in Psychological Anthropology: A Historical Introduction.* San Francisco: W. H. Freeman and Company.

Boster, James 1985 Requiem for the omniscient informant: There's Life in the Old Girl Yet. In *Directions in Cognitive Anthropology*, J. Dougherty, ed. Urbana: University of Illinois Press.

1986 Can Individuals Recapture the Evolutionary Development of Color Lexicons? *Ethnology* 25:1:61–74.

1988 Natural Sources of Internal Category Structure: Typicality, Familiarity, and Similarity of Birds. *Memory and Cognition* 16:3:258–270.

Boster, James, Brent Berlin and John O'Neill 1986 The Correspondence of Jivaroan to Scientific Ornithology. *American Anthropologist* 88:3:569–583.

Boster, James S., and Jeffrey C. Johnson 1989 Form or Function: A Comparison of Expert and Novice Judgments of Similarity among Fish. *American Anthropologist* 91:4:866–889.

Bourdieu, Pierre 1977 *Outline of a Theory of Practice.* Cambridge: Cambridge University Press.

1990 *The Logic of Practice.* Stanford: Stanford University Press.

Bousefield, W. A. 1953 The Occurrence of Clustering in the Recall of Randomly Arranged Associates. *Journal of Genetic Psychology* 49:229–240.

Boyer, Pascal 1993 Pseudo-Natural Kinds. In *Cognitive Aspects of Religious Symbolism.* P. Boyer, ed. Cambridge: Cambridge University Press.

Boynton, Robert M., and Conrad X. Olson 1987 Locating Basic Colors in the OSA space. *Color Research and Application* 12:2:94–105.

Braine, M. D. S., Reiser, B. J., and Rumain, B. 1984 Some Empirical Justification for a Theory of Natural Propositional Logic. *Psychology of Learning and Motivation* 18:313–371.

Briggs, Jean 1970 *Never in Anger.* Cambridge: Harvard University Press.

Brown, Cecil H. 1976 General Principles of Human Anatomical Partonomy and Speculations on the Growth of Partonomic Nomenclature. *American Ethnologist* 3:3:400–423.

1977 Folk Botanical Life-Forms: Their Universality and Growth. *American Anthropologist* 79:317–342.

1979 Folk Zoological Life-Forms: Their Universality and Growth. *American Anthropologist* 81:791–817.

Brown, Cecil H., John Kilar, Barbara J. Torrey, Tipawan Truong-Quang, and Phillip Volkman 1976 Some General Principles of Biological and Non-Biological Classification. *American Ethnologist* 3:1:73–85.

Brown, Roger, and Eric Lenneberg 1954 A Study in Language and Cognition. *Journal of Abnormal and Social Psychology* 49:454–462.

Brugman, Claudia 1981 Story of *Over*. MA thesis, University of California, Berkeley.

Bruner, J. S., J. Goodnow, and G. Austin, 1956 *A Study of Thinking*. New York: John Wiley.

Burgess, Don, Willett Kempton, and Robert E. MacLaury 1985 Tarahumara Color Modifiers: Individual Variation and Evolutionary Change. In *Directions in Cognitive Anthropology*, J. Dougherty, ed. Urbana: University of Illinois Press.

Burling, Robbins 1964 Cognition and Componential Analysis: God's Truth or Hocus-Pocus. *American Athropologist* 66:20–28.

Burton, Michael 1972 Semantic Dimensions of Occupation Names. In *Multi–dimensional Scaling*, Volume II, A. K. Romney, R. Shepard, and S. B. Nerlove, eds. New York: Seminar Press.

Burton, Michael L., and Sara B. Nerlove 1976 Balanced Designs for Triads Tests: Two Examples from English. *Social Science Research* 5:247–267.

Casson, Ronald W. 1983 Schemata in Cognitive Anthropology. *Annual Review of Anthropology* 12:429–462.

Chagnon, Napolean A. 1983 *Yanomamö: The Fierce People.* (3rd Edition) New York: Holt, Rinehart and Winston.

Chapman, L. J. 1967 Illusory Correlation in Observational Report. *Journal of Verbal Learning and Verbal Behavior* 6:151–155.

Chapman, L. J., and J. P. Chapman 1969 Illusory Correlation as an Obstacle to the Use of Valid Psychodiagnostic Signs. *Journal of Abnormal Psychology* 74:271–280.

Chase, W. G., and H. A. Simon 1973 Perception in Chess. *Cognitive Psychology* 4:55–81.

Cheng, Patricia W., and Keith J. Holyoak 1985 Pragmatic Reasoning Schemas. *Cognitive Psychology* 17:391–416.

Chomsky, Noam 1957 *Syntactic Structures*. The Hague: Mouton.

Churchland, Paul 1979 *Scientific Realism and the Plasticity of Mind.* Cambridge: Cambridge University Press.

Clark, Eve 1973 What's in a Word? On the Child's Acquistion of Semantics in his First Language. In *Cognitive Development and the Acquisition of Language*, E. Moore, ed. New York: Academic Press.

Colby, Benjamin, and Lore M. Colby 1981 *The Daykeeper, the Life and Discourse of an Ixil Deviner.* Cambridge: Cambridge University Press.

Cole, Michael 1989 Cultural Psychology: A Once and Future Discipline? *The Nebraska Symposium on Motivation: Cross-Cultural Perspectives.* 37:279–336.

Collins, Allan, and Ryszard Michalski 1989 The Logic of Plausible Reasoning: A Core Theory. *Cognitive Science* 13:1–49.

Collins, A., and M. Quillian 1969 Retrieval Time from Semantic Memory. *Journal of Verbal Learning and Verbal Behavior* 8:240–247.

Conklin, Harold 1954 The Relation of Hanunóo Culture to the Plant World. Unpublished PhD dissertation in Anthropology, Yale University, 1954.

1969 Lexicographical Treatment of Folk Taxonomies. In *Cognitive Anthropology*, Stephen Tyler, ed. New York: Holt, Rinehart and Winston.

Cosmides, Leda 1989 The Logic of Social Exchange: Has Natural Selection Shaped how Humans Reason? *Cognition* 31:187–276.

Cox, J. R., and Griggs, R. A. 1982 The Effects of Experience on Performance in Wason's Selection Task. *Memory and Cognition* 10:496–502.

Craik, Kenneth 1943 *The Nature of Explanation.* Cambridge: Cambridge University Press.

D'Andrade, Roy 1962 Aguacatenango Tzeltal Ethnobotany. Unpublished manuscript.

1965 Trait Psychology and Componential Analysis. *American Anthropologist* 67:5:2:215–228.

1974 Memory and the Assessment of Behavior. In *Measurement in the Social Sciences*, T. Blalock, ed. Chicago: Aldine-Atherton.

1976 A Propositional Analysis of U.S. American Beliefs about Illness. In *Meanings in Anthropology*, K. Basso and H. Selby, eds. Alberquerque: University of New Mexico Press.

1980 U-statistic Hierarchical Clustering. *Psychometrika* 43:1:59–67.

1981 The Cultural Part of Cognition. *Cognitive Science* 5:179–195.

1985 Cultural Terms and Cultural Models. In *Directions in Cognitive Anthropology*, J. W. D. Dougherty, ed. Urbana: University of Illinois Press.

1987a The Folk Model of the Mind. In *Cultural Models in Language and Thought*, D. Holland and N. Quinn, eds. Cambridge: Cambridge University Press.

1987b Modal Responses and Cultural Expertise. *American Behaviorist*: 31:2: 194–202.

1989 Culturally Based Reasoning. In *Cognition and Social Worlds*, A. Gellatly, D. Rogers, and J. A. Sloboda, eds. Oxford: Clarendon Press.

1992 Schemas and Motivation. In *Human Motives and Cultural Models*, R. D'Andrade and C. Strauss, eds. Cambridge: Cambridge University Press.

1993 Towards a Theory of Emotion and Culture. Paper presented at the Emory Mellon Symposium on Emotions.

D'Andrade, Roy, and Egan, Michael J. 1974 The Color of Emotion. *American Ethnologist* 1:49–63.

D'Andrade, Roy, Naomi Quinn, Sara Nerlove, and A. K. Romney 1972 Categories of Disease in American-English and Mexican-Spanish. In *Multidimensional Scaling*, Volume II, A. K. Romney, R. Shepard, and S. B. Nerlove, eds. New York: Seminar Press.

D'Andrade, Roy, and Claudia Strauss 1992 *Human Motives and Cultural Models.* Cambridge: Cambridge University Press.

D'Andrade, Roy, and Myron Wish 1985 Speech Act Theory in Quantitative Research on Interpersonal Behavior. *Discourse Processes* 8:229–259.

Dawes, Robin, and Robert Pearson 1991 The Effects of Theory-Based Schemas on Retrospective Data. In *Cognition and Social Survey Data*, J. Tanur, ed. New York: Russell Sage Press.

DeGroot, A. D. 1965 *Thought and Choice in Chess*. The Hague: Mouton.

De Valois, Russell L., and Karen K. De Valois 1993 A Multi-State Color Model. *Vision Research* 33:8:1053–1065.

Digman, John M. 1990 Personality Structure: Emergence of the Five-Factor Model. *Annual Revue of Psychology* 41:417–440.

Dougherty, Janet (Keller) 1975 A Universalistic Analysis of Variation and Change in Color Semantics. PhD dissertation, University of California: Berkeley.

1978 Salience and Relativity in Classification. *American Ethnologist* 5:1:66–79.

Douglas, R. Gordon Jr., K. M. Lindgre, and Robert B. Couch 1968 Exposure to Cold Environment and Rhinovirus Common Cold: Failure to Demonstrate Effect. *New England Journal of Medicine* 742–746.

Dreyfus, Hubert L. 1987 From Socrates to Expert Systems: The Limits of Calculative Rationality. *Bulletin of the American Academy of Arts and Sciences* 40:4:15–31.

Edmunson, Munroe 1973 The Anthropology of Values. In *Culture and Life: Essays in Honor of Clyde Kluckhohn*. W. W. Taylor, J. L. Fisher, and E. Z. Vogt, eds. Carbondale: Southern University Press.

Eggan, Fred 1950 *The Social Organization of the Western Pueblos*. Chicago: University of Chicago Press.

Eisenstadt, M., and Y. Kareev 1975 Aspects of Human Problem Solving: The Use of Internal Representations. In *Explorations in Cognition*. D. A. Norman, D. E. Rumelhart, and the LNR Research Group, eds. San Francisco: W. H. Freeman.

1977 Perception in Game Playing: Internal Representation and Scanning of Board Positions.In *Thinking: Readings in Cognitive Science*. P. N. Johnson-Laird and P. C. Wason, eds. Cambridge: Cambridge University Press.

Epling, J. P., J. Kirk, and J. P. Boyd 1973 Genetic Relations of Polynesian Sibling Terminologies. *American Anthropologist* 75:1596–1625.

Evans-Pritchard, E. E. 1940 *The Nuer.* Oxford: Oxford University Press.

Fillenbaum, S., and A. Rapoport 1971 *Structures in the Subjective Lexicon*. New York: Academic Press.

Fillmore, Charles 1975 An Alternative to Checklist Theories of Meaning. *Proceedings of the 1st Annual Meeting of the Berkeley Linguistics Society* 1:123–131.

1977 Topics in Lexical Semantics. In *Current Issues in Linguistic Theory*. Roger Cole, ed. Bloomington: Indiana University Press.

Finney, Benjamin R. 1979 *Hokulea the Way to Tahiti*. New York: Dodd, Mead and Company.

Flavell, John J. 1988 The Development of Children's Knowledge about the Mind.In *Developing Theories of the Mind*, J. Astington, P. Harris, and D. Olson, eds. New York: Cambridge University Press.

Fortes, Meyer 1983 *Oedipus and Job in West African Religion*. (2nd Edition) Cambridge: Cambridge University Press.

Fox, Robin 1967 *Kinship and Marriage*. Baltimore: Penguin Books.

1968 *Encounter with Anthropology*. New York: Harcourt Brace Jovanovich.

Frake, Charles O. 1961 The Diagnosis of Disease among the Subanun of Mindanao. *American Anthropologist* 63:1:113–132.

1962 The Ethnographic Study of Cognitive Systems. First published in *Anthropology and Human Behavior.* Washington, DC: Society of Washington.

1964 Notes on Queries in Ethnography. *American Anthropologist* 66:3:2:132–145.

Freeman, L. C., A. Kimball Romney, and Sue C. Freeman 1987 Cognitive Structure and Informant Accuracy. *American Anthropologist* 89:310–325.

Gara, Michael A. and Seymour Rosenberg 1981 Linguistic Factors in Implicit Personality Theory. *Journal of Personality and Social Psychology* 41:3:450–457.

Gardner, Howard 1989 *The Mind's New Science*. New York: Basic Books.

Garro, Linda 1986a Intracultural Variation in Folk Medical Knowledge: A Comparison Between Groups. *American Anthropologist* 88:351–370.

1986b Language, Memory and Focality: A Reexamination. *American Anthropologist* 88:128–136.

1988 Explaining High Blood Pressure: Variation in Knowledge about Illness. *American Ethnologist* 15:98–119.

Geertz, Clifford 1973 *The Interpretation of Cultures*. New York: Basic Books.

Gellner, Ernest 1987 *Culture, Identity, and Politics.* Cambridge: Cambridge University Press.

Gentner, Dedre 1978 On Relational Meaning: The Acquistion of Verb Meaning. *Child Development* 49:988–998.

1983 Structure-Mapping: A Theoretical Framework for Analogy. *Cognitive Science* 7:155–170.

1989 The Mechanisms of Analogical Learning. In *Similarity and Analogical Reasoning,* S. Vosniadou and A. Ortony, eds. London: Cambridge University Press.

Geoghegan, William H. 1976 Polytypy in Folk Biological Taxonomies. *American Ethnologist* 3:3:469–480.

Gerber, Eleanor 1985 Rage and Obligation. In *Person, Self, and Experience*, G. White and J. Kirkpatrick, eds. Berkeley: University of California Press.

Gladwin, Thomas 1970 *East is a Big Bird.* Cambridge: Harvard University Press.

Goldberg, Lewis 1982 From Ace to Zombie: Some Explorations in the Language of Personality. In *Advances in Personality Assessment*, Volume I, C. D. Spielberger and J. N. Butcher, eds. Hillsdale: Erlbaum.

Goodenough, Ward 1953 *Native Astronomy in the Central Carolines.* Philadephia: Museum Monographs, The University Museum, University of Pennsylvania.

1956 Componential Analysis and the Study of Meaning, *Language* 32:195–216.

Gorer, Geoffrey 1964 *The American People*. (Revised Edition). New York: Norton.

Greenberg, Joseph 1966 *Language Universals.* The Hague: Mouton and Co.

Hage, Per 1972 Muncher Beer Categories. In *Culture and Cognition: Rules, Maps, and Plans*, J. Spradley, ed. San Francisco: Chandler.

Hakel, Milton D. 1974 Normative Personality Factors Recovered from Rater's Descriptor: The Beholder's Eye. *Personal Psychology* 27:409–21.

Hamill, James F. 1990 *Ethnologic*. Urbana: University of Illinois Press.

Hamilton, David L. 1988 Understanding Impression Formation: What Has Memory Research Contributed? In *Memory: Interdisciplinary Approaches*, P. R. Solomon, G. R. Goethals, C. M. Kelley, and B. R. Stephens, eds. New York: Springer-Verlag.

Hamilton, S., and B. Fagot 1988 Chronic Stress and Coping Skills: A Comparison of Male and Female Undergraduates. *Journal of Personality and Social Psychology* 55:819–823.

Harris, Marvin 1968 *The Rise of Anthropological Theory.* New York: Thomas Crowell.

Hays, Terence E. 1976 An Empirical Method for the Identification of Covert Categories in Ethnobiology. *American Ethnologist* 3:3:489–507.

Henley, N. M. 1969 A Psychological Study of the Semantics of Animal Terms. *Journal of Verbal Learning and Verbal Behavior* 8:176–184.

Holland, Dorothy 1992 How Cultural Systems Become Desire. In *Human Motives and Cultural Models,* R. D'Andrade and C. Strauss, eds. Cambridge: Cambridge University Press.

Holland, Dorothy, and Margaret Eisenhart 1990 *Educated in Romance: Women, Achievement and College Culture.* Chicago: University of Chicago Press.

Holland, Dorothy, and Debra Skinner 1987 Prestige and Intimacy, the Cultural Models behind Americans' Talk about Gender Types. In *Cultural Models in Language and Thought,* D. Holland and N. Quinn, eds. New York: Cambridge University Press.

Hunn, Eugene 1975 A Measure of the Degree of Correspondence of Folk to Scientific Classification. *American Ethnologist* 2:309–327.

1976 Toward a Perceptual Model of Folk Biological Classification. *American Ethnologist* 3:3:508–542.

Hutchins, Edwin 1980 *Culture and Inference.* Cambridge: Harvard University Press.

1983 Understanding Micronesian Navigation. In *Mental Models,* D. Gentner and A. L. Stevens, eds. Englewood Cliffs: Lawrence Erlbaum.

1994. *Cognition in the Wild.* Cambridge: MIT Press.

1991 The Social Organization of Distributed Cognition. In *Perspective on Socially Shared Cognition,* L. B. Resnick, J. M. Levine, and S. D. Teasley, eds. Washington DC: American Psychological Association.

Hutchinson, J. W., and G. R. Lockhead 1977 Similarity as Distance: A Structural Principle for Semantic Memory. *Journal of Experimental Psychology: Human Learning and Memory* 3:660–678.

Jakobson, Roman, and Morris Halle 1956 *Fundamentals of Language.* The Hague: Mouton & Co.

Johnson, Allen W., and Timothy Earle 1987 *The Evolution of Human Societies: From Foraging Group to Agrarian State.* Stanford: Stanford University Press.

Johnson, Mark 1987 *The Body in the Mind: The Bodily Basis of Meaning, Imagination, and Reason.* Chicago: University of Chicago Press.

Johnson-Laird, P. N. 1983 *Mental Models.* Cambridge: Harvard University Press.

Johnson-Laird, P. N., P. Legrenzi, and M. Legrenzi, 1972 Reasoning and a Sense of Reality. *British Journal of Psychology* 63:392–400.

Kant, Immanuel 1929 *Critique of Pure Reason,* N. K. Smith, translator. London: Macmillian [1781].

Kardiner, Abraham, and Ralph Linton 1949 *The Individual and his Society.* New York: Columbia University Press.

Kay, Paul D. 1975 Synchronic Variability and Diachronic Change in Basic Color Terms. *Language in Society* 4:257–270.

Kay, Paul D., Brent O. Berlin, and William Merrifield 1991 Biocultural Implications of Systems of Color Naming. *Journal of Linguistic Anthropology* 1:1:1225.

Kay, Paul D., and Willet Kempton 1984 What is the Sapir–Whorf Hypothesis? *American Anthropologist* 86:65–79.

Kay, Paul D., and Chad K. McDaniel 1978 The Linguistic Meanings of Basic Color Terms. *Language* 54:610–646.

Keller, Janet D., and F. K. Lehman 1993 Computational Complexity in the Cognitive Modelling of Cosmological Ideas. In *Cognitive Aspects of Religious Symbolism*, P. Boyer, ed. Cambridge: Cambridge University Press.

Kirk, Lorraine, and Michael Burton 1977 Meaning and Context: A Study of Contextural Shifts in Meaning of Maasai Personality Descriptors. *American Ethnologist* 4:734–761.

Kluckhohn, Clyde 1949a *Navaho Witchcraft*. Papers of the Peabody Museum of American Archaeology and Ethnology, 22:2. Cambridge: Harvard University.

1949b The Philosophy of the Navaho Indians. In *Ideological Differences and World Order*, F.S.C. Northrop, ed. New Haven:Yale University Press.

Kluckhohn, Florence, and Fred Strodtbeck 1961 *Variations in Value Orientations*. Evanston: Row Peterson.

Kroeber, A. L., and Clyde Kluckhohn 1963 *Culture: A Critical Review of Concepts and Definitions*. New York: Knopf.

Kronenfeld, David B. 1974 Sibling Typology: Beyond Nerlove and Romney. *American Ethnologist* 1:3:489–506.

Kruskal, J., and M. Wish 1978 *Multidimensional Scaling*. Beverly Hills: Sage Publications.

Kuhn, Thomas 1970 *The Structure of Scientific Revolutions*. (2nd Edition) Chicago: University of Chicago Press.

Kuper, Adam 1983 *Anthropology and Anthropologists: The Modern British School*. New York: Routledge and Kegan Paul.

Labov, William, and David Fanshel 1977 *Therapeutic Discourse: Psychotherapy as Conversation*. New York: Academic Press.

Lakoff, George 1987 *Women, Fire, and Dangerous Things*. Chicago: University of Chicago Press.

Langacker, Ronald 1987 *Foundations of Cognitive Grammar*, Volume I, *Theoretical Perspectives*. Stanford: Stanford University Press.

1991 *Foundations of Cognitive Grammar*, Volume II: *Descriptive Application*. Stanford: Stanford University Press.

Lantz, DeLee, and Volney Stefflre 1964 Language and Cognition Revisited. *Journal of Abnormal and Social Psychology*, 69:5:472–481.

Lave, Jean 1988 *Cognition in Practice*. Cambridge: Cambridge University Press.

Lazarus, Richard S. 1991 *Emotion and Adaptation*. New York: Oxford University Press.

Leach, Edmund R. 1962 Concerning Trobriand Clans and the Kinship Category Tabu. In *Cambridge Papers in Social Anthropology*, Jack Good, ed. 1:120–145.

Lee, Dorothy D. 1940 A Primitive System of Values. *Journal of Philosophy* 7:3:355–379.

1949 Being and Value in a Primitive Culture. *Journal of Philosophy* 48:401–415.

Lee, Richard B. 1984 *The Dobe !Kung*. New York: Holt, Rinehart and Winston.

Lenneberg, Eric 1961 Color Naming, Color Recognition, Color Discrimination: A Reappraisal. *Perceptual and Motor Skills* 12:375–382.

Lenneberg, Eric, and John Roberts 1956 The Language of Experience: A Study in Methodology. *International Journal of Linguistics* Memoir no. 13.

LeVine, Robert 1973 *Culture, Behavior, and Personality.* Chicago: Aldine.

Levinson, David 1991 *The Encyclopedia of World Cultures.* Boston: G. K. Hall & Co.

Levy, Robert I. 1973 *The Tahitians: Mind and Experience in the Society Islands.* Chicago: University of Chicago Press.

1984 Emotion, Knowing, and Culture. In *Culture Theory: Essays on Mind, Self, and Emotion*, R. A. Shweder and R. A. LeVine, eds. Cambridge: Cambridge University Press.

Lewis, D. 1972 *We the navigators.* Honolulu: University Press of Hawaii.

Linder, Sue 1982 A Lexico-Semantic Analysis of English Verb-Particle Constructions with UP and OUT. Doctoral Dissertation, University of California, San Diego.

Lounsbury, Floyd 1956 A Semantic Analysis of the Pawnee Kinship Usage. *Language* 32:158–194.

1964 A Formal Account of the Crow- and Omaha-Type Kinship Terminologies. In *Explorations in Cultural Anthropology*, W. H. Goodenough, ed. New York: McGraw-Hill.

Lucy, John A., and Richard A. Shweder 1979 Whorf and his Critics: Linguistic and Nonlinguistic Influences on Color Memory. *American Anthropologist* 81:581–615.

1988 Language, Memory, and Focality: A Reply to Garro. *American Anthropologist* 90:4:923–931.

Lutz, Catherine 1985 Ethnopsychology Compared to What? Explaining Behavior and Consciousness among the Ifaluk. In *Person, Self, and Experience*, G. White and J. Kirkpatrick, eds. Berkeley: University of California Press.

Lutz, Catherine A., and Lila Abu-Lughod 1990 *Language and the Politics of Emotion.* New York: Cambridge University Press.

McCauley, Robert 1986 Intertheoretic Relations and the Future of Psychology. *Philosophy of Science* 53:179–199.

McClelland, David 1951 *Personality.* New York: Sloane Associates.

McClelland, David, John W. Atkinson, R. Clark, and E. Lowell 1953 *The Achievement Motive.* New York: Appleton-Century-Crofts.

McClosky, H., and A. Brill 1983 *Dimensions of Tolerance: What Americans Believe about Civil Liberties.* New York: Russell Sage Foundation.

Mackintosh, N. J. 1988 Approaches to the Study of Animal Intelligence. *British Journal of Psychology* 79:509–525.

MacLaury, Robert E. 1987 Color-Category Evolution and Shuswap Yellow-with-Green. *American Anthropologist* 89:1:107–124.

1992 From Brightness to Hue: An Explanatory Model of Color-Category Evolution. *Current Anthropology* 33:2:137–186.

McNeill, David 1987 *Psycholinguistics: A New Approach.* New York: Harper and Row.

Mandler, George 1984 *Mind and Body: The Psychology of Emotion and Stress.* New York: Norton 1984.

1985 *Cognitive Psychology: An Essay in Cognitive Science.* Hillsdale: Erlbaum.

Mandler, Jean M. 1984 *Stories, Scripts, and Scenes: Aspects of Schema Theory.* Hillsdale NJ: Erlbaum.

Mead, Margaret 1950 *Sex and Temperament in Three Primitive Societies.* New York; Mentor.

Metzger, Duane, and G. Williams 1963a Formal Ethnographic Analysis of Tenejapa Ladino Weddings. *American Anthropologist* 65:1076–1101.

1963 Tenejapa Medicine I: The Curer. *Southwestern Journal of Anthropology* 19:216–234.

1966 Some Procedures and Results in the Study of Native Categories: Tzeltal "Firewood." *American Anthropologist*. 68: 389–407.

Miller, George 1956 The Magical Number Seven, Plus or Minus Two: Some Limits on our Capacity for Processing Information. *Psychological Review* 63: 2.

Miller, Roy A. Jr. 1974 Are Familists Amoral? A Test of Banfield's Amoral Familism Hypothesis in a South Italian Village. *American Ethnologist* 1:3:515–535.

Minoura, Yasuko 1992 A Sensitive Period for the Incorporation of a Cultural Meaning System: A Study of Japanese Children Growing up in the United States. *Ethos* 20:3:304–339.

Minsky, Marvin 1975 A Framework for Representing Knowledge. In *The Psychology of Computer Vision*, P. H. Winston, ed. New York: McGraw-Hill.

Mischel, Walter 1968 *Personality and Assessment*. New York: Wiley.

Moffatt, Michael n.d. American Friendship and the Individual Self. Manuscript.

Moran, L. J., R. B. Mefferd, Jr., and J. P. Kimble 1964 Idiosyncratic Sets in Word Association. *Psychology Monographs: General and Applied* 78:2:1–22.

Murdock George P. 1949 *Social Structure*. New York: Macmillan. 1957 World Ethnographic Sample. *American Anthropologist* 59: 664–687.

Murray, Harry 1938 *Explorations in Personality*. New York: Oxford University Press.

Nakao, K., and A. K. Romney 1984 A Method for Testing Alternative Theories: An Example from English Kinship. *American Anthropologist* 86:668–673.

Neisser, Ulric 1967 *Cognitive Psychology*. New York: Appleton-Century-Crofts.

Nerlove, Sarah, and A. K. Romney 1967 Sibling Terminology and Cross-Sex Behavior. *American Anthropologist* 74: 1249–1253.

1976 Reaction Time of Semantic Judgments as Predicted from Semantic Distance. *Social Science Working Papers* 90. University of California, Irvine.

Newell, A., J. C. Shaw, and H. A. Simon 1958 Elements of a Theory of Human Problem Solving. *Psychological Review* 65:151– 166.

Nisbett, Richard E. 1993 *Rules for Reasoning*. Hillsdale: Erlbaum.

Norman, Donald A. 1986 Reflections on Cognition and Parallel Distributed Processing.In *Parallel Distributed Processing*, Volume II, J. L. McClelland, D. E. Rumelhart, and the PDP Research Group, eds. Cambridge: MIT Press.

Norman, W. T. 1963 Toward an Adequate Taxonomy of Personality Attributes: Replicated Factor Structure in Peer Nomination Personality Ratings. *Journal of Abnormal and Social Psychology* 66:574–583.

Opler, Morris E. 1937 An Outline of Chiricahua Apache Social Organization. In *The Social Organization of North American Indians*, Fred Eggan ed. Chicago: University of Chicago Press.

Parish, Steven 1991 The Sacred Mind: Newar Cultural Representations of Mental Life and the Production of Moral Consciousness. *Ethos* 19:3:313–351.

Peabody, Dean 1987 Selecting Representative Trait Adjectives. *Journal of Personality and Social Psychology* 52:1:59–71.

Pike, Kenneth L. Pike 1967 *Language in Relation to a Unified Theory of the Structure of Human Behavior*. The Hague: Mouton and Company.

Quinlan, Philip T. 1991 *Connectionism and Psychology.* Chicago: University of Chicago Press.

Quinn, Naomi 1975 Decision Models of Social Structure. *American Ethnologist* 2:1:19–45.

1987 Convergent Evidence for a Cultural Model of American Marriage. In *Cultural Models in Language and Thought*, D. Holland and N. Quinn, eds. Cambridge: Cambridge University Press.

1991 The Cultural Basis of Metaphor. In *Beyond Metaphor: The Theory of Tropes in Anthropology*, J. Fernandez, ed. Stanford: Stanford University Press.

1992 The Motivational Force of Self-Understanding. In *Human Motives and Cultural Models*, R. D'Andrade and C. Strauss, eds. Cambridge: Cambridge University Press.

Quinn, Naomi, and Dorothy Holland 1987 Introduction. In *Cultural Models in Language and Thought*, D. Holland and N. Quinn, eds. New York: Cambridge University Press.

Quinn, Naomi, and Claudia Strauss n.d. A Cognitive Framework for a Unified Theory of Culture. Manuscript.

Radcliffe-Brown, A. R. 1957 *A Natural Science of Society.* Glencoe: The Free Press.

Randall, Robert 1976 How Tall is a Taxonomic Tree? Some Evidence of Dwarfism. *American Ethnologist* 3:3: 545–546.

Randall, Robert, and Eugene S. Hunn 1984 Do Life-Forms Evolve or Do Uses for Life? Some Doubts about Brown's Universals Hypotheses. *American Ethnologist* 11:2:329–349.

Ripps, Lance J. 1990 Reasoning. *Annual Review of Psychology* 41:321–53.

Roberts, John 1964 The Self-Management of Cultures. In *Explorations in Cultural Anthropology*, W. Goodenough ed. New York: McGraw Hill.

Romney, A. K. 1989 Quantitative Models, Science and Cumulative Knowledge. *Journal of Quantitative Research* 1:153–223.

Romney, A. K., William Batchelder, and Susan Weller 1987 Recent Applications of Cultural Consensus Theory. *American Behavioral Scientist* 31:2:163–177.

Romney, A. K., and R. G. D'Andrade 1964 Cognitive Aspects of English Kin Terms. *American Anthropologist*, 68:3:2 146–170.

Romney, A. K., Tom Smith, Howard E. Freeman, Jerome Kagan, and Robert E. Klein 1979 Concepts of Success and Failure. *Social Science Research* 8:302–326.

Romney, A. K., Susan Weller, and William Batchelder 1986 Culture as Consensus: A Theory of Culture and Informant Accuracy. *American Anthropologist* 88:313–338.

Rosaldo, Michelle Z. 1984 Toward an Anthropology of Self and Feeling. *Culture Theory: Essays on Mind, Self, and Emotion*, R. A. Shweder and R. A. LeVine, eds. Cambridge: Cambridge University Press.

Rosch, Eleanor (Heider) 1972 The Structure of Color Space in Naming and Memory for Two Languages. *Cognitive Psychology* 3:337–354.

1973 Universals in Color Naming and Memory. *Journal of Experimental Psychology* 93:10–20.

1975 Cognitive Representations of Semantic Categories. *Journal of Experimental Psychology* 104:192–233.

1976 Cognitive Reference Points. *Cognitive Psychology* 7:532–547.

1978 Principles of Categorization. In *Cognition and Categorization*, E. Rosch and B. Lloyd, eds. Hillsdale: Erlbaum.

Rosch, Eleanor and C. B. Mervis 1975 Family Resemblances: Studies in the Internal Structure of Categories. *Cognitive Psychology* 5:573–605.

Rosch, Eleanor, C. Simpson, and R. S. Miller 1976 Structural Bases of Typicality Effects. *Journal of Experimental Psychology: Human Perception and Performance* 2:491–502.

Rosenberg, Seymour, and Andrea Sedlak 1972 Structural Representations of Perceived Personality Trait Relationships. In *Multidimensional Scaling*, Volume II, A. K. Romney, R. Shepard, and S. B. Nerlove, eds. New York: Seminar Press.

Rosenblatt, Allan D. 1985 The Role of Affect in Cognitive Psychology and Psychoanalysis. *Psychoanalytic Psychology* 2:2:85–97.

Rosenblatt, Allan D., and James T. Thickstun 1977 *Modern Psychoanalytic Concepts in General Psychology*. New York: International Universities Press.

Ruhlen, Merritt 1987 *A Guide to the World's Languages*, Volume II: *Classification.* Stanford: Stanford University Press.

Rumelhart, D. E. 1980 Schemata: The Building Blocks of Cognition. In *Theoretical Issues in Reading Comprehension: Perspectives from Cognitive Psychology, Linguistics, Artificial Intelligence, and Education*, R. Spiro, B. Bruce, W. Brewer, eds. Hillsdale: Erlbaum.

Rumelhart, D. E., and A. A. Abrahamson 1973 A Model for Analogical Reasoning. *Cognitive Psychology* 5: 1–28.

Rumelhart, David E., and James L. McClelland 1986 On Learning the Past Tenses of English Verbs. In *Parallel Distributed Processing*, Volume II, J. L. McClelland, D. E. Rumelhart, and the PDP Research Group, eds. Cambridge: MIT Press.

Rumelhart, David E., Paul Smolensky, James L. McClelland, and Geoffrey. E. Hinton 1986 Sequential Thought Processes in PDP Models. In *Parallel Distributed Processing*, Volume II, J. L. McClelland, D. E. Rumelhart, and the PDP Research Group, eds. Cambridge: MIT Press.

Russell, Bertrand 1945 *A History of Western Philosophy.* New York: Simon and Schuster.

Russell, J. A., M. Lewicka, and T. Nilt 1989 A Cross-Cultural Study of a Circumplex Model of Affect. *Journal of Personality and Social Psychology* 57:5:848–861.

Sahlins, Marshall 1978 *Culture and Practical Reason.* Chicago: University of Chicago Press.

Sapir, Edward 1921 *Language*, New York: Harcourt, Brace.

Schacter, Stanley, and J. E. Singer 1962 Cognitive, Social, and Physiological Determinants of Emotional State. *Psychological Review* 69:379–399.

Schank, Roger C., and Robert. P. Abelson 1977 *Scripts, Plans, Goals, and Understanding: An Enquiry into Human Knowledge Structures.* Hillsdale: Erlbaum.

Scheffler, Harold, and Floyd Lounsbury 1971 *A Study in Structural Semantics: the Surlono Kinship System.* Englewood Cliffs: Prentice-Hall.

1978 *Australian Kin Classification.* Cambridge: Cambridge University Press.

Schneider, David M. 1965 American Kin Terms and Terms for Kinsmen: A Critique of Goodenough's Componential Analysis of Yankee Kinship Terminology. *American Anthropologist* 67:5:2:288–308.

1968 *American Kinship: A Cultural Account.* Englewood Cliffs: Prentice Hall.

Scribner, Sylvia 1977 Modes of Thinking and Ways of Speaking: Culture and Logic Reconsidered. In *Thinking: Readings in Cognitive Science*, P. N. Johnson-Laird and P. C. Wason, eds. Cambridge: Cambridge University Press.

Searle, John R. 1975 A Taxonomy of Ilocutionary Acts. In *Language, Mind, and Knowledge*, K. Gunderson, ed. Minneapolis: University of Minnesota Press.

Shore, Bradd 1993 Feeling our Way: Toward a Bio-cultural Model of Emotion. Paper presented at the Emory Mellon Symposium on Emotions.

Shweder, Richard A. 1972 Semantic Structures and Personality Assessment. Doctoral Dissertation, Harvard University (University Microfilms no. 72–29, 584).

1977 Illusory Correlation and the M.M.P.I. Controversy. *Journal of Consulting and Clinical Psychology* 45:917–924.

1982 Fact and Artifact in Trait Perception: The Systematic Distortion Hypothesis. In *Progress in Experimental Personality Research*, Volume II. New York: Academic Press.

1992 Ghost Busters in Anthropology. In *Human Motives and Cultural Models*, R. D'Andrade and C. Strauss, eds. Cambridge: Cambridge University Press.

1993 Cultural Psychology: Who Needs It? *Annual Review of Psychology* 44: 497–523.

Shweder, Richard A., and Roy D'Andrade 1980 The Systematic Distortion Hypothesis. *New Directions for Methodology of Social and Behavioral Science* 4:37–58.

Shweder, Richard A., and Robert A. LeVine 1984 *Culture Theory: Essays on Mind, Self, and Emotion*. Cambridge: Cambridge University Press.

Shweder, Richard A., Manamohan Mahapatra, and Joan Miller 1990 Culture and Moral Development. In *Cultural Psychology*, J. W. Stigler, R. A. Shweder, and G. Herdt, eds. Cambridge: Cambridge University Press.

Singer, Jerome, and Peter Salovery 1991 Organized Knowledge Structures and Personality. In *Person Schemas and Maladaptive Interpersonal Patterns*, M. Horowtz, ed. Chicago: University of Chicago Press.

Smith, C. A., and P. C. Ellsworth 1985 Patterns of Cognitive Appraisal in Emotion. *Journal of Personality and Social Psychology* 48:4:813–838.

Spiro, Melford E. 1982 *Buddhism and Society: A Great Tradition and its Burmese Vicissitudes*. Berkeley: University of California Press.

1984 Reflections on Cultural Determinism and Relativism. In *Culture Theory: Essays on Mind, Self, and Emotion*, R. A. Shweder and R. A. LeVine, eds. Cambridge: Cambridge University Press.

1987 Collective Representations and Mental Representations in Religious Symbol Systems. In *Culture and Human Nature: Theoretical Papers of Melford E. Spiro*, B. Kilborn and L. Langness, eds. Chicago: University of Chicago Press.

n.d.a Cultural Ideology and Social Reality: An Essay on Cultural Internalization. Manuscript.

n.d.b Narcissus in Asia. Manuscript.

Spradley, James P. 1970 *You Owe Yourself a Drunk*. Boston: Little Brown.

1979 *The Ethnographic Interview*. New York, Holt, Rinehart and Winston.

Stefflre, Volney 1972 Some Applications of Multidimensional Scaling to Social Science Problems. In *Multidimensional Scaling*, Volume II, A. K. Romney, R. Shepard, and S. B. Nerlove, eds. New York: Seminar Press.

Stefflre, Volney, Victor V. Castillo, and Linda Morley 1966 Language and Cognition in Yucatan: A Cross-Cultural Replication. *Journal of Personality and Social Psychology* 4:1:112–115.

Strauss, Claudia 1992a Models and Motives. In *Human Motives and Cultural Models.* In Roy D'Andrade and Claudia Strauss, eds. Cambridge: Cambridge University Press.

1992b What Makes Tony run? In *Human Motives and Cultural Models.* In Roy D'Andrade and Claudia Strauss, eds. Cambridge: Cambridge University Press.

Stross, Brian 1973 Acquisition of Botanical Terminology by Tzeltal Children. In *Meaning in Mayan Languages*, M. Edmunson, ed. The Hague: Mouton.

Suchman, Lucy A. 1987 *Plans and Situation Actions: The Problem of Human Machine Interaction.* Cambridge: Cambridge University Press.

Swartz, Marc 1991 *The Way the World Is: Cultural Processes and Social Relations among the Mombasa Swahili.* Berkeley: University of California Press.

Talmy, Leonard 1978 The Relation of Grammar to Cognition – A Synopsis. *Proceedings of TINLAP – 2 (Theoretical Issues in Natural Language Processing).* Urbana: University of Illinois Coordinated Science Laboratory.

Tulving, Endel 1983 *Elements of Episodic Memory.* Oxford: Oxford University Press.

Turiel, Elliot, Melanie Killen, and Charles C. Helwig 1987 Morality: Its Structure, Functions, and Vagaries. In *The Emergence of Morality in Young Children*, J. Kagan and S. Lamb, eds. Chicago: University of Chicago Press.

Tversky, Amos 1977 Features of Similarity. *Psychological Review* 84: 327–352.

Tyler, Stephen A. 1969 *Cognitive Anthropology.* New York: Holt, Rinehart and Winston.

Vendler, Zeno 1967 *Linguistics in Philosophy.* Ithaca: Cornell University Press.

1972 *Res Cognitans: An Essay in Rational Psychology.* Ithaca: Cornell University Press.

Vogt, Evon Z., and Ethel M. Albert 1966 *People of Rimrock.* Cambridge: Harvard University Press.

Wallace, Anthony F. C. 1956 Revitalization Movements. *American Anthropologist* 58:264–281.

1960 *Culture and Personality.* New York: Random House.

1964 On Being Just Complicated Enough. *Proceedings of the National Academy of Science* 17:458–461.

Wallace, Anthony F. C., and John Atkins 1960 The Meaning of Kinship Terms. *American Anthropologist* 62:58–80.

Wason, P. C. 1968 Reasoning about a Rule *Quarterly Journal of Experimental Psychology* 20:273–81.

Weller, S. C. 1984 Consistency and consensus among informants: Disease Concepts in a Rural Mexican Town. *American Anthropologist* 86:966–975.

Weller, Susan C., and A. Kimball Romney 1988 *Systematic Data Collection.* Newbury Park: Sage.

Weller, Susan C., A. Kimball Romney, and D. P. Orr 1986 The Myth of a Sub-Culture of Corporal Punishment. *Human Organization* 46:39–47.

Wellman, Henry 1990 *The Child's Theory of Mind.* Cambridge: MIT Press.

Werner, Oswald 1987 *Systematic Fieldwork.* Newbury Park: Sage.

Werner, Oswald, K. Y. Begishe, M. A. Austin-Garrison, and J. Werner 1989 *The*

Anatomical Atlas of the Navajo. Window Rock: Native American Materials Development Center, 1989.

Werner, Oswald, and G. M. Schoepfle 1987 *Foundations of Ethnography and Interviewing,* Volumes I and II. Newbury Park: Sage.

Wexler, Kenneth, and A. Kimball Romney 1972 Individual Variations in Cognitive Structures. In *Multidimensional Scaling: Theory and Applications in the Behavioral Sciences*, Volume II, A. K. Romney, R. Shepard and S. B. Nerlove, eds. New York: Seminar Press.

White, Geoffrey 1978 Ambiguity and Ambivalence in A'ara Personality Descriptors. *American Ethnologist* 5:334–360.

1980 Conceptual Universals in Interpersonal Language. *American Anthropologist* 82:759–781.

1987 Proverbs and Cultural Models.In *Cultural Models in Language and Thought*, D. Holland and N. Quinn, eds. Cambridge: Cambridge University Press.

Whiting, Beatrice, and John W. M. Whiting 1975 *Children of Six Cultures*. Cambridge: Harvard University Press.

Whiting, John W. M., and Irvin L. Child 1953 *Child Training and Personality: A Cross-Cultural Study.* New Haven: Yale University Press.

Whorf, Benjamin Lee 1956 Science and Linguistics. In *Language, Thought, and Reality*, J. B. Carroll, ed. Cambridge: MIT Press.

Wierzbicka, Anna W. 1984 Apples are not a Kind of Fruit. *American Ethnologist* 11:313–326.

1992 *Semantics, Culture, and Cognition: Universal Human Concepts in Culture-Specific Configurations*. New York: Oxford.

1993 A Conceptual Basis for Cultural Psychology. *Ethos* 21:2:205–231.

Wiggins, J.S. 1973 *Personality and Prediction: Principles of Personality Assessment*. Reading MA: Addison-Wesley.

Wikan, Unni 1987 Public Grace and Private Fears: Gaiety, Offense, and Sorcery in Northern Bali. *Ethos* 15:4:337–365.

1989 Managing the Heart to Brighten Face and Soul: Emotions in Balinese Mortality and Health Care. *American Ethnologist* 16:2:294–312.

Wish, Myron 1976 Comparisons among Multidimensional Structures of Interpersonal Relations. *Multivariate Behavioral Research* 11:297–325.

Wish, Myron, Morton Deutsch, and Lois Biener 1972 Differences in Perceived Similarity of Nations. In *Multidimensional Scaling*, Volume II, A. K. Romney, R. Shepard, and S. B. Nerlove, eds. New York, Seminar Press.

Young, J. C. 1978 Illness Categories and Action Strategies in a Tarascan Town. *American Ethnologist:* 5:1:81–97.

Name index

General index